REVIVE ME ACCORDING TO YOUR WORD

AN INSPIRATIONAL BIBLE READING GUIDE DESIGNED TO HELP BRING GOD'S WORD ALIVE TO YOU

BRENT CANTELON

CeeTeC

CeeTeC Publishing
Abbotsford, Canada

Revive Me: According to your Word
Copyright 2012
Brent Donald Cantelon
ISBN 978-0-9865749-4-8

Library of Congress Cataloging-in-Publication Data
Cantelon, Brent (Brent Donald), 1959-
    Revive Me: According to your Word / Brent Cantelon.
    p.cm.
    ISBN 978-0-9865749-4-8 (pbk.)

I. Devotional calendars—Pentecostals. I. Title.
BV4811.C36 2012   242.2.C36 2012

PRINTED IN U.S.A.

PUBLISHED BY
CeeTeC Publishing

Canada   United States
PO Box 466   PO Box 1117
Abbotsford, BC V2T 6Z7   Sumas WA, 98285

Phone: 604-853-5352 or 604-807-5831
www.ceeteconline.com
ceetecpublishing@gmail.com

Dedication

The Lord, in mercy, has given me the most wonderful wife and friend in Carina. She is a constant encouragement and motivator for me to share in print some of the things that have been on my heart.

So this work is firstly for the Lord's glory and the love of His Word, but it is secondly, dedicated to Carina.

Acknowledgments

I want to acknowledge Steve Hill and the Brownsville Revival in the late nineties. It was there, through those services and the little devotional guide "On Earth as it is in Heaven" by Robert Murray McCheyne, that I fell in love with the Bible in a way that has continued to transform my life and ministry.

I want to thank my assistant Monica Unger, who has labored with amazing vision and tenacity along side of me in this project, without your help Monica this project would never have happened, thank you. Thank you also to other people who in various ways have helped to get us to this point, Steven Barks, Elodi Kerluke, Nicole Molnar, and Sylvia Quiring.

Thank you to Dr. Dave Demchuk who helped with editing and corrections.

Finally and not least, I want to acknowledge the congregation of Christian Life Assembly, and the Leadership and Executive teams, for the privilege of serving with you. The motivation to embark on this project was entirely out of a desire to serve in stimulating your love and growth in the Word of God.

Bless you today!

Brent Cantelon

Introduction

My prayer is that as you use this Bible reading guide you will grow deeper in your love for the Word of God and will say, "How sweet are Your words…sweeter than honey to my mouth." (Psalm 119:103). My desire is that you will also grow in conviction and confidence that His Word is "very pure", and "established forever". So many people long to read the Bible, yet struggle with various burdens that hinder that desire, from busyness, to difficulty understanding, to bogging down in some of what could be called the "drier" portions. This guide is intended to assist you in receiving a living "word" to your heart from the Bible, a practical life application word for each day.

We will be averaging 85 verses or 3.25 chapters, for about 15 minutes per day. As you read each day, ask the Lord in prayer to reveal a particular word to your spirit. A living "word" to you, a verse that is particularly alive and memorable to you, for that day. Mark it in your Bible, add it to your journal. These words will become a powerful testimony and record in your life of the living power of God to speak a relevant and practical help to you, from the Bible.

Disclaimer for the "Quote of the Day"

I have chosen quotes from many different people and authors, (most of whom I am comfortable recommending). There are occasional quotes that fit the flow of the reading for the day from people I do not know. For this reason it is important to state; because someone is quoted, this does not imply endorsement of everything they have ever said or written.

"I have reasonably assumed that the authors' quotations herein were public domain."

Abbreviations

NKJV – New King James Version
NLT – New Living Translation
MSG – The Message paraphrase
SFLB – The Spirit Filled Life Bible

DAY 1

📖 GENESIS 1 – 3
📖 PSALMS 1, 2

◉ K E Y   T H O U G H T S

- **Genesis 1:1** We know where we come from. God is the Creator, this is the beginning of all time. "In the beginning, God."

- Gen. 2, 3 God's created order and perfection. God's original design and purpose for man was without flaw, the ensuing issues of natural disaster and wickedness that we live with are not "the will of God". The fall of man and the entrance of sin into the world resulted in the disfigurement of all of God's perfect creation.

- Gen. 2:15; Psalm 2:8 A clear declaration of God's heart to send Jesus as the Savior of the world, to conquer the evil one and provide hope for all people. Jesus is given "the nations" as His inheritance – what joy there is to tell the good news to all nations.

- **Psalm 1** Promises to those who delight in the ways of the Lord: like a fruitful/flourishing tree, prosperity.

- The contrast of the plight of the wicked – they are like dust that blows away in the wind.

QUOTE OF THE DAY

"Satan gives Adam an apple (fruit), and takes away Paradise. Therefore in all temptations let us consider not what he offers, but what we shall lose."

Richard Sibbes (1577-1635)

DAY 2

📖 GENESIS 4; 5:1 – 3, 23 – 24, 6
📖 PSALMS 3 – 5

⊚ K E Y   T H O U G H T S

- **Genesis** The sinfulness and wickedness of mankind grieved the heart of God – but Noah found grace in the eyes of the Lord.
- An appeal from us to the Lord to "hear our cry" will always be heard by the Him.
- **Psalm 5:11** "But let those who rejoice in You put their trust in You."

QUOTE OF THE DAY

"Sins are like circles in the water when a stone is thrown into it: one produces another. When anger was in Cain's heart, murder was not far off."

Philip Henry (1631-1696)

DAY 3

📖 GENESIS 7 – 8
📖 PSALMS 6 – 7

⊚ K E Y   T H O U G H T S

- **Genesis 7:1** A beautiful foreshadowing of the safety we have in Christ, the "ark" of His mercy and grace. Also, the concept of *"you and your household"* creates such hope for generations of godliness.
- **Psalm 7:17** The basis of our praise is the Lord's goodness, His unchangeable righteousness – We must sing to the Lord!

QUOTE OF THE DAY

"I care not where I live, or what hardships I go through, so that I can but gain souls to Christ. All my desire is the conversion of sinners, and all my hope is in God."

David Brainerd (1717-1747)

DAY 4

📖 GENESIS 9; 11:1 – 9, 27-32; 12:1 – 9
📖 PSALMS 8, 9

⊛ K E Y   T H O U G H T S

- **Genesis 9:6** The intrinsic value of every human life, from conception to natural death, is established by our being made in the "image of God".
- 12:1-3, 7 The Abramic covenant.
  - a) as believers we are grafted into the promised blessings of this covenant (Gal. 3:13,14)
  - b) in mid-eastern conflicts of our time this "God chosen people" still have His special favor, this covenant is everlasting. (vs.7)
- **Psalm 8:1, 9** *"How excellent is Your Name in all the earth"* – above all names, higher than any other. He alone is worthy of our praise, the Lord alone is God.
- Therefore! "I will praise You... with my WHOLE heart."
- Ps. 9:10 He will not forsake those who seek Him. So, seek Him!

DAY 5

📖 GENESIS 12:10 – 20; 13, 14
📖 PSALM 10

☞ K E Y   T H O U G H T S

- **Genesis 12** Abram engages in the practice of building an altar at significant moments in his life. (When last did you "build an altar" to acknowledge the blessing of the Lord in your life?)
- Melchizedek: This unusual OT character is believed to be the first physical representation or Theophany of Jesus. Abram gives Him the first tithe recorded in scripture. Hebrews 7:1-10 speaks in further detail about this encounter.
- **Psalm 10:14** "You observe trouble and grief.....You are the helper of the fatherless....You have heard the desire of the humble... (vs. 17) (You will) ...do justice to the fatherless and the oppressed." (vs. 18)

QUOTE OF THE DAY

"For there is nothing that makes us love a person so much as praying for them; and when you can once do this sincerely for any man or woman, you have fitted your soul for the performance of everything that is kind and civil towards him."

William Law (1686-1761)

DAY 6

📖 GENESIS 15, 16
📖 PSALMS 11, 12, 13

☞ K E Y   T H O U G H T S

- **Genesis 15:6** The most notable characteristic of Abram is that "he believed" in the Lord.
- 15:18-21 "God's oath was unilateral, unconditional, with no requirements demanded of Abram as his part in this mighty

covenant. Abram simply believed. The Abrahamic covenant is the OT model for the New Covenant in Jesus Christ." (SFLB)

- **Psalm 13** We are sons and daughters who have an intimate relationship with the Father. We can come to Him in times of despair and trouble and unburden our hearts to Him. But notice how in vss. 5 & 6, there is always a return to the character of God, who does not change. The right perspective through trouble is trust, rejoicing and song; *"because He has dealt bountifully with me."*

QUOTE OF THE DAY

"God isn't looking for people of great faith, but for individuals ready to follow Him"

Hudson Taylor (1832-1905 Missionary to China)

DAY 7

📖 GENESIS 17, 18
📖 PSALMS 14, 15

◉ K E Y   T H O U G H T S

- **Genesis 17:7, 8** Note the words "everlasting covenant"
- 18:14 As God asks Abraham regarding the probability of an aged Sarah becoming pregnant; ask yourself regarding your situations.... *"is anything too hard for the Lord?"*
- 18:25 When we do not understand circumstances we remember the words: *"Shall not the Judge of all the earth do right?"*
- **Psalm 14:1** (What has the fool said?)
- 15:2 In answering the question "who may abide in Your tabernacle (presence)?" Meditate on the statement: *"he who... speaks the truth in his heart."*

QUOTE OF THE DAY

"It is good to be humbled. I am never better than when I am brought to lie at the foot of the cross. It is a certain sign God intends that soul a greater crown."

George Whitefield (1714-1770)

DAY 8

📖 GENESIS 19, 20
📖 PSALMS 16, 17

⊛ K E Y   T H O U G H T S

- **Genesis 19:16** Notice how difficult it is for the Lord to drag these people into His mercy. (How attached am I to the things of this world, the ways of the world, (vs. 26) how tempted am I to look back ….. to the "Sodoms" of my life?)
- **Psalm 16:11** Where is *"fullness of joy"* found? Where are *"pleasures forevermore"*?

QUOTE OF THE DAY

"He is no fool who gives up what he cannot keep to gain that which he cannot lose."

Jim Elliot, missionary martyr who lost his life in the late 1950's trying to reach the Auca Indians of Ecuador

DAY 9

📖 GENESIS 21, 22:1 – 19
📖 PSALM 18

⊛ K E Y   T H O U G H T S

- **Genesis 21:8** Abraham's faith in the Lord is completely secure. *"God will provide for Himself."*
- 21:18 The confirmation of the covenant with Abraham is based upon one simple principle, obedience. Notice the promised

blessing that flows from Abraham's obedience.

- **Psalm 18:3** The idea of *"calling upon the Lord"* occurs throughout scripture. We are always free to call upon the Lord!
- 18:30 Meditate on the truth that "His way is perfect; the word of the Lord is proven."

QUOTE OF THE DAY

"How shall I depend on Him for raising my body from the dust and saving my soul at last, if I distrust Him for a crust of bread towards my preservation?"

Joseph Hall (1574-1656)

DAY 10

📖 GENESIS 23, 24

⊙ K E Y   T H O U G H T S

- **Genesis 23, 24** Isaac and Rebekah illustrate the hand of the Lord directing, providing, caring for the important parts of our lives. Note as well, their submission to the Lord's way, allowing Him to work things out.

QUOTE OF THE DAY

"Prayer is as natural an expression of faith as breathing is of life; and to say a man lives a life of faith, and yet lives a prayerless life, is every bit as inconsistent and incredible as to say that a man lives without breathing."

Jonathan Edwards (1703-1758)

DAY 11

📖 GENESIS 25, 26
📖 PSALM 19

◉ K E Y   T H O U G H T S

- **Genesis 26:18** Isaac re-digs the wells that his father had dug. There is wisdom in returning to the faith, to the first love, the days when our foundations were established. The best things are not always the new things.

- 26:22 "Rehoboth" – the name of the well that they did not quarrel over means: "spaciousness". What a great thought – the Lord has a place of spacious blessing for each of us!

- **Psalm 19** One of the beautiful short Psalms. Presenting the two major ways that God communicates:

  a) through the magnificence of His creation;

  b) through the reliability and truth of His Word.

- Memorizing verses 7-11 would be a valuable exercise. At the very least – read this Psalm aloud once or twice today.

QUOTE OF THE DAY

"What a difference in men/women who go into battle intending to conquer if they can, and those who go into battle intending to conquer."

Dwight L. Moody (1837-1899)

DAY 12

📖 GENESIS 27
📖 PSALMS 20, 21

◉ K E Y   T H O U G H T S

- **Genesis 27** Note how in the beginning, lies and deception mark the life of Jacob – it will be decades before he actually overcomes this weakness in his life. Note also the role of parents in guiding children into either integrity or falsehood.

- 27:34-38 some of the saddest, most poignant verses in the Bible – Heb. 12:16 credits Esau with being *"immoral and godless".* He chooses anger and revenge as a way to resolve this family dispute – sowing damaging seeds for his descendants.

- **Psalm 20** A marvelous blessing is pronounced on those who will trust the Lord. Pray this Psalm out loud, pray it upon yourself.

- Ps. 21 The king: the coming Messiah.

- Vs.13 *"Be exalted, O Lord", "we will sing",* be sure, today to exalt the Lord and to lift up your voice and sing - TODAY!

QUOTE OF THE DAY

"A man can no more diminish God's glory by refusing to worship Him than a lunatic can put out the sun by scribbling the word, 'darkness' on the walls of his cell."

C. S. Lewis

DAY 13

📖 GENESIS 28, 29
📖 PSALMS 22, 23 (READ THE 23RD OUT LOUD)

⊙ K E Y   T H O U G H T S

- **Genesis 28:14** the continued renewal of the covenant of blessing upon the "seed" of Abraham. The covenant promised three things – a nation, a land, and the Messiah *(through your seed, all the nations of the earth will be blessed...)*.

- 28:22 the tithe is part of the Abrahamic covenant of grace. Melchizedek (Gen. 14) is a type of Christ, or even an OT appearance of Jesus (King and Priest) (Heb. 7:15ff).

- The ordinance of the tithe runs through the whole of scripture as an acknowledgement of the Lord's provision and authority in our finances.

- Jacob's experience at Bethel (Gen. 28:10-22). (Where is your 'Bethel' – that place where the Lord has revealed Himself to you, spoken to you, called you?)

- Notice how deception (or any sin) impacts many generations- Jacob deceived his father, now he is deceived in the matter of Leah and Rachel.

- **Psalm 22** contains significant Messianic prophecies, foreshadowing the words of Jesus on the cross. (vs. 1, 12-18)

- Vs. 3 The powerful principle of praise – our praises 'enthrone' the presence of God – as we praise and worship, the Holy Spirit is present to work in all the ways that the power of God is able to work, to heal, to restore and encourage, to deliver.

- 22:21b *"You have answered Me"* – notice the capitalization – of 'ME' – the Father did not abandon the Son on the cross, He will not abandon you.

QUOTE OF THE DAY

"There are no crownwearers in Heaven that were not crossbearers here below."

Charles Spurgeon (1834-1892)

DAY 14

📖 GENESIS 30
📖 PSALMS 24, 25, 26

◉ K E Y   T H O U G H T S

- **Genesis 30:22** Such a simple and powerful statement: *"God remembered, ... God listened... God opened."*

- **Psalm 24:33** a classic question, a very clear answer, *"he who has clean hands and a pure heart."*

- 24:10 The Captain of the army of the Lord, the leader of everything in heaven and in earth – that is who He is! As such, He has unquestioned authority.

- 25:14 The secret of the Lord? "with those who fear/reverence/ honor Him."

- 26:8 "I have loved.... Your house, and the place where Your glory dwells."

DAY 15

📖 GENESIS 31
📖 PSALMS 27, 28

⊚ K E Y T H O U G H T S

- **Genesis 31** Consider the provision of God in Jacob's life – do you have a situation in your life that seems unjust? (wage changes 10 times...) God is able to compensate more than fully when we are treated unjustly. He is the just and righteous judge.
- **Psalm 27** is so full of encouraging promises – vss. 13 and 14 are a fantastic decision and encouragement in times of struggle – we could all benefit from the final command: "Wait, I say on the Lord!"

DAY 16

📖 GENESIS 32, 33
📖 PSALMS 29, 30

◉ K E Y   T H O U G H T S

- **Genesis 32:22-32** *"Peniel"* – this classic encounter with the presence of God results in a dramatic change in the life of Jacob. When was your peniel? Have you marked the significant God encounters in your life as reference points for your future? Do you have a need for a fresh peniel?

- **Psalm 30** contains two wonderful promises: "Weeping may endure for a night, but joy comes in the morning", "You have turned for me my mourning into dancing"

- Through the seasons of life's difficulties – there will be an end, there will be a new day of blessing – hold on!

QUOTE OF THE DAY

"If God be your partner, make your plans large."

D.L. Moody (1837-1899)

DAY 17

📖 GENESIS 34, 35
📖 PSALMS 31, 32

◉ K E Y   T H O U G H T S

- **Genesis 34** This chapter shows the exaggeration of "honor", and the depths that racism can fall to. These brothers were reprimanded formally by God for their violence and cruelty (Genesis 49:5).

- Genesis 35:7, 14 Notice how often Jacob builds an altar for worship and thanksgiving.

- Vs. 10 Jacob's name is officially changed to "Israel".

- Vss. 9-13 The Abrahamic covenant is renewed with Jacob/Israel.
- **Psalms 31, 32** These two Psalms provide clear warning regarding the consequence of sin 31:10 *"my strength fails because of my iniquity".*
- and the joy of those who find forgiveness in the Lord.
- 31:24 "Be of good courage, and He shall strengthen your heart."
- 32:1 "Blessed is he whose transgression is forgiven."
- 32:8 This verse is one of the life promises that I have leaned on for many years. The Lord says: *"I will instruct you and teach you... I will guide you with My eye!"*

QUOTE OF THE DAY

"Let the seas roar, the earth be shaken, and all things go to ruin and confusion; yet, the soul that adheres to God will remain safe and quiet, and shall not be moved forever."

Robert Leighton (1613-1684)

DAY 18

📖 GENESIS 37, 38
📖 PSALM 33

◉ K E Y   T H O U G H T S

- **Genesis 37, 38** The long trickling down effect of dishonesty and sin upon a family.
- Polygamy was never God's best for families. The rivalry and hatred among siblings and "wives" was a constant thorn and stumbling block and point of contention.
- Yet God in His wisdom proves Himself a redeeming God through every botch up of man – His plans are always being perfected.
- **Psalm 33:6** The creative 'word' of the Lord is the starting point of everything that is. He is the first cause, His initiative and His word set all the world in motion.

QUOTE OF THE DAY:

"The greatness of a man's power is the measure of his surrender."

William Booth (1829-1912)

DAY 19

📖 GENESIS 39
📖 PSALM 34

"IF POSSIBLE READ THIS PSALM OUT LOUD — HEAR YOUR OWN VOICE DECLARING THESE MARVELOUS PROMISES OF GOD."

⊖ KEY THOUGHTS

- **Genesis 39** One of the great chapters in the Bible on <u>character</u>.

- The base line principle is that the hand of the Lord was upon Joseph – the Lord does have favor to bestow upon us!

- Integrity; patience; purity; steadfastness through injustice

- Looking past momentary gratification (sin with Potiphar's wife) to long term and more global consequence – *"How could I do this great wickedness and sin against God?"*

- Through every mistreatment – the favor, the hand of the Lord continues to prosper this great example – no matter what, the Lord is able to transform difficulty into blessing if we will trust Him first!

QUOTE OF THE DAY

"I feel it is far better to begin the day with God, to see His face first, to get my soul near Him before it is near another."

Robert M. McCheyne (1813-1843)

DAY 20

📖 GENESIS 40, 41
📖 PSALM 35

⊙ K E Y   T H O U G H T S

- **Genesis 40, 41** The Lord is at work for the preservation of His chosen people (the covenant of Abraham, Isaac and Jacob).

- Joseph has spent years languishing, he must have asked the Lord many times…. (When will the dreams you have given me come to pass?)

- In one day, seemingly with a few hours, Joseph arises from a prison to be second in authority in a great Kingdom!

- Faithfulness to God is the pathway to advancement and influence – He will make a way!

- **Psalm 35** It is the Lord who vindicates when we have enemies rising against us or we are treated with injustice. Put your trust in Him to vindicate your cause, He is able to clear your name. Interesting how this truth was just illustrated in the life of Joseph!

QUOTE OF THE DAY

"He that takes no care to set forth God's portion of time in the morning, doth not only rob God of His due, but is a thief to himself all the day after, by losing the blessing which a faithful prayer might bring from heaven on his undertaking (behalf)"

William Gurnall (1617-1679)

DAY 21

📖 GENESIS 42, 43
📖 PSALM 36

⊙ K E Y   T H O U G H T S

- **Genesis 42, 43** Although Joseph's actions are a bit confusing to understand, the underlying principle is his processing of forgiveness.

- A godly heart is always challenged with the practical outworking of forgiveness, what does it really look like when applied to family relationships?

- **Psalm 36:5, 6** Notice these four characteristics of God; mercy, faithfulness, righteousness, judgments.

- 36:9 Where is the fountain of life? Where do we see light?

QUOTE OF THE DAY

"Do all the good you can,
By all the means you can,
In all the ways you can,
In all the places you can,
At all the times you can,
To all the people you can,
As long as ever you can."

John Wesley

DAY 22

📖 GENESIS 44, 45
📖 PSALM 37

◉ K E Y   T H O U G H T S

- **Genesis 45** This chapter of Joseph's life illustrates that there is an overwhelming release once the restoration of a relationship happens, when everything gets 'into the light' there is freedom.

- **Psalm 37:1-8** Bedrock principles of trust – "do not fret, trust in the Lord, delight yourself in the Lord, Commit your way to the Lord, Rest in the Lord, Cease from anger"

- 37:23, 24 This is a promise – always expect that the Lord will *"uphold you with His hand"*.

"I have but one passion: It is He, it is He alone. The world is the field and the field is the world; and henceforth that country shall be my home where I can be most used in winning souls for Christ."

Count Nicolaus Ludwig von Zinzendorf, founder of the Moravian Missionary Society

DAY 23

📖 GENESIS 46:1 – 7, 27 – 34; 47
📖 PSALM 38

⊙ K E Y   T H O U G H T S

- **Genesis 46** Great illustration of God's provision for His people – His faithfulness to the covenant to Abraham – even through the trials of Joseph.
- **Psalm 38:3-8** there will be times when we feel discouraged to the point of being overwhelmed. Our sinful behavior is usually the cause, they feel like wounds.
- A repentant heart will always find comfort in the presence of the Lord (vs. 18) *"I will be in anguish over my sin"*.
- True repentance includes grief, not a smug, casual indifference. In those moments the Lord's grace and mercy are so sweet as He *"restores our soul"*.

QUOTE OF THE DAY

"It's amazing what can be accomplished if you don't worry about who gets the credit."

Clarence W. Jones

DAY 24

📖 GENESIS 48
📖 PSALMS 39, 40

⊙ K E Y   T H O U G H T S

- **Genesis 48** The power of blessing: there is a prophetic element to these blessings pronounced by Jacob/Israel. (Have you released blessing upon your family? Your friends? What increase are you speaking over your children?)

- There is no long term benefit in withholding words of life and blessing from those we love, be generous with words of encouragement and blessing, make it a plan.

- **Psalm 39** The theme today is about the tongue in both sections of our reading: (vs. 1) *"I will guard my ways, lest I sin with my tongue".*

- Ps. 40 *"I waited patiently for the Lord.... And He heard my cry."* The Lord our God is a prayer hearing and prayer answering God!

- The power of corporate worship, the importance of gathering together: 40:10 *"I have declared Your faithfulness ....in the great assembly."*

- 40:17 Poor and needy "yet the Lord thinks upon me... do not delay, O my God."

QUOTE OF THE DAY

"Atheists don't believe in hell and neither do most Christians."

Leonard Ravenhill

DAY 25

📖 GENESIS 49, 50
📖 PSALM 41

☉ K E Y T H O U G H T S

- **Genesis 50:15, 20** True forgiveness does not rehash and repay the past offenses that have been brought under the blood.

- 50:20 This verse is a great comfort to any who have suffered unjustly. God is able to transform tragic circumstances into good. We do not cross the line into saying God caused the evil, or the injustice. Those evil things result from the fallen condition of man and our world. But because of the Lord's power and authority, He is able to bring glory to Himself with any surrendered heart no matter what the difficulty or circumstance – He 'turns' it, confounding the devil's plan. God is much bigger than the devil! (Rom. 8:28)

- **Psalm 41:1** Consider this promise of blessing: "blessed are those who consider the poor".

- 41:9 Notice this prophetic foreshadowing of the role of Judas Iscariot.

- Vs.12 The Lord knows the heart. When there is integrity of heart regardless of the outward misunderstandings, He will uphold you in your integrity.

QUOTE OF THE DAY

"Our greatest fear should not be of failure but of succeeding at things in life that don't really matter."

Francis Chan, 'Crazy Love'

DAY 26

📖 EXODUS 1, 2
📖 PROVERBS 1

⊙ K E Y   T H O U G H T S

- **Exodus 2:23-25** God remembers, and God hears. We can have confidence that the Lord does not forget His promises to us. He is faithful, in His time – He will "acknowledge" us.
- Proverbs 1 Wisdom is personified much of the time in Proverbs, speaking in the first person.
- **Proverbs 1:33** summarizes the chapter – "…whoever listens… will dwell safely… will be secure, without fear."

QUOTE OF THE DAY

"God has communicated to man, the infinite to the finite. The One who made man capable of language in the first place has communicated to man in language about both spiritual reality and physical reality, about the nature of God and the nature of man."

Francis Schaeffer

DAY 27

📖 EXODUS 3
📖 PROVERBS 2

⊙ K E Y   T H O U G H T S

- **Exodus 3** The burning bush passage contains many applicable principles for us – God reveals Himself in Holiness.
- *"The place where you are standing is Holy"* – there will be moments in our lives where the Holiness of God is overwhelming. (Am I in a place where when He calls my name I say "Here I am"?)
- (Have I had a 'holy ground' experience this past year, will I

seek His presence this coming year?)

- 3:7 A verse of great comfort: *"I have seen the oppression, I have heard their cry, I know their sorrows."* The same is true for you who are struggling today.
- Vs. 14 One of the foundational names of God "I AM" – no beginning, no ending – He always was and always will be. This name is a key characteristic of what makes Him truly the only God.
- **Proverbs 2:10-12** "When wisdom enters your heart and knowledge is pleasant to your soul". Two benefits result (fill in the blanks):

    1) Discretion will _____.

    2) Understanding will _____.

- Immorality is personified in three alliterated characteristics. The immoral person...

    1) Flatters

    2) Forsakes

    3) Forgets

- Vss. 18, 19 The end of sexual immorality is death, (something always dies!)
- Notice that regaining the "path of life" is most difficult. We know that the power of Jesus and the cross bring restoration from sexual immorality. But, these dire warnings are to preserve you from the inevitable consequences that flow from sexual impurity.
- These proverbs are diametrically opposed to the sexually permissive and sexually saturated culture we live in. They are a breath of fresh air for those who desire to live in the fullest anointing and grace of God.

QUOTE OF THE DAY

"Catch on fire and others will love to come watch you burn."

John Wesley

DAY 28

📖 EXODUS 4, 5, 6:1 – 9
📖 PROVERBS 3:1 – 6

◉ K E Y T H O U G H T S

- **Exodus** There was a clear promise of deliverance and blessing by God, accompanied by miraculous signs ... *"the people believed"*.

- However the fulfillment of the promises and the timing became very confusing and challenging to the people.

- The promise had not changed, but the hardship in between the promise and its fulfillment caused real disillusionment and discouragement.

- The re-statement of the covenant promises in the past and the specific promises addressed to their captivity is a powerful encouragement, it should have lifted their spirits.

- **6:9** There will be times of trouble in our lives when it seems difficult to hear God or sense His presence. This verse gives us two things that cause us to lose perspective: *"anguish of spirit and cruel bondage"*. God has not changed, has not forgotten and is at work to fulfill His Word, even when the trouble and pain of our lives make it difficult to hear Him or see His hand. Persevere! He is at work.

- **Proverbs 3:5, 6** ought to be memorized – instead of further reading today, give some time to memorizing these powerful, encouraging promises.

QUOTE OF THE DAY

"I continue to dream and pray about a revival of holiness in our day that moves forth in mission and creates authentic community in which each person can be unleashed through the empowerment of the Spirit to fulfill God's creational intentions."

John Wesley, How to Pray: The Best Of John Wesley

DAY 29

⊚ K E Y   T H O U G H T S

- **Exodus 7:1-7** We learn that the result of Moses and Aaron speaking to Pharaoh will be that his heart will remain stubborn He will not listen to God's voice. In spite of this hardness of heart God will still be glorified through miraculous signs and a great deliverance.

- 8:15, 32 Often when we receive "relief" from the Lord, or our situation improves we are quick to forget the promises we made in the time of trial.

- Notice: Pharaoh again, hardened his heart.

- What a powerful relationship between Moses and God, the power of prayer, entreatment and obedience.

- **Proverbs 3:9, 10** There is specific blessing promised to those who will honor the Lord with the first-fruits of their possessions.

- Vs. 11, 12 During a season of chastening or correction, receive it with thankfulness. The Lord is shaping character and protecting from further trouble in the future.

- Vs. 27-30 Excellence of business practice, an open handed integrity with our neighbors (community).

QUOTE OF THE DAY

"Loving God - really loving Him - means living out His commands no matter what the cost."

Charles Colson

DAY 30

📖 EXODUS 9, 10
📖 PROVERBS 4

◉ K E Y   T H O U G H T S

- **Exodus 9:4** The Lord is able to differentiate between those who are His and those who are not. We can have confidence in the Lord's protection and care even when things around us are being destroyed.

- 9:34 A consistent characteristic of a sinful heart is "hardness". A hardened heart is a sinful heart.

- Pharaoh, like any unrepentant person is fully responsible for the hardening and rebellion of his own heart. His pride and self-sufficiency (this was a battle between gods, Pharaoh considered himself a god and was worshipped by his people as such), were the battle ground.

- God's part in the hardening of Pharaoh's heart was in providing the miracles that occasioned his own (Pharaoh) rebellious and proud decisions.

- **Proverbs 4:18** The ever rising promise for "the just" is contrasted with, and sandwiched between the description of the future of the wicked.

QUOTE OF THE DAY

"The work of a Christian lies not in the depth of speculation, but in the height of practice."

Thomas Manton (1620-1677)

DAY 31

📖 EXODUS 11, 12
📖 PROVERBS 4

◉ K E Y   T H O U G H T S

- **Exodus 11** We see again, Moses' issue with anger (11:8). His first angry outburst resulted in murder. This event does not have any recorded consequence, but one of his next incidents keeps him from the Promised Land. Scripture has much to say about anger, particularly the damage an uncontrolled temper can produce.

- Ex. 12 The Passover is instituted. The powerful foreshadowing of the Lord Jesus Christ as the *"Lamb of God who takes away the sins of the world"* (John 1:29), is clear in the Passover remembrance.

- "It is characterized by selecting a Lamb, which is sacrificed four days later and eaten as part of a major commemorative meal. A feast of hope and life, the Passover represents deliverance and new beginnings; in many of its elements, it is a type of Christ our Redeemer, the Lamb of God." (SFLB)

- **Proverbs 4:7** "Wisdom is the principle thing; Therefore get wisdom!"

- 4:13 "Take firm hold of instruction, do not let her go!"

- Wisdom is found in God's Word, (Proverbs is a part of the Bible's wisdom literature) – foolishness is with wickedness, (vs. 19) *"they do not know what makes them stumble."*

QUOTE OF THE DAY

"There are two kinds of people: those who say to God, "Thy will be done," and those to whom God says, "All right, then, have it your way.""

C. S. Lewis

DAY 32

⊛ K E Y   T H O U G H T S

- **Exodus 14:13** *"Stand still, and see the salvation of the Lord, which He will accomplish for you today."* In the most pressing circumstances (sea in front, armies in the rear) –the instruction of the Lord was to be still and watch the power of God at work.

- The Lord will fight for you. It is the Lord who vindicates His own children – think of "the Lord" fighting on your behalf!

- **Proverbs 5** A very clear portrayal of the characteristics of the seducer and the seduced, when it comes to sexual immorality, specifically adultery (married people having sexual relations with someone other than their spouse).

- The depiction of the dire consequences of immorality is very stark and shocking. The adulterer loses their ability to think beyond the moment, sin causes temporary insanity, they will give up everything in their life that they love for a moment of indulgence.

- 5:18 A great command of wisdom for a happy life, and a blessed life – <u>rejoice</u> in the wife of your youth, in the husband of your youth.

QUOTE OF THE DAY

"I ought to spend the best hours of the day in communion with God. It is my noblest and most fruitful employment, and is not to be thrust into any corner."

Robert M. McCheyne (1813-1843)

DAY 33

📖 EXODUS 15, 16
📖 PROVERBS 6:1 – 19

⊙ K E Y   T H O U G H T S

- **Exodus 15: 20, 21** A wonderful picture of celebration at the victory the Lord has brought to Israel. (How are you at celebrating? Does song and dance ever flow enthusiastically from your life?)

- We are continually bumping into the "complaining and grumbling" of these people. It seems that at every reversal, their allegiance wavers from the Lord.

- This fundamental flaw, or indulgence of the flesh appears repeatedly through this history – are we different? (What is our default position when things are not clear, or there is some pain or struggle? Complaining, grumbling, longing for the good old days of bondage?)

- **Proverbs 6:16-19** (Do you find yourself anywhere in this list of seven things that the Lord "hates"? (strong feelings!)).

- (What does *one who sows discord among the brethren* mean to you? What have you observed in others or yourself?)

QUOTE OF THE DAY

"Forgiveness lies at the heart of the Christian faith. It can heal broken families, it can restore friendships and it can reconcile divided communities. It is in forgiveness that we feel the power of God's love."

Queen Elizabeth II (Christmas speech 2011)

DAY 34

📖 EXODUS 17, 18
📖 PROVERBS 6:20 – 35, 7

☉ K E Y   T H O U G H T S

- **Exodus 17, 18** The people have begun to put their trust in the man Moses, their eyes are away from the Lord (who will not fail). 17:4 shows the inevitable result of trusting in man – they were disillusioned and ready to stone him.

- Tempting the Lord – assigning characteristics to God that are the opposite to His revealed character. 17:7 *"is the Lord among us?"* God had promised to always be among them – He is faithful, He will be faithful, we must remain faithful to Him through the times when we suffer or struggle.

- Aaron and Hur are a wonderful illustration of those who decide to walk along-side leaders to strengthen their hands for victory over the enemy. This picture of lifting up heavy hands is a lasting call to stand in unity.

- Ex. 18 Jethro's wisdom is from the Lord for the good of the people. Identifying leaders who are *"able men, such as fear God, men of truth, hating covetousness"* (vs. 21), and appointing them to lead differing sized groups of people is still effective to care for a growing congregation.

- **Proverbs 6 & 7** Further descriptions, warnings and consequences of sexual immorality. These graphic warnings should dispel any doubt about the rightness or wrongness of sexual activity outside of marriage.

- 7:14 is a stunning example of someone being religious technically and using it as justification for sin. Jesus has no compassion for this type of heart. Matt. 23:23, speaks to someone who is obeying the letter of the law and ignoring the weightier matters of obedience. This also speaks to the person who tries to split hairs on what is immoral and what is not. Being committed to Christ requires a higher standard than looking for technicalities and loopholes to indulge the flesh.

- 7:27 The "house" of immorality "is the way to hell, descending to the chambers of death."

- 6:32 *"He who does so destroys his own soul."*

- These Proverbs contain warnings that are proven true over and over again through history – learn from the sad examples of others and listen to the wisdom of the Lord. You will be blessed if you do!

- To those who have fallen into sexual immorality, true repentance and transparency are the pathway to restoration. Do not delay. Bring it into the light, with God and with trusted others.

QUOTE OF THE DAY

"Lukewarm living and claiming Christ's name simultaneously is utterly disgusting to God."

Francis Chan, 'Crazy Love: Overwhelmed by a Relentless God'

DAY 35

📖 EXODUS 19
📖 PROVERBS 8, 9

◉ K E Y   T H O U G H T S

- **Exodus 19:5** This verse gives the principle of God's ownership of all the earth. The earth and all the peoples of the earth are His, He has the authority to choose one people as *"a special treasure to Me."* God's authority over the earth and its peoples must be understood to grasp global issues that appear to be unfair to man (Ps. 24:1). He is the ultimate authority, He is good, He does as He chooses to do, without malice and with total and perfect wisdom.

- The people are not to come near the mountain of God; praise God that through Jesus blood we are able to enter the very presence of God *"the Presence behind the veil"*. (Heb. 6:19)

- **Proverbs 8:13; 9:10** *"The fear of the Lord."* Two clear examples are given:

    a) *"The fear of the Lord is to hate evil."*

b) *"The fear of the Lord is the beginning of wisdom."*

- Willingness to receive reproofs, instruction, advice with humility all build into the fear of the Lord.
- "The words "wisdom" or "wise" and "understanding" occur over 140 times in Proverbs." (SFLB)
- Wisdom is knowing the truth and how to apply it to any given situation.
- This is why Proverbs continually exhorts us to *"get wisdom"*.

QUOTE OF THE DAY

"Can you worship a God who isn't obligated to explain His actions to you? Could it be your arrogance that makes you think God owes you an explanation?"

Francis Chan, 'Crazy Love: Overwhelmed by a Relentless God'

DAY 36

📖 EXODUS 20; 21:12 – 27; 22:16 – 31
📖 PROVERBS 10

⌖ KEY THOUGHTS

- **Exodus 22:21** The treatment of strangers and the poor is an important component in the culture of God's people. The values of a people need to be built upon the Lord's redemptive actions in their past, *"for you were strangers"* at one time.
- 22:29 As we are learning to be givers in line with the Word of God we find the principle of not "delaying" to bring our tithes and offerings. Perhaps you have found this in the past that to delay with the firstfruits often means that we do not bring the firstfruits. Bring them to the Lord without delay.
- **Proverbs 10:12** The power of love, not to overlook sin, but to forgive. Not a leniency with sinful living but a grace to restore when someone loved stumbles. Thank God for the wideness of His grace with us!
- Pursue the *"blessing of the Lord"* (Prov. 10:22). There is no sorrow added when we receive the riches of the Lord.

"We think sometimes that poverty is only being hungry, naked and homeless. The poverty of being unwanted, unloved and uncared for is the greatest poverty. We must start in our own homes to remedy this kind of poverty."

Mother Teresa

DAY 37

📖 EXODUS 23, 24
📖 PROVERBS 11

☉ K E Y   T H O U G H T S

- **Exodus 23, 24** The people of God are to remember His faithfulness and provision with three annual celebrations where "all the males" are to present themselves before the Lord. The principle of "not forgetting" the goodness of the Lord is a huge component of living faithfully before the Lord.

- **24:9-18** A powerful description of time with the Lord, "on the mountain". As we spend time daily with the Lord we should set a standard that we will encounter His presence each day. We never want our time with the Lord to become religious or lifeless.

- **11:24, 30** Two encouraging benefits for those who build godly character. To the generous; supernatural principle of sowing and reaping – even though it seems as though giving is reducing our resource, yet, with God it actually increases our supply.

- Soul winning is equated with wisdom, the fruit of those who walk with God is a tree of life! *"He who wins souls is wise"*, is a powerful motto to live by.

QUOTE OF THE DAY

It has been said that our anxiety does not empty tomorrow of its sorrow, but only empties today of its strength.

Charles Spurgeon

DAY 38

📖 EXODUS 29, 31:1 – 11, 18
📖 PROVERBS 12

⊙ K E Y   T H O U G H T S

- **Exodus 29, 31** The details of the construction of the tabernacle, the ark, all the garments and furniture are precise and specific.

- The purpose of this elaborate preparation was to make a place for the presence of the Lord to dwell.

- 29:43-46 God's purpose was to give Israel a place where His glory would dwell, a place where He could be "among them".

- This is always God's heart for His people, to be among us, to dwell with us – the Holy Spirit is Jesus' provision for us now.

- John 14:16 *"And I will pray to the Father, and He will give you another Helper, that He may <u>abide with you forever</u> - 17 the Spirit of truth, . . . but you know Him, for <u>He dwells with you and will be in you</u>"*.

- **Proverbs 12:25, 26** *"Anxiety causes depression"* – such a straightforward statement of wisdom. Notice that the solution is a "good word" from one to another.

- The power of words of encouragement is that they are transforming to the hearer. Grow in this ministry – encourage someone today!

- The importance of choosing godly friends – those whose hearts are after God in a way that encourages, motivates and brings the best out in you. Two important thoughts:

  a) Who is challenging you?

  b) Who are you challenging to godliness?

QUOTE OF THE DAY

"Do all the good you can, in all the ways you can, to all the souls you can, in every place you can, at all the times you can, with all the zeal you can, as long as ever you can."

John Wesley

DAY 39

📖 EXODUS 32
📖 PROVERBS 13

🔘 K E Y   T H O U G H T S

- **Exodus 32** A number of key principles and examples are contained in this famous chapter.

- The tendency of people to wander from the true God to "gods" made with hands – something more tangible, something that still is god-like but has less demands on their lives.

- Humanity is always looking for ways to blend true worship with humanly designed worship. God has defined true worship, but man prefers to design his own way so that he can do what he wants rather than submit to the ways of the Lord. *"To obey is better than sacrifice."* (1 Sam 15:22)

- The role of an intercessor: Moses stands in the gap for the people of Israel. God listens to Moses' petition and "relents", or is moved to pity. We are never out of order to petition the Lord for mercy – He is the one who will perfectly balance justice and mercy – we are free to ask.

- 32:26 This ultimatum should always bring challenge to our hearts – *"whoever is on the Lord's side?"*

- 32:33 We will all be accountable for our own sins, no other human can take our place. *"Whoever has sinned against Me, I will blot him out of My book."*

- Praise God for the substitutionary work of Jesus on the cross. *Jesus is the one who is able*, He is the one who has made a way for us to receive forgiveness! (Isaiah 53:5, 6; Colossians 2:24)

- **Proverbs 13:24** *"He who loves him (son/daughter) disciplines him promptly"*. Loving, godly discipline is essential to the character development of our children. We are never to harm, injure or correct in anger. We are to treat our children as we are treated by God – *"those the Lord loves, He corrects."*

"Education without values, as useful as it is, seems rather to make man a more clever devil."

C. S. Lewis

DAY 40

📖 EXODUS 33, 34
📖 PROVERBS 14

☀ K E Y   T H O U G H T S

- **Exodus 33** describes a nation in revival. There was a place called the tabernacle of meeting, the meeting was with the presence of the Lord.

- There is great value in setting aside time specifically for the purpose of meeting with the Lord. Camp meetings, special times of prayer and fasting, conferences, all have value in refocusing our spiritual vitality and vision.

- 33:17 God knows us "by name" – have you thought recently of the significance of God knowing your name? How personal, how meaningful is this "friend" called Jesus.

- 34:26 *"Do not boil a young goat in its mother's milk"* – just for interest sake, this most likely had to do with a pagan Canaanite fertility rite. The people were to have nothing to do with any ungodly idolatry or associations. They were to be holy, separated unto the Lord.

- **Proverbs 14:12** Man has always put forward his own ways, ways that seem right in "his own eyes." Those who are determined to follow the Lord are concerned with following the ways of the Lord and walking in His commands.

QUOTE OF THE DAY

"We are all missionaries...Wherever we go, we either bring people nearer to Christ, or we repel them from Christ."

Eric Liddell

DAY 41

📖 EXODUS 35:20 – 36:7
📖 PROVERBS 15

⊚ K E Y   T H O U G H T S

- **Exodus 35, 36** This is one of the giving highlights of the entire Bible. This phrase used is repeatedly; *"whose heart was stirred, and in whose spirit was willing, ... And they brought"*, is a beautiful picture of the heart of a giver.

- These gifts are freewill offerings, unprescribed amounts, out of their own hearts. The corporate desire of the people to build the house of the Lord was overwhelming.

- This zeal for the Lord's house was so contagious that for the first and the only time in the Bible, the people are told to stop giving, there was too much given for the necessary work to be completed.

- (How is your heart for the house of the Lord? Is your heart stirred and your spirit willing?)

- Like the children of Israel, our attitude to giving is a very reliable indicator of spiritual growth. It is impossible to be filled with the Spirit of the most extravagant God and maintain a miserly heart toward His house and His people.

- **Proverbs 15:16, 17** On the theme of contentment and financial position. Great treasure does not buy happiness, great feasting is no substitute for 'love'.

- The repeated, consistent teaching of scripture regarding finances is to honor and obey the Lord first *("the first of the firstfruits")*, to trust Him completely *("not our own wisdom")* – and then we will see His blessing, financially and in the family order where love reigns! So many homes are conflicted over finances, if only they would surrender to the wisdom of the Lord.

QUOTE OF THE DAY

"When it's hard and you are doubtful, give more."

Francis Chan, 'Crazy Love: Overwhelmed by a Relentless God'

DAY 42

📖 EXODUS 37:7 – 9; 40:12 – 38
📖 PROVERBS 16

⊛ K E Y   T H O U G H T S

- **Exodus 37** The mercy seat: a beautiful physical representation of the mercy of God. In the case of the ark of the covenant "mercy" actually had a physical location. Now, because of the precious blood of the Lord Jesus we are able to find mercy *"in time of need."*

- Hebrews 4:16 *"Let us therefore come boldly to the throne of grace, that we may obtain mercy and find grace to help in time of need."*

- The glory of the Lord – how we long for this experience in our lives! "Lord, I want to know your glory, show me your glory I pray."

- **Proverbs 16:18, 19** Pride is almost impossible to self-diagnose. That is the nature of pride, it is like carbon monoxide, difficult to detect until it is too late.

- (Have you observed pride in someone else's life that can be an example to you, or, have you seen the consequences of pride in your own life in the past that you can learn from?)

- The pursuit of genuine humility, as in the example of Jesus, is a very good life goal!

- Uncontrolled anger is identified often in the wisdom literature as a destructive trait.

- (How do we measure up in these two warnings, pride and anger? Is there work to be done in our character by the Holy Spirit?)

QUOTE OF THE DAY

"Meaninglessness ultimately comes not from being weary of pain but from being weary of pleasure."

G.K. Chesterton

DAY 43

📖 MATTHEW 3, 4
📖 PROVERBS 17

⊛ K E Y   T H O U G H T S

- **Matthew 3:8, 10** The theme of fruitfulness is used a lot through the NT (New Testament). The measure of our lives in Christ is not so much in what we say or how we appear, but in the fruit that our lives produce

- In this case the fruit is to be 'in keeping' with repentance, a change of course, evidence of true repentance is a change of behavior… not just pious sounding words.

- **Proverbs 17** Much wisdom pertaining to the tongue, to words, to tale-bearing.

- The Bible is very concerned with relationships, how to be a good friend, how to avoid strife and conflict. (vss. 4, 9, 14, 17, 27, 28)

- (Is my life characterized by these traits? Would an outside observer call me 'wise' or a 'fool' in these matters?)

QUOTE OF THE DAY

"Experience: that most brutal of teachers. But you learn, my God do you learn."

C. S. Lewis

DAY 44

📖 MATTHEW 5
📖 PROVERBS 18

⊛ K E Y   T H O U G H T S

- Wow! Today we have two of the most amazing chapters in the whole of scripture

- **Matthew 5** Some of Jesus most famous words – the Beatitudes and many of His upside down instructions.

- Jesus demonstrates in this sermon that His followers will be decidedly different from those in the world.

- Vs. 14 Jesus commands us to let our lights shine, not to hide the light of the gospel that is in our hearts. In order for the good works of our lives to point people to Christ, as followers of Jesus we must be recognizably different from those who are not following His ways.

- (Do they know us to be followers of Jesus?)

- Vs. 44 Loving and praying for our enemies, or those who have mistreated us is surely one of the most effective ways to realize forgiveness and healing. It also disarms the opposition - how can you oppose love?

- Jesus' standard of the kingdom is not one of degrees, but is rather a clear radical call to obedience in the heart! He is not about external appearances, but purity on the inside. It is a high standard.

- **Proverbs 18** Take a few extra moments to meditate on the wisdom and help found in these verses: 1; 13; 16; 21; 22; 24. If we lived all these principles we would have a very fulfilling life!

QUOTE OF THE DAY

"Holy solitaries' is a phrase no more consistent with the Gospel than holy adulterers. The Gospel of Christ knows no religion but social; no holiness, but social holiness."

John Wesley

DAY 45

◻ MATTHEW 6
◻ PROVERBS 19

◉ K E Y   T H O U G H T S

- **Matthew 6** Jesus' teachings on giving and prayer are not to establish strict rules that giving must always be anonymous, and prayer must only be offered in secret.

- He is coming against the hypocritical practice of public display for personal glory, which misses the point of these actions completely.

- The purpose of alms-giving is for the blessing of the poor, not for the commendation of the giver.

- The purpose of prayer is communion and intercession with God, not to gain the admiration of other people, who see you as a great "pray-er".

- Giving to the poor is to be done in a way that honors the recipient, quietly, without ostentation. Other types of giving are done publicly for the encouragement of all.

- 6:14, 15 Jesus' teaching about forgiveness is strong. If we refuse to forgive others, we should expect the same reception from God. How inconsistent to expect mercy, expect grace, claim to have received God's mercy and yet have none to share with others.

- **Proverbs 19:17** Think of this! Lending to the Lord, of course He will pay back! What a powerful motivator to sacrifice for those in need around us. The debt from this care for the poor becomes God's own debt to the giver.

- 19:22 Kindness . . . *"what is desired in a man/woman is kindness"* – how radical and simple.

QUOTE OF THE DAY

"He measures our lives by how we love."

Francis Chan, 'Crazy Love: Overwhelmed by a Relentless God'

DAY 46

📖 MATTHEW 7
📖 PROVERBS 20, 21

⊛ K E Y   T H O U G H T S

- **Matthew 7** This third chapter in Matthew's account of the sermon on the mount contains one foundational principle after another:

- The plank in our own eye – (those who easily take offense but are blind to their own need of mercy)
- The power of simple asking prayer mixed with faith (7,8)
- The practical promise of the Holy Spirit – (c.r. - Luke 11:13), *"How much more...."* This is the heart of our Father in Heaven.

- Vss. 15-23 Those true followers of Jesus are known by the fruit of their lives, and their heart, rather than by the words they speak or the appearances they present.

- Vs. 23 *"you who practice lawlessness"* – hypocrisy, private disobedience, a heart that is secretly self-centered instead of submitted to Christ's Lordship, the true measure of the soul... that is what will be evaluated on that day.

- External religious behavior, or popular thought on righeouness, (such as politcal correctness) will not save us.

- Building on the Rock. (vss. 24-29) The key words are *"hears these sayings of Mine <u>and does them</u>."*

- **Proverbs 20:14** Have you ever bartered with a vendor in the Old city of Jerusalem? Carina had this experience with a shop merchant: "Oh you are very beautiful, you have beautiful eyes, come in to my shop". After the bartering process, as he handed her the vase and a bag he said "ugly old woman!"

- 21:30 No earthly wisdom, understanding or counsel will stand against the Lord! Follow His ways.

QUOTE OF THE DAY

"with all prayer (Eph. 6:18)" All sorts of prayer- public, private, mental, vocal. Do not be diligent in one kind of prayer and negligent in others... let us use all."

John Wesley 'How to Pray: The Best Of John Wesley'

DAY 47

⊙ K E Y   T H O U G H T S

- **Matthew 8:13** *"As you have believed"* – also vs. 26 *"why are you fearful, O you of little faith?"*

- Jesus places significant value upon faith, believing. There is no denying that believing faith coupled with asking is taught by Jesus as a kingdom principle.

- We often feel weak in this area. Perhaps looking at our lack of answers we conclude that we have no faith or that we are rejected for lack of faith. Our posture should be instead – "Lord, increase my faith!" – "Help my unbelief"

- Never allow condemnation for a lack of faith, to define unanswered prayer. Never say "it's my fault" – always ask, always knock – never shut the door of God's possibilities because of personal fear of failure!

- *"Be believing, not unbelieving!"*

- Healing (8:17) – Jesus is our provision for healing (quoting Isa 53:4, 5). Christ's cross and the blood that He shed gives us the boldness and the promised provision to seek all types of healing, physical, emotional, mental.

- Jesus, you are my healer!

- **Matthew 9:37, 38** This declaration of truth by Jesus must take root in our hearts, as we live in a disinterested culture of secularism!

- There is, among us, a ripened harvest. It is a fact!

- There is a need for workers, laborers to work in the harvest! This need is also a fact!

- Pray for workers. "Oh God, speak to people's hearts, call them to the harvest!" "Speak to my heart, Lord."

"Some wish to live within the sound of a chapel bell; I wish to run a rescue mission within a yard of hell."

C.T. Studd

DAY 48

📖 MATTHEW 10
📖 PROVERBS 23

⊛ K E Y   T H O U G H T S

- **Matthew 10** Jesus gives authority to those that He commissions to do His work, to heal, to cast out demons and to testify.

- 10:28 The "fear of God" is a large recurring theme through the whole of scripture. God's holiness and character are the sources of this reverence. The response of one who fears God is obedience and worship. An unwavering conviction that the ways of the Lord are right.

- 10:32-39 In dealing with challenging verses, always balance them with the rest of the scripture and the recorded words of the speaker. Jesus is not against family! The whole of his teaching, including His words from the cross regarding His own mother show us that family is highly valued and "religion" must never be used as an excuse to be irresponsible with our family members.

- This teaching and others like it are directing us to the first place of our commitment to follow Christ. In Jesus' setting, those who would choose to follow Him would pay a high price even among their families. Think of someone leaving the Jewish faith, (or any faith for that matter) to follow Jesus – there will be opposition.

- Vs. 39 How to find life is clearly defined – submission to the Lordship of Jesus is truly the source of real life!

- **Proverbs 23:17** Our world is obsessed with envying/admiring "sinners". Just look at our choices for entertainment and music!

If you are tempted in this way, it will only discourage your soul, envy and covetousness are powerfully destructive forces. Counter this with zeal for the Lord "all the day".

- 23:29-35 Drunkenness is never condoned in the Bible – nowhere! This is a consistent theme from the family strife caused by Noah's drinking to Lot's incestuous grandchildren to the Ephesian believers being instructed to *"be not drunk with wine wherein is excess/dissipation (a ruined life)."* Eph. 5:18

- Drunkenness is included in lists of sins: (Luke 21:34; Rom. 13:13; 1 Cor. 6:10; Gal 5:21; 1 Peter 4:3)

- Love in the body of Christ holds one another accountable – drunkenness is not funny. It is important to realize it does lead to ruin.

QUOTE OF THE DAY

"It is always a good proof that your convictions and desires are from the operation of the Spirit when you are willing to conform to God's order."

William Jay (1769-1853)

DAY 49

📖 MATTHEW 11
📖 PROVERBS 24

⟳ K E Y   T H O U G H T S

- **Matthew 11** The report to John, of what the ministry of Jesus is accomplishing is a clear measurement of effective ministry today.

- 11:12 *"forcefully advancing"* – *"violent take it by force"*.

- "The kingdom of God makes its penetration by a kind of violent entry opposing the human status quo. It transcends the "softness" (vs.8) of staid religious formalism and exceeds the pretension of child's play (vss. 16, 17). It refuses to "dance to the music" of society's expectation that the religious community provide either entertainment ("we played the flute") or dead traditionalism ("we mourned"). ... The upheaval caused by the kingdom of God is not caused by political provocation or armed advance. It is the result of God's order shaking relationships, households, cities, and nations by the entry of the Holy Spirit's power working in people." Jack W. Hayford (The Spirit Filled Life Bible)

- 11:28 Is someone weary today, someone burdened heavily by the struggles or failures of your life in reaching godly objectives? Jesus calls us to Himself, to a relationship with Him, much more than to a list of rules. Let Him be that friend to you today.

- **Proverbs 24:11** Those who know Jesus have an accountability to the Father for those people we know, who will say "surely we did not know".

- We are clearly instructed to *"deliver those who are drawn toward death"*, and *"hold back those stumbling to the slaughter."*

QUOTE OF THE DAY

"We are debtors to every man to give him the gospel in the same measure in which we have received it"

P.F. Bresee, founder of the Church of the Nazarene

DAY 50

📖 MATTHEW 12
📖 PROVERBS 25

⊙ K E Y   T H O U G H T S

- **Matthew 12:31, 32** The unpardonable sin. Many people have come upon these verses and heaped fear upon themselves. "Have I committed the unpardonable sin?" This is not a rash word of blasphemy, a cursing string of anger against God. It is someone who has decidedly purposefully determined to assign evil to God and good to evil. Someone who has closed their heart entirely to the wooing of the Holy Spirit, they have removed any measure of softness to the conviction of God. In fact conviction is a key sign you have not committed the unpardonable sin.

- Any person who is convicted of their sin and confesses their sin will be forgiven. The mere fact that a person is concerned that they may have gone over the line on this topic is evidence that they have not. Those who have so hardened their hearts against God to have crossed over to this sin are not even aware that they are in that place.

- Their issue is not that they wouldn't be forgiven if they asked, the issue is they will not ask.

- Vss. 34, 35 illustrate this —*"out of the heart the mouth speaks..."*

- While it is true that there are times where we speak hastily or unwisely, you hear people say, "I didn't mean that", or , "I take that back," yet... we should be asking ourselves when we sin with our mouths; "where did it come from?"

- Vss. 36, 37 *"Out of heart the mouth speaks"* – we will be accountable for every word spoken. That is why we are encouraged to be; *"quick to listen, slow to speak, and slow to get angry."* James 1:19

QUOTE OF THE DAY

"A word fitly spoken is like apples of Gold in settings of silver. Like an earring of gold and an ornament of fine gold is a wise rebuker to an obedient ear."

King Solomon Prov. 25:11, 12

DAY 51

📖 MATTHEW 13
📖 PROVERBS 26

◉ K E Y   T H O U G H T S

- **Matthew 13** contains what is called "The Parable of the Sower".

- Parables: There are two time frames to keep in mind when interpreting the parables of Jesus. There are kingdom principles that are *"now"*, and kingdom principles that are *"not yet", or "then."*

- "This complete view allows for our understanding and applying the principles of "kingdom come" without falling into the confusion of expecting now what the Bible says will only be then." Jack Hayford (SFLB)

- When interpreting the parables of Jesus, "a general approach would be to find the primary point (using grammatical historical principles and staying consistent with the original purpose and message of the parable). Then move on to secondary points of application, using the whole of the Scripture's revelation to guide interpretation." (SFLB)

- The seed and the sower: there will always be a varied response to the gospel, our part is to continually be sowing the "good news", allowing the word/testimony itself (the seed) to take root and grow by God's miraculous working.

- 13:22 Notice the triple threat to the soul: 1) the cares of this world/life, 2) the deceitfulness of riches, 3) pleasures of life (Lk. 8:14)

- 13:58 Unbelief has amazing power! Even to the point of limiting the "mighty works" of Jesus Himself. No wonder Jesus encourages us to not be unbelieving, but to have faith!

- **Proverbs 26** is filled with wisdom on how to avoid contention and conflict. This is very different from the current attitude of our culture:

  - Vs. 17 Meddling in a quarrel not your own

- Vs. 20-22 The power of not gossiping is that the strife ceases, it is not stirred up further.

- Listening to 'tale-bearing' affects the very "inmost" part of us, we have responsibility to not speak in a "tale-bearing" way, and to not listen to those who are "talebearers".

"Go to poor sinners with tears in your eyes, that they may see you believe them to be miserable, and that you unfeignedly pity their case. Let them perceive it is the desire of your heart to do them good."

Richard Baxter (1615 – 1691)

DAY 52

📖 MATTHEW 14
📖 PROVERBS 27

⊛ K E Y   T H O U G H T S

- **Matthew 14:5** At least five of Jesus healing miracles were directly attributed to the motivation of "compassion". The heart of Jesus is sensitive to needs of those who are hurting – we are to have this same heart – the same eyes to see.

- Vss. 22-33 There is someone reading this account today and you are in a storm. Be encouraged!

- You are able by faith to walk upon the waves of the storm with Jesus

- Even if you doubt and begin to falter, there is additional grace from Jesus to reach out and pull you up! I love the fact that Jesus does not let Peter sink, just to teach him a faith lesson – he reaches out His hand and catches him.

- Vs. 36 *"As many as touched it (the hem of His garment), were made well"*. Notice the active faith, there was a physical act of faith, believing enough to go to Him, reach out, push through the crowd and actually touch His garment. Faith is action, not just thinking or feeling!

- **Proverbs 27:6, 10, 14, 17** (What is the status of your friendships? Are you a faithful friend? Have you developed friendships that 'sharpen' you?)This is a decision not an accident, pursue friendships that cause you to grow, not ones that drag you down.

"Expect great things from God; attempt great things for God."

William Carey, who is called the father of modern missions.

DAY 53

📖 MATTHEW 15, 16
📖 PROVERBS 28

🌀 K E Y   T H O U G H T S

- **Matthew 15** The key to understanding the challenging dialogue between Jesus and this woman asking for help for her daughter is the result! Jesus did respond, He did heal her. He did not reject her faith. Don't miss the result by taking offense over ancient cultural nuances of language.

- Vs.19 This verse is very challenging – it addresses our authenticity before the Lord. How often we are quick to blame someone else, something else, for the sinful issues of our lives that we are accountable for; "out of the heart".

- The word 'fornications' comes from the root word "porneia"' The modern words pornography, pornographic etc… all have their root in "porneia". Our world is awash in obscene material – accept Jesus challenge today! Search your heart, examine your mind – seek to walk in purity before the Lord. If you are struggling with this issue – seek help today.

- **16:2-27** Meditate on Jesus' meaning in *"deny himself, and take up his cross, and follow Me"*.

- (Is there a higher calling on your heart – is there anything that could possibly be an "exchange for your soul" in practice?)

- We know that nothing can be exchanged for our soul, but how do we live in light of that truth? Think of all the people you know who have sold their eternity for some sin, some pleasure, some prideful rebellion.

- "Lord, I want nothing to come between me and You, nothing!"

"The world needs Christians who don't tolerate the complacency of their own lives."

Francis Chan, 'Crazy Love: Overwhelmed by a Relentless God'

DAY 54

📖 MATTHEW 17, 18
📖 PROVERBS 29

◎ K E Y   T H O U G H T S

- **Matthew** Jesus often uses the teaching method of *"how much more…"*

- What is more important, the use of a hand or an eye, or freedom from sin? (Matt. 18:6-9)

- Jesus is not encouraging mutilation to overcome the flesh, but rather the clear teaching that sin is the most serious matter and must be dealt with aggressively.

- 18:14 The heart of God is for every "little" one on earth, that none should perish – compare this with 2 Peter 3:9 *"The Lord is . . .longsuffering toward us, not willing that any should perish but that all should come to repentance."*

- 18:15-17 How to settle conflicts in a godly manner – (we would interpret, "bring it to the church" as bringing it before the elders in some form, rather than a public exposure).

- 18:19, 20 The power of agreement – this principle needs to be applied, practiced. The phrase, "let's agree together", is a godly one.

- **Proverbs 29:11** Have you heard someone say "I always speak my mind"? The complication of some kind of higher commitment to honesty misses the point of the wisdom of this statement in Proverbs. There is a time to hold back, comment or feelings.

- The reason is often that there is more to the story that we have not yet heard.

"This generation of Christians is responsible for this generation of souls on the earth!"

Keith Green

DAY 55

📖 MATTHEW 19, 20:1 – 19
📖 PROVERBS 30

⊛ K E Y   T H O U G H T S

- **Matthew 19** The heart of God is broken by unfaithfulness in any circumstance and unfaithfulness in our relationship with Christ is a tragedy. Israel's frequent worship of idols, being unfaithful to God in the process, is the subject of much of the OT, fueling many prophetic warnings.

- In marriage, unfaithfulness breaks God's heart and causes great damage to the family and society. Jesus gives clear direction as to "grounds" for divorce – however:

- The heart of God would always be for reconciliation wherever possible. For those already divorced, you are not rejected for your failed marriage. The Lord has restoration and a future for you just as He does for any other person suffering from the brokenness caused by sin.

- 19:27 Peter is usually blurting out his thoughts before he takes sufficient time to think – the phrase *"what shall we have?"* has always jangled in my heart. I want to follow the Lord for His sake, not for what I can "have."

- Vss. 29, 30 If you have never visited your brothers and sisters around the world, you are missing out on the present day fulfillment of this promise. You have millions of brothers and sisters who would gladly share all they have with you.

"God's definition of what matters is pretty straightforward. He measures our lives by how we love."

Francis Chan,' Crazy Love: Overwhelmed by a Relentless God'

DAY 56

📖 MATTHEW 20:20 – 34; 21
📖 PROVERBS 31

⌖ K E Y   T H O U G H T S

- **Matthew 20:26ff** Becoming great in the Kingdom of heaven: the key to understanding Kingdom greatness is the sentence (vs. 28) *"just as the Son of Man did not come to be served, but to serve…"*

- 21:9 This is such a colorful picture of spontaneous, joyous worship. It erupts at the presence of Christ riding into Jerusalem on the donkey.

- How does your heart respond in worship – do you ever allow yourself to step over the line of personal comfort and with abandon, worship *"He who comes in the Name of the Lord"?*

- 21:21-22 The promise of answered prayer – such strength in Jesus words.

- The keys to understanding the balance between promised blessings and practical results (when it appears that our prayers are not answered, or in fact we receive a different result than our request)

- Stand in what we know: we know we are permitted to ask freely, often and with perseverance. So ask and keep on asking.

- The Lord is free to answer with yes, no or wait – all are answers, all are His prerogative. We will be disappointed if we wrongfully assume that every petition we bring to the Lord will automatically result in a yes. God is wiser than our greatest wisdom – He does know what is best.

- **Proverbs 31** "The Proverbs 31 woman" – be comforted sisters, vs. 30 is the key to this lofty passage; *"Charm is deceitful and beauty is passing, but a woman who fears the Lord, she shall be praised."*

Quote of the Day

"Thanksgiving is inseparable from true prayer; it is almost essentially connected with it. One who always prays is ever giving praise, whether in ease or pain, both for prosperity and for the greatest adversity. He blesses God for all things, looks on them as coming from Him, and receives them for His sake- not choosing nor refusing, liking or disliking, anything, but only as it is agreeable or disagreeable to His perfect will."

John Wesley, 'How to Pray: The Best of John Wesley'

DAY 57

📖 MATTHEW 22, 23

⊛ K E Y   T H O U G H T S

- **Matthew 22, 23** In these chapters Jesus is taking much time to expose the religious emptiness of the religious leaders of His day. They followed external practices and rituals without the inner purity of the heart.
- 22:1-14 The Parable of the Wedding Feast:
- "There are two ways of sinning against God's merciful gift: the one is refusing to accept it; the other is taking it in outward, but continuing in sin. The former was the sin of the Jews; the latter is the sin of nominal Christians." (<u>Expositions of Holy Scripture</u> – Alexander Maclaren)
- The man who is present at the wedding without the "wedding garment" – some important points to consider in this small detail of the whole parable:
- The king sees this one individual among the whole gathering, there is no escaping the true judgment of our Lord – He truly sees the heart, there is no hiding from Him.
- This man is not unjustly treated, the whole parable gives us assurance that this person knew what the wedding garment, (or, proper preparation in godliness and holiness) was.

- "This man who "did not have a wedding garment on" is the nominal Christian, who says that he has accepted God's invitation, and lives in sin, not putting off 'the old man with his deeds,' nor putting on 'the new man, which is created in righteousness." Expositions of Holy Scripture – Alexander Maclaren
- 22:13 One of Jesus' most clear and terrible descriptions of the reality of eternal hell.
- 22:14 Not that there is a limitation to who is chosen, but rather that not many who are given the opportunity will choose to make the preparations, or surrender to the requirements of true discipleship.

QUOTE OF THE DAY

"It remains for the world to see what the Lord can do with a man wholly consecrated to Christ."

Henry Varley (1835-1912)

DAY 58

📖 MATTHEW 24
📖 ROMANS 1

⊚ K E Y   T H O U G H T S

- **Matthew 24** "In His private teaching to the disciples on the Mount of Olives, Jesus responded to three questions, concerning 1) the destruction of the temple, 2) His Second Coming, and 3) the End. These topics are interwoven and sometimes it is difficult to determine which event is being described. This difficulty is partially resolved with the realization that most prophecy is capable of both a near and a future fulfillment. Jesus uses the tragic events surrounding the destruction of Jerusalem as a picture of conditions preceding His own return. One should bear this in mind throughout the chapter." (SFLB)
- 24:13 Endurance to the end, or faithfulness to Christ is required for one to be saved. Our current relationship to Jesus is the

measurement, not some distant bright moment in the past that we are hoping will "get us through".

- Living for Jesus is an ongoing relationship not a ritual.

- 24:14 Such a motivating truth for evangelization and missions here at home and around the world. There is much work to be done!

- **Romans 1:4** It is Christ's resurrection from the dead that declares Him to be the Son of God. Jesus rising from grave is absolutely central to His divinity.

- 1:16 *"Not ashamed of the gospel"* – I am always challenged and convicted by this declaration. Couple this verse with Jesus teaching: *"For whoever is ashamed of Me and My words, of him the Son of Man will be ashamed when He comes in His own glory."* (Luke 9:26)

- Vss. 18-32 As believers holding a high view of the inspiration of the scripture this passage is one of the thresholds of conflict between the wisdom/culture of the world and the unchanging truth of God's word.

- You will have to choose in a very practical way, "will I honor God's revelation of truth, or bend to the culturally accepted wisdom of today?"

- Sexual lust, and immorality in any form is forbidden in Jesus teaching and in the whole of scripture, this clearly includes both heterosexual and homosexual immorality.

QUOTE OF THE DAY

"Has your relationship with God changed the way you live your life?"

Francis Chan

DAY 59

📖 MATTHEW 25
📖 ROMANS 2

◉ K E Y   T H O U G H T S

- **Matthew 25** In chapters 24 and 25 Jesus instructs us to be watchful, to be ready, to be diligent as we await His return.

- 24:36; 25:13 and other passages make it very plain, *"no one knows" when the day of the Lord is, when His return will be"*. In spite of this people still try to set the time of the Lord's return, and present reasons why it is this date or that date – do not go there! Just be ready at all times!

- 25:40 *"the least of these"* – how motivating to know that through the challenges of finding ways to minister to the least and the last (it is not a simple task) – we are actually ministering to Jesus, kindness, mercy, charity are unto Jesus first – therefore it is always valid and noted in heaven!

- 25:41, 46 Jesus repeats the word "everlasting" when referring to punishment – there is no second chance.

- **Romans 2** This important passage gives insight into the universal question: "what about those who have never heard?" Everyone will face the judgment, all will be judged based on the knowledge they have, not the knowledge they do not have.

- Satan has been accusing God of unfairness and imperfect judgment since the Garden of Eden. We must come to peace with the perfect balance of God's goodness and mercy with His Holiness and justice.

- Remembering our readings in Genesis – how exciting to see the truth of Rom. 2:29, that there is a place in Christ to become a Jew "inwardly" (part of the Abrahamic covenant). Such magnificent promises of His blessing in our lives through Jesus Christ.

"There is always the danger that we may just do the work for the sake of the work. This is where the respect and the love and the devotion come in - that we do it to God, to Christ, and that's why we try to do it as beautifully as possible."

Mother Teresa

DAY 60

📖 MATTHEW 26

☾ K E Y   T H O U G H T S

- **Matthew 26:39, 42** Learn from the way Jesus prays and interacts with the Father. There is the freedom to petition. We always have the permission to ask, to express our hearts to the Lord.

- But then, like Jesus, we also, must surrender our will to His will. In learning to pray, there is much to learn, boldness with humility, freedom with surrender.

- If Jesus prays, *"not as I will but as You will"* – we should pray from that place as well.

- When we do that, we are essentially saying, here is my list of requests, desires and needs – but, You are God and I am not, You are good and I am not – Blessed be the Name of the Lord!

- Vs. 40 *"Could you not watch with Me one hour?"* (How is your prayer life? Is it growing? When last did you watch for even one hour?)

- Vss. 69-75 (How does your heart respond to Peter?) I feel so many things as I read this tragically human account. The sting of mockery, the fear of rejection, the failure of denial – the instant remorse and repentance.

- Thank God, the Bible does not exclude the many illustrations of men and women, just like us who stumble and yet are mighty in God – and useful in His kingdom.

- There is something so freeing and healing in Peter's weeping, true repentance must touch the deepest core of our lives to truly allow the Holy Spirit to transform us.

- There is nothing glib, no rationalization of sin in Peter's humble return to the path of discipleship.

QUOTE OF THE DAY

"We all want progress, but if you're on the wrong road, progress means doing an about-turn and walking back to the right road; in that case, the man who turns back soonest is the most progressive."

C. S. Lewis

DAY 61

📖 MATTHEW 27, 28

⊚ K E Y   T H O U G H T S

- **Matthew 27** (What are the things that stand out to you as you read of Christ's trial, torture and crucifixion?)
- *"Why have you forsaken Me?"* 27:46 (quoting Ps. 22:1) This powerful moment reminds us of the awfulness of sin, as Jesus began to bear the burden of the sins of the entire world.
- John Wesley helps with this: "and a most distressing sense of His (the Father's) letting loose the powers of darkness upon Him (Jesus), withdrawing the comfortable discoveries of His presence, and filling His soul with a terrible sense of the wrath due to the sins which He was bearing." 'Explanatory Notes upon the New Testament'
- Jesus truly bore our sins. He paid the most terrible price, for you and for me.
- Christ is Risen! The resurrected Christ is the central doctrine of the church – He must be risen from the dead to have the authority to offer eternal life. There are many recorded instances of Jesus appearing to various people, in various settings, from individuals to a group of five hundred at one time. (1 Cor. 15:3-8)

- *"And if Christ is not risen, then our preaching is empty and your faith is also empty."* (1 Cor. 15:14)

- The resurrection separates Christianity from all other religions. Jesus, crucified and raised from the dead is the Rock on which our faith is built! Praise God.

- Matt. 28:18-20 These verses are a blueprint for purpose in our lives. So often we ask the Lord, "What do you want me to do with my life?"

- His answer is so clear, "make disciples of all nations, baptize them, I will be with you!"

- There is room for every believer to be a part of this commission in one way or another! Are you?

QUOTE OF THE DAY

"I have but one passion - it is He, it is He alone. The world is the field and the field is the world; and henceforth that country shall be my home where I can be most used in winning souls for Christ."

Count Zinzindorf (founder of the Moravian missionaries)

DAY 62

📖 ROMANS 3, 4, 5:1 – 5

⟳ K E Y   T H O U G H T S

- **Romans 3** All have sinned! There is no way around this truth, regardless of the philosophies of man, the arguments of unbelievers – all have sinned and all are in need of salvation from sin.

- Beside Rom. 3:23, in the margin of your Bible, write the reference 6:23. In the margin by 6:23 write 5:8, then in the margin by 5:8 write the reference 10:9, 10.

- This is the 'Romans road' - a simple verse by verse, step by step plan of salvation. When you have the opportunity to share your testimony or have a spiritual conversation with someone, walk them through these verses. Ask them to read them out loud with you. The gospel has power, the word of God has power – let it do its work in people's hearts. Take courage!

- 4:20 *"he did not waiver at the promise.... Fully convinced that what He (God), had promised He was also able to perform."*

- (How is your faith today? Where is your faith based? Who has promised?) There is the reference for our faith – the One who has promised.

- 5:5 Allow the love of God to be poured into your heart by the Holy Spirit. This is one of the blessed works of the Holy Spirit - assurance given through the love of God that we are His, He is with us. We are loved. Hallelujah!

- Many refer to the lofty heights of the book of Romans. It is truly one of the high points of the whole Bible.

QUOTE OF THE DAY

"You may stand on the banks of many mighty rivers, but except you be born again you never can see the river that bursts from the Throne of God and runs through His Kingdom."

Dwight L. Moody (1837-1899)

DAY 63

📖 ROMANS 5:6 – 21; 6
📖 LEVITICUS 10:1 – 7; 16:1 – 22, 30 – 34

☉ K E Y   T H O U G H T S

- **Romans 5:12** This passage, (this verse specifically), is important for our understanding of the imputed sinful nature that all are born with.

- Death (sin) spread to all through (because of) Adam's sin. We are both born in sin, (sinful nature) and then we choose to sin as soon as we are able.

- Vss. 17-21 Let us get some help from the commentary in the Spirit-Filled Life Bible: "we are in Adam by birth, but we are in Christ by faith. In Adam by birth we are condemned and die, but because of Christ's redemptive work we can be justified and live if we are in Him by faith."

- "The second 'all men' (vs. 18b), refers to all who were represented by Christ, namely, all who would believe in Him"
- "if we do not think it fair that we were counted guilty for Adam's sin, then we also should not think it fair that we are counted righteous for Christ's obedience." (SFLB)
- **Leviticus 10:3** *"by those who come near Me, I must be regarded as Holy"* – this is a key to understanding all of the rituals contained in the book of Leviticus. Our God is Holy. Prior to Christ there were elaborate rituals to ensure the purity of the priests and illustrating the holiness of God.
- Vs. 16 The day of atonement. This is a marvelous and specific foreshadowing of Jesus providing for our atonement on the cross.
- Whereas the priest only made atonement once a year – we have access to Christ's atoning work at any time, personally, without the need of any other intermediary! Heb. 4:16 *"Let us therefore come boldly to the throne of grace, that we may obtain mercy and find grace to help in time of need."*

QUOTE OF THE DAY

"One smile from Jesus sustains my soul amid all the storms and frowns of this passing world. Pray to know Jesus better."

Robert M. McCheyne (1813-1843)

DAY 64

📖 ROMANS 7, 8:1 – 11
📖 LEVITICUS 17:6 – 16

◉ K E Y   T H O U G H T S

- **Romans 7:15** Thank God that even the mighty Apostle Paul struggled with this inner conflict of temptation, struggle and even failure to do what he wanted to do inwardly. He uses the word "flesh" to describe that part of his life that struggled to live apart from God.

- This battle is faced by all honest followers of Christ – and yet where is the hope? Vs. 25 "I THANK GOD – THROUGH JESUS CHRIST OUR LORD!!"
- 8:6 There is a clear pathway to "life and peace". It is in being spiritually- minded, not carnally-minded.
- The help for our flesh, the strength for our weakness is found through the indwelling presence of the Holy Spirit. There is a literal life brought to our mortal bodies through the inner presence of the Spirit.
- We do not have to be slaves to sin any longer – there is power for overcoming victory through Jesus.
- Renew the battle my friend. You can be victorious. Do not say… "this one sin, or this area, has defeated me, I will give up and just live with it." NO – invite the Holy Spirit right now to help you! He will.
- **Leviticus 17:7** Idolatry is interaction with demons – it is not insignificant, or culturally cute. There are spiritual realities connected with idol worship.
- 17:11 The significance of the blood:
  - a) it makes atonement for the soul (the blood of Jesus cleanses us from all unrighteousness (1 Jn. 1:9).
  - b) Vs. 14 The life of all flesh is in the blood. The value of blood to human life is directly related to the "precious blood" of Jesus that was shed.
- His 'transfusion' of purity, forgiveness, eternal life.

QUOTE OF THE DAY

"The greatness of a man's/woman's power is the measure of his/her surrender."

William Booth (1829-1912)

DAY 65

📖 ROMANS 8:12 – 10:5

📖 LEVITICUS 18 (YOU MAY CHOOSE TO READ OR NOTE THE SUMMARY COMMENTS BELOW)

◉ K E Y   T H O U G H T S

- **Romans 8:13** The *"deeds of the flesh"* are put to death by *"the Spirit in you."* The result of allowing the Spirit to work in us to conquer the flesh is to "live."

- The contrast between sin and obedience to the Spirit is the contrast between life and death.

- Vss. 15-17 The liberating life-giving role of the Holy Spirit in our inner man, the confirming presence of the Holy Spirit with our spirit gives us great confidence in our standing with God. Consider the breadth of the thought of being a joint heir with Jesus!

- Vss. 26-28 The devotional power and benefit of praying in tongues. How fantastic when we do not know how things will work out (vs. 28) to know that when we pray in the Spirit, He is interceding on our behalf in accordance with the will of God! Read vs. 28 out loud!

- Vss. 29-30 Although God has complete knowledge of all of time in an eternal 'present' tense – yet He still allows man the freedom to choose. We are not pressed into His plans without any choice – we are free moral agents, God's sovereignty and wisdom is not frustrated by our submission or rebellion.

- "These two verses outline a sequence of events and indicate that everyone who has begun the sequence will complete it." (SFLB)

- Vs. 31 Who is for us? Who then can be against us?

- 35-39 One of the loftiest groupings of promises in the whole Bible – You are safe in the loving hands of God!

- I recommend you purchase the song "How He loves" by David Crowder Band, (album: "Church Music") and play it loud! "He loves us, oh how He loves us!"

- I am thinking of some big guy in a truck – let the God of universe

love you today! Or some kid in the middle of a family break up
– He, the Lord God, Abba – loves you!

- Rom. 9-10:5 Paul's heart is for his own people, although God
has a special purpose for Israel – vs. 32 is a key – *"they did not
seek (righteousness) by faith."*

- 10:4 Christ is the end of the law …. salvation is *"for everyone
who believes."*

- **Leviticus 18** The entire spectrum of sexual immorality is
identified and forbidden; from fornication, adultery, incest,
homosexuality to bestiality – very graphic, very clear.

- If there is any doubt of the validity of these instructions for
today – cross reference Jesus' words in Matt. 5:28 and
Romans 1:27ff.

- Two purposes:

  a) the people of God were to have nothing to do with the
  wickedness of the surrounding peoples

  b) 19:2 *"You shall be holy, for I the Lord your God am holy."*

QUOTE OF THE DAY

"My soul longs, yes, even faints for the courts of the LORD; My heart and my flesh cry
out for the living God."

The sons of Korah: Psalm 84:2

DAY 66

📖 ROMANS 10:6 – 11:36
📖 LEVITICUS 19:9 – 11, 14, 17, 18, 32 – 34

◉ K E Y   T H O U G H T S

- **Romans 10:8-17** This passage "preaches". By that I mean,
the gospel is contained here in marvelous language.

- Confession with the mouth, belief in the heart, whoever believes
will not be *"put to shame"*, whoever calls *"will be saved"*.

- The need of global evangelization (vss. 14, 15).

- The source of faith is 'hearing the Word'.

- Take courage brothers and sisters, the gospel has power, the word will speak. Those who come to Jesus through your faithful sharing will declare your feet 'beautiful' – the feet that carried the gospel to them!

- Romans 11 can be challenging, however, there are a number of beautiful truths to be found.

- "First, the Bible calls us to honor the fact that since they (the Jews), were the national avenue by which messianic blessing has come to mankind, (9:4, 5), there should be a sense of duty to "bless" all Jewry (Gen. 12:3), to "pray" with sincere passion for them (Rom. 10:1), and to be as ready to "bear witness" to any Jew as graciously and sensitively as we would to any other human being." (1:16,17) (Jack Hayford: Spirit Filled Life Bible)

- Rom. 11:19-22 contains a solemn warning of the necessity of perseverance, or continuing in the faith.

- Vss. 33-35 The writer seems to throw up his hands toward heaven and with awe declares the mysterious, wonderful and unquestionable "judgments and ways" of our God!

- *"...to whom be glory forever. Amen."*

- **Leviticus 19** Selected verses that contain timeless wisdom particularly relating to the poor, handicapped, neighbors, the elderly and foreigners (strangers). All of these groups are affirmed in the NT.

QUOTE OF THE DAY

"Remember you are not a tree that can stand alone; you are only a branch, and it is only while you abide in Him, as a branch, that you will flourish."

Robert M. McCheyne (1813-1843)

DAY 67

📖 ROMANS 12
📖 LEVITICUS 20:22 – 27

⊛ K E Y   T H O U G H T S

- **Romans 12:1, 2** We could stop right here today! If you are willing, memorizing these two verses would be a valuable use of time.

- Notice: *"present your BODIES."* These vessels are to be holy, for His pleasure.

- J.B. Phillips renders it: "Don't let the world around you squeeze you into its own mold."

- Contrast, 'conforming' with 'transforming'. Search your life. Would you say, with honesty, that you are being conformed by the world, or, are you in the process of being 'transformed'?

- Renewing the mind by the Word of God: John 15:3; 17:17; Eph. 5:23.

- Psalms 19:8 (NKJV)

- Vs. 8 *"The statutes of the LORD are right, rejoicing the heart; the commandment of the LORD is pure, enlightening the eyes."*

- 12:6 *"let us use them"*. The value of spiritual gifts is in using them, not possessing them.

- Our behavior toward our Christian brothers and sisters is described in detail; kindly, affectionate, honor, of the same mind, live peaceably etc. Our relationships are a precise indicator of the measure of God's grace in our own lives.

- Vs. 21 Connect this verse with vss. 1, 2 *"be not conformed but be transformed"*. There are practical ways to do this - overcome evil with good.

- **Leviticus 20:23** The nations that the Lord was displacing were ungodly and wicked. Their idolatrous and immoral practices were to have no place in Israel's worship and day to day life.

- The phrase *"I am the Lord your God who has separated you from the peoples"*, is a key to understanding the judgment toward the ungodly and the rituals establishing Israel's unique worship.

- Lev. 23 There are seven feasts recorded in Leviticus. Of the seven three were major feasts where all the males of Israel were to present themselves at the tabernacle/temple annually.

- The three major feasts were:

  a) Passover/feast of unleavened bread

  b) Weeks or Pentecost and

  c) Tabernacles.

- They commemorate the Passover and exodus from Egypt, the first harvest in spring (and the day of Pentecost for Christians), and the forty years in the desert or booths (dwelling in tents).

QUOTE OF THE DAY

"He did what He taught, and He taught what He did. He came to serve and to give, and His whole life was marked by those two things, from the manger to the cross."

Charles H. Mackintosh (1820-1896)

DAY 68

📖 ROMANS 13, 14
📖 LEVITICUS 26:1 – 26

☉ K E Y   T H O U G H T S

- **Romans 13:7** Followers of Christ are to honor authority, pay taxes and customs and show reverence for God, by reverencing those earthly authorities that God has placed in their lives.

- 13:10 Treatment of "neighbors", those around us, is a reliable indicator of the measure of the work of the Holy Spirit in our life. A heart filled with the love of Christ will treat "neighbors" with love, fulfilling all the commands of Jesus and the law.

- 13:14 Consider the application of *"make no provision for the flesh"*. How does this work practically in our lives? (For example, the places we go….)

- 14:10 Each of us is accountable for *"the things we have done"*. This judgment (the Judgment seat of Christ) does not determine entrance or denial into heaven but rather refers to the degrees of reward relating to faithfulness and fruitfulness in Christ's kingdom work.
- Rom. 14 The Law of Love. This chapter contains principles that remove the technical loopholes of selfish living. We are to modify our freedoms based on the impact that our indulgence will have on those around us.
- Freedom without love, without relational accountability or concern for the effect of our actions on others will cause harm.
- 14:21 summarizes this kind of Christ-like love. The answer to questionable, or debatable practices is not about me, my freedom. It is about the good of the whole, a higher standard of love, rather than a legalistic adherence to my personal privilege. (example of Jesus: Phil. 2:5-11)
- **Leviticus 26** lists the benefits of following God's ways and the consequences of rebellion to His ways. A stark spectrum of results should motivate us to live in His ways. The promise is *"blessing"* and *"I will walk among you and be your God."*
- Vs. 8 *"Five will chase a hundred, and a hundred will chase ten thousand of your enemies."*

QUOTE OF THE DAY

"Nothing, in such a world as this, can be more foolish than to renounce a friend because we have found him to be imperfect."

Susan Huntington (1791-1823)

DAY 69

📖 ROMANS 15, 16
📖 LEVITICUS 26:40 – 46

◉ K E Y   T H O U G H T S

- **Romans 16:5**

  a) Churches that meet in homes, they had no other places to meet. The high value of "cell" groups, or home groups, small gatherings of believers where prayer, fellowship and the word are shared.

  b) Notice how the Holy Spirit includes the name of one person who came to Christ! The first convert to Jesus in all of Asia is recorded. Never minimize the value of one soul, one life. Every heart is the seed of a greater harvest, every life has a circle that they influence for God.

- 16:17, 18 Divisive people are severely denounced, they are to be avoided!

- 16:19 A good rule for life: *"be wise in what is good, and simple concerning evil"*.

- **Leviticus 26:40-46** *"but if they confess... accept their guilt, (and return to Me)"*

- *"Then I will remember My covenant"*. The re-activation of God's blessing corresponds to our obedience, keeping our relationship with Him alive, vibrant and pure.

QUOTE OF THE DAY

"Do you know that nothing you do in this life will ever matter, unless it is about loving God and loving the people he has made?"

Francis Chan 'Crazy Love: Overwhelmed by a Relentless God'

DAY 70

📖 NUMBERS 6:22 – 27; 9:15 – 23
📖 JOHN 1:1 – 13

⊛ K E Y   T H O U G H T S

- **Numbers 6:24ff** Speaking words of *"blessing"* is something that ought to be practiced among our families and our fellowship. This is one of the classic blessings of the scripture.

- Num. 9:15ff The pillar of cloud and the pillar of fire. These two signs served as the directive of God for the people's journeys. We ought to expect today, that the Holy Spirit is able to lead us in meaningful ways.

- God has both timing and destinations in His heart for our good, learning to listen to the promptings of the Holy Spirit and to *"keep in step with the Holy Spirit"* (Galatians 5:25) are both invaluable benefits to the believer.

- **John 1** Magnificent revelation regarding who Jesus is and what He does.

- 1:1 Christ existed from eternity.

- 1:3, 10 Christ's role in creation.

- 1:4, 5 He is life; He is light.

- 1:12 By receiving Him, we have the 'right' to become children of God (born again). Many people will say "we are all God's children" and while we are all His children, in that we are all given the breath of life by Him, we only have the 'right' to be His spiritual children through faith in Jesus Christ.

- 1:17, 18 Jesus is the expression, the declaration, the articulation of God. We can know who God is, what He is like by knowing Jesus! How wonderful!

- There is actually a way to personally know the Creator of the universe! It is through seeing and knowing Jesus.

"Obedience deepens our intimacy with Jesus. If we want to know the Father, we must not only love Him, but also obey Him. Scripture is clear that it is important to know the Father through His Word, and if we want to be a part of what the Father is doing and to be able to see where He is moving then it is clear that we must obey His commands. It is important to be biblically literate, but we must also be biblically obedient!"

John Wimber

DAY 71

📖 NUMBERS 11
📖 JOHN 1:15

⊛ K E Y   T H O U G H T S

- **Numbers 11** Longing for the land of bondage: *"we remember fish, cucumbers, melons, leeks, onions and garlic – which we ate freely"*. Selectively forgetting the beatings, the oppression, the murder of children….the severe bondage of captivity.

- Memory is unreliable. Somehow the people were completely missing the point of God supernaturally and daily providing food (miraculously nutritious food) for them that tasted like pastry prepared with oil.

- Moses expresses the challenge that every person who leads people faces – *"how can I bear these people"*. It might be just a family or a Life Group, or a few employees but it is always a burden that is much lighter when shared with others.

- Num. 11:17 This impartation is an ordination for the functioning office of elder, not necessarily a permanent transference of gifting. The function is to share in the work of giving leadership and care to the people – a marvelous example of sharing and delegating, releasing ministry in a body.

- 11:20 The dissatisfaction and 'cravings' of the people caused them to forget the goodness of the Lord, and to prefer the sinful past of bondage, to deliverance and God's blessing.

- (Has walking in obedience to God's ways become 'loathsome' to us?)

- When the quail arrive, instead of trusting the Lord for each day and rejoicing in the blessing, the people hoard the meat. The one who gathered the least gathered around 2000 liters! They would not rely upon the Lord to provide for them.

- They would not believe His promises, they would not let Him be their sufficiency.

- **John 1:33** It is Jesus who baptizes us with the Holy Spirit! Ask Him, simply pray, "Jesus baptize me with the Holy Spirit" and then receive by faith (Acts 2:4, 10:44-47; 19:2-7).

- Jn. 1:37-51 This is the first passage of personal evangelism in the NT – a good title for this 'method' of bringing people to Jesus would be, *"Come and see"*.

- Personal testimony and allowing Jesus' power and work to speak for itself (through sharing your personal experience, bring them to where the presence of Jesus is), are always effective ways to bring someone to Christ.

QUOTE OF THE DAY

"Has this world been so kind to you that you should leave with regret? There are better things ahead than any we leave behind."

C. S. Lewis

DAY 72

📖 NUMBERS 12
📖 JOHN 2; 3:1 – 21

⊙ K E Y   T H O U G H T S

- **Numbers 12** Dissension, criticism, personal ambition – all of these characteristics are unseemly for a leader of God's people.

- What an amazing description of Moses' leadership and character: "Now the man Moses was very humble, more than all men who were on the face of the earth."

- **John 2:24, 25** Jesus does not crave the approval of man, knowing that the heart of man is fickle and most often self-interested.

- Jn. 3 The Nicodemas session. Jesus uses the illustrations of physical birth and the blowing of the wind to explain spiritual birth to this learned man.

- 3:16 Such marvelous, generous, embracing love – that *"whosoever"* … (KJV) (Who is the whosoever in your life?)

- 3:20, 21 Jesus speaks of bringing things into the light. As we search our lives and our hearts, are there any dark places in our life? Any matters that are concealed, hidden from the light?

- Freedom is found in bringing these dark things into the light of Jesus' Holy presence. The key phrase is "practicing evil".

- 3:17 *"but that the world through Him might be saved"*.

- Add Acts 4:12 *"There is salvation in no one else! God has given no other name under heaven by which we must be saved."* (NLT)

- Jesus is God's only provision for the salvation of humanity.

- "Thank you Lord, for this transforming blessing."

QUOTE OF THE DAY

"By salvation I mean not "barely", according to the vulgar notion of deliverance from hell or (merely) going to heaven, but a present deliverance from sin, a restoration of the soul to its primitive health, its original purity, a recovery of the divine nature, the renewal of our souls after the image of God in righteousness and true holiness in justice mercy and truth."

John Wesley

DAY 73

📖 NUMBERS 13; 14:1 – 25
📖 JOHN 3:22 – 36

◉ K E Y   T H O U G H T S

- **Numbers 13:18** Everyone answers before God for their own sins, we are not held accountable for the sins of our ancestors. However, when there has been great sin, or long term sinful behavior there will be a cascading of consequences that future generations will carry.

- The children of an alcoholic often pay a heavy price, sometimes even the grandkids or beyond suffer because of sin's ripple effect. In the cases of abuse, crime, family breakup over infidelity – generations will suffer.

- Caleb brings a good report – 13:24. He had a 'different' spirit in him. Caleb is promised an inheritance in the land of promise. He has to wait 40 years to see it come to pass.

- A word of faith or a promise can be certain, without the timing being known. Caleb does receive this promise! He was faithful and God was faithful (see Joshua 14:6ff).

- **John 3:36** The instructions and means of receiving everlasting life are very clear.

- *"He who believes in the Son has everlasting life. He who does not believe in the Son shall not see life, but the wrath of God (against his unredeemed sin) remains upon him."*

QUOTE OF THE DAY

"When there are dissensions, and jealousies, and evil speakings among professors of religion, then there is great need of a revival. These things show that Christians have got far from God, and it is time to think earnestly of a revival."

Charles Finney

DAY 74

📖 NUMBERS 16
📖 JOHN 4:1 – 38

☞ K E Y T H O U G H T S

- **Numbers 16** Korah is rebelling against the civil authority of Moses' leadership, the main complaint being the turnaround at the Promised Land.

- Dathan and Abiram are rebelling against the priestly authority of Aaron and his descendants. These men already had responsibilities in the temple, but they wanted to expand into the priestly role, which God had chosen exclusively for Aaron's progeny.
- Vss. 41-50 A most remarkable complaining! This incident reminds us that there have always and will always be people who accuse God of injustice. It is a classic case of "We know what they did was wrong, but did you have to deal with it THAT way?"
- *"You have killed the people of the Lord."* There was a strange gap in these people's knowledge of the holiness and power of God, and their rebellious, complaining hearts.
- **John 4** Jesus assures us that the water that HE gives, will satisfy the soul, *"never thirst again"*. Spiritual satisfaction in following Jesus is a deep well of continuous refreshing for the inner longings of a person.
- Vss. 35-38 Being engaged in Harvest work is urgent – it is ripe right now – we are not to procrastinate. Now is the day of salvation!
- Partnership between sowers and reapers involves the principle of encouragement. One sows, another reaps – both rejoice in the harvest!
- We are to focus on reaping – others have been sowing, their seed is now ready for harvest. We should never reduce our focus so much that we exclude ourselves from working in all aspects of the kingdom.
- How many people have said, "I don't have the gift of evangelism" and ignored obedience to Jesus' clear command to be involved in the harvest? There is someone you know who is ready to receive Jesus. (Will you look? Will you notice?)

QUOTE OF THE DAY

"Go straight for souls, and go for the worst."

William Booth

DAY 75

📖 NUMBERS 17
📖 JOHN 4:39 – 5:23

◉ K E Y   T H O U G H T S

- **Numbers 17:8** A miracle is just that, a miracle. Aaron's staff, not only budded, it blossomed and produced ripe almonds! In one night! When our God works a miracle never call it coincidence or luck.

- We are slow to believe, God can do whatever He chooses – *"nothing is impossible with God."*

- **John 4:39-42** This poor, immoral woman becomes the messenger (a flawed messenger) that eventually sees "many" in that city come to faith in Christ.

- Every person who comes to Jesus has a "city" somewhere, a city of people that their testimony will influence. Fresh testimony, without sophisticated structure is effective – *"now... we ourselves have heard."* – in the very least to pique interest and inquiry.

- Jn. 5:14 Sin and its consequences bring a worse fate than being physically sick for 38 years!

- 5:18 (also 4:26) There is no doubt, both from Jesus' own declarations and from the conclusions of the religious leaders of the day – Jesus makes Himself equal with God! He is God.

- There is no ambiguity on this subject, Jesus own words speak it plainly, *"I am He (Messiah)"*. His actions, by making God His father and offering the forgiveness of sins, demand we recognize his divinity. The other alternatives are that He was a liar, or a lunatic, or just a legend (myth). None of those alternatives bear any credibility.

- He is the Christ, the Messiah, the Son of the Living God. He is fully God, fully Man – the Savior of the World!!!

- Song recommendation – "Savior of the World" – Ben Cantelon (itunes).

"I gave in, and admitted that God was God."

C. S. Lewis

DAY 76

📖 NUMBERS 20
📖 JOHN 5:24 – 6:14

⊛ K E Y   T H O U G H T S

- **Numbers 20** This rejection, by the descendants of Esau (Edom), comes up later when the children of Israel actually enter to occupy the land.

- It is difficult from this far away to fully understand the severity of Moses' sin and rebellion in this instance.

- This act of anger and willful rebellion is why Moses does not enter the Promised Land.

- We do know that in spite of the result, (abundant water for the people and their flocks), the manner, or delivery of the miracle was displeasing to the Lord. Interesting illustration that the end doesn't always justify the means. (Num. 20:11)

- "The measure of success in the Lord's eyes is not the outcome of the effort, but the obedience of His servant." (SFLB)

- **John 5:39** It is possible for someone (the religious leaders in this case) to be very knowledgeable and yet miss the point entirely. Especially when the point is toward surrender to Jesus. Many people reject Christ, not because of evidence, but rather because of a prior commitment to another ideology or lifestyle.

- 5:44 Two things to note in this verse; we are to seek honor only from God, not from others! Secondly, Jesus is very clear that there is only one God, *"the only God!"*

- Feeding of the 5000, (6:1-14) Put yourself into the picture of this miracle, think as if you were one of the disciples seeing this marvel transpire.

- (What would you be thinking, feeling?)
- (With where you are at right now, in your walk with God, how would seeing this miracle affect you?)
- (Why do you think Jesus made sure that there was enough left over for one basket for each disciple?)

DAY 77

📖 NUMBERS 21
📖 JOHN 6:15 – 71

⊛ K E Y   T H O U G H T S

- **Numbers 21** The fiery serpents, (either the symptoms of being bitten or the appearance of the snakes) – again, this judgment comes from grumbling and complaining against God and His leaders.
- The mercy of healing for the people – the imagery is clearly connected, by Jesus, to Himself providing healing atonement on the cross. (John 3:14, 15)
- We have access to the promise of physical healing – Look to Jesus and Live! *"when he looked, ... he lived."* (vs. 9)
- At this point in Numbers, we start meeting all the various "ites" – all of these peoples have origins that connect in their combined histories.
- The people of Moab and Ammon are descended from the incestuous children of Lot. The rebellion, idolatry and aggression of these people was most often the reason for their judgment.
- The defeats of kings, Sihon and Og, are referred to over

and over in the history of Israel; these are lands east of the Jordan.

- **John 6:18-20** Jesus walks to the disciples, on the water, through a storm and says *"It is I, do not be afraid."* Jesus is Lord of the universe! Vs. 29 There is no doubt about work that pleases God. It is <u>believing</u>!

- Vs. 35 How many people are still hungering and still thirsting by seeking sustenance in things that cannot satisfy. Only Jesus can satisfy the soul, only He can fill the ache on the inside.

- We understand this challenging passage on the blood and body of Jesus best when we apply it to His other teachings about communion. This symbolic instruction to eat His flesh and drink His blood have to do with the work that His death accomplished on the cross.

- Authority to give eternal life, healing, forgiveness and cleansing of sins are all offered through Christ's atoning work on the cross.

- Vs. 63 Jesus' words are "spirit" and they are "life".

- Vs. 68 Some of Peter's wisest recorded words - we would do well to repeat these to ourselves often... *"You (alone), have the words of life."*

QUOTE OF THE DAY

"God proved His love on the Cross. When Christ hung, and bled, and died, it was God saying to the world, "I love you.""

Billy Graham

DAY 78

📖 NUMBERS 22:18 – 40
📖 JOHN 7

◉ K E Y   T H O U G H T S

- **Numbers 22** This unusual prophet is hired by the King of Moab, to curse Israel. The request itself should have been clear enough for him to have had nothing to do with it.

- His donkey speaks (God can do anything!)

- His prophetic words all bless Israel. Chapters 22-24 contain marvelous blessings upon Israel (you may choose to read the whole passage).

- The NT gives us insight into the sin of this prophet;

  a) he was for hire, loved money

  b) even though he blessed Israel prophetically, he advised Moab to tempt Israel with idolatry and sexual immorality (Rev 2:14)

- Later on, Balaam is sought out for judgment and death with the Midianites.

- **John 7:38** This description of the fruit of believing is alive with imagery of life. It is a continuous supply, a river from within – a source of strength – purity. The access to all these blessings? Believing in Jesus!

- 7:42 Jesus fulfilled all the prophecies (Mic. 5:2), that the leaders keep referring to; they would not have known that He was born in Bethlehem (because of the census) – but grew up in Nazareth.

- Neither would they know that His lineage of both mother, and father (earthly parent, though not blood parent), were traced directly to King David.

QUOTE OF THE DAY

"We are a supernatural people, born again by a supernatural birth; we wage a supernatural fight and are taught by a supernatural teacher, led by a supernatural captain to assured victory."

James Hudson Taylor (1832-1905)

DAY 79

📖 NUMBERS 25; 27:12 – 23
📖 JOHN 8:1 – 36

⊘ K E Y   T H O U G H T S

- **Numbers 27:14** A little more insight into Moses' sin given here – he did not 'hallow/reverence' the Lord 'before their eyes'. The inference being that Moses took glory to himself, rather than allowing all the glory to be to God.

- Vss. 18-23 Inauguration, or ordination – setting someone apart for service or ministry by the laying on of hands. There is something special about the acknowledgment of 'grace' upon a life through the laying on of hands.

- **John 8:12** Jesus is the light of the world. Following Him will result in having the 'light of life'. All others will walk in darkness.

- Vs. 24 A clear statement of the pathway to eternal life. There is no wiggle room in Jesus' teaching on sin and death. Believing in Jesus as the Son of God is the way to freedom from sin.

- Vs. 29 We should set our hearts to follow Jesus' example to live 'always' in the will of the Father, no question, or equivocating - just 'always', yes Lord!

- Vss. 31-36 This progression of abiding, knowing the truth (Christ and His Word), and freedom is great hope for all of us.

- If we invite Jesus to make us free, 'the Son' will 'make' us free INDEED! (surely) Free from sin, free from condemnation, free from guilt and shame, free from fear, free from isolation and confusion. Freedom in Christ is true freedom.

QUOTE OF THE DAY

"A rule I have had for years is: to treat the Lord Jesus Christ as a personal friend. His is not a creed, a mere doctrine, but it is He Himself we have."

Dwight L. Moody

DAY 80

📖 NUMBERS 33:50 – 56
📖 JOHN 8:37 – 59; 9

✺ K E Y   T H O U G H T S

- **Numbers 33:50-56** God gives clear instructions to His people, what to do and why. Dispossessing the inhabitants was necessary. The action was a fulfillment of His promise to Israel, and His judgment upon the wickedness and idolatry of the nations.

- God's holiness and purity of worship is uppermost. To compromise with the people of the land would mean a mixing of idolatry and pure worship of God. It would be the demise of many of the tribes in the future.

- By compromising, the people would have the judgment of the Lord fall upon them for their wickedness just like the idolatrous nations living in Canaan.

- **John 8:44** Learn to recognize the language of the devil – he only speaks one! There is NO truth in him (Satan).

- Healing of the blind man (washing in the pool of Siloam) – the Pharisees were skilled at missing the point (religion is like that).

- 9:24 *"We know that this Man is a sinner."* Many people approach Jesus with their minds already made up, many unbelievers come with preconceived notions of the Bible, God, Jesus, the way of salvation. The starting point of a search for truth is critical, and a humble spirit won't steer you wrong!

- These people were not about to be confused by the facts!

- Enjoy the man's simplicity and sarcasm... *"one thing I know; that though I was blind, now I see."* (they were badgering him about knowledge and pedigree – quite intimidating) This guy just stands up with his testimony.

- Intellectual and religious 'knowledge' is often a hindrance to true, childlike faith. These highly educated, very religious people were those who said 'we see' or 'we are the ones who understand'. It was to be their blindness, they could not get past their pride to see Jesus.

DAY 81

📖 NUMBERS 35:9 – 34
📖 JOHN 10

◉ K E Y   T H O U G H T S

- **Numbers 35:9-34** Cities of refuge – this passage gives a very clear description of both pre-meditated and accidental murder. Also the penalties for both are clearly prescribed.

- There were always to be at least two witnesses. There was punishment (like a house arrest) for the one guilty of manslaughter.

- The city of refuge is also a marvelous picture of our ability to flee to Jesus when our soul needs refuge. He is our hiding place, it is to Him that we can run in time of need or transgression.

- **John 10:9, 10** Another 'I AM' statement by Jesus – He is the doorway to peace with God.

- Vs. 10 take time today to <u>memorize this verse</u>. There is no clearer verse in scripture to contrast the works of the devil and the works of Jesus in our lives.

- Jesus is the good shepherd – *"gives His life for the sheep."*

- 34, 35 *"you are gods"* – "the reference, taken from Ps. 82:6 does not attribute deity to the judges to whom it refers, but was a title of commendation, noting the God-given capacities of human life and will – the fruit of being made 'in His image.'" (SFLB)

"God is the only being who is good, and the standards are set by Him. Because God hates sin, He has to punish those guilty of sin. Maybe that's not an appealing standard. But to put it bluntly, when you get your own universe, you can make your own standards."

Francis Chan, 'Crazy Love: Overwhelmed by a Relentless God'

DAY 82

📖 DEUTERONOMY 1
📖 JOHN 11

⊛ K E Y   T H O U G H T S

- **Deuteronomy 1:6** There are times to stay at the mountain, and there are definitely times to move on in faith and take what has been given/promised!

- 1:8 "Go in and possess the land." Moses exhorts the people to this action thirty five times in Deuteronomy. Thirty four times he reminds them this is the *"land the Lord is giving you"*.

- 1:21 When facing a challenge or needing to conquer, we are strengthened by the Lord when He *says "do not fear or be discouraged"*.

- Vs. 36 Caleb is a tremendous example of a man of faith who endured forty years of desert wanderings because of other's sins – yet he endured, and is called a man who *"wholly followed the Lord"*.

- Vs. 38 As Moses instructed the people as to how to treat their leader we should also take this advice and "encourage" our leaders.

- **John 11:25** *"I am"* – this time the resurrection and the life!

- Only Jesus has the authority through His own resurrection and conquest of death to offer eternal life to those who will "believe".

- 11:42 Jesus gives us insight into His prayer relationship with the Father. *"I know that You always hear Me."* We can have this same confidence when we pray – He always hears us.

- *"Lazarus come forth."* Is there some area of your life that seems as dead and decayed as Lazarus was? Let your faith increase and call it forth!
- Jesus is the One who brings the glory of God to those who will believe. (vs. 40)

QUOTE OF THE DAY

"Anxiety does not empty tomorrow of its sorrows, but only empties today of its strength."

Charles Spurgeon

DAY 83

📖 DEUTERONOMY 3:21 – 29; 4:1 – 14
📖 JOHN 12

⊛ K E Y   T H O U G H T S

- **Deuteronomy 3:22** It is God Himself who fights the enemies of His people. Take courage in your fight that the Lord is the one who is the best warrior!
- Moses has such a close relationship with the Lord that he appeals God's decision to refuse him entry to the Promised Land.
- This interaction reveals an intimacy of relationship that is truly beyond any religious ritual.
- 4:9, 10 The Scripture commands godly men and women to teach their children the ways of the Lord, to recount the goodness and the deeds of the Lord.
- Our world proposes foolish means of raising children, "let them discover their own wisdom, their own gender, their own way."
- The wisdom of God is to teach your children and grandchildren the ways of the Lord. Instruct them, show them so that they will be blessed in knowing how to walk in God's ways.
- **John 12:3** This extravagant act of worship by Mary is so emotional, so expressive, so full of love. It is almost

embarrassing to put yourself in that room, and yet Jesus completely receives it and honors her devotion.

- Vss. 24-26 The recurring theme of dying to live, that self and self-will must succumb to the crucifying of the flesh. This is in order to have true life now, and eternal life forever.

- Vs. 26 A simple and yet profound instruction – *"If anyone serves Me, let him follow Me."* I can understand that… "help me now, Holy Spirit to live this way."

- Vss. 31, 32 "all peoples" praise God. The gospel is not limited to Jew, or Greek, or Canadian! It is good for all peoples – all the world.

- Vss. 28, 47-50 Jesus' obedience and submission to the Father is so challenging to our stubborn insistence that we "know what to do." Jesus is absolutely humble in His immediate choices, to do and say as the Father has said to do and say.

QUOTE OF THE DAY

"The world may frown – Satan may rage – but go on! Live for God. May I die in the field of battle."

James B. Taylor (1801-1829)

DAY 84

📖 DEUTERONOMY 4:15 – 43
📖 JOHN 13 – 14:6

◉ K E Y   T H O U G H T S

- **Deuteronomy 4** We must not miss the strong and consistent injunctions against idolatry. The human heart's tendency to substitute a god of our own shaping/making is always the downfall of a true relationship with God.

- Although physical idolatry is not as clear a line of demarcation in our culture (Although Buddhas seems to be increasingly fashionable), idolatry is no less present.

- Idols of material things, money, pleasure, position, children, appearance…

- 4:24, 35 express that the Lord requires absolute singleness of heart and that *"there is none other besides Him"*. In other words, all other so called, 'gods' are false gods, not real.

- Vs. 39, 40 *"there is no other"* – keep His commandment. Why? *"That it may go well with you and with your children after you!"* And, that you may "prolong" your days. Having it go well for you and your children and a long and blessed life sounds like a good plan.

- **John 13:3** This powerful verse on identity gives us insight into true Christ-like character. Notice how the security of Jesus' identity in the Father, (Jesus knew where He had come from, and knew where He was going) results in action! Servanthood!

- Jesus was absolutely secure in the Father therefore He was absolutely free to serve in one of the most menial of tasks, a task reserved for the lowest of slaves and servants. Servanthood flows out of nearness to the Father.

- 13:35, 36 A new commandment – a powerful, radical radiating commandment – love one another. The world will know something is different – they will know who we belong to by how we treat each other.

- Vs. 38 I wish I could have heard the tone of Jesus' voice as He asked this question. (Keep in mind His love for Peter) My guess is that it was a knowing, soft spoken sadness. I hear Him asking you and me today: "Will you lay down your life for My sake?"

- 14:6 Memorize this verse – it will keep you grounded when the winds of "all roads lead to god" blow against you!

QUOTE OF THE DAY

"When our affections are alive to other things, they are dead to God, therefore the less we let loose our hearts to these things, the more lively and cheerful in the work of obedience."

Thomas Manton (1620-1677)

DAY 85

📖 DEUTERONOMY 5 – 6:9
📖 JOHN 14:7 – 24

⊕ K E Y   T H O U G H T S

- **Deuteronomy 5** The Ten Commandments – we seek to honor the timeless ordinances given to us for all time and yet be sensitive to certain commands that are rescinded in the NT. Look for the commands that Jesus and the other NT authors endorse or remove.

- We are to keep a Sabbath rest for our good, but many NT scriptures make it certain that actual Sabbath keeping as prescribed in the law are no longer binding upon the follower of Jesus.

- Rom. 14:5 "The Christian's Sunday is not a Sabbath in the sense of the old covenant Sabbath. The first day of the week was set apart by the resurrection of our Lord Jesus. On that day He appeared to His disciples. The Christians broke bread on that day (Acts 20:7), and on that day they brought their offerings to the Lord (1 Corinthians 16:2). The first day of the week is the Lord's Day. We are not told exactly how to keep the day, but it is to be observed in worship as a special day." 'The Complete Biblical Library – Romans-Corinthians'

- Deut. 6:4, 5 This magnificent summary verse is one of Jesus' most famous OT quotes. Jesus adds *"and you shall love your neighbor as yourself"*. (Matt. 22:37,38)

- **John 14:12ff** We must catch Jesus' strong teaching regarding the role of the Holy Spirit in our lives. Greater works, *"because I go to the Father"*, the power of asking prayer, the promise of hearing and answering. Say with me out loud please, "Greater works!"

- The next great theme is the proof of love for Jesus: obedience to His commands vs. 21 *"and keeps them, it is he who loves Me"*. This is the measurement of our love for Jesus!

- The gift of the Holy Spirit as "another Helper". In its literal meaning: "one besides Me and in addition to Me but one just like Me. He will do in My absence what I would do if I were physically present with you." (<u>SFLB</u> - Word wealth 14:6)

- He (the Holy Spirit) is also the "Spirit of Truth". How we need Him today when our society denies the existence of objective truth.

- 14:24 Meditate on this beautiful metaphor for relationship with the Father and the Son - *"We will come and make our home with him"*. Our hearts/lives are the 'home' of God – every room, every part open to His presence.

QUOTE OF THE DAY

"One evening I invited Jesus Christ into my heart. What an entrance He made. It was not a spectacular emotional thing, (although for some there is great emotion – neither experience need be prescriptive), but very real. It was at the very center of my life. He came into the darkness of my heart and turned on the light. He built a fire in the cold hearth and banished the chill. He started music where there had been stillness, and He filled the emptiness with His own loving, wonderful fellowship. I have never regretted opening the door to Christ, and I never will – not to eternity."

Robert B. Munger 'My Heart Christ's Home'

DAY 86

📖 DEUTERONOMY 6:10 – 7:11
📖 JOHN 14:25 – 31

⊙ K E Y   T H O U G H T S

- **Deuteronomy 6:12** This instruction is a timeless warning to the human nature we all possess. When prosperity comes, when times are peaceful, without tangible stress – we are inclined to "forget".

- We forget where He has brought us from, forget what He has done for us, forget the principles of holiness that we are commanded to abide by. Israel's history is a motivating example of what happens when a people 'forget' God and specifically begin to worship at the feet of other gods.

- 7:1-11 God has chosen His own people, He has *"set His love upon them"* (vs.7). He has a divine plan for them and for their overall role in His plan of redemption.

- Many people stumble at how Israel was to treat the nations dwelling in the land that was promised by God, to them. (Israel). While from our cultural perspective it seems harsh and very politically incorrect (since our culture rejects absolute truth and God's authority altogether) it was in the purpose of God.

- Israel was not to compromise with pagan nations, living in blatant rebellion to God. They were to be holy before the Lord. Further, they (Israel), were to be the instrument of God to bring judgment/punishment to these rebellious nations who would have been able to trace their recent history's to the same ancestors as Israel. They were nations of heinous wickedness and idolatry – their immorality and barbarity was almost inconceivable.

- 7:9, 10 reminds us of who God is. This is the lens to look through, who <u>God</u> is. Not who we are or what we think should happen.

- **John 14:26** The "Helper" – the "Spirit of Truth" – *"He will teach you all things"*. What encouraging promises from Jesus. We can trust the Holy Spirit to teach us.

- Many of us may feel inadequate academically, maybe even intimidated because of a lack of formal training. Embrace and enter in to your relationship with the Holy Spirit – He is going to teach you from your spirit outward. Deep things, truthful things, wisdom that only God can give. Praise God.

- *"Peace I leave with you"* (vs. 27). Notice - *"not as the world gives"*. This inner peace with God is the rock from which all peace is built.

- (Will you accept Jesus' command?) *"Let not your heart be troubled, neither let it be afraid."* (How are you doing with that today?)

- Christ's followers, true followers, will choose to walk in a place of confidence and peace. The Lord is in control, He will return – we are His!

"We don't get to decide who God is."

Francis Chan 'Crazy Love: Overwhelmed by a Relentless God'

DAY 87

📖 DEUTERONOMY 7:12 – 8:3
📖 JOHN 15

⊕ K E Y   T H O U G H T S

- **Deuteronomy 17** Large themes: there will be evident and multiplied blessings upon those who walk in obedience to the ways of the Lord.

- As well, there is to be no compromise with the wicked or the ways of the world. These examples serve us by showing that loyalty to God, and singleness of heart in serving and worshipping Him – is right!

- Vss. 18 & 21 When we face enemies or obstacles that seem insurmountable we are assured of the Lord's help and we are not to fear. This is a challenge, *"You shall not be terrified of them".* Why? *"The Lord your God, the great and awesome God, is among you."* Ok then...yes Lord.

- Vs. 26 There are times to search our home and see if we have brought in any abominations. (Is there anything present that we know is displeasing to the Lord?)

- God's provision of manna is a strong teacher regarding daily dependence upon the Lord. His heart is always for relationship with us. There will be times when we have trials that the Lord is looking to see what is truly in our hearts.

- 8:3 Jesus quotes this verse – here we find life: in *"every word that proceeds from the mouth of the Lord."*

- **John 15** This is a very rich chapter, so full of inspiration for spiritual growth.

- It is the heart of God that we, the 'branches', would be very fruitful! This fruitfulness only flows through us, as we are connected to, and 'abiding' in, the Vine, (Jesus).

- "Abide": remain, to live in, *"to make our home in Christ, as He makes His home in us."* (MSG)
- Vs. 6 When seeking to be a follower of Jesus, we must receive His teaching. He says that branches that do not abide (remain connected), will wither, the withered will be burned. There is no uncertainty in Jesus plain words.
- God is glorified when in answer to prayer, we bear "much" fruit.
- Joy (vs. 11) is the natural byproduct of fruitfulness. This is why there are so many joyless Christians, they have ceased bearing fruit and are frustrated at the insipid benefits of trying to live in two worlds.
- The command of Jesus is to love one another (vs. 12 & 17). (Just a question, are you in relationship with brothers and sisters on a spiritual level, where true godly love can blossom, are you in community – consistently? A home group - Life Group?)
- The Holy Spirit is "the Helper". "Help us today Holy Spirit."

QUOTE OF THE DAY

"When sinners are careless and stupid, and sinking into hell unconcerned, it is time the church should bestir themselves. It is as much the duty of the church to awake, as it is for the firemen to awake when a fire breaks out in the night in a great city."

Charles Finney

DAY 88

📖 DEUTERONOMY 8:4 – 20
📖 JOHN 16

☉ K E Y   T H O U G H T S

- **Deuteronomy 8** Prosperity has a seductive quality about it, a dangerous inference that "I" have gotten this for myself.
- Vss. 7-16 recount the blessings of the land that the Lord is

bringing the people into and then comes the caution.

- Vss. 17, 18 It is only the Lord who gives anyone the power to get wealth, and through this provision prove the establishment of His covenant with us.

- Moses uses the word "forget" many times in these farewell instructions to Israel. (Have you forgotten any of the goodness of the Lord? Are we looking to any other 'gods' for our security or joy?) He alone is sufficient to meet our needs and longings.

- **John 16** Jesus takes significant time to explain, promise and encourage us regarding the coming of the Holy Spirit.

- Vs. 7 A key verse to understand the undeniable importance of our having a relationship with the Holy Spirit. Jesus actually says *"it is better that I go away"* – because? Then the Holy Spirit will come to you.

- Think this way – having the Holy Spirit with us now is better than if Jesus had stayed on the earth. In light of this, there is so much more to know of this blessed person, the Holy Spirit.

- Vss. 8-11 "The ministry of the Spirit to <u>unbelievers</u> is that of conviction. Specifically, He uses their unbelief to prove the gravity of sin (9), the triumphant work of Christ to prove the availability of righteousness (10), and the defeat of Satan to prove the solemn certainty of judgment (11)." (SFLB)

- Vs. 24 Note the power of asking. Go ahead, ask in His Name!

- Vs. 33 Take heart, even though there are troubles in this life, Christ has overcome – and in Him, full of the Holy Spirit, so will you!

QUOTE OF THE DAY

"In using all means, (methods of evangelism, church work, witnessing, altar calls) seek God alone. In and through every outward thing, look only to the power of His Spirit, and the merits of His Son. Beware you do not get stuck in the work itself; if you do, it is all lost labor. Nothing short of God can satisfy your soul. Therefore, fix on Him in all, through all, and above all....."

John Wesley 'How to Pray: The Best of John Wesley'

DAY 89

📖 DEUTERONOMY 9 – 10:5
📖 JOHN 17

◉ K E Y   T H O U G H T S

- **Deuteronomy 9:4-6** Three times the Lord reminds the children of Israel that it is not their own righteousness that entitles them to the land, rather, it is the wickedness of these "nations" and God's commitment to fulfill His promises to Abraham, Isaac and Jacob.

- The gifts and blessings of God are always about His grace. The benefits we receive are such a testimony to His goodness and love.

- (I don't want to be called 'stiff-necked' – how about you?)

- At least 7 specific rebellions or grumblings are recorded in chapter 9.

- Vs. 29 Sighs with relief – *"Yet they are Your people, Your inheritance..."*

- **John 17:3** Jesus makes the way to eternal life very plain and simple. Not many ways, not great complicated rituals filled with uncertainty...

- Vs. 5 Jesus is the 'eternal' Word (visible expression, communication of God) – *"before the world was"* – He had glory!

- Vss. 13-18 Meditate on this beautiful prayer of Jesus – it is a prayer for you, today. Jesus prays that you may have:

  - His joy.

  - Protection from the evil one.

  - His sanctifying (ongoing purifying cleansing)

  - His purpose in your heart – we are sent ones.

- Vs. 26 This is so deep – the same love that the Father has for the Son – is that "love" Jesus prays for us to have "in us".

- Remember that you are so loved by God. An everlasting love, a deep and wide love, a love with feeling and commitment.

"How deep the Father's love for us, how vast beyond all measure. That He should give His only Son, and make a wretch His treasure."

Song: 'How Deep the Father's Love'

DAY 90

📖 JOHN 18, 19

⊚ K E Y   T H O U G H T S

- **John 18:11** Jesus' absolute surrender to the will of the Father, and the purpose for which He had come to the earth is so inspiring.

- Vs.18 The phrase *"Peter stood with them and warmed himself."* (The fires of the world are the wrong place to seek warmth.)

- Don't be too hard on Peter, and yet see the pathos and struggle in this disciple's life – afraid for his life, failing badly in the moment – recovering so well at Pentecost and beyond. (vss. 18, 25, 27, Acts 2:2 ff *[following forward verses]*)

- Jesus lovingly, powerfully restores him, (Jn. 21:15-19; Mark 16:7)

- 18:28 The religious leaders are plotting murder, but are very careful to not defile themselves ceremonially. Religion is so blind, so devoid of heart and integrity. Only a living relationship with Jesus, and the indwelling authority of the Holy Spirit can set us free!

- Vs. 37 *"Everyone who is of the truth hears My voice."* Jesus is truth - eternal, unchangeable, reliable. Make Him the measurement of all so called 'truth' in our time. Ask - how does this opinion line up to Jesus?

- Vss. 38 and 19:4 Note that twice Pilate "finds no fault".

- Allow the majesty and love of Jesus' crucifixion to move your heart to worship.

- His care for Mary from the cross banishes any misinterpretation of earlier teaching regarding the value of family love. (Matthew 10:37)

- 19:30 *"It is finished."* Once, for all time, the price has been paid! Perhaps the greatest three words in the Bible. He left nothing undone, He shrank from none of the pain, He left no loopholes in the plan of redemption, the debt was paid in full, the chains were completely broken. Hallelujah! Such depths of love – such heights of victory. We worship you Jesus!

QUOTE OF THE DAY

"Let the seas roar, the earth be shaken, and all things go to ruin and confusion; yet, the soul that adheres to God will remain safe and quiet, and shall not be moved forever."

Robert Leighton (1613-1684)

DAY 91

📖 DEUTERONOMY 10:12 – 11:3, 18 – 28
📖 JOHN 20

⊙ K E Y   T H O U G H T S

- **Deuteronomy 10:12ff** This pathway of blessing is always valid. This instruction in relationship with the Father will bring blessing to our lives regardless of which 'testament' (old or new) we live in.

- Vs. 18 The heart of God is always engaged and active in the care for widows and orphans. This is the root of Jesus' teaching in the New Covenant and connects directly to the *"pure and undefiled religion"* passage (James 1:27).

- 11:18ff The importance and insistence upon the teaching of children. Parents, you are the primary vehicle for the transfer of spiritual knowledge and experience. Do not leave or delegate that responsibility to anyone else. Look to supplement your input, (with teachers, youth workers) but the significance of your role can never be fully replaced by someone else.

- **John 20:21** A blessing of peace, and a sending out. There is always an application in practical living that will flow from inner peace.

- 22, 23 Anticipating the outpouring of the Holy Spirit in Acts, and the impact of presenting the gospel Those who hear as a result of Spirit empowered preaching/testimony will truly have the opportunity to receive forgiveness. Without the gospel – they remain in their sins.

- 20:30, 31 Testimony and this testament are presented by the writer (John) so *"that you may believe"*.

- Believing results in Life!

QUOTE OF THE DAY

"For I do not seek to understand in order that I may believe, <u>but I believe in order to understand</u>. For this too I believe, that "unless I believe, I shall not understand."

(Isa. 7:9)

Anselm (a medieval church Father around 1100)

DAY 92

📖 DEUTERONOMY 12:1 – 11, 29 – 32; 13:1 – 10
📖 JOHN 21

⊙ K E Y   T H O U G H T S

- **Deuteronomy 12:8** sounds like modern secular views of a relationship with God – *"every man doing whatever is right in his own eyes."*

- False gods are not to be worshipped. One of the abominations is identified – the human sacrifice of children.

- Our God is a loving compassionate God, not a malicious angry god requiring appeasement.

- **John 21** How easily discouragement moves Peter to return to his old ways ... *"I'm going fishing"*.

- The miraculous catch of fish contains so much hope and encouragement. How many times have we toiled and felt that our labor was fruitless. If Jesus guides us in the work, if we use His methods and ways:

- The catch will be large, and the nets won't break!
- Persistence in serving the Lord is often the key that moves it from failure to great harvest.

- Jesus showed Himself alive many times after His resurrection – this is the third time (21:14).

- Try to imagine, if the gospel writers included all these events, how many more there must have been. And Jesus still said *"greater works than these"* – such amazing promises.

QUOTE OF THE DAY

"Believers who have the gospel keep mumbling it over and over to   themselves. Meanwhile, millions who have never heard it once fall into the flames of eternal hell without ever hearing the salvation story."

K.P. Yohannan, founder of Gospel for Asia Bible Society

DAY 93

DEUTERONOMY 14:22 – 29; 15:7 – 18
ACTS 1:1 – 8

KEY THOUGHTS

- **Deuteronomy 14:23** Notice the outcome that comes to people when they commit to the tithe – *"that you may learn to fear the Lord your God always."*

- We believe that the tithe is an ordinance (timeless, established practice). Affirmed first by Abraham to Melchizedek (Gen. 14 - a type of Christ), then not removed, but affirmed by Jesus (Matt. 23:23).

- In the NT, this principle greatly expanded into generosity and heartfelt giving led by the Spirit. It was never rescinded by any of the Apostles.

- Tithing is a tutor that leads to generosity.

- Our treatment of the poor is always a reliable indicator of our own heart condition.

- **Acts 1** Key words:
- Infallible proofs – undeniable evidence of Jesus' resurrection
- Promise of the Father – the Holy Spirit
- Baptized with the Holy Spirit.
- Power, witnesses – to the ends of the earth (Acts 1:8 is the theme of the entire book).
- This instruction is so important. Jesus' last words and only clear instruction are relating to their staying in Jerusalem for the single purpose of the baptism in the Holy Spirit. This event in their lives was so important that nothing else of the future plan mattered enough to mention.
- This same baptism, this same power is for you. Every follower of Jesus is qualified and commanded to receive this most important relationship with the Holy Spirit.
- Enter in, draw near, welcome the Holy Spirit to your heart and life.

QUOTE OF THE DAY

"It does not say, make your light shine. If it is really a light it will shine in spite of you – only don't hide it under a bushel. Let it shine. Confess Christ everywhere."

Dwight L. Moody (1837-1899)

DAY 94

📖 DEUTERONOMY 18:9 – 22; 19:14 – 21
📖 ACTS 1:9 – 14; 2:1 – 4

☉ K E Y   T H O U G H T S

- **Deuteronomy 18** There is to be no compromise for those who would follow the Lord fully. No mixing of practices, no inclusion of the occult with the genuine worship of God.
- Purity is the heart of God in calling His people to reject profane and abominable practices.

- 18:15 is a prophetic reference fulfilled in Jesus Christ. Peter quotes this verse in Acts 3:22, 23 stating that Jesus is the fulfillment.
- True principles for the administration of justice. We seem to have lost our way in the modern world, the simplicity and straightforward application of justice when under the authority of God is refreshing.
- **Acts 1:14** All continued, one accord – prayer, supplication. They obeyed the instruction of Jesus, they were united, they were willing to persevere for the reception of the promise, the Holy Spirit.
- 2:1-4 This coming of the Holy Spirit, the baptism in the Holy Spirit of the 120 is a massive marker in the life of the church. The church age begins – the believers are empowered, the manner of God's dealing with man changes significantly.
- This is the first recorded instance in Acts of people being filled with the Spirit.
- We need to long for a fresh infilling of the Spirit. (Would you invite the Holy Spirit right now? Simply begin praying with faith, "Come Holy Spirit", "fill me Holy Spirit", "I long for more of You.")

QUOTE OF THE DAY

"The only way to keep a broken vessel full is to keep it always under the tap."

Dwight L. Moody (1837-1899)

DAY 95

📖 DEUTERONOMY 20; 21:22, 23; 22:1 – 12
📖 ACTS 2:5 – 41

☞ K E Y   T H O U G H T S

- **Deuteronomy 20:3, 4** When we have enemies, or are facing a battle of any kind, this promise will sustain us – *"the Lord your God is He who goes with you, to fight for you!"*

- 21:23 This is quoted by the Apostle Paul in Galatians 3:1. He (Jesus) became the curse for us, so that we could experience freedom from the terrible consequences of the curse. Praise God!

- 22:1-12 Fascinating list of miscellaneous laws; honesty, gender definition and clarity, work place safety, and purity in everything.

- **Acts 2** Peter preaches that the phenomenon they were currently experiencing was the fulfillment of Joel's prophecy from hundreds of years prior, *"This is that"* meaning that this was the beginning of the outpouring the Holy Spirit for *"all flesh"*.

- There is so much in this message – it contains a few recurring themes in Acts:

- Vs. 21 *"whoever,* (KJV says "whosoever") *calls on the name of the Lord shall be saved!"* There is such a wide reach of God's grace, for any person, any color, language or status – *"shall be saved"*. Never minimize the powerful spiritual transaction of salvation through the confession of someone who "calls".

- Vs. 32 In just about every sermon in Acts there will be a reference to the resurrection of Jesus. This was the pivotal proclamation that separated Christianity from all other philosophies and religions.

- The Holy Spirit is *"poured"* out, a favorite terminology, He is "the Promise". "Peter's words clearly extend to every believer in every era everywhere, full reason to expect the same resource and experience that was afforded the first believers who received the Holy Spirit at the birth of the church." (SFLB)

- Repentance brings the remission of sins. Then, (subsequently, following after, a separate experience), you will receive the gift of the Holy Spirit, or baptism in the Holy Spirit. (vs. 38)

- A mighty harvest of 3000 "souls", notice the description, not people, "souls". A living, eternal being of infinite value.

- What a day, what a beautiful fulfillment of the promise Jesus made – *"if I go I will send the Comforter"*. (John 16:7) He surely has come and is among us!

"All the resource of the Godhead are at our disposal!"

Jonathan Gofarth

DAY 96

📖 DEUTERONOMY 26 – 27:10
📖 ACTS 2:42 – 47

☉ K E Y   T H O U G H T S

- **Deuteronomy 26:11** In teaching the people to tithe, God brought many significant benefits to them. This one is so powerful: through the practice of returning the tithe (the holy tithe vs. 13) they would be able to…

  - *"Rejoice in every good thing which the Lord your God has given to you and your house."*

  - Because an accurate tithe brings us to the awareness of all that the Lord has provided, we actually have to calculate how blessed we are! It is a remembrance before the Lord, He does not fail, He does prosper His people. Tithing reminds us that every pay period, every bonus, every blessing is from the Lord. Thank you God, for your extravagant blessings!

- 27:10 How do we identity a people of God? They *"obey the voice of the Lord and obey His commandments"*. Jesus said: *"If you love Me, keep my commandments."* (Jn. 14:15)

- **Acts 2:42ff** (We need to slow our reading down a little at this point in Acts… less verses and more thought, receiving and action.) Oh how we long to be among a community of Spirit-filled believers who live this way!

- Continued steadfastly:

  a) doctrine, teaching

  b) fellowship, gatherings

  c) breaking of bread, some form of communion probably accompanied by a meal

  d) prayer

- Many wonders and signs – causing great reverence for God and the Holy Spirit.
- A common level of care, a practical love for one another. They lived as travelers on the earth headed to a different land, so sharing possessions and caring for fellow sojourners was natural.
- Daily – encouraging one another.
- Vs. 46 introduces the "house to house". Biblical foundation for smaller spiritual gatherings in homes – fellowship – lots of food!
- In this environment *"the Lord added DAILY"*.
- Pray aloud with me if you are able: "Oh, Holy Spirit, fall on us in this same powerful way. We long to know all of your power and to share together to see people being added 'daily' to your kingdom."

QUOTE OF THE DAY

"Our greatest fear as individuals and as a church should not be of failure, but of succeeding at things in life that don't really matter."

Francis Chan, 'Crazy Love'

DAY 97

📖 DEUTERONOMY 28:1 – 47, 63, 68
📖 ACTS 3:1 – 10

☀ K E Y   T H O U G H T S

- **Deuteronomy 28** This chapter is a graphic picture of the contrast between the "blessings" of God and the "cursings" that fall upon the people/person who:
  - Obeys and walks in the ways of the Lord and the person who disobeys and abandons the ways of the Lord.
- The blessings will "overtake" (vs. 2).
- The cursings will "pursue and overtake" (vs. 45).

- Vs. 47 *"Because you did not serve the Lord your God with joy and gladness of heart."*

- Vs. 29 No more tragic picture exists in Scripture. If God's covenant people (the ones on whom He has set His love) walk in disobedience and serve other gods, they will eventually find themselves:

  - *"offered as slaves...to your enemies...but no one will buy you."* Rebellion and disobedience to God's ways leaves us destitute and alone. Picture a slave standing on the auction block, the bid goes lower and lower until it is zero, still no one takes you – cast off, unwanted, hopelessly alone.

- **Acts 3:6** This is the same Peter who just a short time ago was "warming" by the fires of the world, denying he had ever known Jesus! Now since his encounter with the Holy Spirit he is filled with faith, bold to declare healing in the name of Jesus Christ!

- Peter's transformation from the tempestuous, stumbling disciple into the 'Rock' is such an encouragement to you and me! Filled with the Holy Spirit, walking in faith. In that power he truly 'became' the man of God that Jesus saw him to be.

- Jesus sees in you that same potential. It is so good, and so much more – a high blessing. Take heart today – the Lord is far from finished with you!

- Welcome all of His means of transformation in your life.

QUOTE OF THE DAY

"How quickly we forget God's great deliverances in our lives. How easily we take for granted the miracles He performed in our past."

David Wilkerson

DAY 98

📖 DEUTERONOMY 29
📖 ACTS 3:11 – 4:4

⊕ K E Y   T H O U G H T S

- **Deuteronomy 29:5, 6** The Lord's supernatural provision for the travelers had a specific purpose: *"that you may know that I am the Lord your God."*

- God's purpose in drawing us into a relationship of dependency is always so that we may know Him, His goodness, faithfulness, and love! Drawing near is always for our blessing.

- Vs. 18 To serve the 'gods' of the nations around us places us in danger of having a poisonous root bringing bitterness placed in our lives. Dabbling with other gods or the world's ways is not harmless or innocent – poisons, kills, maims and destroys.

- Vs. 19 This statement is a classic exposure of a rebellious heart. "Even though I am going my own way, living my life by my own will – ignoring God's ways and commandments – I'm still expecting everything to work out well – 'I shall still have peace.'" With such an attitude, a rude awakening is ahead.

- **Acts 3:14, 15** The resurrection is central to the authority to heal.

- "Through faith in His Name" has granted this "perfect soundness." Complete healing!

- Vs. 19 The fruit of repentance is a "time of refreshing". How true. Sin burdens us, causes heaviness and clouds of discouragement. Repentance lifts and refreshes the spirit as we enter in to the grace and love of our wonderful Jesus. (1 Jn. 1:9)

- 4:4 In spite of persecution we must take note that all through the birth and growth of the NT church there was consistent and vehement opposition to the gospel! It was never without resistance.

- "HOWEVER!!" (vs. 4) If people have a chance to hear the 'Word' there will always be those who will believe.

- Never be discouraged by opposition or resistance, continue to share the good news. Silence is the only way that the seed will not bear fruit and that is only because it is "still in the barn".

DAY 99

📖 DEUTERONOMY 30
📖 ACTS 4:5 – 22

KEY THOUGHTS

- **Deuteronomy 30:6** When backsliders return to the Lord not only is the heart of the wanderer 'reshaped' but so is the potential for the descendants to be followers of God.
- Sin and rebellion are so rooted in selfishness that most backsliders give no thought to the ripple effect upon their children and grandchildren. Live for God because it is right and good for you, but also it is a heritage of blessing that you can give to your generations to follow.
- Vss. 11 - 14 The ways of walking with the Lord are not hidden, they are not too complicated to understand – or too lofty to be obeyed. The word is 'near'… our part is to do it.
- Vss. 14 – 20 I recently heard that a friend had died from a drug overdose. This man was one of the reasons that our church is now involved in recovery ministry. His life verse was Deut. 30:19. This sad story is a testimony to the tragedy of departing, or being drawn away from the ways of the Lord. The eventual result of rebellion against God is always *"that you shall perish"*. (vs.18)
- Vs. 20 summarizes it all. That you may *"love…obey…cling to Him"* for He is your *"life and length of your days."*

- **Acts 4:8** There are a few things that you should note and mark every time you see them in Acts. *"Filled with the Spirit"* is one of those things. This filling was not a once for all experience, it was once a baptizing and then always more filling! Continue to be filled, keep on being filled. (Eph. 5:18)
- 4:10 Note here the fifth reference in Acts to the resurrection. We will stay true to the NT way if our teaching, preaching, leading and witnessing is always anchored in the reference point of the resurrection.
- 4:12 Read this out loud, memorize this verse if you will. This statement runs absolutely against the current of the accepted 'truth' of our culture.
- Vs. 13 One simple reason for the boldness of these disciples – *"they had been with Jesus."*
- Vs. 15 In spite of the effectiveness and authority of the message, the religious leaders were aggressively trying to stop the spread of the gospel.
- Don't be surprised when someone aggressively tries to silence you. We are no different from the first believers.
- Vs. 19 & 20 (Who are we taking our cue from when it comes to sharing our faith? "you" the world, the culture, Hollywood, godless philosophers) or "God"?
- Vs. 20 *"We cannot help but speak the wonderful works of God."* Just tell what wonderful things God is doing in your life.

QUOTE OF THE DAY

"The gospel is only good news if it gets there in time."

Carl F. H. Henry

DAY 100

📖 DEUTERONOMY 31:1 – 8, 22 – 29; 32:3 – 4, 11 – 12, 15 – 18, 48 – 52

"28 VERSES IN TOTAL. IN AN INSTANCE LIKE THIS, WHERE WE ARE PICKING HIGHLIGHTS IN A CHAPTER, BEFORE YOU BEGIN YOUR READING GO THROUGH THE PASSAGE AND MARK THE SELECTED VERSES FOR THAT DAY."

📖 ACTS 4:23 – 37

☉ K E Y   T H O U G H T S

- **Deuteronomy 31:6, 8** This promise is reiterated many times to Joshua and to the people. Jesus makes the same promise to us (In Heb. 13:5 the writer quotes Jesus).

- When all seems lost, or there is great discouragement it is wise to recite this promise to ourselves. Be reminded just as these people were to be reminded – He will not leave, He will not forsake, He will not fail!

- "Jeshurun" - a symbolical name for Israel. It is most likely derived from a root signifying "to be blessed." (Smith's Bible Dictionary)

- **Acts 4:24** This practice should be ours as well. Whenever we are faced with trouble - *"they raised their voice to God with one accord"*. A powerful release of God's power will follow.

- Vs. 29-30 Notice the specific request – boldness, signs and wonders – always an appropriate prayer!

- Take special note of the response of the Holy Spirit – *"and they were ALL filled with the Holy Spirit"*. Ongoing, continuous fillings in times of need, the result?

- They *"Spoke the word of God...with boldness."* Praise God.

- Vs. 32 The power of unity, a community that cares, shares. Their faith is practical, benevolent and unselfish.

- The giving was without designation. Laid it at the Apostles feet. Further indication that the tithe, and offering has its first place at the gathering point, or house of God.

- This illustrates a principle of bringing our tithes and offerings and allowing spiritual elders to distribute where the need is most acute.

"The Bible, prayer, the House of God – these are the golden pipes through which the golden oil is poured.

Robert M. McCheyne (1813 – 1843)

DAY 101

📖 DEUTERONOMY 33:26 – 29; 34
📖 ACTS 5

☉ K E Y   T H O U G H T S

- **Deuteronomy 33:27** We must always keep the definitions and descriptions of our God within the revealed parameters of the Bible and of God Himself.

- When we start listening to the mockery and derision of the "nations around us" (culture, media, wisdom of man), we will become discouraged even as Israel was. But when we remind ourselves of the revealed truth of who God is we will be supported underneath by "everlasting arms".

- Moses, in spite of his failings, is remembered as someone who was unique in all Israel as a prophet. Our legacy is so important to prepare for. (What will be said of you, of me?)

- **Acts 5:3** Lying to the Holy Spirit illustrates in a clear way that the Holy Spirit is a person. Ours is a relationship with the person of the Holy Spirit not with an aura or 'force'.

- He is a friend who is present for the purpose of communion, relationship, encouragement. Lying to, grieving (Eph. 4:30) ignoring any friend will damage, and stunt the blessings of that friendship.

- 5:11 You think? Vs. 12 More descriptions of unity.

- Vs. 15-16 It's like a 'river' of healing and miracles had been released. It is our expectation and practice to seek the same flow of ministry of healings, miracles, deliverance, signs and wonders.

- At the same time great opposition was arising; imprisonment, threats, gag orders.

- Vs. 29 There are situations where civil disobedience is justified. Where would our world be if Bibles had not been smuggled, if underground churches had not been planted, if people had not stood up for their faith and continued in the face of the threat of death to proclaim the gospel?

- Vs. 39 *"But if it is of God, you cannot overthrow it."* Always true. Resisting the moving of God, when it is God, is futile. He will have His way.

- Vs. 42 More house meetings. They were together daily. You get the distinct feeling that these people, in the midst of a world changing revival, just loved being together!

QUOTE OF THE DAY

"But God doesn't call us to be comfortable. He calls us to trust Him so completely that we are unafraid to put ourselves in situations where we will be in trouble if He doesn't come through."

Francis Chan, 'Crazy Love'

DAY 102

📖 JOSHUA 1
📖 ACTS 6, 7:37, 51 – 60

☉ K E Y   T H O U G H T S

- **Joshua 1:2** *"Moses my servant is dead."* For Joshua, those words were important for a few reasons:
  a) Joshua was truly the leader and the past was indeed the past
  b) there was no one but God to look to and depend upon
  c) Joshua would have to learn to move in his own gifting's of ministry and leadership

- The recurring theme of this chapter of assignment to Joshua is: *"be strong and of good courage, very courageous"*. Three times in the first nine verses.

- The reason for this courage and strength of purpose was also very specific – *"for the Lord your God is with you wherever you go."*
- You too can be strong and courageous in the same promises of God. The land before us is not too big, the task is not beyond us – whether it is an issue of personal obedience, or our vision as a church – we must advance and take the "land" that the Lord has promised!
- Note: the tribes of Reuben, Gad, and the half tribe of Manasseh received their allotted inheritance on the east side of the Jordon, across from Jericho. (There will be a number of incidents to follow that hinge on that information.) Their soldiers were to cross over with the rest, conquer the land and then return to their own possessions.
- **Acts 6** The selection of the first deacons. The apostles were the spiritual elders of the church. The deacons were the 'active young men' who were selected to help with the serving roles needed.
- "The deacons or "young men" at Jerusalem as (were) preparing the rooms for meetings, distributing alms, maintaining order at the meetings, baptizing new converts, distributing the elements at the Lord's Supper". (Smith's Bible Dictionary)
- This description of the qualifications in 6:3, 5, 8 – should be a call to all who desire to serve in the Lord's work. c.r. (cross reference) 1 Tim. 3:8-12.
- Particularly *"full of the Holy Spirit"*. Evidently full, continuing to be increasingly filled, a seeker, one with recognizable spiritual zeal and hunger.
- When we are filled with the Holy Spirit there will be an anointing upon us with the result that those hearing us testify *"will not be able to resist the wisdom and the Spirit"* by which we speak! (6:10)

QUOTE OF THE DAY

"It is possible for the most obscure person in a church, with a heart right toward God, to exercise as much power for the evangelization of the world, as it is for those who stand in the most prominent positions."

John R. Mott

DAY 103

📖 JOSHUA 2
📖 ACTS 8:1 – 25

◉ K E Y   T H O U G H T S

- **Joshua 2** Rahab – there are many applications to be made from this seemingly insignificant incident.

- Rahab, in a godless city, through what she has heard of the conquests of Israel, has come to have enough faith to put her trust in God. In every place/city there is someone who is reaching in faith toward the Lord. Their faith may be immature (Rahab seems to lie with ease) but there is something stirring in their heart that if nurtured could blossom into full-fledged discipleship.

- The scarlet cord: this is a beautiful foreshadowing and illustration of the redemptive theme of the whole of scripture. It is a type of the blood of Jesus, the scarlet cord of Christ's saving work.

- The scarlet cord was the symbol of safety for all of Rahab's family. When one person in a family begins the chain of faith, often over time the gospel permeates the whole clan.

- Rahab, of questionable reputation and character, becomes one the ancestors of the royal line of David and ultimately Jesus. When Jesus gets a hold of a life, the transformation and legacy can truly be stunning.

- **Acts 8:4-8** The ongoing work of the church. Another deacon, Philip, takes the gospel (as do all who were scattered by the persecution) to Samaria.

- Miracles, deliverances, salvations, baptisms in the Holy Spirit all followed. This is our expectation of the church today as we are 'scattered' among our people.

- 8:12 These people had believed and been baptized. Their experience with the Holy Spirit was described in these ways:

- *"Laid hands on them"* and prayed that they might receive the Holy Spirit *"for as yet He had fallen upon none of them."* (vss. 15, 16)

- Their receiving was accompanied by evidence that Simon saw. He wanted to purchase the ability to impart this gift. (Many commentators believe these people spoke with tongues.)

- If there was no observable evidence of a baptism happening, Simon, (who was the first biblical 'clamorer' after signs and wonders , rather than seeking the Giver of those signs and wonders) would not have wanted to purchase the same ability to impart this gift.

- Simon is a challenging character. It says he believed and was baptized, and yet he is aggressively rebuked by Peter. He represents those people who are near the things of God, but who have never completely surrendered to His Lordship. Character, humility, submission, honesty, selfless ministry, lack of proud ambition – these are the signs over time that indicate a truly surrendered heart.

- Bitterness is poison – nothing less. We cannot harbor bitterness without it poisoning our spirits, our attitudes and our motives.

QUOTE OF THE DAY

"Character is what a man is in the dark."

Dwight L. Moody

DAY 104

📖 JOSHUA 3; 4:1 – 9, 20 – 24
📖 ACTS 8:26 – 9:22

◉ K E Y T H O U G H T S

- **Joshua 3:5** This is a recurring theme in the scripture – preparing today for what the Lord will do tomorrow. *"Sanctify yourselves"*…points to a setting apart, a time of preparation.

- The Lord is always preparing 'wonders'. It is what He does best. (How many of us miss the wonders of God by being unprepared in the spirit to receive them, to take the step of faith, to risk for God?)

- We believe in miracles! A miracle is beyond the natural, so the Jordan river standing 'in a heap', up river, the Red Sea opening, manna from heaven, the healing of sickness, financial provision in a crisis, protection on the highway, favor in business are all evidence of the miraculous. Believe in them all, not just the ones we can logically get our minds around.

- Memorial stones might be difficult in your neighborhood, but a journal, a plaque, a picture or video of some great deliverance by the Lord is a powerful reminder so that you will know (4:24) that *"the hand of the Lord is mighty, that you may fear the Lord your God, forever."*

- **Acts 8:29, 35** Philip, (another deacon) is flowing in the Holy Spirit, listening to the voice of the Spirit in his inner man.

- Then *"opening his mouth"* he tells the man about Jesus. What a fantastic phrase - *"opened his mouth"*. It speaks of faith, of obedience, of reliance upon the Holy Spirit.

- Next time you are in a situation where the Lord opens the door just "open your mouth" and let the Holy Spirit fill you with the right words about Jesus.

- Saul is so overwhelmed by the glory of Jesus that he falls to the ground. The holiness of God is blinding. Try to put yourself into Saul/Paul's thoughts for those few days of blindness. He went from being a murderer to one gripped by a jolting revelation of the truth of Jesus and the lies of his own life.

- No wonder he was so open to be baptized/filled with the Holy Spirit when Ananias laid hands upon him. (vs. 17)

- Vs. 20 Another of the evidences of the filling/baptism in the Holy Spirit is a passion for the telling of the gospel – the missionary zeal of God to publish the good news to all people. Pentecost launches the gospel out of the classroom, out of the four walls of the church building into *"all the world"*. Praise God.

QUOTE OF THE DAY

"The Spirit of Christ is the spirit of missions. The nearer we get to Him, the more intensely missionary we become."

Henry Martyn, missionary to India and Persia

DAY 105

📖 JOSHUA 5:10 – 15; 6
📖 ACTS 9:23 – 43

⌖ K E Y   T H O U G H T S

- **Joshua 5:12** The manna ceases the day after they eat of the produce of the land. God's provision is 'seldom early, but it is never late.'

- The heart of God is to always be our source. The trust we have in Him, is the foundation of our relationship – His promises do not fail – if one provision ceases it only means that another is on its way!

- 5:14 The Lord, Commander of the army of the Lord! An angel, (theophany of Jesus) – the point is, any encounter with an enemy is not ours to fight alone. There is a higher authority, a higher source of power. *"The Lord will fight for you."*

- Further information on Rahab – she is identified as a harlot or a prostitute. Thank God for His ever embracing grace!

- Note: The power of quiet intercession (for six days), accompanied by the powerful explosive power of praise – *"Shout!"*

- What a shout that must have been. A declaration of the glory and power of the Lord, over that enemy territory. (Is there a stronghold in your life that needs a mighty shout of the Lord's victory over it today?)

- **Acts 9:27** Our first meeting of Barnabas, an unusual man of encouragement. He has the ministry of strengthening the hands of others – lovely gift to the church.

- 9:31 "The church". This verse gives such hope for us all today. When the church *"walks in the fear of the Lord"* (holiness, obedience, unity) and in *"the comfort of the Holy Spirit"*, (fullness, wisdom, gifts) – we will multiply!

- Healing gifts bring glory to God, and point people to Jesus when they are ministered with the right spirit. (vs. 35)

- Does our faith even extend to asking for the dead to rise? These newly 'filled with Spirit' believers, had that kind of faith.

"You have to stop loving and pursuing Christ in order to sin. When you are pursuing love, running toward Christ, you do not have opportunity to wonder, "Am I doing this right?" or "Did I serve enough this week?" When you are running toward Christ, you are freed up to serve, love, and give thanks without guilt, worry or fear. As long as you are running, you're safe."

Francis Chan, 'Crazy Love'

DAY 106

☐ JOSHUA 7
☐ ACTS 10 – 11:18

☾ K E Y   T H O U G H T S

- **Joshua 7** Achan, through covetousness and lies, single-handedly bore the responsibility for one of the few losses in battle for Israel – notably their second battle, following Jericho.

- His family is also condemned, most likely because of complicit knowledge of his sin and disobedience.

- We all have a responsibility to the whole body. There are times, particularly in ministry, when you wonder why something is not being blessed – there could be a pretender among the soldiers.

- The point for each of us is the call to walk in integrity before God, not to go looking for the 'Achan'. Our sins affect those around us, often times with disastrous effects.

- **Acts 10** Cornelius and Peter. Cornelius is a godly man with limited understanding. His heart and prayers made him a candidate to be a part of a significant moment in church history.

- 10:39, 40 Testimony to the resurrection – effective ministry is rooted in the resurrection and its power for believers.

- This household of Cornelius being baptized in the Holy Spirit – *"just as we have"* (vs. 47) with the same evidences, results in the gospel being released to the gentile world. It was the observance of Spirit baptism that convinced the Jews in Jerusalem that the gospel was indeed for all! Hallelujah! (11:17, 18)

- The baptism or filling with the Holy Spirit is God's marvelous gift to all believers. Jesus will not withhold the Spirit from you. By faith ask right now for a fresh 'baptism' with the Holy Spirit. Expect everything that you see in the Scripture!

- You are a part of those who are "afar off" (Acts 2:39). Open your heart and your mouth wide - be filled with the Holy Spirit - continue to be filled and let Him overflow through your life!

QUOTE OF THE DAY

"Hearing God is not all that difficult. If we know the Lord, we have already heard His voice - after all it was the inner leading that brought us to Him in the first place. But we can hear His voice and still miss His best if we don't keep on listening. After the what of guidance comes the when and how."

Loren Cunningham, 'Is That Really You, God? Hearing the Voice of God'

DAY 107

📖 JOSHUA 8:1 – 8, 26 – 35
📖 ACTS 11:19 – 30; 12

⊛ K E Y   T H O U G H T S

- **Joshua 8** As we follow the conquest of the Promised Land with Joshua and the children of Israel, it is important to keep in mind the previous instructions given to God's covenant people.

- The defeat and destruction of these peoples was because of their own wickedness and idolatry. As well, there was to be no intermingling of the religious and cultural practices with the people of the land – Israel was to be holy to the Lord.

- The variations in plans were to keep their dependency upon the wisdom and leading of the Lord at the forefront of their military strategy. It was to be the *"Lord who would fight for them."*

- **Acts 11:19ff** The persecution and dispersion of the Christians is the reason for the rapid spread of the gospel. Now there are gentiles taking the gospel to the Greeks (Hellenists) (vs. 2) *"and a great number believed and turned to the Lord."*

- Barnabas enters the narrative again and continues in his ways of building up, encouraging.

- This passage also contains a clear outlining of the responsibility of one congregation to others around it *"each according to his ability."*

- The collection for the struggling saints in Jerusalem – because of the closed Jewish economy and community – those who were believers would have been absolutely shut out of any opportunity for buying and selling.

- The persecution would have extended to business and simple things like buying food.

- 12:5 *"Constant prayer"*. We must take heart in prayer and continue. So much is missed from God by a lack of prayer. The application? Without this prayer the result for Peter could have been very different.

- Herod, the same one who killed the baby boys at the time of Jesus' birth, dies a gruesome death. Unbridled pride was his final downfall.

- Vs. 24 No matter what! The gospel is advancing around the world! Growing, multiplying at a phenomenal rate. Do not be discouraged if it seems slow or small where we are. God is at work as never before. We will be part of it!

QUOTE OF THE DAY

"If you take missions out of the Bible, you won't have anything left but the covers."

Nina Gunter

DAY 108

📖 JOSHUA 9
📖 ACTS 13

⊙ K E Y   T H O U G H T S

- **Joshua 9** The Gibeonites represent a great lesson in whether we should rely on our own powers of wisdom and observation or *"ask counsel of the Lord."* (vs. 14)

- Joshua and the leaders were deceived by these people. If they had sought the Lord, or prayed about it they could have avoided the ongoing challenges that the Gibeonites presented to Israel – we will meet them numerous times. They will continue to be a problem for Israel.

- Note also in vs. 24 that the Gibeonites acknowledge God's authority and His right to dispossess the land of its inhabitants.

- **Acts 13: 2, 3** Out of fasting and prayer comes the ordination/ commissioning of the first Apostolic missionaries. One of the key identifiers of Apostolic ministry is its ability to break new ground, to take the word and work of God where it has not been before.

- The continual "filling" of the Spirit (13:9) is essential for effective ministry and penetration into our culture. The proconsul "believed". People in all walks of life will come to Jesus when presented with spirit-filled ministry.

- Vss. 30, 33, 37 Preaching always includes the resurrection and testimony to the living Christ – this is what marks the gospel.

- Vss. 38, 39 Through Jesus is the opportunity for the forgiveness of sins!

- Vs. 44 After just one week of person to person word of mouth *"almost the whole city gathered to hear"*. The power of simply telling what God is doing.

- Vs. 52 Such a marvelous and simple description of life in the church when we are full of the Spirit – *"filled with joy!" "Filled with the Spirit!"* A totally sufficient provision for the "good" life is available to you today! Come Holy Spirit.

"For some years it has been my abiding conviction that it is impossible to enjoy true happiness without being entirely devoted to God."

David Brainerd (1717-1747)

DAY 109

📖 JOSHUA 10:1 – 15; 11:16 – 23
📖 ACTS 14

⊙ K E Y   T H O U G H T S

- **Joshua 10** This narrative provides some of the most dramatic 'support' that God gives to Israel in their quest to conquer the Promised Land.

- Our belief in the supernatural must extend to those miracles that confront our natural reasoning – in other words – some miracles seem to have a plausible explanation, others, like the sun and the moon standing still are wildly miraculous!

- God is able to order His own creation and to override His own natural laws to bring glory to Himself. He is the God of miracles and we are people who believe in Him and in His miracles!

- **Acts 14** See beyond the travelogue of ministry to the growth, structure and challenges of growing the early church.

- The Holy Spirit continues to minister healing through the Apostles. The people of Lystra try to worship Paul and Barnabas. When they refuse, the people quickly turn from worship to stoning! Amazing the fickle hearts of those who do not truly receive the transforming power of Jesus.

- 14:22 *"Through many tribulations enter the kingdom of God."* There will be difficulties and trials as we follow Jesus, "The Bible teaches that suffering, trial, and all order of human difficulty are unavoidable; but God's Word also teaches they may all be overcome. The presence of the King and the power of His kingdom in our lives make us neither invulnerable nor immune to life's struggles. But they do bring the promise of victory; provision in need, strength for the day, and healing, comfort, and saving help." Jack W. Hayford (SFLB)

- Notice that the elders were 'appointed' in every church. Recognition of spiritual grace upon a life and calling that person to serve in leadership is one of the great joys of the church. When the Lord calls you accept the appointment and see the work of God increase in your life.

QUOTE OF THE DAY

"Preparation for old age should begin not later than one's teens. A life which is empty of purpose until 65 will not suddenly become filled on retirement."

Dwight L. Moody

DAY 110

📖 JOSHUA 13:1, 2, 13; 14:6 – 15; 15:13 – 19
📖 ACTS 15

⊛ K E Y   T H O U G H T S

- **Joshua 13** *"Very much land yet to be possessed"*. When God gives us an assignment accompanied by a promise, and we do not fully embrace and enter into His vision for us, there will always be unfortunate consequences that are unnecessary.

- Note: the Philistines', through Judges and Kings - how much better it would have been for Israel to have completed the task they were given in the beginning.

- Caleb, one of the great inspirational leaders of the Bible. He was 40 when he spied the land. After 45 years of waiting and putting up with the whining and complaining of his contemporaries here he is now at 85 asking for the "hill country".

- Vigorous for God in his old age, fully planning to fulfill God's purpose on his life – regardless of age! What a hero of the faith!

- **Acts 15** This section deals with the growing conflict between Judaism and Christianity (15:11) *"we believe that through the* *grace of our Lord Jesus Christ we shall be saved."*

- No addition of the ceremonial law, be it diet or circumcision is necessary for salvation – there are no "add-ons" to Jesus!

- Legalism is an ever present scourge upon the grace of God. The instructions to the churches from the Jerusalem council were not given to assist in obtaining salvation but rather: "they represent a basic separation from glaring paganism and its practices..." (SFLB)

- Godly leaders will have conflicts occasionally (vss. 36-41). The result of this disagreement was the forming of a second missionary team. This break in relationship is healed up later. (2 Tim. 4:11)

- Often, after a bit of time, either more information will surface or perspective will have cleared – allowing a healing of relationships. If there is someone you have had a falling out with, seek within your power to bring it to healing!

QUOTE OF THE DAY

"I wasn't God's first choice for what I've done for China...I don't know who it was... It must have been a man...a well-educated man. I don't know what happened. Perhaps he died. Perhaps he wasn't willing...and God looked down...and saw Gladys Aylward...And God said - "Well, she's willing."

Gladys Aylward

DAY 111

📖 JOSHUA 15:63; 17:13; 21:43 – 45; 23
📖 ACTS 16

☞ K E Y   T H O U G H T S

- **Joshua** The Israelites did not completely drive out the inhabitants of the land as they had been commanded. This becomes an ongoing scourge and complication for the people through the years to follow.

- **21:45** This declaration is repeated numerous times and is a significant point of faith for us today. It is stil! true that none of the words of the Lord have failed, He cannot fail. All His words of promise come to pass!

- The timing and the way in which He fulfills His promises are unknown to us but delay or the unexpected by no means indicate failure. They simply indicate our limited view of the whole picture (23:14).

- Going back (21:11, 12) We are to *"take careful heed to ourselves"* to love the Lord or else if we cling to the past, to the things that do not bring life, the consequence will be very painful.

- **Acts 16** Note that there are identified 'churches' in every city, appointed elders, gatherings of believers. Many today are critical of "the church". Yet the Christians in Acts formed churches. They did more than "have a personal private faith and meet with God on the golf course, or at a coffee shop."

- The "Church" has a valued place in God's purpose for our lives – the Bible says so!

- Two "households" come to faith in this chapter – Lydia's and the Philippian jailer's "household".

- We must have faith and prepare for whole clans of people to come to Christ. When one receives Christ, there is such hope for the whole group. Let's pray today for unsaved family members, "Lord bring them to Yourself, give me grace and wisdom to shine for You."

QUOTE OF THE DAY

"A Christian is growing when he elevates his Master, talks less of what he himself is doing, and becomes smaller and smaller in his own esteem; until, like the morning star, he fades away before the rising sun."

Horatius Bonar (1808-1889)

DAY 112

📖 JOSHUA 24:11 – 33
📖 ACTS 17

◉ K E Y   T H O U G H T S

- **Joshua 24:14** Two words of instruction from Joshua as to how to reverence and serve the Lord. Do so with "sincerity" and in "truth". This speaks to the inner motives and secret places of the heart – externals, rituals and appearances are not the measure of a true relationship with the Lord.

- 24:15 *"But as for me and my house, we will serve the Lord."* Husbands, wives, fathers, mothers – you are the key to whether your 'house' will serve the Lord. There is a God given responsibility to pass on your faith to your 'household'.

- The world lies to families and says "let everyone choose for themselves, all truth is valid, all ways are equal and lead to God." You choose this day, you serve the Lord and lead your family in the ways of the Lord and you WILL experience the blessings of God.

- 24:19 *"You cannot serve the Lord."* A stern warning this is no small task it cannot be a casual promise. This requires all our resolve, all the power and help of the Holy Spirit and the community of others supporting us. We cannot do it alone!

- **Acts 17** Note the different responses in different cities. The message consistently included testimony to the resurrection of Jesus.

- The situation in Athens is interesting – not all cities experienced revival – there is no large response, no church mentioned, no letter to the Athenians.

- There was also consistent opposition, false accusations and persecution that accompanied the proclamation of the gospel. Evangelism, missions, reaching our cities is no easy task – we must not be discouraged by small results, mockery or opposition – it has and always will be so!

"If you found a cure for cancer, wouldn't it be inconceivable to hide it from the rest of mankind? How much more inconceivable to keep silent the cure from the eternal wages of death."

Dave Davidson

DAY 113

📖 JUDGES 1:12 – 36
📖 ACTS 18

⊙ K E Y   T H O U G H T S

- **Judges 1:12-15** Caleb is honored again as a leader among the people.

- The key words in this passage – "nor did _____ drive out the inhabitants of _____."

- This is a record of the incomplete conquest of the land. They did not fully enter in. There were compromises and allowances made all throughout – all of which come back later to be a thorn in the side of the people.

- Procrastination, compromise, apathy, laziness – they are all characteristics of those who live only for the moment, only for the short term. Most of us need improvement in this area.

- When it comes to obedience to the Lord or a life of holiness there is no benefit in waiting – the action must be now and it must be complete.

- **Acts 18:9, 10** These are powerful words of Jesus to Paul. There are always people in our city that the Lord is preparing, stirring up the soil of their hearts to receive the good news.

- How wonderful the phrase: *"many people in this city"*. It is true in your city! Say it with me… "many people!"

- 18:26 Aquila and Priscilla, a wonderful couple committed to hospitality and mentoring. Notice how they take in Apollos and share the 'full gospel' with him.

- 19:1-10 A very clear, very instructive experience with the Holy

Spirit – subsequent to conversion, evidenced by spiritual language – a missional heart is birthed with passion

- The result? Vs. 10 *"all who dwelt in Asia heard the word of the Lord Jesus."*

QUOTE OF THE DAY

"People who don't believe in missions have not read the New Testament. Right from the beginning Jesus said the field is the world. The early church took Him at His word and went East, West, North and South."

J. Howard Edington

DAY 114

📖 JUDGES 2 – 3:6
📖 ACTS 19:11 – 41

⊙ K E Y   T H O U G H T S

- **Judges 2:10** Another generation arose who did not know the Lord! How was that possible, and who was responsible to tell them? We are always just one generation away from losing the gospel – training children and youth is not an option, it is an absolute must!

- Unfortunately we now meet Baal and Asherah – both Canaanite fertility and nature gods – the male and female versions. Idolatrous, immoral, blasphemous practices accompanied their worship.

- Vs. 18 Even during times of rebellion and idol worship the Lord is still moved with compassion by their groanings under the consequences of their sin.

- Vs. 19b summarizes their behavior well *"they did not cease from their own doings nor from their stubborn ways."*

- 3:6 Intermarriage and syncretistic religious practices signal the decline of Israel.

- **Acts 19:12, 19** Descriptions of two of the practices that we would follow on occasion:

a) believing in the healing power of the prayer of faith, the 'prayer cloth' was simply a symbol of faith, there was no inherent power in the cloth.

b) purging our lives of godless material, (actual burning is not out of line!) print, video, audio, online – is always beneficial as we seek to walk in closer relationship with the Lord, and a more intimate fellowship with the Holy Spirit.

QUOTE OF THE DAY

"Seek much personal holiness and likeness to Christ in all the features of His blessed character. Seek to be lamb-like, without which all your efforts to do good to others will be as sounding brass or a tinkling cymbal."

Robert M. McCheyne (1813-1843)

DAY 115

☐ JUDGES 3:7 – 31
☐ ACTS 20

☞ K E Y   T H O U G H T S

- **Judges 3** The book of Judges gives us the most dramatic ups and downs of Israel – in short succession you see judges rise up during times of slavery or oppression, then,

- The people 'forget', rebel and worship other gods. The result is always conquest by a foreign power and the worship of their idols. As their sins become burdensome the people cry out to the Lord and He answers!

- 8 years of slavery, 40 years of peace, 18 years of slavery 80 years of peace. (We may be disappointed by the fickle heart of the people, but are we any different?)

- **Acts 20** What may appear to be nothing more than a travelogue is actually a valuable instruction on how to birth, nurture and grow new congregations.

- The description of the interaction with the Ephesian elders (Timothy was to become their pastor) is very tender and shows the depth of relationship that ought to exist in our church.

- 20:24 In spite of troubles and persecutions, we must let "none of these things" move us! Not counting our own lives dear, but laying them down for the work of the Lord!

- We are to take heed – there will be attempts by enemies of the gospel from without and within to discourage and slow the advance of the kingdom. Take heed, stick with the basics and the gospel that you received at the beginning.

- 20:35 Paul quotes Jesus, if we desire blessings then we must give, the joy of giving far surpasses the joy of receiving.

QUOTE OF THE DAY

"Faith makes all things possible... love makes all things easy."

Dwight L. Moody

DAY 116

" WHEN WE HAVE A READING THAT MOVES FORWARD A LITTLE FASTER, CHECK THE DAY'S VERSES OFF BEFORE BEGINNING YOUR READING. "

📖 JUDGES 4; 5:1 – 3, 31
📖 ACTS 21:1 – 14, 37 – 40; 22:1 – 21

☉ K E Y   T H O U G H T S :

- **Judges 4 & 5**. Deborah, one of the key spiritual leaders in Israel. A gifted and willing leader, affirmed by all those under her care.

- "She is described as a prophetess, song writer/poet, a patriotic leader who judged Israel for 40 years, she was a military commander, and the first woman "supreme court judge." (SFLB)

- Interesting to note that Deborah is the wife of Lapidoth (we know nothing of him other than his name), she also endeavors to have her military commander step up to do his job, she is not striving for power, but willing to serve and lead when called upon.

- The other hero in the chapter is also a woman, Jael. This is one lady I wouldn't want to argue with … Sisera's fate was firmly decided. Hard to imagine singing this song today with tambourines and dancing (5:24-27).

- **Acts 21** We meet more women of God. The Holy Spirit is directing our study today that both our passages would contain clear affirmation of women in ministry roles – the four daughters of Philip are known to prophesy.

- The only reason for Luke (Acts author) to mention this would be if their gifts and ministry were being received and affirmed in the gatherings of the believers. Rise up sisters! Serve the Lord, allow the Holy Spirit to fill you and flow through you to the glory of God!

- 22:21 The expansive heart of God for the good news to be spread throughout all the world – His heart is that none should perish but that all should come to repentance. (2 Peter 3:9)

QUOTE OF THE DAY

"The Great Commission is not an option to be considered; it is a command to be obeyed."

Hudson Taylor

DAY 117

📖 JUDGES 6
📖 ACTS 22:22 – 30; 23:11 – 24, 31 – 35

⊛ K E Y   T H O U G H T S

- **Judges 6** A picture of revival! The people cry out to God, a prophet arises, a man is called, wickedness is destroyed – the Lord's name is lifted up – deliverance is close at hand.

- 6:12 The Call of God is always to something beyond what we see in ourselves at the moment.

- The natural fleshly response is "If God is with us, why is all this happening?" Even when we do not see Him, He is with us, He is at work – He is not frustrated or paralyzed!

- Vs. 14 *"Go in this might of yours."* Gideon was asking… "what might of mine?" Then we get the answer – *"Have I not sent you!"*

- Whenever we are sent – we are equipped with His might! That is all we need. Notice later in vs. 34 Gideon has the Spirit of the Lord *"come upon him"!* Our equipping for service, and for tasks beyond our own confidence will be the Holy Spirit – He is able, He is mighty!

- Vss. 25-27 The purging of idolatry in the land– there was a radical call to repentance which included the destroying of the actual idols of Baal and Asherah. Gideon is fearful (he acts at night) but he still obeys and takes the bold step of faith.

- Even though we often hear of the fleece of Gideon, this patient provision of God was specific to Gideon and not something to be adopted as a practice.

- When we need confirmation from the Holy Spirit, He will give it to us. The point of the fleece is to illustrate the gracious heart of God to give Gideon what He needed to be encouraged in the task of rising as a leader.

- God will provide with the same grace and encouragement for you, leave Gideon's fleece with Gideon. Ask the Holy Spirit to confirm His work in you in a way that is unique to your need.

- **Acts 22** When God has a purpose, even if people rise up to assassinate it, the Lord has ways of protecting and keeping His plan on track. Do not fear, when our lives are in the Lord's hands, when our kids' lives are in the Lord's hands, they are in the safest place possible!

QUOTE OF THE DAY

"The greatness of God rouses fear within us, but His goodness encourages us not to be afraid of Him. To fear and not be afraid – that is the paradox of faith."

A.W. Tozer (1897-1963)

DAY 118

📖 JUDGES 7
📖 ACTS 24:10 – 25:12

⊙ K E Y   T H O U G H T S

- **Judges 7** This famous and remarkable victory is characterized by the statement in 7:2 *"lest Israel claim glory for itself against Me, saying, 'My own hand has saved me.'"*

- The reduction of the army (those using their hands to scoop water to their mouths were considered more alert and ready for battle) was for the sole purpose of acknowledging God's victory.

- No army of 300 could conquer the armies of Midian without God's direct intervention. The point is – regardless of the odds against you, when God is for you, who can be against you!

- **Acts 24** God is always at work with those who are submitted to His purposes for their lives. Through these imprisonments and trials Paul is allowed to testify repeatedly to high governing officials.

- As with Joseph: Genesis 50:20 "you meant evil against me; but God meant it for good".

- Even this appeal to Caesar has an amazing result leading to the expansion of the Kingdom – although on the outside it appears to be a mistake (regarding Paul's freedom).

- When we cannot see what is happening, the Lord is still powerfully at work. So many times, we see after the fact how God has been doing what we would never have planned, and yet it is so much better. (Rom. 8:28)

QUOTE OF THE DAY

"The more obstacles you have, the more opportunities there are for God to do something."

Clarence W. Jones

DAY 119

📖 JUDGES 8
📖 ACTS 26 – 27:12

⊚ K E Y   T H O U G H T S

- **Judges 8:23** The people ask Gideon to be their ruler – he answers well *"the Lord shall rule over you."*

- It is difficult to understand why Gideon, showing so much wisdom and leadership, suddenly decides to shape an 'ephod' (similar to the breastplate worn by the priests) out of the offerings of gold.

- Often a memorial or remembrance of something great in the past becomes a stumbling block to the things yet to come in the future. By looking back, even worshipping this object the people fell into idolatry. Anything that steals our affections from God is a false god and should not be tolerated.

- **Acts 26:18** Our mission: *"to open their eyes, to turn them from darkness to light, from the power of Satan to God, and that they might receive forgiveness of sins AND an inheritance".*

- Vs. 20 The components of the evangelistic gospel: "repent, turn to God, do works that are befitting (evidence of change) of repentance."

- Once we have submitted to the Holy Spirit and repented of sin, we then must continue to live as a changed person, not going back to those things we have been freed from. True repentance means a change of direction, not just a glib "sorry".

- Vs. 23 A summary of the gospel – suffering (sacrifice for sins), first to rise from the dead (authority to grant eternal life), light to all the world (provision of spiritual birth).

QUOTE OF THE DAY

"We are told to let our light shine, and if it does, we won't need to tell anybody it does. Lighthouses don't fire cannons to call attention to their shining - they just shine."

Dwight L. Moody

DAY 120

📖 JUDGES 9:22 – 57
📖 ACTS 27:13 – 44

◉ K E Y   T H O U G H T S

- **Judges 9** Abimelech is a son of Gideon by a concubine (female slave). In an effort to consolidate power he murders his 70 half-brothers at one time, on one stone.

- His story teaches that treachery and violence bring the same results to us – Abimelech's death is tragic and violent – the people are left with nothing but sad memories.

- **Acts 27: 21-25** Paul becomes a prophetic voice of hope and encouragement to the people on the ship.

- The Lord is able to take us from the lowliest place (a prisoner) to being the one to advise the captain. The light of the Holy Spirit through our lives should bring:

  - Hope, encouragement, wisdom to our work and community.

  - The operation of the gifts of prophecy and faith in this dangerous situation, result in the saving of all 276 persons.

- A Christian, filled with the Holy Spirit, ought to have this type of influence on their situations.

- We may not be on a literal sinking ship, but wherever we are we can trust the Holy Spirit to give us creativity and insights into how we can bring solutions and betterment to our world.

- We ought to be the hardest working, most loyal, most joyful, most helpful people because of what Jesus has done for us and because of the empowering of the Holy Spirit within us!

QUOTE OF THE DAY

"When you're sitting in a dark room, you can either sit and curse the darkness—or you can light a candle."

Leonard Ravenhill

DAY 121

📖 JUDGES 10:1 – 29
📖 ACTS 28:1 – 10, 17 – 31

⊛ K E Y   T H O U G H T S

- **Judges 10** Jephthah: this chapter contains important reminders and insights into the ancient conflict over the land of the Middle East.

- Vss.14-24 A recap of the process of possessing the land – It was the Lord God of Israel who gave them the land, not any man's ambition or political maneuvering.

- Vs. 29 *"The Spirit of the Lord came upon Jephthah"* – he was empowered by the Holy Spirit for the task ahead.

- Jephthah's vow (vss. 30-40) is a sad example of a lack of wisdom with the tongue. Many times people value their own words (vows) above the clear direction of God. In this case, human sacrifice is clearly forbidden by God. An unwise vow or statement should be repented of in humility, not carried out in pride because of 'principle'.

- **Acts 28** The marvelous impact of this little evangelistic team, newly formed by trial. Notice the progression and development of what would become a church on Malta.

- A miracle, the gospel, time together, more healings and ministry.

- Honor, selfless provision, and care are the results as the team leaves for Rome.

- Vs. 24 Some were persuaded, some disbelieved. There will always be a mixed result to the gospel – it is truly a leavening that gradually, steadily mixes and grows.

- The kingdom of God is always expanding, even when it appears that the gospel will cease due to imprisonment – yet it continues (vs. 31) *"with all confidence, no one forbidding him."*

- Do not be discouraged by slow progress or small results – the kingdom of God is expanding, the Lord is glorified – He is at work!

"It has always been my aim, and it is my prayer to have no plan as regards myself; well assured as I am that the place where the Savior sees fit to place me must ever be the best place for me."

Robert M. McCheyne (1813-1843)

DAY 122

☐ JUDGES 13:1 – 5, 24, 25; 14
☐ LUKE 3:1 – 22

⊙ K E Y   T H O U G H T S

- **Judges 13** We meet two very well-known Bible characters today – Samson and John the Baptist, both used of God in different eras and in different ways.

- The key verse to understanding Samson's confusing and very carnal life is 13:5 … *"he shall begin to deliver Israel out of the hand of the Philistines."*

- Samson is one of the OT servants of the Lord who is marked by the phrase *"and the Spirit of the Lord began to move upon him."* 13:24

- 14:6 *"and the Spirit of the Lord came mightily upon him,"* vs. 19 *"then the Spirit of the Lord came upon him mightily".*

- In spite of Samson's weak resolve and failings, still the Lord was able to work through him, and the Holy Spirit did come upon Him at specific times for specific tasks.

- **Luke 3** John the Baptist – declares the coming of the Messiah. He challenges people to change their behavior. Three groups of people ask *"what shall we do?"* 1) the people 2) tax collectors 3) soldiers – His answers?

- Care for the poor, no longer be dishonest, do not intimidate or accuse falsely and be content with your wages.

- John also introduces the idea of "fruits worthy of repentance" – true repentance will bring about a change in behavior.

- Jesus is introduced almost exclusively in terms of the Holy Spirit's operation in and through Him. Jesus will be the One who *"baptizes with the Holy Spirit"*. (Luke 3:16)
- At Jesus' own baptism a dove (the symbol of the Holy Spirit) is clearly seen to descend upon Him. Since Jesus is anointed by the Spirit for His work and ministry, how much more should we seek for Jesus to baptize us with the Holy Spirit as has been promised!

QUOTE OF THE DAY

"Give me one hundred preachers who fear nothing but sin, and desire nothing but God, and I care not a straw whether they be clergymen or laymen; such alone will shake the gates of hell and set up the kingdom of heaven on Earth."

John Wesley

DAY 123

📖 JUDGES 15, 16
📖 LUKE 4:1 – 15

⊛ K E Y   T H O U G H T S

- **Judges 15, 16** Samson's great strength and purpose in Israel were to demonstrate the power of the Holy Spirit and to bring judgment against the wicked Philistines.
- His strength depended upon his consecration to the Lord (Nazarite vow, symbolized by his uncut hair).
- We cannot ignore Samson's relational weakness – he is defeated by his compromise with ungodly women.
- Both men and women, particularly those coming out of a lifestyle of sin, will often sacrifice the goodness of the Lord for an unwise or ungodly relationship.
- Moral compromise will ultimately bring destruction – Delilah is a graphic illustration of every immoral, adulterous relationship. From the pleasures and... comforts of her seductions – Samson is defeated!

- 16:20 This verse causes me to shudder every time I read it... *"he did not know that the Lord had departed from him."* So distracted, so blinded by his sin – he had no sensitivity left to even know that he was out from under the Lord's anointing – he was on his own!

- **Luke 4** In each of the temptations of Jesus, Satan starts it off with a lie!

- In two of the temptations he questions Jesus' divinity *"if you are the Son of God."* If anyone knew who Jesus was it was Satan and yet, as the father of lies he will always seek to plant doubt, to question God, to undermine His goodness.

- 4:1 The secret to Jesus' strength to overcome these temptations is found here – *"Jesus, being FILLED with the Spirit...... and LED.... by the Spirit."* You too can be 'filled' and 'led' by the Holy Spirit – this is our hope and promise to walk in victory! Receive more of the Holy Spirit today!

- The enemy is strategic – we need to learn and be prepared for the fact that temptation comes to us in 'opportune' moments of vulnerability and weakness – that is when temptation is most successful. Prepare for it, keep alert to those times when you may be exposed. Weariness, discouragement - even times of great victory are often times when we let down our guard. Notice also how Jesus referred to God's word as he stood strong through temptation. (It is written = it stands written, and remains so.)

- New levels of 'power' in the Holy Spirit will follow victories over temptation – there is a benefit! (4:14)

QUOTE OF THE DAY

"God delights to be fully counted upon and largely used. The deeper the need, and the darker the surrounding gloom, the more is He glorified by the faith that draws upon Him."

Charles H. Mackintosh (1820-1896)

DAY 124

📖 JUDGES 21:25 (SEE KEY THOUGHTS)
📖 LUKE 4:16 – 5:11

☞ KEY THOUGHTS

- **Judges 17-21** is an addendum to the time of the Judges – it is a history of:

    a) the religious depravity of Israel (Micah's idolatry)

    b) the moral depravity and chaos of the story of the Levites concubine – everything is very confused and messed up.

- 21:25 is a precursor to the coming times of the Kings.

- **Luke 4:18-19** Every believer should be familiar with this beautiful description of Jesus' purpose in coming (a quote from Isa. 61:1-2) – there is an unwavering commitment to the "poor, brokenhearted, captives, blind, oppressed" of this world. They are why Jesus came, they are what we should be about as well.

- 4:35 On numerous occasions Jesus will forbid demon spirits to declare any information about Him. It is not that the things they say are untrue – it is that He will not sanction anything spoken by the unreliable witness of a demon. Satan is the father of lies!

- Even if the words contain truth, there is a twist somewhere making it harmful rather than helpful.

- The healing, delivering heart of Jesus and the gospel are fully in front of all Jesus does. (4:40)

- 5:1-11 I love this passage! There is so much for us to receive.

- The beautiful parallels between literal fishing and fishing for souls.

- Frustration at the difficulty in seeing results.

- Jesus' simple command to *"launch into the deep, and let down your nets for a catch"*. (5:4)

- This command runs contrary to local fishing knowledge (fishing happened in the shallows generally).

- When Jesus is involved in the process there will be "a catch".
- We have nothing to fear in seeing such a big catch that the boats are almost sinking! Don't worry about the 'afterwards' details – just catch fish! (vs. 10)
- Jesus values the souls of men and women above all else in this world!

QUOTE OF THE DAY

"If the Great Commission is true, our plans are not too big; they are too small."

Pat Morley

DAY 125

📖 RUTH 1 – 4

ⓒ K E Y   T H O U G H T S

- This little book, a literary jewel, a love story, a delightful relief from the sadness and decadence of the previous season of our reading in Judges.
- Ruth is of such character and charm that you wonder "where did she come from all of a sudden?" God is always preparing individual people for moments of greatness in His great plan.
- Family integrity – Ruth is unusually loyal to her mother in law. (1:16, 17) She repeated chooses loyalty and integrity over personal ambition or gain.
- 2:12 *"under (His) wings"* – by her actions Ruth was evidently choosing to place herself under the care of the 'wings' of the Lord – safety, provision, blessing are all inferred.
- The threshing floor scene – 3:11 *"you are a virtuous woman"* makes it clear that nothing improper happens at the threshing floor.
- Vs. 9 Again the image of *"under your wing"*.
- "This is the most tender point of the account, and the most liable to misconstruction. The culture of the ancient Middle Eastern world involved the practice of the casting of a garment

over one being claimed for marriage, a tradition to which Ruth clearly refers." (SFLB)

- Boaz is older, and perhaps not very attractive, he appreciates her principles in making her heart known to him. (vs. 10)
- The conclusion of the story is a beautiful fulfillment of God's "best" for relationships – they are united in marriage, they are blessed with children, they are blessed by family and friends. Ruth is rewarded greatly for her patience, loyalty and integrity.
- Boaz is the great grandfather of King David. Ruth, a Moabite, is grafted into the lineage of the Lord Jesus Christ Himself.
- Never limit what God is able to do. The longings of our heart, the best for our lives will always be found when we surrender fully to God's ways and let Him be the "restorer" even when everything may appear to be lost!

QUOTE OF THE DAY

"The more able to wait long for answers to our desires and prayers, the stronger faith is."
William Gurnall (1617-1679)

DAY 126

📖 1 SAMUEL 1
📖 LUKE 5:12 – 39

☉ K E Y T H O U G H T S

- **1 Samuel** 1 Barrenness is a theme which often occurs through the scripture – it is referred to in spiritual and in literal terms.
- Hannah's barrenness became the motivation for a life of intercession and prayer.
- The Lord hears her prayer, she keeps her promise of bringing Samuel to the temple – he serves God's purpose faithfully.
- Would you join me today in offering a special prayer for fruitfulness?
- For those couples seeking to have a child – "Lord provide

children for those longing for them – give them a season of abundance and fruitfulness."

- For our church and the spiritual lives of all within our circle of relationships: "Lord break through the barrenness and burst forth with great joy in fruitful living. Pour out Your Holy Spirit upon us, open the gateways that lead to many 'children'."

- **Luke 5:13** Jesus is "willing" – knowing that we have needs to bring, what wonderful comfort to know that in general He will say *"I am willing; be cleansed"*.

- Jesus heals the man let down through the roof - thank God for those committed friends! But, the power of this incident is seen in Jesus' authority to forgive sins!

- Vs. 24 He has power on earth to forgive sins! This is a statement of his Divinity, only God can forgive sins, no man, no ordinary man has that authority.

- Jesus is not just a teacher, or a good man – He is the Son of God sent into the world (vs. 32) to bring healing to the spiritually sick, to *"call sinners to repentance"*.

- Vss. 36-39 (Am I stuck in an old rut in any area of my spiritual life? Is the Lord trying to bring some new wine into my life? Am I resistant?)

- It is a beautiful thing when an older person has retained a supple, sweet disposition toward the new, the young – the next generation. How sad when the old wine skins insist that "the old is better." The Holy Spirit is always bringing fresh new blessings – welcome the new wine of the Spirit.

QUOTE OF THE DAY

Christianity, if false, is of no importance, and if true, of infinite importance. The only thing it cannot be is moderately important.

C. S. Lewis

DAY 127

📖 1 SAMUEL 2:1 – 11
📖 LUKE 6:1 – 26

⊙ K E Y   T H O U G H T S

- **1 Samuel 2** (A shorter reading today because of the depth of material to absorb.)

- Hannah's prayer and thanksgiving – as you walk through her poem/hymn/song – identify the depth of her perspective on who God is!

- "Horn" is a metaphor for strength – the strength of a great horned ox, or bull or even thinking of our knowledge today of the rhinoceros – their horn is their strength.

- Vs. 2 *"No one is holy like the Lord"*. When we face trouble and disappointment, if we can keep the foundations secure as to who God truly is, we will overcome.

- Vs. 8 *"He raises the poor from the dust"*. Our God is able to elevate even the lowest to places of great influence – think of those who once lived on the streets, but now are testifying before people of great power.

- Think of the children of Uganda (Watoto) singing before the president of the USA, and the Queen of England!

- **Luke 6** The beatitudes: a general rule for understanding and applying these beautiful words is to keep in mind that Jesus is contrasting the temporary with the eternal. The values of this life vs. the values of His Kingdom.

- What appears to be poverty, mourning, hunger, persecution in this life is so small in comparison to the blessings of heaven. We can rejoice in our present sufferings because of our faith and spiritual life.

- Those who have their "reward" in this life, have chosen the lesser good. The eternal, the spiritual, the everlasting things are what truly matter.

- Humility that leads to the "kingdom" is highly valuable even though the world admires material wealth more.

"Some flowers must be broken and bruised before they emit any fragrance. All the wounds of Christ send out sweetness; all the sorrows of Christians do the same."

Robert M. McCheyne (1813-1843)

DAY 128

📖 1 SAMUEL 2:12 – 36
📖 LUKE 6:27 – 49

⊙ K E Y T H O U G H T S

- **1 Samuel 2** Eli and his sons: the sons' primary sin was – *"the men abhorred* (hated, had no reverence for), *the offering of the Lord"*. They were also immoral, disobedient bullies. (2:13-17)

- Eli's sin is his lack of action – he scolds the sons but does nothing to discipline them, knowing full well that they are continuing in their sin. (2:25) *"The Lord was resolved to kill them, because of their wickedness"*.

- When Eli dies we learn that he was "very" heavy, it appears that he was rebuking his sons on one hand and accepting all the meat from the offerings on the other!

- Contrast this with the young boy Samuel – during this time of evil and polluted worship we see Samuel: "grew before the Lord". (vs. 21) and that he *"grew in stature and in favor both with the Lord and men."* (vs.26)

- It is difficult to see wickedness come into power and influence – do not despair, the Lord is even now raising someone up who will *"do what is in My heart and in My mind."* (vs. 35)

- **Luke 6** Again, look for the contrasts being taught; Vss. 31-34, in each case the contrast is that "even sinners do the same". The standard of love, the bar for a disciple of Jesus is higher, different from the standards of the world.

- No true follower of Jesus will be unrecognized in the world, because of the inner transformation from Jesus' Spirit within us

– we should be as obvious as the contrast between darkness and light.

- 6:38 This verse is so radically life changing when lived out in faith. Consider the size of the measure you use when you give – do you get excited to receive with that same measure?

- Vss. 43-45 True righteousness is evident in time, all fruit trees will eventually reveal their true character. The heart is the source for our speech. Religious people will often dismiss ungodly behavior by covering it up with high sounding speech.

- The application is always in the doing. The formula is in vs. 47 a) comes to Me, b) hears My sayings, c) does them!

- Is your house being built on a true foundation?

QUOTE OF THE DAY

"Beware of no man more than of yourself; we carry our worst enemies within us."

Charles Spurgeon

DAY 129

📖 1 SAMUEL 3, 4
📖 LUKE 7:1 – 35

☙ K E Y   T H O U G H T S

- **1 Samuel 3, 4** God is able to speak, even to children. When you sense a word from the Lord to your heart, always be willing to say *"speak Lord for your servant is listening"*.

- Think of the challenge for Samuel when his first prophetic word is judgment upon Eli, consider also God's confidence in this developing young leader to trust him with such a message and responsibility.

- A trustworthy leader is the one known by God for his/her heart, not always the oldest one in the room!

- I'm hoping this poor child had a second name! Ichabod strikes fear into the heart even when it is spoken.

- "Oh God, never take Your glory from me, from us. I pray you will never declare that word over my life."

- **Luke 7** Jesus heals a centurion's servant, raises the dead, the lame walk, lepers are cleansed, the deaf hear and the poor have the 'good news' preached to them (the poor were usually ignored or considered unworthy).
- STILL – the Pharisees and lawyers – *"rejected the will of God for themselves"*. (vs. 7:30)
- As we read of Jesus' life and impact we must take careful notice of the divergent responses to His life and ministry. We should not be surprised or discouraged when we experience the same range of results.
- There will always be people who respond joyfully and readily to the gospel, and there will always be those who no matter what is said or done as testimony, will remain unmoved.
- The results or lack or results should not determine our faithful proclamation and living of the gospel.

QUOTE OF THE DAY

"What lust is so sweet or profitable that is worth burning in hell for? Is any lust so precious in thine eye that thou canst not leave it behind thee, rather than fall into the hands of God's justice?"

William Gurnall (1617-1679)

DAY 130

📖 1 SAMUEL 5
📖 LUKE 7:36 – 8:18

⊛ K E Y   T H O U G H T S

- **1 Samuel 5** The ark of God is taken to the house of the Philistine god Dagon, (said to be the father of Baal, head and torso of a man, from the waist down a fish).
- The supremacy of God is displayed in this interesting passage – Dagon, falls twice before the ark of God, the second time the words used indicate a dismemberment (cutting off), not

a breaking. God's authority over all man-made gods is a continuous theme that is being reinforced.

- The superstitious Philistines miss the point completely, their response is to make a law to never step on the threshold "instead of worshipping the living God!"

- **Luke 7:47** This statement is not so much a numbering of our sins, (no one has any right to claim fewer sins than the next person) but rather it is a challenge to those who begin to trust in self-righteousness rather than the merciful grace of Jesus.

- We are in spiritual danger of losing that vibrant sense of love when we begin to feel we are arriving spiritually, not in "need" quite so much. Self-righteousness is the death of love – we are and ever will be needy of the gracious forgiveness and restoration of our loving Lord. Thank you Jesus.

- Parable of the Sower – the seed is scattered. There must be planting and sowing first and foremost, of the word of God,(the message of the gospel). Never hesitate to share the gospel, allow the seed itself to make its way into the soil. Too often we try to evaluate the soil before we will sow the seed. Let the Holy Spirit work the soil – we must get the seed to the soil all around us!

- Four types of soil: hard – interest but no response. Stony or shallow soil, a quick perhaps an emotional response but no depth or effort at growth. Thorny, weed infested: a joyful response, genuine 'in the heart' response – yet through a gradual process the gospel is *"choked"*. Note what does the choking: (fill in the blanks with examples from your life)

- Cares:_____.

- Riches:_____.

- Pleasures of life:_____.

- The good soil! Praise God – the good response to the gospel multiplies and bears fruit with patience (30, 60 and 100 times Matt. 13:23)

- Vs. 18 *"Take heed how you hear"*. Those who hear and believe will find their capacity to grow increases, those who hear and do not believe will become increasingly hardened to the truth.

"Lost people matter to God, and so they must matter to us."

Keith Wright

DAY 131

📖 1 SAMUEL 7:2 – 17
📖 LUKE 8:19 – 9:6

⊙ K E Y   T H O U G H T S

- **1 Samuel 7** The beginning of Samuel's ministry results in a spiritual revival among the people. They get rid of all of their idols and *"served the Lord only".* (vs. 7:4)

- As soon as the revival begins, the enemy is stirred up and begins an intensified opposition. Satan will never stand by idly and watch us be blessed, we must be prepared. In our spirits we must withstand the enemy, even as we are advancing in revival.

- God is going to bring about a marvelous victory for Israel as they returned to Him, the cities that Israel had lost to the Philistines were retaken, there was peace in the land. (vs. 14)

- The *"Ebenezer"* stone was a memorial remembering the goodness of God and that it was He who had helped them. It will help us to have memorial points or markers to be reminded in times of hardship of former times of the Lord's help – He will not fail us now!

- **Luke 8** The simple application – when you are in a storm, Jesus is with you in the boat, He even has authority over the physical wind and waves – Jesus' question *"where is your faith?"* (vs. 25) is a good one to ask right now.

- **8:39** The power of testimony is encouraged by Jesus. When God has done something great for you – tell it, tell it as often as you can to as many as you can!

- **Vs. 50** A word to you today: *"do not be afraid; only believe"*. Someone is reading this and this is a living, meaningful, forceful, applicable, current word for you today – receive it and go forward.

- 9:6 A colorful and encouraging picture of Spirit-filled ministry – *"preaching and healing everywhere"*.

QUOTE OF THE DAY

A revival is nothing else than a new beginning of obedience to God."

Charles Finney

DAY 132

📖 1 SAMUEL 8
📖 LUKE 9:7 – 50

☉ K E Y   T H O U G H T S

- **1 Samuel 8:3** Even though Samuel was a godly man, his sons did not walk in his ways. Two thoughts on this:
  a) There will be godly people whose child/children make their own choices and rebel against the Lord. Our posture should be prayer and support – believing that those kids will return!
  b) The fact that we live for God is not a guarantee that our kids will, it takes diligence, integrity and lots of communication and prayer.
- Israel's demand for a King is a clear rejection of God as their ruler – they wanted to be *"like all the nations"*. How tempting for us to *"be like all the nations/people"* around us instead of a person ruled and led by God alone.
- **Luke 9** Feeding the 5000 (men) – Jesus is able to multiply! (What do you need multiplied today? Finances, reconciliation, wisdom, bread?)
- 9:20 If your confession is as Peter's, speak the words out loud, let it ring in your spirit: *"You are the Christ, the Son of the Living God."* (John 6:69)
- Vs. 23 (What does it mean today, for me to *"take up (my) cross*

and follow Him?" What am I seeking to gain of this world that might endanger my soul?) (vs. 25)

- Vs. 35 A supernatural affirmation from heaven of the identity of Jesus Christ – *"Hear Him!"*

- Vs. 48 The Kingdom of God requires "childlikeness", we, like children, need His help. We require assistance and cannot enter the kingdom on our own merit. We must also trust like a child, faith that is simple, without the discoloration of cynicism.

- Vss. 57-62 We know from the rest of Jesus' teaching and of the scriptures that Jesus is not against family care – this is a challenge to His followers against

    a) the love of material things above love for Christ. (vs. 56)

    b) procrastination in obedience to the commands of Christ. (vs. 60)

    c) double mindedness, instead of a firm and final commitment – we cannot live in two worlds. (vs. 62)

QUOTE OF THE DAY

"As to gold and silver, I count it dung and dross; I trample it under my feet I esteem it just as the mire of the streets. I desire it not and I seek it not; I only fear lest any of it should cleave to me, and I should not be able to shake it off before my spirit returns to God."

John Wesley (1703-1791)

DAY 133

📖 1 SAMUEL 9
📖 LUKE 10

☀ K E Y   T H O U G H T S

- **1 Samuel 9** What appear to be random events in the life of Saul are included to show how the Lord is able to order our lives for His own purpose – the whole point of the donkey account is to get Saul to Samuel.

- Never be afraid of whether the Lord can accomplish His good purpose in our lives – He is able to arrange things!

- Remember these humble beginnings in the life of Saul, his is a life of very sad instruction to us.

- **Luke 10:2** The harvest IS great! The need is for laborers, there is a harvest around us, it is great and the prayer need is for the workers. Church! We are to be those workers.

- The 70 are sent to do two things – heal the sick and proclaim the kingdom of God (the good news). The ministry of healing is for all to minister, not just a few.

- 10:20 Our greatest rejoicing ought to be in our salvation, not in any gifts or manifestation that might flow through us on occasion.

- Vs.21 Jesus experienced great joy in the Spirit, His joy came from the ministry of His followers. There is a marvelous joy in raising and releasing others into the work of the Lord. All of us can have this kind of joy by investing and sharing in love in the lives of those around us.

- The lawyer is trying to complicate the simple question- Jesus turns it around and challenges us all – are we a neighbor to the one in need? Anyone in need is our neighbor. Are we proving to be that one that Jesus honors in this parable?

- Vss. 29 and 36 Summarize the matter for us.

QUOTE OF THE DAY

"I must assert in the most unqualified way that it is primarily and mainly for the sake of saving the soul that I seek the salvation of the body."

William Booth

DAY 134

📖 1 SAMUEL 10
📖 LUKE 11:1 – 13

⊙ K E Y   T H O U G H T S

- **1 Samuel 10** Samuel gives Saul a number of signs to look for as confirmation of his selection as king.

- 10:7 *"the Spirit of the Lord will come upon you, and...(you will) be turned into another man."*

- Vs. 9 *"God gave him another heart".* The Holy Spirit is working all throughout the history of God's relationship with man. The result of a full encounter with the Holy Spirit will always be a change – it is not possible to truly have the Holy Spirit come upon us and to stay the same. He, the Holy Spirit, changes hearts even to the point of us becoming "new". Praise God.

- This possibility is available daily. (What do you need today, what is it in your life that is longing for 'newness'?) Invite the Holy Spirit right now... "Holy Spirit, make me a new man/woman by Your power".

- **Luke 11** Prayer – the Lord's Prayer is much more than a template to be repeated mindlessly. Each of the phrases represents an aspect of prayer and intercession relating to the Kingdom – *"Thy kingdom come, Thy will be done on earth as it is in heaven".* As we pray, this is the heart of what we are asking – that heaven's rule, heaven's way would intervene and bring order to our world, our lives.

- "All kingdom ministry begins with, is sustained by, and will triumph through prayer." Jack W. Hayford

- Vss. 5-8 Perseverance in prayer is commended – we are not to give up asking, we are permitted, even encouraged to petition with tenacity. Don't give up friend – our God is much greater in goodness than an uncaring friend.

- Vss. 9-13 These verses would be included in the "top 10" of insights into our relationship with the Holy Spirit.

- Ask, seek, knock – what arrogance in us would disobey this direction? What independence inside a proud heart would say, "I will not ask, or seek, or knock". Our relationship with the Holy Spirit is a beautiful dependency that acknowledges our need and His supply.

- The prayer promises here should stop us in our tracks – these are strong motivations to pray!

- The heart of God for you, for every person is that we would be filled with the Holy Spirit and His power! Ask right now, seek right now, knock .... right now!

• Come Holy Spirit.

DAY 135

📖 1 SAMUEL 11
📖 LUKE 11:14 – 54

⊙ K E Y   T H O U G H T S

- **1 Samuel 11** Saul's early activity as King reveals an ongoing relationship with the Holy Spirit (vs. 6). The anointing of the Spirit is an equipping to deal with the current situation – a righteous indignation at this unjust attack results in action, not just emotion.

- Saul also shows a magnanimous grace toward those who had opposed his appointment as king. (vs. 13)

- There is the simple ability to celebrate and rejoice in the goodness of God's blessing. *"Saul and all the men of Israel rejoiced greatly"* (vs.15).

- **Luke 11:33-36** "The lamp of the body is the eye" – a review of what we are looking at is a healthy exercise.

- Consider Jesus' words: *"when your eye is good, your whole body also is full of light".*

- Jesus has little patience with religiosity and putting on a good outward appearance. The whole of Jesus teaching is about the heart, the inner man.

- Our challenge as followers of Jesus is to live a life that is integrated – every aspect, every section and corner of our lives connected with the others. Jesus must be the center of our lives; all of who we are and what we do must flow from that surrendered place of His Lordship.

- Vs. 52 The person who chooses rebellion against Christ and then tries to influence others to the same place is most harshly rebuked by Jesus, both here and in other teaching. (Luke 17:2)
- Seeking to persuade others to join us in sin or rebellion is one of the most serious offenses to Jesus. So many people are a bad influence so that they will at least have some company on the road to hell. Be an encourager, build up people's faith, call them on – don't be the one who knocks them off the road.

QUOTE OF THE DAY

"How can you pull down strongholds of Satan if you don't even have the strength to turn off your TV?"

Leonard Ravenhill

DAY 136

📖 1 SAMUEL 12
📖 LUKE 12

☻ K E Y   T H O U G H T S

- **1 Samuel 12** Samuel speaks of prayer, rather of not praying as sin against the Lord – an amazing verse of insight into prayer. (vs. 23)
- I wonder, is there anyone that we have failed to pray for? In so doing consider that it is sin against the Lord! Such power and importance is afforded to prayer.
- **Luke 12:3** Another verse highlighting our accountability for every word that we speak, hypocrisy is going to be exposed eventually, the true heart, the true motive will show itself. You are no exception, I am no exception.
- 12:15 Whenever we come across Jesus saying *"take heed and beware"* we ought to stop in our tracks and seriously consider what He is instructing us about – in this case, it is covetousness.

- *"Life does not consist in the abundance of the things he possesses."*
- Vs. 29 *"nor have an anxious mind."* This little five word phrase seems so large a task – the only way to having a mind that is not anxious is absolute trust that the Lord is truly in charge of even the most minute detail – He knows all about it.
- Vs. 31 Seek first – this is the key!
- Vss. 44-48 The most severe judgment is for those who are knowing and yet not doing. (What do you think it would mean to be *"beaten with many stripes"* in God's judgment?)
- Vs. 48 Those who are given much have much required of them – much blessing, much knowledge, much opportunity, much prosperity. The blessings and privileges of God are for our enjoyment but not for our exclusive use – we are to spread them (blessings) to others – with words, deeds, compassion, generosity, love…

QUOTE OF THE DAY

"Choose rather to want less, than to have more."

Thomas a Kempis (1340-1471)

DAY 137

📖 1 SAMUEL 13 – 14:23
📖 LUKE 13

⊛ K E Y T H O U G H T S

- **1 Samuel 13** When we come under pressure the temptation is always to take matters into our own hands and abandon the clear commands of the Lord.
- Saul makes many excuses (13:12), he also blames the people, *"I felt compelled"*. Saul doubted the Lord's promises to him as the leader, he was struggling with trust.
- This is the beginning of the end for Saul.
- Every time we come across the phrase *"a man after His (God's)*

own heart" – it stirs a desire in me to be that man. Pray, "Lord teach me to be that kind of man, (or that kind of woman)".

- 14:6 In the face of insurmountable odds, Jonathan shows us what trust looks like *"For nothing restrains the Lord from saving by many or by few."*

- It was the Lord at work on Israel's behalf (vs. 23). God is always able to help, to save, to deliver – the circumstance is not what determines His help. Our faith, our faithfulness to His ways and our faith-filled action brings the results.

- **Luke 13:1-5** The theology of the day taught that when bad things happened to someone it was judgment for their sin, Jesus says emphatically – No! It was also taught that a prosperous person was a righteous person, this is also false.

- The outward is not a true indicator of the inward heart. (the fig tree)

- 13:16 Jesus often shows compassion for individual situations – *"think of it"* or in our language, "imagine 18 years!" The gospel is always spread one person at a time.

- Vss. 22 -30 How many people are around us that would say if asked about eternity: "I'm a good person, I think I have a pretty good chance"? The way to eternal life is not based on personal merit or on a comparative scale – it is through Christ alone!

- Would Jesus have wept over my city, He must be weeping even now. Such need, such brokenness, such spiritual lostness.

QUOTE OF THE DAY

"If Jesus Christ be God and died for me, then no sacrifice can be too great for me to make for Him."

C.T. Studd

DAY 138

📖 1 SAMUEL 14:24 – 52
📖 LUKE 14

⊙ K E Y T H O U G H T S

- **1 Samuel 14** Jonathan summarizes his father's leadership, Vs. 29 – *"My Father has troubled the land."* Saul continues in a headstrong, temper-filled manner.

- His lack of wisdom shows that he was impatient, unwilling to accept counsel and unrepentant when shown to be wrong.

- To leaders studying this passage – there is much in Saul's style of leadership that we should avoid!

- **Luke 14** (When Jesus calls you, do you make excuses?) (14:18)

- Vs. 26 Jesus is for the family! However there is often a cost in family relations to follow Christ. The story is told many times over of the first one in a family that follows Jesus, a season of persecution and hardship and then, one by one the others begin to follow Christ as well.

- (The question is one of approval – are we more concerned with approval on earth or approval in heaven?)

- Vs. 33 A strong, pointed definition of true discipleship - nothing can be above Jesus in our heart!

QUOTE OF THE DAY

"I believe many backsliders are still Christians outwardly, but they have been moving away in heart. They neglect secret prayer and become very formal in public devotion."

Dwight L. Moody (1837-1899)

DAY 139

📖 1 SAMUEL 15
📖 LUKE 15

⊙ K E Y   T H O U G H T S

- **1 Samuel 15:9** Notice that they destroyed all the *"worthless and despised things"* but kept the "best" of the sheep and oxen…

- The excuse for disobedience was that they had a better idea! We will disobey God, because we have a better idea. "What a waste, why destroy all this good stuff, let's keep it and make sacrifices instead."

- Saul is self-deceived *"I have performed the commandment of the Lord."* (vs. 13)

- 15:22, 23 Underline these verses, meditate upon them – there is a wealth of teaching in these two verses.

  - Rebellion is as _____.

  - Stubbornness is as _____.

- Vs. 24 Saul identifies the reason why he sinned - *"feared the people and obeyed their voice"*. Peer pressure, image, keeping up appearances…

- This tragic saga finds Saul trying to at least "save face" in front of the elders and the people. (vs. 30)

- **Luke 15: 7, 10** What brings joy to the angels in heaven?

- How valuable is one soul to God?

- 15:2 What a wonderful upside down denunciation! Jesus eats with sinners and receives them! Praise God, aren't you glad He does? (Do we have His heart for those 'sinners' around us?)

- Prodigal Son: find a few points of application for yourself in this most famous of Jesus' parables – (where do you find yourself? With the prodigal? With the Father? With the older brother?)

- This chapter finishes on the same theme as it began (vs. 32) *"It was right that we should make merry and be glad, for your brother was dead and is alive again, and was lost and is found."* Will you believe with me that there will be much more of "making merry" in the house of God and the lives of His people?

QUOTE OF THE DAY

"He is no fool who gives up what he cannot keep to gain that which he cannot lose."

Jim Elliot, missionary martyr who lost his life in the late 1950's trying to reach the Auca Indians of Ecuador.

DAY 140

📖 1 SAMUEL 16
📖 LUKE 16:1 – 18

◉ K E Y   T H O U G H T S

- **1 Samuel 16** David is chosen and anointed to be the next King.

- Vs. 7 *"For the Lord does not see as man sees; for man looks at the outward appearance, but the Lord looks at the heart."*

- This truth is encouraging and challenging at the same time. God is able to see through our behavior, which is faltering at times and see that our heart truly desires to serve Him.

- At other times, when our outward appearance presents well, the Lord knows what is really in our heart.

- The key to understanding vss. 14-23 is vs. 14: *"But the Spirit of the Lord departed from Saul,"* The distressing spirit was either demonic or the conviction of God upon Saul's mind. This distress was caused when Saul's communion with the "Spirit of God" ceased.

- **Luke 16** Parable of the unjust steward – Jesus is not endorsing fraud (that would be inconsistent with all of Jesus other teaching on integrity). It may have been within this steward's authority to grant a discount, or even to choose to have some things go "on sale". He may have had that discretion.

- The point Jesus is making (with parables, there is usually a main point of teaching or a key reason for the parable beyond the details of the story), is money, wealth is to be used for the good of others. Its value to do good is only present in this life, use it wisely and generously.

- Vss. 11-13 are three of the most pointed and clear verses in the Bible when it comes to our responsibility with money and the prospect of God's blessing upon our finances.
- The matter of integrity with money is a sure indicator of a trustworthy heart able to bear the "true riches" – the blessings and authority of God.
- We cannot serve God *AND* money – there must be a choice!
- Vs. 16 *"pressing into the kingdom"* "1) an impassioned pursuit of prayer, 2) confrontation with the demonic, 3) expectation of the miraculous and 4) a burning heart for evangelism." (Jack W. Hayford, SFLB)
- Vs. 18 See Matthew 5:32, even though divorce was customarily accepted and widespread – Jesus and the kingdom of God set a higher standard.

QUOTE OF THE DAY

"When I have any money, I get rid of it as quickly as possible, lest it find a way into my heart."

John Wesley (1703-1791)

DAY 141

📖 1 SAMUEL 17
📖 LUKE 16:19 – 31

☙ K E Y   T H O U G H T S

- **1 Samuel 17** So many lessons and encouragements in this chapter – you could preach ten sermons on just this account. Fabulous!
- David's character has been forged in worship and solitude, he has a powerful grasp on the authority of God, *"the armies of*

the living God".

- Note carefully – vs. 33 Saul's restrictive warning: *"for you are a youth".* Yes, he was a youth, young enough to believe, young enough to act, young enough to engage the enemy with abandon and trust in his God!

- We must not hold back the youth, we must release, encourage and strengthen them, they are a precious treasure.

- When all the army of Israel, all the big guns, the older, wiser more experienced warriors were paralyzed with fear – the youth just did it!

- Goliath was about 9'9" tall, his coat of mail weighed 126 pounds, his spear head weighed about 15 pounds – this was one magnificent warrior!

- David's confidence is in the Lord proven by the Lord's faithfulness in the past. (lion and the bear)

- Vs. 47 *"Then all this assembly shall know that the Lord does not save with sword and spear; for the battle is the Lord's and He will give you into our hands."* (What is your battle?)

- (Are you allowing it to be "the Lord's"?) He is able to save you, protect and deliver you.

- **Luke 16:19ff** Jesus is addressing a number of issues in the religious leaders of the day; our financial standing is not an indicator of our standing with God. It is only through a personal relationship with Christ that we gain entrance to heaven.

- Jesus teaches strongly on the blessings of heaven and the horrors of hell – do not water it down, remember whose mouth is uttering these words, we must not temper Jesus teaching with modern softness. These are serious realities, not interesting points of dialogue!

- Once in hell there is no second chance.

- Those whose minds are already made up – not having believed the scriptures, will not believe even if the sign was a resurrection (foreshadowing Jesus' own death and resurrection, which the religious of the day did not accept).

"Never think that Jesus commanded a trifle, nor dare to trifle with anything He has commanded."

Dwight L. Moody

DAY 142

📖 1 SAMUEL 18
📖 LUKE 17

⊚ K E Y   T H O U G H T S

- **1 Samuel 18** When the Lord is with someone, even a hostile strategy to cause failure will result in victory! David has the favor of the Lord on his life.

- Michal loves David – notice how Saul and his children are on such different pages, both Jonathan and Michal have given their allegiance to David – Saul's behavior drove a wedge between himself and his children.

- **Luke 17:4** Forgiveness is not something that we can refuse to give – Jesus' illustration is not an exact science. The point is to forgive whenever we are requested to forgive. We are seeking to be like our Lord, who never rejects us when we come to Him for cleansing.

- Vss. 5-10 This parable is the answer to modern day entitlement. This teaching flows out of the disciples request for an "increase" in their faith.

- The way to increase our faith is to serve faithfully in the work of the Lord, doing what is our duty to do, without thought of injustice or hardship – we are blessed to serve.

- The master (our Lord Jesus Christ), will always take care of the compensation.

- Vs. 27ff The common denominator when it comes to understanding the urgency of the end times is "preparedness or readiness".

- The unexpected return of the Lord will catch many people unawares.
- *"The coming of the Son of Man"* will be sudden, taking people by surprise. Once that day has come, the whole order of things changes permanently – there are no second chances!
- "Watch" – be anticipating, expecting Christ's return, be ready, have your life and values in order in the present – procrastination is the opposite of readiness – make your preparations today!

QUOTE OF THE DAY

"A state of mind that sees God in everything is evidence of growth in grace and a thankful heart."

Charles Finney

DAY 143

📖 1 SAMUEL 19
📖 LUKE 18

◉ K E Y   T H O U G H T S

- **1 Samuel 19** Saul is losing his grip on reality, he relents from his murderous plans only to pick up his spear once again.
- Michal, although protecting David in this instance, begins to show a willingness to lie, charging David with threats of violence.
- Vss. 23 – 24 Saul's behavior is to be understood here in a tragic and desperate sense – the answer to the rhetorical question *"is Saul also among the prophets?"* is clearly, no!
- **Luke 18** The parable of the persistent widow is a study in contrasts, the unjust judge (not God) gives way to persistence, "how much more" will our loving heavenly Father respond to His children.
- Vs. 8 Faith on the earth? (Are we trusting that the Lord is indeed intervening for His glory, and are we bringing our requests to him?)

- Vs. 14 Humility is one foundational value in the kingdom of God.
- Vss. 24-30 Riches in this life are a strong deterrent to complete surrender to Christ - with God it is not impossible, but the struggle for authority in a life can be fierce.
- Vss. 35-43 (What would your answer be today if Jesus was to ask you; "what do you want me to do for you?")
- This man knew his most immediate need. Jesus is able to meet our need, His heart is to meet our need – we need the faith to ask and then believe that He will answer.

QUOTE OF THE DAY

"If we are obeying the Lord, the responsibility rests with Him, not with us. We must obey the Scriptures and trust God to be faithful to His pledged Word."

James Hudson Taylor (1832-1905)

DAY 144

📖 1 SAMUEL 20
📖 LUKE 19:1 – 27

⊛ K E Y   T H O U G H T S

- **1 Samuel 20** Jonathan is a man of amazing integrity and character, respectful of his father and yet selflessly willing to acknowledge that David has been anointed as King.
- The friendship of David and Jonathan is a very powerful example of selflessness and surrender to God's will and purpose. These were friends who were like brothers.
- David keeps his vow and when he is king he is very kind to the household of Jonathan.
- **Luke 19** Zacchaeus. (As you are reading this narrative, who do you identify with the most?
- Are you seeking to see who Jesus is? Willing to go to almost any lengths to get close to Him?)

- Are you willing to be a guest with someone who would be considered 'a sinner'?
- (What do you feel about Zacchaeus' restitution? Is he too over-zealous?)
- Who has Jesus come to seek and save? (How much of my life is devoted to this cause?)
- A mina was the equivalent of about three month's wages, so actually quite a lot of money was entrusted to these servants.
- Many parables have a "now and not yet" application – the now application was anticipating that the 'Kingdom of God' would not come in its final fulfillment until a later date. The "not yet" application was to teach the responsibility of diligence and even risk taking – venturing something great for God.
- Notice that the reward for faithful service is greater opportunity and trust.

QUOTE OF THE DAY

"No reserves. No retreats. No regrets."

William Borden

DAY 145

📖 1 SAMUEL 21 – 22:5
📖 LUKE 19:28 – 20:19

◉ K E Y   T H O U G H T S

- **1 Samuel 21** Jesus mentions this incident with the holy bread in Matt. 12:3, 4. Jesus taught that He was Lord of the Sabbath and that human need had to be considered before religion or rituals.
- This gathering of 400 men is described in an unflattering but encouraging kind of way: *"everyone who was in distress, in debt or discontented"*.
- As time went on some of these became known as David's mighty men, people of valor, character and bravery. Often

times, a good leader or influence can transform a rag tag band of people into something good and positive. Jesus does this with all of us!

- **Luke 19:37** The people were rejoicing, *"for all the mighty works they had seen"*. (Have you seen the Lord do any mighty works? Is there a genuine heart of rejoicing, thankfulness? Celebration?)
- The Lord Jesus Christ will be praised, He will be worshipped – what a tragic picture, that stones would have to cry out because the people with the freedom to worship refused to do so.
- (What hinders us from abandoned joyful worship? What would be able to shut our mouths?)
- Vss. 9ff The chief priests and the scribes were being given the opportunity to believe, they were being offered the first chance of salvation – their religion had become such blindness that they missed their opportunity for salvation completely.
- Jesus came that we might have life and have it abundantly – not a religious bondage that leaves us captive and cold.

QUOTE OF THE DAY

"I cannot imagine how religious persons can live satisfied without the practice of the presence of God."

Nicolas Herman, (Brother Lawrence 1611-1691)

DAY 146

📖 1 SAMUEL 22:6 – 23
📖 LUKE 20:20 – 21:4

⊛ K E Y   T H O U G H T S

- **1 Samuel 22** Saul's leadership has degenerated into paranoia and wickedness. Doeg seems to be a ruthless man who attaches himself to Saul in a time of vulnerability.
- We must always be careful of who has our ear. (Who do we allow into the council of our inner circle? Where are we getting

our information?)

- The downfall of many great leaders has been a lack of wisdom when it comes to who they listen to. Success breeds a deafness, especially of hearing correction.

- **Luke 20:27** There will always be people around who do not believe in life after death. Jesus makes it abundantly clear, there is a life after death, it will be a conscious life, a life where we recognize one another – (Abraham, Isaac, Jacob).

- And it will be a life that will be in fellowship with God.

- 21:1-4 This unnamed widow is amazingly famous for her giving. And yet, the amount she gave was so small it seems strange to mention it.

- Jesus teaches that sacrificial giving is measured by the amount remaining not by the amount given. The religious people of the day made a big show of their giving – *"to be seen by men"* so that they would be considered righteous.

- This widow understood that true giving is from the heart. It is to be seen by God, who knows the heart and it is God Himself to keeps track of what we give – rewarding accordingly.

- Notice that Jesus stood near enough to the offering box that He could see what was being put in. Our giving is an accurate gauge of our heart - to refuse to give, to resent giving, to be miserly or manipulative in our giving all indicate a heart problem.

- (How does the giving gauge read in your life? Is the dial anywhere near the "widow's" standard?) Start a new practice today - begin to give, Jesus is watching! It does matter.

QUOTE OF THE DAY

"Men do not drop into the right way by chance; they must choose it, and continue to choose it, or the will soon wanders from it."

Charles H. Spurgeon (1834-1892)

DAY 147

📖 1 SAMUEL 23
📖 LUKE 21:5 – 38

◉ K E Y   T H O U G H T S

- **1 Samuel 23** David shows, right from the beginning of his reign (even as a fugitive with a band of non-descript followers) a dependency upon the Lord.

- 23:10 He sought the Lord for wisdom and direction – we ought to sincerely seek the Lord when we have important decisions to be made.

- Learning to listen to the voice of the Holy Spirit is an invaluable skill – a large part of successful hearing is the willingness to receive something contrary to our preferences.

- People will often equate only the favorable response, or the easy route as being from God, He will often speak things to guide us that do not make total sense at the time. Remember also the counsel of trusted godly advisors.

- (Don't you wish you had a Jonathan in your life?) What a man of integrity, what a gift of encouragement (vs. 16), *"he strengthened his (David's) hand"* – even though he (Jonathan) would not be king!

- (Who can you be a Jonathan to, today?)

- The stronghold at En Gedi is known as Masada today.

- **Luke 5:13** Many situations that appear to be bad will turn out as *"an occasion for testimony"*. Be watching for those moments and when they happen, open your mouth, the Holy Spirit will fill it!

- Jesus prophesies many things, including the destruction of Jerusalem (fulfilled in A.D. 70). This passage corresponds with Matt. 24 and others – warning of the signs of the times.

- The central intent of these passages is to stir up a watchful attitude, to be ready, to be aware of the signs, to be looking up.

- Vs. 34 This strong warning – *"Take heed to yourselves"*. Note the specific warnings, and the description of a heart that gets "weighed down" instead of a heart that is light and free.

- Carousing – drunkenness, the general attitude of partying, wild living, getting drunk is universally condemned in the scripture – it is not a gray area! The danger inherent in drunkenness is that one's sensibilities are impaired, which leads to many worse problems.

- The overall sense is a life completely focused on the moment, even drowning the future realities in alcohol to avoid the sober truth.

- And cares of this life. The distractions of material things, material pursuits. Every luxury you add also adds more work, more time, more concern.

- Jesus' point is that we should be sharp, keen-eyed, aware, with our lives 'in order' so that we are ready for that moment when the 'Day of Lord' happens.

QUOTE OF THE DAY

"The only time you can really say that 'Christ is all I need,' is when Christ is all you have. The Bible is either absolute, or it's obsolete."

Leonard Ravenhill

DAY 148

📖 1 SAMUEL 24
📖 LUKE 22:1 – 46

⊛ K E Y   T H O U G H T S

- **1 Samuel 24** Notice the respect and restraint that David shows toward Saul, even though his men were encouraging him to take advantage of the situation.

- There is a remarkable honor in David's heart toward a man who is literally trying to kill him. David's trust in the Lord and his respect for the 'anointing' upon Saul is a challenge to us when we come across leaders who are less than perfect.

- **Luke 22:33** Peter is sincere in this moment, I believe his intentions were noble, however when pressure was applied, Peter gave in.
- Vs. 40 (What does Jesus identify as a factor in overcoming temptation?)
- The complete surrender of Jesus' will to the will of the Father is the standard and example that we should strive to follow.
- *"Not My will, but Yours, be done."*
- (Have you ever felt like the disciples when it comes to spending time in prayer?)
- (Isn't it a challenge to your heart to realize that the very Son of God took time to pray?) You would think that of all people Jesus would not need to pray, and yet His life is significantly marked by prayer.
- Surely we would benefit ourselves and God's work by an increase in our prayer life.

QUOTE OF THE DAY

"A long time out of Christ's glorious presence is two deaths and two hells for me. We must meet. I am not able to do without Him."

Samuel Rutherford (1600-1661)

DAY 149

📖 1 SAMUEL 25
📖 LUKE 22:47 – 71

☉ K E Y   T H O U G H T S

- **1 Samuel 25** Abigail – this woman of wisdom and integrity is a significant example of loyalty and action. Firstly, she saves her husband's household from a great slaughter.
- Notice how she has perspective to share with David in 25:31, that his tempestuous actions will result in *"grief and offense of heart"* after he has become ruler of all Israel.

- She was able to share this perspective with David – he, wisely, listened.
- (Who will you listen to? Will you listen to wise counsel – do you seek wise counsel?)
- **Luke 22:47ff** We are entering in to Luke's account of the trial, crucifixion and resurrection of Jesus.
- Notice how Jesus never loses His focus on people throughout every stage. He heals the man's severed ear. (vs. 48)
- Peter's heart wrenching denials - truly we are people like Peter. (Do you ever feel pressure from mockery or opposition? Are you ever pushed into a corner of circumstances where you feel that silence or outright denial will provide a way out of an awkward situation?)
- Vs. 61 Even in custody, Jesus makes eye contact with Peter to restore him. This look is not to condemn or reject – it is a look of love, a look of powerful restoration.
- When we fail the Lord, there will always be a "look", some twinge or memory from the Holy Spirit to restore us to fellowship – accept the loving embrace of the Father – return, don't run.
- Vs. 70 A key statement of Jesus' divinity – *"are You then the Son of God?" "You rightly say that I am."*
- Jesus is God, everlasting, all powerful, fully God and fully man. There is no one else like Him, He alone is the provision of God for our salvation.

QUOTE OF THE DAY

Acts 4:12 "Nor is there salvation in any other, <u>for there is no other name under heaven given among men by which we must be saved</u>."

(NKJV)

DAY 150

📖 LUKE 23 – 24:35

✪ K E Y T H O U G H T S

- **Luke 23** Allow yourself to be transported to the scene
- All your senses: sight, sound, smell … put yourself right there.
- He is unjustly accused, He is mercilessly beaten and humiliated, He is associated with criminals, and yet…
- When the thief asks Him for entrance into His kingdom Jesus response is full of grace and promise – *"today you will be with Me in Paradise"*.
- He is Risen! In fulfillment of His own prophetic words, 24:6, 7.
- The apostles do not believe, but Peter (vs. 12), runs to the tomb! Peter is the early adopter, all in, all in first – love his heart.
- I am struck by Jesus' patience and grace toward unbelief and spiritual blindness – He takes the time needed to bring people to understanding. There is no single way that a person comes to believe – the Holy Spirit directs the path uniquely for each person.
- For the two men from the road to Emmaus, it was when Jesus broke the bread…
- When you struggle with discouragement or even unbelief, the Lord will give you what you need to be strengthened in your faith if you will receive it. He is so patient with our doubting and struggling – there will always be sufficient intervention toward you if you are open and childlike.
- When you have been strengthened – do like these two guys did… get to some people that you can testify to. Encourage the faith of others with how the Lord has met with you! (vs. 33)

*"Do not think me mad. It is not to make money that I believe a Christian should live.
The noblest thing a man can do is, just humbly to receive, and then go amongst others
and give."*

David Livingstone

DAY 151

📖 1 SAMUEL 26 – 28:2
📖 LUKE 24:36 – 52

☉ K E Y   T H O U G H T S

- **1 Samuel 26:21** We are hopeful that Saul is finally coming out of his dazed perspective, *"indeed I have played the fool and erred exceedingly"*.

- David is living all this time with the knowledge that he is the next anointed king do Israel and yet he will do nothing to force God's timing of that event.

- **Luke 24:38** Hear Jesus' words to all of us today: *"why are you troubled? And why do doubts arise in your hearts?"*

- Vs. 39 We are given insight into the nature of a resurrection body – it is a tangible re-created body that will live forever!

- Vss. 46 – 48 A powerful statement of Christ's identity and of the great commission – *"you are witnesses of these things"*.

- Vs. 49 This instruction of Jesus gives us the measure of importance of "the Promise", the Holy Spirit. There is nothing more important for these disciples to do than to receive the baptism of the Holy Spirit in the days ahead.

- For all of us believers, receiving and living in the overflowing fullness of the Holy Spirit is the most important "enduement of power" that is available to us.

- More important than gaining great knowledge, more important than position – be filled with the Holy Spirit (and keep on being filled).

- Jesus' ascension into heaven assures us of the coming

of the Holy Spirit. Jesus said, *"it is better that I go away"* – better because then the Holy Spirit will come and be with you always.

DAY 152

📖 1 SAMUEL 28:3 – 29
📖 1 CORINTHIANS 1

◉ K E Y   T H O U G H T S

- **1 Samuel 28:3 - 24** Saul has killed the priests of the Lord, he has banished spiritists and mediums, so there is no one left to help him seek direction. He resorts to a plot of disguise and intrigue – utter desperation and self-deception.

- "Before they can do anything Samuel appears, not a dead ghost conjured up, but a prophet of God again delivering God's message to the king. It is clear that the medium has not called him up, but that the Lord has again stepped into the life of Saul to speak to him. The woman was terrified and **cried out**, literally "screamed in terror," shocked at Samuel's appearance. Far from giving credence to any kind of spiritualist activity or contacting the dead, this passage shows that God is supreme. The medium is left terrified and Saul is paralyzed in fear, as both of them are rejected by the living God." (Spirit Filled Life Bible vss. 11-19)

- **1 Cor. 1:10-17** Sectarianism. When you are joined to a local church, be faithful to that body. There are so many "teachers" about in our Christian world, TV, internet, radio – it is easy to attach yourself to a particular teacher/preacher and begin to say: *"I am of Paul, I am of Apollos, I am of Peter".*

- Be faithful to your church, be faithful to the Bible through your own reading and study, be faithful to the leadership of your pastor. All these other teachers are a distant voice in your life, you cannot know them, you cannot receive care from them, and everything sounds so perfect outside of the context of daily living and relationship.

- It is Christ who unifies the body – notice in vs. 17 – the power of the gospel is not with *"words of wisdom"*. It is a simple gospel, a practical gospel, a gospel centered in the cross.

- Vs. 18 should be a treasured verse – how we love the cross, its message, its deep treasures are the power of God unto salvation. Praise God.

- Vs. 24 Christ: *"the power of God and the wisdom of God."*

- Vs. 26 I fit into this category, so do you – but, we are "called"!

- Three important words:

  1) <u>Righteousness</u>: a term from the courts – transference of His Perfection, Holiness, *"rightness"* to us, acquittal from all charges.

  2) <u>Sanctification</u>: the process of cleansing from pollution (a temple term), accomplished by the power of the Holy Spirit.

  3) <u>Redemption</u>: a slavery term, buying back someone in hopeless (sin) debt that could never be re-paid. Ultimately fulfilled in the redemption of our physical bodies in the final resurrection.

- This is all "<u>IN CHRIST</u>". TAKE A FEW MOMENTS TO THANK THE LORD AND WORSHIP HIM, RIGHT NOW!

QUOTE OF THE DAY

"God cannot give us a happiness and peace apart from Himself, because it is not there. There is no such thing."

C. S. Lewis

DAY 153

📖 1 SAMUEL 30
📖 1 CORINTHIANS 2

☉ K E Y   T H O U G H T S

- **1 Samuel 30** Notice the action of David when he faced the anger and rebellion of the people, *"he strengthened himself in the Lord"*.

- (What is your usual course of action when you face discouragement or setbacks? What would you think it means to strengthen yourself in the Lord?)

- Vs. 22 There always seems to be "wicked and worthless men/women" around. They have bad ideas to share.

- One of the qualities of David that makes him a *"man after God's own heart"* is GENEROSITY. (vss. 24, 26)

- Vs. 24 is a marvelous principle of leadership whether in business or ministry – it takes both those out front as well as those who "stay by the supplies" to make any venture a success.

- **1 Corinthians 2:11** We learn about God by the Spirit of God. When the godless go off opining about what God is like, remember, they do not know Him. They have not been taught by the Spirit. Just as the spirit of man knows the insides of a man's heart, so when we are filled with the Spirit of God we are taught by Him. We learn what He is truly like.

- Do not be intimidated by the rantings of the godless against the Lord – they don't know what they are talking about!

- 2:16 *"but we have the mind of Christ."* (Is there a developing mind in you? The mind of Christ? Are all thoughts, opinions, decisions filtered through a 'Christ' perspective?)

- Vs. 13 The Holy Spirit *"teaches"* - one of the beautiful roles of the Holy Spirit is to instruct us, guide us – give us spiritual insights that would not be available otherwise.

- Ask the Holy Spirit today to instruct you, as you pray and commune with the Spirit, allow Him to give you insight.

"Remember God never gives light for two steps at a time. If He has given thee light for one step, then in the fear and love of His Name, take that one step, and thou assuredly will get more light."

Charles H. Mackintosh (1820-1896)

DAY 154

📖 1 SAMUEL 31 – 2 SAMUEL 1
📖 1 CORINTHIANS 3

◉ K E Y   T H O U G H T S

- **1 Samuel 31** There can be nothing but sadness at the demise of Saul and his three sons, it is a tragic, ignominious ending to a forty year reign.

- Squandered potential, generational destruction, spiritual and self-delusion, and ultimately suicide leave Saul as one of the most emotional and dramatic examples of rebellion's consequences in all the scripture.

- **2 Samuel 1** Note how the young messenger was trying to impress David with his lies. What do we learn from this?

- **1 Corinthians 3** Continuing on this theme *"I am of Paul, I am of Apollos"* - the evidence of wisdom and maturity is respect and unity in a person's circle of relationships.

- True spiritual knowledge does not come from being the disciple of a favorite celebrity 'teacher' – it comes from personal growth and study of the Bible, without external assistance other than the Holy Spirit.

- The evidence of spiritual depth will be the fruit of a person's life in their family, their business life, and their reputation among friends who know them well.

- Knowledge, data, information, appearances – are meaningless if the meat of the word is not producing good and visible fruit in my life. The popular phrase: *"how is that working for you?"* – is a good one to remember.

- Anyone can present themselves well, what do those closest to you say? How are your relationships, as they describe them? (not as you describe them)
- We can receive the good from many sources – but fundamentally, we must be grounded in the word and in Christ – not in some other teacher. We do not follow gurus, we follow Christ and Him alone.

QUOTE OF THE DAY

"A man ought to live so that everybody knows he is a Christian... and most of all, his family ought to know."

Dwight L. Moody

DAY 155

📖 1 CORINTHIANS 4, 5
📖 2 SAMUEL 2 – 3:1

⊛ K E Y   T H O U G H T S

- **1 Corinthians 4:2** What is the key characteristic of a 'good' steward? A steward is someone who has been trusted with the resources of another. Faithfulness is not negotiable.
- 4:6 *"Puffed up on behalf of another"* – the most difficult offense to overcome is a second hand offense. When a wife picks up the offense of her husband it will take her much longer to get over it, if she ever does. The same goes for a husband.
- Vs. 20 The kingdom of God is not just talk, semantics or clever phrasing – the kingdom of God is advanced by the power of God operating through His people.
- Immorality is universally condemned in the scripture. While the specific sin of incest is grossly outside of God's will, the bigger issue for the church was their apathy toward discipline by allowing the situation to go uncorrected.
- Church discipline is an important aspect of the accountability of belonging to a local church – knowing that those who love

us will challenge us should we get off track.

- 5:9-11 is a very practical guide for how we should live in an immoral world. Some had made the mistake of cloistering themselves from anyone in the world who was living immorally – Paul's evangelist heart comes through loud and clear – to separate yourself from all who are sinful… *"then you would need to go out of the world".*

- The issue is within the church, those who persist in blatant, unrepentant, sinful ways; do not fellowship with them as if all is well. Find ways to lovingly bring correction, leadership roles are out, profile must be removed – the goal is always restoration, however, if a person refuses to accept a restorative path in humility – they must be cut loose to their own destructive path of sin.

- Take careful note of the list in vs. 11.

- **2 Samuel 3:1** There will always be evidence of the grace of God upon a life, Saul's heritage was corrupted, David was the Lord's choice. When looking for leaders, look for those who have an evident grace upon them, what they put their hand to prospers.

QUOTE OF THE DAY

"Lukewarm living and claiming Christ's name simultaneously is utterly disgusting to God."

Francis Chan 'Crazy Love'

DAY 156

📖 1 CORINTHIANS 6 – 7:9

◉ K E Y   T H O U G H T S

- **1 Corinthians 6** The moral life of the believer is important. The backdrop for this passage was a widely held belief at this time that a person's lifestyle did not affect their spiritual life, that the spirit and the body were separate.

- So suing one another, cheating and sexual immorality were seen as unrelated to one's spiritual life.

- Paul addresses this head on, particularly in his list of sins that will disqualify someone from the kingdom of heaven.

- This is not a condemnation of anyone who has ever committed one of these sins, but rather a judgment against those who persist, willfully, knowingly rebelling against a purified life – all the while insisting that they are fit for the kingdom.

- In our current season of controversy over the Christian 'lifestyle' – you have dear one, to face the challenge of authority. (Will you accept God's Word, His authority – or will you waiver under cultural pressure?) This list is particularly relevant in North American culture.

- This is also not a condemnation of one who is struggling to be free in an area, whose heart is toward the Lord, whose desire is to live a pure and holy life before the Lord. There is grace for those who, with damaged pasts or confusing experiences wrestle, particularly with sexual issues. God is able! You are loved! He will walk with you to wholeness and to freedom – don't give up, be encouraged today!

- 6:18 There can be no misinterpretation of this – "flee" is an action, not a time to dialogue.

- The chapter finishes with a reminder of why this is so important. You are valuable, you have been purchased by the precious blood of Christ – so, glorify God in your body.

- 1 Cor. 7 – Some were zealously concluding that even sexual relations in marriage were to be ended – that is not so, husbands and wives are to honor one another by lovingly providing for the sexual needs of their spouse.

QUOTE OF THE DAY

"Christianity was simple: fight your desires in order to please God."

Francis Chan 'Crazy Love'

DAY 157

📖 1 CORINTHIANS 7:10 – 40
📖 2 SAMUEL 3:2 – 39; 4

💿 K E Y   T H O U G H T S

- **1 Corinthians 7:14** "The ultimate reason for keeping a mixed marriage together is the holy influence of the believer's life on the unbelieving partner, resulting in the possible salvation of the entire household." (SFLB)

- Vs. 35 This verse gives us the key point of the whole passage – *"that you may serve the Lord without distraction."*

- Some were using their Christianity as an excuse to be irresponsible in their marriages and occupations.

- Some were quitting their work, leaving their marriages, all in the name of Christ – vs. 24 gives clear counsel – stay where Christ found you and be an influence for His glory.

- (Ask yourself today: "is there anything in my life right now that has become a distraction to my serving the Lord?") Anything that usurps Jesus' rightful place as Lord over all, needs to be examined and dealt with in a straightforward and loving manner.

- **2 Samuel 3ff** Abner is a good man! Joab (note this man, he is a controversial figure throughout the whole reign of David), on the other hand displays anger, revenge, ambition.

- Note David's description of Joab and his brothers; *"too harsh for me."*

- Yet David's response is to trust the Lord to repay the wickedness.

QUOTE OF THE DAY

"A man who is eating or lying with his wife or preparing to go to sleep in humility, thankfulness and temperance, is, by Christian standards, in an infinitely higher state than one who is listening to Bach or reading Plato in a state of pride."

C. S. Lewis

DAY 158

2 SAMUEL 5:1 – 16
1 CORINTHIANS 8, 9

KEY THOUGHTS

- **2 Samuel 5** David is finally acknowledged as the sole ruler of Israel. This has been a long time coming, and is truly a remarkable reign.

- Enemies are often overconfident, not realizing that they are not only fighting just another army, but they are actually fighting against God.

- Always remember:

  - Romans 8:31 *"If God is for us, who can be against us?"*

- **1 Corinthians 8:4, 6** Powerful statements regarding the supremacy of God. "There is one God." Even though there are many 'gods' – there is only one God and one Lord Jesus Christ.

- Christ's deity is clearly expressed by the phrase: *"through whom are all things, and through whom we live"*.

- When it comes to the believer's liberty, "what are we allowed to do?" That is not the real question, the real question is "how much love do I have, and how will my actions (liberty) affect those around me?"

- The key to walking in liberty is the understanding that we are all responsible to one another – the misuse of 'liberty' always comes from a "self-first" view.

- 8:13 Concern and love for the brothers and sisters is the standard.

- 9:12 Enduring all things *"lest we hinder the gospel"*.

- Vss. 16, 19 Compelled by love to preach the gospel.

- Vss. 24-27 These are life verses – verses to build a godly life around.

- Temperate in all things – ask, "is this true of me?"

- A higher set of priorities – "to obtain an imperishable crown" –

ask, "is this my priority grid?"

- Discipline of the body – ask, "is there evident discipline of the flesh so that the spirit is free to serve?"
- Vs. 27 *"lest when I have preached to others, I myself should become disqualified."*

QUOTE OF THE DAY

"Holy ones, in every age, have lived near to God in secret. It is this that fits one to live a holy, self-denying, cross bearing life before the world."

James B. Taylor (1801-1829)

DAY 159

📖 2 SAMUEL 5:17 – 6:23
📖 1 CORINTHIANS 10

⊚ K E Y   T H O U G H T S

- **2 Samuel 5:24 and 6:2** We must never lose sight of the fact that our Lord is *"the Lord of Hosts"*. Our God has armies! Hosts of heavenly beings that are under His authority for the purpose of fulfilling His will.
- This marching in the mulberry tree tops, is a memorable image giving us courage to know, we do not fight against the enemy alone!
- The judgment upon Uzzah (vs. 6:3) seems harsh, however, the ark was being transported in a disobedient manner, (on a cart). The next time we see the ark being transported, it is carried on the shoulders of the priests. David and the priests would have known how the Lord had commanded things to be done.
- 6:14 *"danced before the Lord with all his might"* – how fantastic! (When last, your heart filled with abandoned joy and thankfulness to God, did you dance before the Lord – "with all your might"?) Why not put on a great worship song and do it right now!!! You will be blessed and the Lord will be pleased!

- Michal is a sad example of the withering consequences of bitterness (vs. 23).

- **1 Corinthians 10: 1-13** Old Testament examples – we are completely free to benefit spiritually from the examples and teaching of the OT. Always filtering the commands in light of the NT teaching.

- Vs. 20 The spiritual impetus behind idolatry is demonic – idols although powerless and mute, have a demonic strategy of bondage working through them…we are to have nothing to do with any idol. Perhaps you have retained some trinket or souvenir, or past religious artifact – a housecleaning is always in order.

- Vss. 23-33 Give practical guidelines for determining matters of conscience. Vss. 24, 29, 33 – all echo the same theme… our decisions are to be based on the good, the wellbeing of the **other**, not our own liberty.

- This is consistent throughout the Scripture – ask yourself, "does this behavior, activity or liberty edify?" Then ask, "how does this behavior, activity or liberty profit or hinder those around me?" These are the governing principles of a person committed to love. A more complex series of question to answer instead of simply saying - "there's nothing wrong with it."

- 11:1 (Who would you feel free to say this to?) If this statement makes you uncomfortable, the solution is to imitate Christ more.

- Like it or not, sons, daughters, friends, colleagues, observers will be imitating you –are you a helpful model?

QUOTE OF THE DAY

"I make it a rule of Christian duty never to go to a place where there is not room for my Master as well as myself."

John Newton (1725-1807)

DAY 160

2 SAMUEL 7
1 CORINTHIANS 11

KEY THOUGHTS

- **2 Samuel 7:8** Never fear that your beginnings or your past disqualify you from greatness in God's kingdom. The Lord delights to use people with a humble and willing heart. If the credentials do not impress the world, but the impact of one's life is undeniable – the Lord is glorified!

- Vss. 10 & 22-24 remind us that Israel has a very special place in God's heart and God's redemptive plan. Modern political winds do not alter God's covenant heart with His people. We are told to pray for Israel, remember His people.

- **1 Corinthians 11:3-16** There were cultural issues at play during the time of the writing of this "head covering" passage. Although we live in a different time and there are few remaining taboo's relating to hats and hair – yet the principles underlying this passage remain.

- We are to be aware of how our appearance either glorifies God or exalts an ungodly culture above what is appropriate. (What are we saying by what is seen? Or what are we identifying ourselves with by what we are showing?)

- An independent spirit between husband and wife is always harmful. Disrespect, independent indifference to the other's feelings is a sign of a deeper rebellion that will express itself in more harmful ways if not addressed (vs. 11:11).

- There is a consistent theme throughout the epistles to the churches; divisions, factions, schisms are not pleasing to the Lord. Disunity and a party spirit – "I'm with these people not with 'those' people" – does not build up the church.

- Societal levels of standing, wealth/poverty, professional/laborer, educated/illiterate – are to have no bearing on the fellowship at the Lord's table. Before God, and within the fold of God's grace and mercy we are all on the same level.

- If God sees us this way, we ought to see one another this way too. Both to those we would consider above us, and those we would consider below (hard to even say those words, yet it happens) – in Christ we are all one family!

- Prejudice is never attractive or godly.

DAY 161

📖 2 SAMUEL 9
📖 1 CORINTHIANS 12

⊙ K E Y   T H O U G H T S

- **2 Samuel 9** There are many indicators of David's 'heart'. He voluntarily shows kindness to those who would be considered his enemies – the son of Jonathan, lame, unable to contribute in any way is brought to the very table of the King.

- David and Jonathan as kindred spirits bonded together through adversity, remain a strong example of the power of godly friendship.

- **1 Corinthians 12** This is a very significant chapter. Contextually there were some issues of misuse of 'gifts' in this church. Those who are anti-charismatic will use terms like "wildly immoral, out of control" etc. to describe this church. This is an exaggeration based on interpretive bias.

- The Apostle is bringing needed guidance – however he is not shutting down the gifts, the Holy Spirit is providing wisdom for the proper operation of the gifts, saying in essence; *"these are given by God, these are necessary for the body to be healthy, learn to use them in love."*

- 1 Cor. 12:7 is a key verse to understanding this whole chapter:

"But the manifestation of the Spirit is **given to each one for the profit of all.**"

- These gifts are for the benefit of the whole body, utilized in public ministry, they are to be exercised in submission to the whole body. No one gift is to be elevated above the others – (the usefulness of all the parts of the body is a key theme here).

- "Paul identifies a spiritual gift as a supernatural ability bestowed on an individual by the Holy Spirit, not as a heightened natural ability. Thus, each gift is a manifestation of the Spirit, that is, visible evidence of His activity. The Holy Spirit bestows the gifts to whom He wills as the occasion recommends from the divine viewpoint." (SFLB)

- As Spirit-filled believers we identify both the: 1) personal use of spiritual language (speaking with tongues as evidence of the baptism of the Holy Spirit Acts 2) 2) and a public gift of tongues (vs. 12:10). The blessing of speaking with tongues for personal edification is available to all believers, to commune with God, spirit to Spirit, building up the inner man, (1 Cor.14:14). This does not mean that all must exercise the public ministry gift of tongues. This gift must be accompanied by interpretation [similar to prophecy] so that all those hearing may be edified.

- Vss. 29-31 in no way discourages the use of spiritual gifts. The point being made is to encourage the balanced use of all the gifts without elevating one above the other as a badge of spiritual superiority – the point is to desire gifts that edify the body.

- 1 Cor. 14:5, 18 indicate a whole-hearted enthusiasm for the personal use of tongues for all believers, using Paul himself as the example.

- 12:31 *"desire the best gifts"* – is not a ranking of the value of the gifts based on the previous list's numbering... (tongues being the last) – it is an appeal to desire the gifts that flow in each life for the benefit of all, ministered in love.

- Public/ministry gifts are not to become a source of spiritual pride, or a personal validation of being better than someone else – they are always under the authority of the Holy Spirit and for the benefit of others.

"Holy ones, in every age, have lived near to God in secret. It is this that fits one to live a holy, self-denying, cross-bearing life before the world."

James B. Taylor (1801-1829)

DAY 162

📖 2 SAMUEL 11
📖 1 CORINTHIANS 13

⊛ K E Y   T H O U G H T S

- **2 Samuel 11** One of the most infamous sins in the whole of scripture, not only adultery, but lying and murder to cover up the first sin.

- Rather than judging David's weaknesses and despising his flaws – consider how persistent and devious are the enemy's temptations. Let us all be cautioned. None of us are above or beyond such danger, we must be vigilant, transparent and active in the Lord's work.

- Age is not a guarantee of freedom from sin's destructive tentacles – finishing well is a worthy goal!

- **1 Corinthians 13:1-3** The main point of this chapter is to elevate the place of love as the grid that all gifts must pass through. Tongues, prophecy, understanding, knowledge, faith, generosity to poor, martyrdom are not being forbidden or diminished! But ministry without love in spite of any gifting becomes negative.

- The solution is not the cessation of the gifts – but rather the application of love – this is the flow of these next verses.

- Enjoy the New Living Translation of these verses (vss.4-7) *"Love is patient and kind. Love it not jealous or boastful or proud or rude. It does not demand its own way. It is not irritable, and it keeps no record of being wronged. It does not rejoice about injustice but rejoices whenever the truth wins out. Love never gives up, never loses faith, is always hopeful, and endures through every circumstance."*

- Vss. 10, 12 are keys to understanding this passage – *"that which is perfect"*, and *"see face to face"*, both refer to the return of Christ and the believers being with Him forever.

- The appeal is that our understanding now is limited by our humanity – the way to address this lack is to cover all ministry and personal interaction with love. This is not calling gifts childish, or immature, or intimating that gifts will cease while we are on this earth.

- Once in heaven, these gifts for the blessing of the body of Christ, will no longer be needed. But for now, looking at the state of the church, we need all the gifts, all the power and help of the Holy Spirit that we can get.

- Love is an earthly and heavenly commodity that 'abides'. An eternal element, lasting, beautiful and so desirable. Pursue love!

QUOTE OF THE DAY

"Maturity comes from obedience, not necessarily from age."

Leonard Ravenhill

DAY 163

📖 2 SAMUEL 12:1 – 15
📖 PSALM 51

◉ K E Y   T H O U G H T S

- **2 Samuel 12:8** The heart of the Lord is always to bless and to provide the highest good to His children. Notice the phrase: *"and if that had been too little I also would have given you much more!"*

- Vss. 9-1 Even though David will repent fully and be fully forgiven, with this sin (as with all sin) there are earthly consequences.

- Sin ripples, sin has a splash to it, our sin gets 'on' others. Notice how many other people will be affected by David's sin!

Some people have a casual attitude to sin saying: "I'm only hurting myself." This is never the case – our sin seeps from us to those around us.

- Others will not answer to God for our sin, but they will suffer from the residue of our sin in this life. Often the ones most affected are the ones we say we love the most, our family.

- David understands that our sins are *"against the Lord"*.

- **Psalm 51** learn this great prayer of repentance and humility.

- Be encouraged that the Lord does forgive freely (1 John 1:9), He does restore, there can be greater days in the future.

- God is able to use you in His service and ministry (51:14).

- The exercise of intentional praise and worship to God following repentance is a critical phase in God's restoration of joy and will strengthen your certainty of acceptance in His presence.

- Lift up your voice and read verses 15 -17 out loud, and then let your spirit pour forth praise with a grateful and full heart of love.

QUOTE OF THE DAY

"Let the wicked forsake his way, And the unrighteous man his thoughts; Let him return to the LORD, And He will have mercy on him; And to our God, For He will abundantly pardon."

Isaiah 55:7

DAY 164

📖 1 CORINTHIANS 14

✺ K E Y T H O U G H T S

- **1 Corinthians 14** is primarily concerned with the public gatherings of believers and with the gifts, tongues/interpretation and prophecy, being used for the edification of the whole gathering.

- There was a misuse of the personal practice of speaking with other tongues, apparently to speak with tongues had become a public display of spirituality, a kind of "look what I can do" situation. People were gaining control of a meeting and showing their gift of tongues – without interpretation, the result was confusion.

- 14:1 "Neither love nor gifts come automatically and should not be a passive matter of indifference. Believers should desire especially to prophesy, as compared to speaking in tongues in public (vvs.2-5). Tongues are primarily for self-edification and depend on the companion gift of interpretation when exercised in public. Tongues are permitted but prophecy is preferred (vs. 39)." (SFLB).

- Vss. 14-19 Paul reveals the place of tongues in his own personal prayer life. Praying in tongues is praying from the spirit instead of the intellect, and the same is true of singing praises. For Paul, praying and singing, both in tongues and in everyday language, were normal and regular parts of prayer and praise. There is no suggestion of hysteria, emotionalism, or abnormality of any kind." (SFLB).

- The church (the public gathering) is to be edified by any use of spiritual gifts – they are not to credential a person as spiritual or superior.

- There also should be sensitivity to those who are not believers in the gathering not a removal of the gifts, but a coherent use of gifts that do display the supernatural to those who are still seeking.

- Vss. 39 & 40 summarize the point of this chapter – the gifts are to be released in the church, but not in a disorderly confusing manner – respect and submission to spiritual authority is always a good indicator of an authentic gift from the Holy Spirit.

QUOTE OF THE DAY

"Pursue love, and desire spiritual gifts."

The Apostle Paul, 1 Cor. 14:1

DAY 165

2 SAMUEL 12:16 – 31; 13
1 CORINTHIANS 15:1 – 34

☺ K E Y   T H O U G H T S

- **2 Samuel 12** Notice how David processes the sentence of death upon this first child of Bathsheba, fasting, prayer – requesting of God for mercy.

- But once the child has died, he receives the reality of the situation and looks forward to a heavenly reunion (vss. 22, 23).

- The Amnon, Tamar, Absalom incidents read like a dramatic movie script – but it's what they show us that is troubling.

- The larger theme to learn from this passage is the price of David's (their father), unwillingness to bring discipline and correction to his children.

- It could be that because of his own failure(s), he lost his confidence to correct his own children. Perhaps he felt unqualified. This hesitance to consistently parent his kids becomes one of David's defining characteristics later in his life.

- The consequences to himself and his kingdom are immense.

- **1 Corinthians 15:2** "<u>HOLD FAST</u>" - simple yet powerful instruction to all believers.

- Vss. 3-8 A magnificent creedal statement of the truth, and the witnesses to the truth, of Christ's resurrection.

- Vs. 17 establishes the absolutely essential nature of the bodily resurrection of Jesus Christ. Praise God, He is Risen! Therefore we are no longer in our sins, having come to Him for forgiveness and cleansing from our sins.

- Vs. 32 A worldview devoid of eternal perspective only leads to a hedonistic lifestyle – "party hard and enjoy the moment."

- Vs. 33 An important proverb, with very deep truth.

- Vs. 34 There were false teachers and enemies of Christ who were seeking to subvert the truth of the resurrection and the need of living a holy life – the Apostle Paul does not mince words – "Awake to righteousness!"

DAY 166

📖 2 SAMUEL 14
📖 1 CORINTHIANS 15:35 – 58; 16

⊘ K E Y   T H O U G H T S

- **2 Samuel 14** David continues his ways of avoiding issues requiring action within his family. His inactivity results in significant dysfunction among his children.

- There seems to be an overemphasis upon physical appearance in these passages, Saul, David, Absalom and Tamar are noted for their appearance – when David was chosen there was a specific statement by God, that "man looks on the outward appearance but God looks on the heart."

- We should always be careful to see the inner person not just the exterior – it is a mistake to judge a book by its cover.

- **1 Corinthians 15:49** *"Bear the image of the heavenly man"*, the resurrection body, the return of Christ, the resurrection of the dead are all central truths to Christianity.

- Death has been overcome by Jesus' triumph – this life is not all that there is. We are to have a long view perspective, an eternal perspective.

- Vs. 58 Perhaps you have become discouraged in your *"labor in the Lord"* - it is NOT in vain, so be steady, remain committed and grow in your ministry unto the Lord!

- Be encouraged that the Lord's work, whatever expression you give it, is the only thing from this life that will truly go with us into heaven. But once in heaven it will translate into rewards!

- 16:2 This is a very simple, straightforward instruction about preparing our giving for our Sunday gatherings. Notice that the standard used is not equal among all people, so it's not like paying dues. The standard is the measure of how the Lord has prospered you.

- Those who have prospered greatly are to give more largely, those with less, smaller gifts – *"as each one has prospered"* – indicates that when all do what is within their capacity, then the need is more than met.

- I love Stephanas – it is so encouraging to have the man who was the first convert in Asia listed in Scripture. Think of Asia, there was a "first" Christian among those who are now billions – the gospel always starts with one.

QUOTE OF THE DAY

"We talk of the Second Coming; half the world has never heard of the first."

Oswald J. Smith

DAY 167

📖 PSALM 42, 43, 44

" AS WE RETURN TO THE PSALMS, BE SURE TO PUT THESE PRAYERS AND HYMNS INTO THE FIRST PERSON (I). DO NOT JUST READ THEM AS IF THEY ARE IN THE THIRD PERSON (HE/SHE) - MAKE THEM YOUR OWN. PRAY THE PRAYERS, CRY THE CRIES, SING THE SONGS — ENGAGE WITH THE LIVING GOD IN WORSHIP. THAT IS WHY THE BOOK OF PSALMS WAS WRITTEN. "

⊙ K E Y T H O U G H T S

- **Psalm 42:1** This is a picture of an animal of the field that is in the heat without water, longing desperately for a drink that will satisfy. (Do you know this longing for God?)

- (Is there a soul thirst for God in your life? Are you pursuing the Living God in the same way that someone dying of thirst would pursue water?)

- These Psalms give us the proper strategy for dealing with enemies and those that oppose us, we are to bring them to the

Lord and allow Him to be the vindicator, the judge.

- 42:11 & 43:5 are a repeated refrain, actually speaking to the cast down soul, with a solution.
- *"Hope in God"* and *"Praise Him"* because? He is our help!
- *"I shall yet praise Him"* – indicates a persevering life of praise in the midst of hard times. He remains worthy of praise when we do not understand how things will be resolved.
- He will restore our hope through praise and worship.
- 44:23-26 shows us how the Lord is willing to hear our cry when we are in desperate situations – we are permitted to call upon Him, we are welcomed to bring our needs and pains to Him.
- Reminding the Lord and ourselves of His character is always a good source of encouragement: *"redeem us for Your mercies sake."*

QUOTE OF THE DAY

"He is the best friend at all times, and the only friend at sometimes."

Joseph Caryl (1602-1673)

DAY 168

📖 2 SAMUEL 15
📖 PSALM 45, 46

◉ K E Y   T H O U G H T S

- **2 Samuel 15** Absalom's rebellion: again, David would have known of Absalom's behavior, but his pattern of non-involvement, non- correction brings bad results, (again).
- Parents, even though you are not perfect, when you see a pattern of behavior developing in your son or daughter – love them more than you love yourself and do your best to bring correction to them.
- Even if they do not respond immediately, they will recall your voice and your wisdom in a more contemplative time.

- **Psalm 45:6** The eternity and authority of God is forever and ever! He does not change!
- Ps. 46:1-3 These verses are well known and much loved, there is enough wisdom and comfort in these three verses to carry you in times of crisis and trouble.
- A refuge – somewhere that we can run for safety.
- A strength – when our own strength is insufficient for the challenge.
- A help – how often do we say "a little help please?"
- Trouble – everyone has trouble… the question is, what do we do when we're in trouble, where do we go?
- Vss. 10, 11 Some wonderful counsel – *"Be still and know that I am God."* Stop running, stressing and sweating long enough to know … God.
- Even when it seems that the nations are oblivious to God's ways – *"He will be exalted"* – be encouraged in the Lord.
- His "kingdom" will come, His "will" will be done on earth as it is in heaven.

QUOTE OF THE DAY

"When wealth is lost, nothing is lost; when health is lost, something is lost; when character is lost, all is lost."

Billy Graham

DAY 169

📖 2 SAMUEL 16, 17
📖 PSALM 47

⊛ K E Y   T H O U G H T S

- **2 Samuel 16** This incident of conflicting counsel teaches us that God is able, even in situations that seem hopeless.
- If Absalom had followed Ahithophel's advice, it is assumed that they would have been victorious and defeated David.

- (Do you have a situation that seems hopelessly against you? Is there someone giving counsel to someone you love that is leading them from God or from you?) Pray that the Lord will put another voice into their life who will speak, like Hushai.

- We prayed very hard for our children's associates – praying that the Lord would bring positive influences into their lives, voices for good, we tried to help them understand the value of positive people, positive friends.

- Notice that despite Ahithophel's wisdom there is a strong root of pride, the rejection of his advice brings a selfish and proud response to end his own life. Pride will often cause a person to take drastic action that actually marginalizes them unnecessarily – but they are blinded by their pride.

- **Psalm 47** The thrust of application of this Psalm is the exhortation to sing praises! Repeated over and over again, *"sing praises"*.

- Put on some worship music, or get to a place where you will feel free and offer up singing and praises to the Lord today.

- He is the *"King of the earth, He reigns over the nations, He is on His Holy Throne – He is greatly exalted!"*

- Sing praises!

QUOTE OF THE DAY

"I will praise God whether He deals with me in a way of justice or in a way of mercy, when He hath thunder in His voice, as well as when He hath honey under His tongue."

Stephen Charnock (1628-1680)

DAY 170

📖 2 SAMUEL 18 – 19:8
📖 PSALM 48, 49

◉ KEY THOUGHTS

- **2 Samuel 18** Leadership requires proper perspective, David's mourning and display over Absalom's death causes his loyal people and soldiers to become demoralized.

- Joab's evaluation is very perceptive (vss. 5-7). David is still struggling with his own issues of family leadership, except in this instance he over reacts after the fact, and almost loses the whole kingdom.
- **Psalm 48** The imagery of the power and strength of God, compared to a great city with great walls – is used often throughout the OT.
- The comparison is made for encouragement – God is mighty, strong, safe, impenetrable – the enemies of God will not prevail – we can run to Him, we can hide in Him, we can have confidence in Him as in a great city with walls.
- Ps. 49 describes the confidence of the foolish – the description of the ungodly wealthy is poignantly perceptive.
- Vs. 11 "their inner thought is that their houses will last forever."
- Vs. 17 *"for when he dies he shall carry nothing away."*
- Vs. 20 *"yet does not understand"* – this strong summary gives us a key – without understanding of God and submission to His ways, the man/woman who receives honor in this life will come to nothing.
- Think of great people of the past who are gone, if honor in this life is all that there is, it feels very shallow and temporary.
- In God's economy there is a lasting value to 'His' honor on our lives – an eternal value, a lasting blessing.
- Consider what you are building in this life, is it something that will translate into reward and honor in the next life? (Where is your treasure? Is it earthly, fleeting, temporary or will it last?)

QUOTE OF THE DAY

"There is no happiness in having or in getting, but only in giving. Half the world is on the wrong scent in pursuit of happiness."

Henry Drummond (1851-1897)

DAY 171

📖 2 SAMUEL 19:9 – 43
📖 PSALM 50, 52

⊚ K E Y   T H O U G H T S

- **2 Samuel 19:22** David's repeated statement *"what have I to do with you, you sons of Zeruiah?"* indicates the nature of these men. They were consistently violent, vengeful and harsh.

- David distinguishes himself as a leader by his mercy, not his vengeance. We should beware of those in a place to counsel us, those who have our ear. What is the nature of their counsel? Often those who counsel saying "it is for your good" have a personal or ulterior motive at heart.

- **Psalm 50** What should our action be in the 'day of trouble'? The phrase – *"call upon Me"* and *"call upon the Lord"* are used often in the scripture. (Is this invitation something that you have accepted? Are you one who is "calling" upon the Lord?)

- 50:23 A memorable verse of instruction and wisdom for a relationship that is near to the Lord.

- 52:8, 9 The wicked and the righteous are contrasted. The healthy, vibrant olive tree is a picture of a living relationship with the Lord – the foundation of such a relationship is *"I will trust in the mercy of the Lord, forever and ever."*

- *"I will wait on Your Name, for it is good."*

QUOTE OF THE DAY

"Men do not drop into the right way by chance; they must choose it, and continue to choose it, or they will soon wander from it."

Charles H. Spurgeon (1834-1892)

DAY 172

📖 2 SAMUEL 20
📖 PSALM 53, 54

◉ K E Y   T H O U G H T S

- **2 Samuel 20:5** Amasa's issue was procrastination, *"he delayed longer than the set time which David had appointed him."*
- This good man was David's choice to lead. His flaw was timing – he did not seize the moment. I wonder what his excuse would have been for the delay. Family, business, laziness? Whatever, because of this weakness his role ends with the treachery of Joab (a son of Zeruiah).
- Note the level of political intrigue in those verses. It is easy for us to judge from our distant perspective – David was still the greatest leader that the kingdom of Israel ever had!
- **Psalm 53:1** Meditate on the precise wording used here, those who say there is no God are "fools". This is a strong indictment of the godless – there is none who does good. *"no not one."* The "righteousness" of the ungodly amounts to nothing in the eternal economy of God.
- Ps. 54 When we are in trouble we can "cry out" to God to save, to vindicate and hear our prayers.
- At the same time, while in the difficult season we are to "freely" offer our sacrifices of praise! (vs. 6)

QUOTE OF THE DAY

"The core problem isn't the fact that we're lukewarm, halfhearted, or stagnant Christians. The crux of it all is why we are this way, and it is because we have an inaccurate view of God. We see Him as a benevolent Being who is satisfied when people manage to fit Him into their lives in some small way. We forget that God never had an identity crisis. He knows that He's great and deserves to be the center of our lives."

Francis Chan

DAY 173

2 SAMUEL 21:15 – 22; 22
PHILIPPIANS 1:1 – 18

KEY THOUGHTS

- **2 Samuel 22:2-4** Through all of David's experiences he has gained an accurate and strong view of who God is: *"rock, fortress, deliverer, strength, shield, horn of salvation (strong), stronghold, refuge, SAVIOR"*. (Do you see the Lord this way?) This is who He is!

- Vs. 4 Our resolve ought to be to *"call upon the Lord"* – our prayers are effective and necessary in the economy of God.

- Vs. 30 Even when the odds are against us, with the help of the Lord we can advance against a "troop".

- Vs. 31 *"As for God"*... what are His ways?

- Vs. 34 When we are challenged by having to climb high places, mountains in our lives – the strength of the Lord is able to make us move as easily as a deer (or mountain sheep), upon the heights.

- Vs. 47 Declare this loudly today: "THE LORD LIVES, BLESSED BE MY ROCK! LET GOD BE EXALTED."

- **Philippians 1:6** Be confident today. All that the Lord has begun in you is His joy to continue and complete. The Lord is working in you, receive His work with enthusiasm and joy.

- He is able to complete it! You will not remain an unfinished work of art.

- Vs. 18 Competition in the body of Christ: we must concern ourselves with the spread of the gospel, not with minor differences among those proclaiming Christ.

- Paul was able to rejoice that *"Christ is preached"*. Too many Christians get all wrapped up in controversy toward those who, although different in nuances or distinctive doctrines (which we all are free to hold), yet are preaching Christ.

- Unity does not necessarily mean uniformity – we are free to be who we are, without limiting those who are of a different stream – yet preaching Jesus.

"When there is a spirit of controversy in the church or in the land, a revival is needful. The spirit of religion is not the spirit of controversy. There can be no prosperity in religion, where the spirit of controversy prevails."

Charles Finney

DAY 174

📖 2 SAMUEL 23
📖 PHILIPPIANS 1:19 – 30

◉ K E Y   T H O U G H T S

- **2 Samuel 23:3** A key principle for leadership – when the Lord gives you responsibility over others, exercise your leadership with justice.

- 23:8-38 David's mighty men – this is an amazing litany of heroic and brave deeds. A real "man" passage. Men, be strong in the Lord, allow your life and your deeds to be spoken of with this type of respect and honor.

- We do not fight with swords and primitive weapons of battle, but we are in a war – fight with courage, stand with honor – the Lord will help you!

- Coming through all of this study of David – we must remember the captivating designation that he was a *"man after God's own heart"* – through all the successes and failures, he was first and foremost a friend of God. His heart was toward the Lord, very human – yet a great leader, a man of God and a reference point for all who would follow. Greatness is not perfection, greatness is staying near the foot of the cross and allowing Him to establish you.

- **Philippians 1:21** Are we able to say: *"For to me, to live is Christ"?* What would it mean to me, today – to live in Christ, all that I do, all that I am, long for, live for is Christ. "I pray today Lord, help me to live this way."

- Vs. 27 The exhortation to unity, *"one mind" striving,* for the faith of the gospel – the spread of the gospel of Christ, the evangelization of the world – this we are to be united on.

- This is conduct worthy of the gospel – in spite of opposition.
- Living *"worthy of the gospel"* – necessitates perseverance through opposition and hardship – Christ paid with His own blood, died upon the cross. Hardship and difficulty accompanied the purchase of our salvation.
- We ought not to be discouraged or surprised when the gospel costs us something, - persecution (not everybody thinks Christianity is a wonderful thing) is to be expected. Jesus was persecuted to death for the gospel.

QUOTE OF THE DAY

"No Christian is in a right condition, if he is not seeking in some way to bring souls to Christ."

Charles H. Mackintosh (1820-1896)

DAY 175

📖 2 SAMUEL 24
📖 PHILIPPIANS 2

✹ K E Y   T H O U G H T S

- **2 Samuel 24** David shows his humanness and his heart in this final chapter of 2 Samuel.
- Notice how he repents, no denial, no blaming – *"I have sinned greatly...I have done very foolishly."* True repentance is transparent and accurate.
- We also see his 'pastor's' heart as well, willing to receive punishment himself instead of "the sheep".
- 24:24 is a classic passage on the way to bring an acceptable offering to the Lord – *"I will not give that which costs me nothing."*
- Our giving should be a) our best, b) the first c) generous. (How is your practice of giving? Has there been a transformation in

your heart so that giving flows from your life?) Or is our giving something like prying a penny from the hand of a little child… remember, God loves a 'cheerful' giver.

- **Philippians 2:1-4** The dream of any leader would be this description that you would be of *"the same love, being of one accord, of one mind."*
- Vs. 4 This is a worthy verse to live by – it is a true indicator of a transformed heart to live for others. Jesus is our example of this type of selfless life (vs. 5ff).
- Vs. 16 There are many references throughout the epistles to the need to *"hold fast"* to the gospel. To continue in the faith, to be firm, to stand, to not leave the first teachings.
- Perseverance is a vital characteristic of true followers of Christ.
- Vs. 20 reveals the joy of raising up "like minded" disciples who will "sincerely care" for the state of the people.
- Vs. 13 Be encouraged, it is God who is working in you! It is the Holy Spirit who is shaping, changing, growing you.
- He works in us BOTH to "will" – to have our minds, our motivations changed, and "to do" - to actually execute the things He calls us to do – much more than mere words or promises. ACTION.

QUOTE OF THE DAY

"People who do not know the Lord ask why in the world we waste our lives as missionaries. They forget that they too are expending their lives … and when the bubble has burst, they will have nothing of eternal significance to show for the years they have wasted."

Nate Saint, missionary martyr

DAY 176

📖 PSALMS 55, 57
📖 PHILIPPIANS 3:1 – 16

🕮 K E Y   T H O U G H T S

- **Psalms 55, 57** There are a number of Psalms that express the writer's heart during times when enemies were troubling his life. The action in times of persecution or opposition is always the same:

- Express your heart freely to God, be fully transparent with the Lord as to how you are feeling.

- Allow the Lord to judge and to vindicate, always conclude with praise and worship.

- 55:22 *"Cast your burden on the Lord, and He shall sustain you."*

- 57:7-11 Read this hymn of praise out loud to the Lord today. Allow your perspective to shift from the problems to the greatness of our God!

- **Philippians 3** Outward physical acts of religious devotion do not equate to inward nearness to God – He looks upon the heart.

- 3:12, 14 – *"press on, lay hold"* these few verses are a rallying cry for all believers.

- We are not perfect, we are still pressing toward the love of Christ, there are rewards in store for those who are faithful.

- To know Him, to attain to the *"fellowship of the resurrection"*.

- *"Forgetting the things that are behind"* – land on this thought for a few minutes: what are "the things that are behind?"

- Our successes, accomplishments – basis for pride.

- Our failures – this is more likely the challenge for us… to truly be able to believe and live in the grace of God, that He has forgotten, He has renewed us.

- We must grant ourselves the same grace in God to carry on, to continue in the relationship of a disciple with his master.

"Had I cared for the comments of people, I should never have been a missionary."

C.T. Studd

DAY 177

📖 PSALMS 60, 61
📖 PHILIPPIANS 3:17 – 4:7

⊙ K E Y   T H O U G H T S

- **Psalms 60, 61** Notice how many times in the Psalms the pattern is one of discouragement and despair at the beginning and then a turn around to praise and confidence in the character of God by the close of the Psalm? This is a good way to live, freedom to feel pain, not denial, but then a conscious turning of our perspective to the greatness and faithfulness of God.

- 60:1 A cry for the Lord to "restore" – what type of restoration is needed in your life or the lives of those in your circle? Call upon the Lord today and ask Him to *"save with Your right hand, and hear me."* (The right hand represents strength in the OT.)

- Vs. 12 *"Through God"* – we will do valiantly!

- 61:1, 2 Always return to the Rock, the unchanging, faithful one who is higher – sees farther, knows all things, is ever at work!

- **Philippians 4:1** *"Stand fast"* – have you been wavering? (Has discouragement found a gap in your amour?) Often the victory is very near, if you will just "stand fast".

- Is there anyone that you know of that you are not *"of the same mind"* with? These two women were both respected in church leadership and yet there was a fight between them, we do not know what it was over.

- The apostle urges them to work it out, and he urges the other believers to 'help' them to get through it. Reconciliation and harmony are essential to experiencing the full blessings of God.

- Vss. 4, 5, 6, 7 are classic exhortations that ought to be

foundations for our lives.

- The way to be anxious for nothing is to found in vs. 6 – there is a way to live in Christ without anxiety:
  - *"By prayer,*
  - *And supplications,*
  - *With thanksgiving,*
  - *Let your requests be made known to God."*

QUOTE OF THE DAY

"Expect great things from God. Attempt great thing for God."

William Carey

DAY 178

📖 PSALMS 62, 63
📖 PHILIPPIANS 4:8 – 23

⊙ K E Y   T H O U G H T S

- **Psalm 62:8** (Is it part of your relationship with the Lord the ability to *"pour out your heart before Him?"*)
- (Do we treat the Lord as a refuge?) He is a place that we can go to where there is acceptance and understanding, as well as the power to do something about the things that we share.
- Psalm 63 is a powerful chapter to read out loud, if you are able, read these words audibly and listen to the strong exhortation.
- What definition would you give to *"lovingkindness"*? (vs. 3)
- An intimate relationship with God will result in a praise-filled, expressive life of worship – *"I will lift up my hands in Your name… my mouth shall be satisfied."*
- **Philippians 4:8** This list of things to think about defines a thought life under the authority of Jesus – this is not just a passing 'thought' we are exhorted to *"meditate",* on these things, think deeply, spend some time on them.
- Vs. 12 (Have you learned "both"? How to abound and how to

be abased?)

- MEMORIZE vs. 13 and vs. 19. These highlight life verses will strengthen you and give you a foundation in times of trouble.
- Vs. 21 If it is not your practice, make it a new commitment to *"greet every saint in Christ Jesus."* When you are in church, greet every person you see, don't walk by anyone! You are brother and sister in Christ!

QUOTE OF THE DAY

"God's part is to put forth power; our part is to put forth faith."

Andrew A. Bonar

DAY 179

📖 1 KINGS 1
📖 PSALMS 64, 66

⊙ K E Y   T H O U G H T S

- **1 Kings 1** We are introduced to the reign of Solomon (note that David has no immoral relations with Abishag).
- Note the role of those who are faithful, Benaiah is such a respectable man. Unknown to most of us, yet a mighty warrior (2 Samuel 23:20-23), and a man faithful to leadership. It is a good thing to honor godly leaders that the Holy Spirit has placed in authority.
- **Psalm 64:1** *"Preserve my life <u>from fear of the enemy</u>."* Not necessarily from the enemy, living in the fear of what "might" happen is often worse than what actually happens.
- In the Lord we can be confident that HE will hide us, protect us and take us through tough seasons.
- 66:13, 14 (Have you offered promises to the Lord when you were in trouble, when you called upon the Lord in times of need?) "Lord if you help me, I will...."
- If we do not fulfill those promises we are in danger of an irreverent heart, trying to manipulate or fool the Lord with

promises leads to a dysfunctional relationship. Keep your word and learn in the process to be cautious with what you speak.

- 66:18 An important principle of prayer – when we approach the Lord in prayer with unconfessed or known hidden sin, this verse teaches that *"the Lord will not hear."*

- We must be in a right place as we bring our petitions. The state being described is of the person who knowingly, willingly lives in rebellion to God's ways and yet continues to pray for blessing and favor from the Lord.

- The Lord will always answer a prayer of repentance, always hear a cry for restoration, He loves a "contrite" or humble heart willing to admit need.

- Vs. 20 A great reason to bless the Lord – *"He has not turned away my prayers!"*

QUOTE OF THE DAY

"Lose not your confidence of making progress toward the things of the Spirit; you still have time, the hour is not yet past."

Thomas a Kempis (1380-1471)

DAY 180

📖 1 KINGS 2
📖 PSALMS 67; 68:1 – 6, 18 – 20

⊙ K E Y   T H O U G H T S

- **1 Kings 2** Solomon completes some of the work that David had left unfinished. His throne and reign are established without the political crisis that were a part of David's reign.

- **Psalm 67:6** Blessing comes from God.

- When God is lifted up His enemies are scattered. There is powerful authority in the Name and in the presence of our Lord. See the picture of a group of enemies scattering like rats from a sinking ship.

- Ps. 68:5, 6 This is a very lovely passage describing the Father heart of God.

- (Are you fatherless? Have you experienced abandonment or loss?) He is your Father, He is your defender.
- The body of Christ is to be the family of the solitary – isolation and loneliness are not in the Father's heart for you.
- Receive His design for you today: to put you in His family, to break any bondage and turn that to prosperity.
- The only instruction is to live in submission and peace to God. Rebellion results in dryness, an arid land (a picture of poverty and hopelessness).
- 68:19, 20 More of the blessings of walking with the Lord - *"loads us with benefits"* – the picture of someone so overwhelmed with gifts that they can't carry them all...
- *"escapes from death"*. The Lord is our protector – He watches over us. (Has there been an escape from death in your life – have you given God glory for preserving your life?)

QUOTE OF THE DAY

"Our faith as to the present is revived by glad memories of the past."

Charles H. Spurgeon (1834-1892)

DAY 181

📖 1 KINGS 3; 4:20 – 34
📖 PSALMS 69, 70

◉ K E Y   T H O U G H T S

- **1 Kings 3** Solomon chooses wisely when asked by God, *"what shall I give you?"*
- The heart of God is for the good of His children, as a loving father would be to a son or daughter. God our Father chooses to give more than what was requested!
- The "best" is what God longs to bring to us – His desire is to bless us.

- Vs. 14 In just about every promise of blessing you will find an "if". *"If you walk in My ways."* This is the key to blessings.
- **Psalm 69** (What is your response when you face troubles? When you feel as if you are about to go under?)
- Vs. 1 I wonder if Peter recollected this Psalm when he was beginning to sink while walking on the water with Jesus – *"Lord save me!"* (Matt. 14:30)
- 70:5 There is nothing wrong with crying out for help when you are feeling that you are in trouble, it is not weak to acknowledge need.

QUOTE OF THE DAY

"Church attendance is as vital to a disciple as a transfusion of rich, healthy blood to a sick man."

Dwight L. Moody

DAY 182

📖 1 KINGS 5; 6:1
📖 PSALMS 71, 72

☞ K E Y   T H O U G H T S

- **1 Kings 5** Solomon is about to build the temple – a significant event in the history of Israel. The temple became the center piece of Israel's worship.
- The stones of the temple's foundation are absolutely astonishing! Buried far beneath the surface of Jerusalem are magnificent, perfectly hewn stones so precise that it is difficult to slide a single sheet of paper into the joints.
- **Psalms 71, 72** As we read these two Psalms, it is important to be reminded of the heart of David – for God!
- We have just finished reading of his life and reign, the overall impression we are left with is of his failures and not his victories.
- These Psalms give us the heart of David, the reason why

he was called the man after God's own heart. In spite of his humanness and his failures, David was an enthusiastic worshipper, he loved God with all he had, he was faithful to the Lord and expressed it in these magnificent hymns of praise.

- Ps. 71:1 *"In You oh Lord I put my trust."* Vs. 3 *"for You are my Rock and my fortress."*
- Vs. 20 *"You…. shall revive me again, and bring me up again from the depths of the earth."*
- Ps. 72:8 This verse is chiseled into the stone arch over the door to the parliament buildings in Ottawa, Canada. Let us pray together that in our nation, truly, *"He shall have dominion also from sea to sea, And from the River to the ends of the earth."*
- 72:18 As this group of Psalms comes to a close, David is transported to heights of praise to the God, *"who only does wondrous things."*

DAY 183

📖 1 KINGS 8

⊛ K E Y   T H O U G H T S

- **I Kings 8:10 - 11** The cloud of the glory of the Lord filled the newly completed temple. The presence of God was so intense that the priests could no longer continue their 'service' – they had to stop what they were doing and be in the presence of God.
- Solomon's prayer of dedication is a masterpiece of humble petition.
- The theme of the prayer is *"then hear in heaven"*. Solomon gives numerous scenarios for when the people will need God's

hearing and intervention:

- "when anyone sins….."
- "defeated before an enemy" etc…
- When the Bible speaks of *"God hearing"* it assumes He also will do something. *"Then hear in heaven… and forgive, act, maintain their cause, have compassion, listen".* God is a living, hearing, acting God – not a lifeless, unresponsive, vengeful deity.
- Vs. 48 A prescription for returning to the Lord after a season of backsliding and unfaithfulness. How should we return to the Lord?
- "…with all (our) heart and with all (our) soul."
- Recalling the faithfulness of God is a good thing to do while in prayer (vs. 56) – *"THERE HAS NOT FAILED ONE WORD OF ALL HIS GOOD PROMISE."*
- Vs. 61 A strong exhortation to people of all times. (What does it mean to you, to maintain a *"loyal"* heart to the Lord? Is your heart loyal today?)
- The sacrifice and feast of the dedication of the temple is staggering in size – 22,000 bulls, 120,000 sheep! A fourteen day feast for ALL the people - now that's a celebration!

QUOTE OF THE DAY

"Many Spirit-filled authors have exhausted the thesaurus in order to describe God with the glory He deserves. His perfect holiness, by definition, assures us that our words can't contain Him. Isn't it a comfort to worship a God we cannot exaggerate?"

Francis Chan, 'Crazy Love'

DAY 184

📖 1 KINGS 9
📖 2 CORINTHIANS 1, 2

◉ K E Y   T H O U G H T S

- **1 Kings 9:4** "If" … "integrity of heart and in uprightness, to do according to all that I have commanded you…. keep My statues and judgments."

- The promise of having a descendent on the throne has conditions – regrettably, a sorry history of succession follows.
- **2 Corinthians 1:4** There is comfort from the Lord when times are tough. We also can be supported by God in difficult days.
- 1:12 A clear conscience is supported by conduct that is marked by *"simplicity and godly sincerity"*.
- 1:22 The seal of the Holy Spirit in our hearts – the presence of the Holy Spirit in our hearts is like God making a deposit on a purchase. You make a deposit only if you intend to complete the purchase. The Holy Spirit is God's deposit that the work He has started in each of us is going to be completed.
- 2:11 Forgiveness must be ongoing and ever available to other people – because there will always be new offenses.
- Perhaps however, there is a long standing hurt or wound or sin against you. Sometimes the old wounds, left unforgiven are the hard ones to let go of – we are the only ones being hurt by the unforgiven offense. Unforgiveness is like drinking poison, and expecting it to kill the other person…
- Satan loves to take advantage of us, by leveraging bitterness against us, limiting our freedom, hampering our growth in God. Release the offense to God, forgive the offender.
- Vss. 14-17 In a Roman victory procession, both the victors and the conquered were part of the parade. It was common for the air to be filled with aromatic incense and burning spices.
- To the conquerors it was a pleasant, joyful aroma of victory (the gospel to those who are being saved), to the conquered it was an unpleasant repulsive, smell that reinforced their captivity. The gospel to the unbeliever is a sentence of death unless they turn to Christ and repent.

QUOTE OF THE DAY

"Being a Christian is more than just an instantaneous conversion - it is a daily process whereby you grow to be more and more like Christ."

Billy Graham

DAY 185

📖 1 KINGS 10 – 11:13
📖 2 CORINTHIANS 3, 4

◉ K E Y   T H O U G H T S

- **I Kings 10** All of Solomon's wisdom, all of Solomon's wealth could not keep him from *"loving many foreign women"*.

- This is a tragic fall into idolatry, not only idols, but the most depraved and hideous, including child sacrifice, all manner of sexual perversion in worship – truly astonishing.

- Wealth, education, status are not indicators of godliness – a heart after God, a loyal heart is the only true factor.

- **1 Corinthians 3:16** When you come to Jesus there is a veil of spiritual darkness and religion that lifts from your mind and heart – things formerly hard to understand or insignificant suddenly come to light.

- Vs. 17 In Christ, by the Holy Spirit there is liberty, freedom – true freedom.

- 1 Cor. 4:1 *"we do not lose heart"!* - since we have received mercy. The fact that we have received the mercy and love of God to our hearts is a guarantee that the Lord will be faithful regardless of the challenges we face.

- Vss. 8, 9 There will be times when we are "hard-pressed, perplexed, persecuted, struck down" but we are NOT "crushed, in despair, forsaken, destroyed" – praise God!

- Vs. 16 Again… *"we do not lose heart!"* There is an inward renewal that comes from focusing not on the moment but looking to the things that are "unseen".

- Be reminded today that the things that are unseen are "eternal". The things of the Spirit, the works of obedience to Christ, the perseverance in the midst of discouragement – these things… plus the souls of men, women, children, youth – these remain… kindness, compassion, love…. These remain!

- (How much of our lives are devoted to the unseen? How much is devoted to the seen?)

"If God calls you to be a missionary, don't stoop to be a king."

Jordan Groom

DAY 186

📖 1 KINGS 11:14 – 43
📖 2 CORINTHIANS 5

◉ K E Y   T H O U G H T S

- **I Kings 11** God continues to honor David by placing his descendants on the throne because *"he kept My commandments and My statutes."*

- **2 Corinthians 5** is a mountain peak chapter – so much wonderful, encouraging truth packed into these verses.

- Vs. 8 *"we walk by faith not by sight"*. We are so resistant to living by faith. We struggle living by what is unseen, what is promised and yet not attained, living by trusting rather than by having a 'show me first' attitude.

- Vs. 10 (Are you aware as a follower of Jesus that you will stand before the *"judgment seat of Christ"?*) Believers will be required to give an answer for the things done in the body *"whether good or bad"*.

- Our salvation is secure in Christ alone, but the level of reward that we receive is variable depending on the level of our obedience and 'labor' in the Lord.

- It is the love of Christ that 'compels' us, motivates us to share the gospel, to love people, to be 'ambassadors' (vs. 20).

- 5:17 Meditate on the things that were old that have gone, and on the things that are new that have 'come' into your life since coming to Jesus, and as you have been growing in the Lord.

- Vss. 18-21 This powerful description of the heart of God, expressed in magnificent language – gives us a clear mandate for evangelism.

- The work of Christ in the cross, gives us the resources to deliver on the promises of the gospel, the heart of love (compelling us), and the job description, an ambassador – imploring/pleading with people to make peace with God.
- We all are called to this ministry of reconciliation. Hallelujah!

QUOTE OF THE DAY

"If you die wrong the first time, you cannot come back to die better a second time. If you die without Christ, you cannot come back to be converted and die a believer – you have but once to die. Pray that you may find Christ before death finds you."

Robert M. McCheyne (1813 – 1843)

DAY 187

📖 1 KINGS 12
📖 2 CORINTHIANS 6, 7

⊛ K E Y   T H O U G H T S

- **I Kings 12** Rehoboam is Solomon's son, his choice for the throne – however, because of Solomon's idolatry and rebellion the kingdom is going to be divided (as judgment).
- We need to notice how many times a leader or individual is led astray by foolish advice – in this case Rehoboam listens to the young aristocracy instead of the elders. The sense of entitlement is very evident – it is God who gives authority to govern, to lead.
- Vss. 25 - 33 are a description of how man-made religion starts:

  a) It is politically, or personally advantageous to the creator.

  b) It contains elements of the original true faith.

  c) It is for the convenience of the people (closer, gods they can see).

- The establishment of Jeroboam's high places will become a recurring measurement of the apostacy of leaders that will follow and their destruction the true indicator of when revival breaks out.

- **2 Corinthians 6:2b** "NOW" – there is an urgency to the gospel. Vs. 3 the character of our lives is absolutely vital in the presentation of Christ. How many times have we heard "if that is what Christianity is like (referring to a faulty character or behavior) I don't want anything to do with it"?

- Vss. 14 – 18 This passage gives specific instruction on separation from the world. Remember this is not telling us to have nothing to do with the world (1 Cor. 5:10), but rather we are being taught not to enter into intimate relationships with those who are unbelievers. Marriage, business partnerships (not forbidden but requiring extreme wisdom, counsel and confirmation) etc. A simple way of thinking about it is… "if the starting points are miles apart how probable is the chance of the relationship succeeding, when the most critical part, the spiritual, does not connect."

- 7:10 Repentance leads to good things! Doctrine that removes the place of repentance in the believer's life is robbing us of a beautiful promise and relief.

QUOTE OF THE DAY

"Some people stumble over their intellect and say they can't understand religion. Many parts of the Bible I don't understand, but I am not going to fight against my Lord with my puny reason."

Dwight L. Moody (1837-1899)

DAY 188

📖 1 KINGS 13
📖 2 CORINTHIANS 8

⊛ K E Y   T H O U G H T S

- **1 Kings 13:2** A stunning prophecy of promise for renewal. The child is mentioned by name, Josiah, he is born 300 years later and led Israel through their greatest season of national revival.

- This account, although a bit confusing has a straightforward message – the man of God had a word from the Lord. It was a clear direction, he fully understood it, saw it confirmed miraculously and began to live in obedience to it.

- Later in the account, someone else came along saying – "I have a word from the Lord, actually from an angel"- change to my word from the word you received! Ultimately, that false prophet was destroyed by God.

- The second man is lying! When God gives you a clear word, works in your life, teaches you something or you experience a blessing from God, and then someone else says "that is wrong" – stick with what God has done in your life! Do not be intimidated by someone else's word!

- We see this in the NT when the believers were beset by "Judaizers", who wanted the believers to add religious ceremony and circumcision to the grace of God. Paul exhorts them;

    "Are you so foolish? Having begun in the Spirit, are you now being made perfect by the flesh?" Galatians 3:3

- **2 Corinthians 8** A classic passage on the heart of giving.

- 8:7 As you are abounding in all the goodness and blessings of God, are you likewise "abounding" in the grace of giving? Honestly?

- 8:11 We often have a heart to give, we intend to give but we lack the finish – we haven't completed what the Lord stirred in our hearts to do – if this is so, pick it up where you left off, continue, don't give up.

- Vs. 12 Here is the key to giving – *"according to what one has not according to what he does not have".* This levels the playing field, we are not judged in giving by what others do, we are to respond within our capacity but, we are to be faithful and truthful with God about our capacity!

- The principles of accuracy and consistency are important guides – if we are faithful to give when our capacity is small we will be able to give when our capacity is large.

- Vs. 24 The apostle actually challenges the believers to show proof of their love by their giving. Much more than words, love is always provable by action.

"Let us remember, that while we are in this world, we sojourn (live temporarily) in a strange land, and are at a distance from our home; and, therefore, do not let us be inordinately affected with anything in it."

Philip Doddridge (1702 – 1751)

DAY 189

📖 1 KINGS 14
📖 2 CORINTHIANS 9

⊚ K E Y   T H O U G H T S

- **I Kings 14:8** David: *"who followed Me with all his heart, to do only what was right in My eyes"*. This standard of commitment to God is the reference point for all the kings that follow.

- 2 Corinthians 9 Continuing with principles of generosity in giving. Not out of *"grudging obligation"*. The whole principle of heart felt giving is gratitude, a reciprocal heart that is willing to give lavishly as we have received lavishly.

- Vss. 6-8 Meditate on the principle of sowing and reaping. The words "sparingly" and "bountifully" could not be any more contrasted.

- Vs. 7 (Why would God love a cheerful giver? Why wouldn't He love just a "giver"?)

- The system of rules and regulations, obligations, grudging duty had ground the people into all manner of crazy ways of meeting the letter of the law but missing the spirit entirely.

- God is interested mostly in our hearts – if out of a joyful, thankful full heart a person cheerfully gives – then the Lord is pleased! Generosity is certainly a high standard that surpasses the tutor of tithing.

- NT giving is well beyond any minimum requirement of the tithe, tithing is a wonderful starting point as a reference and tutor in elementary giving – generosity could not possibly be a standard less than a tithe.

- Vss. 10 - 11 The blessing of our whole life is influenced by our giving. Our giving is accurate in evaluating the condition of our heart, the level of trust that we have in God and the transformation of our character from selfishness to focus on others.

- Vss. 12 -15 Others are blessed in multiple ways by our giving – there is much 'thanksgiving' to God (others' faith is encouraged), they glorify God, they offer much prayer as a result.

- Giving is truly a powerful, accurate sign of an inner work of God in our lives.

QUOTE OF THE DAY

"Give me five minutes with a person's checkbook, and I will tell you where their heart is."

Billy Graham

DAY 190

📖 1 KINGS 15; 16:29 – 34
📖 2 CORINTHIANS 10 – 11:4

☉ K E Y   T H O U G H T S

- **1 Kings** A lot of treachery, consolidation of power through violence, one good King Asa, yet he had no impact on spiritual life long term.

- We meet Ahab and Jezebel. 16:29ff – very significant and wicked team. The practice of marrying for political expedience results in religious syncretism and much wickedness. Compromise in spiritual things will never bring a good result.

- **2 Corinthians 10:3-6** "Our warfare is not 'against flesh and blood' (Eph. 6:12); therefore, carnal (weak, worldly) weapons will not do. We need weapons that are God-empowered (mighty in God). Their purpose is for pulling down [demolishing] strongholds (anything opposing God's will).

- Here Paul refers specifically to warfare in the mind, against arrogant rebellious ideas and attitudes (which he terms arguments), and against every high thing (pride) opposed to the true knowledge of God. The aim is to bring every disobedient thought into…. obedience to Christ." (Spirit Filled Life Bible)

- Ranking our spiritual progress by comparing ourselves with other believers/people is never a beneficial route to take (10: 12).

- 10:12 – 11:4 There is great value in keeping in mind how you came to Jesus, who introduced you to Christ, what your spiritual heritage is. Many will come along and try to move you to a "better" way.

- This phrase in 11:3 is a huge caution and warning – so many people are moved away and 'corrupted' by departing from "the simplicity of the gospel".

- Another Jesus, another gospel, a higher level of learning – saying in essence, "what you first believed is not right, this is a better way".

- Dear brother, dear sister – trust the working of the Holy Spirit in your life, think of this – there were people who were corrupting the church in Corinth saying that the teaching of the Apostle Paul was too simple, too basic… Paul!

- If it was happening then, with the greatest Apostle of all as the target, it will happen now – do not assemble many teachers around your head to fill it with complicated ideas that stroke our pride, stick with "the simplicity of the gospel"!

QUOTE OF THE DAY

"All your carnal reasoning and logical subtleties can never overthrow the plain Word of God."

John Fletcher (1729-1785)

DAY 191

📖 1 KINGS 17
📖 2 CORINTHIANS 11:5 – 12:13

🌐 K E Y   T H O U G H T S

- **I Kings 17** Elijah is one of the favorite prophetic characters of the Bible. He had amazing authority and yet a humanity that we can all relate to.

- With the widow of Zarephath – he utters this wonderful promise of miraculous provision, vs. 14: "The bin of flour shall not be used up, nor shall the jar of oil run dry, until the day the Lord sends rain on the earth."

- In other words – when all the rest of the earth is in need the Lord is able to take care of you supernaturally. This whole passage features encouraging testimony to God's power to provide, (the ravens feeding Elijah).

- (Are you anxious or fearful about having food to eat, clothing to wear and a place to lay your head?) When you are fully in the care of the Lord there is no need to be afraid, He will keep His promise to you!

- Honor the Lord with your tithes and offerings, trust Him and see how He is faithful.

- **2 Corinthians 11** There have always been, and there will always be, people, 'prophets', leaders who will come along and try to convince you that they have something you don't, they have a revelation that you need, they are going to lead you into "the truth".

- Paul is so reluctant to defend himself, as he finally wades into some of his credentials he chooses things that others would consider weaknesses – he says (paraphrasing), *"I was too weak to mistreat you, I assumed you would value the supernatural signs of apostolic authority, these have been my sufferings, the cost I have paid for you having the gospel."*

- 11:14 It is the work of Satan to transform himself into a false 'angel of light' and try to deceive. Beware when:

- teaching confuses you, causes fear, bondage, heaviness –

exclusivity (you and your little circle are the only ones who are right) – when the joys you once knew start to be lost, worship, reading the word, prayer, - all for fear of doing something wrong, or not "knowing" enough

- People you have known and trusted for years use the 'wrong' words, and you break fellowship from those who brought you to Christ because they aren't 'deep' enough…

- There is no preacher that you can listen to except your latest 'super teacher' – you have walked into a situation like Paul is addressing here.

- Return to your first love, return to love and the experience of God's presence and grace – don't continue to be "puffed up" in knowledge. (1 Cor. 8:1; 13:4) Bring someone to Jesus, care for the poor – stop the endless debate and all the talking, do something!

- 12:9 (Is there a difficult issue in your life that is not going away? Perhaps a physical pain or limitation?) Receive Jesus' word today *"His grace is sufficient for you, His strength is made perfect in weakness"*.

QUOTE OF THE DAY

"Oh let every trial teach me more of Thy peace in my conscience, and more of Thy love in my heart, that I may keep on in a steady course, walking humbly with my God."

William Romaine (1714 – 1795)

DAY 192

📖 1 KINGS 18
📖 2 CORINTHIANS 12:14 – 21

◉ K E Y   T H O U G H T S

- **I Kings** The showdown between the 'gods' of Baal and Asherah, both the most frequently mentioned idols of Bible times – they were supposedly gods of fertility and weather, the practices of both were extremely wicked and immoral.

- Vss. 26 & 29 says it all, *"but there was no voice, no one answered, no one paid attention"*. What seems to be a bit theatrical is actually a prophetic illustration of the power of the true God.
- God answers immediately, powerfully, supernaturally and undeniably in answer to prayer.
- Answered prayer: "first, even though we have a promise for God's provision, we are not to stop praying for its fulfillment (vs. 41). Second, we see one of the postures of prayer as we read that he bowed down on the ground, and put his face between his knees (vs. 42). Third, we learn the importance of persistence in prayer as we read that Elijah prayed seven times (vs. 43). And fourth, we understand the necessity of faith as we pray by realizing that Elijah believed his prayer was answered before the answer actually came (vss. 44-45).
- James 5:17, 18 explains that the prayer of a Christian can be as effective as the prayer of Elijah!" (Spirit Filled Life Bible)
- (How is your prayer life? Why not determine today that you will grow in prayer, that you will believe enough in prayer to actually practice this powerful weapon which brings spiritual victory?)
- (Is there something that you stopped praying for after six times?) Is there something where a small indicator of an answer has appeared (cloud the size of a man's hand – hardly a rain storm yet) – press into that thing in prayer – pursue it until the answer comes fully – be encouraged and strengthened that our God is a prayer hearing and prayer answering God!
- **2 Corinthains 12:20, 21** These lists of things that ought not to be present in the church should be a challenge to our hearts. These items *"contentions, selfish ambitions, backbiting are…. etc.)* are the fruit of something other than the Spirit of Christ at work in our character.
- Justifying our behavior on the grounds of 'cause' or 'principle' is not adequate to avoid this exhortation – to cease.

QUOTE OF THE DAY

"The more able to wait long for answers to our desires and prayers, the stronger faith is."

William Gurnall (1617-1696)

DAY 193

📖 1 KINGS 19
📖 2 CORINTHIANS 13

⊚ K E Y   T H O U G H T S

- **I Kings 19:1-10** This emotional and poignant description of the mighty prophet in a season of discouragement is most instructive.

- Discouragement often runs contrary to the facts, when we are discouraged we can't evaluate the data correctly. Elijah is very tired, he's a fugitive on the run for his life.

- And yet – he is visited by an angel twice. The angel supplies him with food and water – supernatural food that equips him for a 40 day journey! And yet.....

- He wants to die, has lost perspective completely and is overcome with self-pity.

- God is faithful, He will not fail you, He will provide sufficient strength, you will get through it, He will protect you, you are not alone!

- In times of discouragement rather than seek mighty manifestations of power, look for His voice of love and tenderness – He will reveal Himself in relationship. That is what we need in down times, to hear His voice, and to know that He loves us.

- **2 Corinthians 13** "Those who seek "proof" from Paul (vs.3) should examine and test themselves rather than him. If they know that they are genuine Christians, they should know that Paul is a genuine apostle (3:1-3). If they are not disqualified (counterfeit, unapproved, failing the test), neither is Paul. Whether he is approved (qualified, genuine, passing the test) or thought to be disqualified, Paul's main concern is their right behavior, not their opinion of him." (SFLB)

- It is a fruitless trap to spend time trying to determine who is 'really' right with God and who is not. The energy of our spiritual lives must be spent examining ourselves not judging other's walk with God – He (the Lord) will do that very accurately.

- Vs. 11 "....be joyful. Grow to maturity. Encourage each other. Live in harmony and peace." (NLT)
- Great counsel for us all.

DAY 194

📖 1 KINGS 21
📖 MARK 1

⊜ K E Y   T H O U G H T S

- **I Kings 21:25** Jezebel's influence is powerfully negative in Ahab's life and in the religious life of Israel. (Who are the influences in your life? What are they influencing you toward?)
- We are wise if we surround ourselves with people who call us on in the things of the Lord. There is a time to sever ties with a person or people who consistently try to pull us away from the Lord.
- There is no shame in acknowledging that certain influences are bad – we can continue to pray for them, but not allow them to pull our hearts from the Lord.
- **Mark 1:8** Jesus is baptized in water. (Have you been baptized in water?)
- Vs. 15 Note the simple message: "repent and believe in the gospel."
- Vs. 17 When we follow Jesus He promises that He will "make you become" fishers of men. One of the transforming works of Jesus is to cause our hearts to be toward those around us who are lost. This is a consistent theme of purpose that Jesus gives

to His disciples/followers.

- Vss. 27, 34 Jesus has authority both to teach, and, to cast out demons.

- Vs. 35 Prayer - Jesus made prayer part of His life – the Son of God found benefits in prayer, had the need to pray, took time to pray. (What place does prayer have in our lives?)

- Vs. 38 (What does Jesus say His purpose was in coming?)

- Vs. 41 *"Moved with compassion"*, we encounter this description of Jesus' motivation. Make a note of every time you come across it – God's heart is moved by the needs of His people.

- Vs. 41 *"I am willing"* - when it comes to healing, this is the posture of God toward our sickness. He is willing, we do not need to fear when we ask, we do not need to 'cover' for God. When the sick receive prayer, approach the Lord with this conviction – He is willing.

- Allow the answer of healing or not to be His responsibility, He can handle it. Let us not fail by trying to "pre-think" God, His timing, His ways. Let us be the ones who simply ask in faith.

QUOTE OF THE DAY

"Unless I had the spirit of prayer, I could do nothing."

Charles Finney

DAY 195

📖 1 KINGS 22
📖 MARK 2:1 – 17

◉ K E Y   T H O U G H T S

- **I Kings 22** The demise and disrespectful end of Ahab – both Jehoshaphat and Josiah, (good kings), engage in a battle that is not their own – it is usually not wise to jump into someone else's battle.

- **Mark 2:1-12** Read this account of 1) the full house because Jesus is there, 2) the four friends bringing 3) the paralyzed man, 4) digging through the roof, 5) healing, 6) testimony and forgiveness of sins.

- (Put yourself in the story, who do you identify with the most, where would you be at this point in your life in this story? The friends? The sick man? The people thronging Jesus for more?)

- (Who do you know that needs your help to get to Jesus?) Who is paralyzed by sin, or life, or hurts – do all you can – through even a solid barrier like a roof, to get them to the presence of the One who has the answer to their need.

- Mark 2:17 Jesus makes such a clear statement regarding the self-righteousness of the religious people – those who are trying to make themselves right before God will never succeed – Jesus has come for those who recognize their need of Him.

- He also has come to those who will receive Him most readily, "the sick" – this includes those who will listen, those who know that they are in need. This is who we should go to first.

- Children receive Him gladly, youth are willing to believe, the poor, the broken, the outcast – Jesus spent much of His ministry with these people – we ought to do the same.

- Reach out to someone today – there is someone who is waiting for some good news!

QUOTE OF THE DAY

"What are we here for, to have a good time with Christians or to save sinners?"

Malla Moe

DAY 196

📖 2 KINGS 2
📖 MARK 2:18 – 3:6

✪ K E Y T H O U G H T S

- **2 Kings** continues with the history of the divided kingdoms of Judah and Israel. "There were nineteen regents in Israel, all of them bad. In Judah, there were twenty rulers, only eight of them good. Second Kings records the last ten kings in Israel, and the last sixteen rulers in Judah." (SFLB)

- We will focus on the eight good Kings of Judah – they represent a revival spirit. We will see clearly enough the consequences of the bad kings' spiritual decline in the measures the good kings take to right the spiritual life of Judah.

- 2 Kings 2 Notice how Elisha refuses to be distracted from his purpose of being mentored by Elijah. Elisha was determined to be with this man of God, he put himself in a place to be mentored by proximity. Get yourself around other people of God, make the effort to have people of maturity and wisdom speak into your life.

- It is our responsibility to be mentored, not theirs to mentor us! Take initiative, find someone whom you admire in the Lord, and get near them, even from a distance you will learn and grow.

- Elisha has a deep desire to go beyond Elijah spiritually, (double portion), Elijah is not threatened. It should be the desire of every parent and every spiritual leader that those who follow us would go beyond us in spiritual things.

- **Mark 2:22** "The joy of the new message cannot be contained within Jewish legalism any more than fermenting wine can be held by brittle old wineskins." (SFLB)

- Jesus is the original and godly revolutionary against religion. There is a lot of bravado and big talk from people about being against 'religion' – even hating religion – unfortunately many people lump everything relating to spiritual life and church under the heading of 'religion'.

- It is not right to judge the heart of a person who wears different clothes yet loves the Lord and label them 'religious'.

- It is not right to dismiss everything "church" and elevate completely self-serving brands of spirituality that digress into coffee cliques.

- Jesus was bringing a radical new message of relationship and grace into a stifling religious environment that had lost its way.

- Jesus is God, He is all wise – He has the perspective to

determine what is religious and what is not.

- The essence of true religion is all about a heart for God. Our focus is not all the stuff we are against, or all the 'religious' people that are so very wrong. That ends up being just another form of an equally religious spirit.

- Be a follower of Jesus in spirit, in every way – show who you are by what you are 'for'.

DAY 197

📖 2 KINGS 3:5 – 27
📖 MARK 3:7 – 4:20

☞ K E Y T H O U G H T S

- **2 Kings 3** Johashaphat rightly calls for Elisha. Looking for confirmation of important decisions is a wise thing to do. Confirmation can come from reading the word, from a brother or sister, or in prayer by a confirming inner witness of the Holy Spirit.

- The wickedness of the Moabite king is shown in his desperate burnt offering (sacrifice) of his eldest son – God was always against human sacrifice.

- This principle makes the sacrifice of Jesus so very significant – the love of God for humanity was so great that He gave His one and only Son so that we could have eternal life. (John 3:16)

- **Mark** As we read of Jesus ministry, notice how many times the phrases "He healed many, He healed them all", are used. Jesus' heart was very generous with bringing comfort and healing to people (Mk. 3:9 – 12).

- 3:13 *"called to Him those He Himself wanted"*. The call of God is extended to so many.
- 3:20 – 22 During this time, so many wonderful things are happening through the ministry of Jesus. This would be called a revival today. But whenever God is moving the enemy stirs up opposition and trouble – it should not surprise us when during times of blessing there is a corresponding challenge that arises. Do not be disheartened, the Lord's strength is sufficient for both!
- 3:28 The unpardonable sin: "not so much an act as a state of sin, a settled attitude that regards good as evil and evil as good....Willful blindness and rejection of the truth had resulted in such spiritual insensibility that they could no longer recognize the truth and were immune to its convicting power." (SFLB)
- The only sin that Jesus will not forgive is an unconfessed sin, or a sin unrecognized through continual hardening of the heart. (1 John 1:9)
- 4:1-20 The Parable of the Sower.
- 4:8 Hear the language and the expectation of the harvest: "Yielded a crop that … increased and produced" – "thirty, sixty and one hundred times".
- When it comes to harvest, the kingdom heart of Jesus for His church is that it be multiplied.
- When the word of God is sown faithfully, it will "yield increase and produce". If there is never any fruit we have good reason to examine the seed we're using. Or worse, that we have put the seed away completely – we're not even sowing!
- Vs. 17 Watch for one another – tribulation and persecution cause people to stumble – encourage each other.
- Vs. 19 Underline the three things that Jesus names that "choke" the word so that it is "unfruitful."
- In our work for the Lord we should always be looking for the "good soil". Put energy into the good soil, the harvest will far surpass any of the losses on other kinds of soil.

"Let no cross be considered too heavy to be borne in following Christ; no loss too great to be sustained for Christ; and no path too holy in going after Christ."

James B. Taylor (1801 – 1829)

DAY 198

📖 2 KINGS 4:1 – 7
📖 MARK 4:21 – 32

🔑 K E Y   T H O U G H T S

- First thought today: "Do you believe in miracles?" If so, do you only believe in miracles that you can understand? An important threshold of faith to cross is this, believing in a miracle is believing in the One who performs it, He (the Lord) is able to do anything. ANYTHING!

- Never approach a supernatural miracle from a naturalistic perspective – it is an intervention into the normal order of things by the Author of all things. If we accept and believe in creation, then Noah's ark, Jonah's whale, the manna, the walking on the water… are all within His ability to do.

- I believe in miracles!

- **2 Kings 4:6** I've always wondered if they really exhausted all the possible sources for 'vessels'. When there were no more containers to hold the blessing, the miracle provision stopped.

- The old song urged: *"bring your vessels not a few."* Always be an open vessel for more of the blessing of God, the oil of the Holy Spirit – the power of His working in us.

- **Mark 4:21ff** – Jesus emphasizes the power of the "seed" (the word of God, the gospel), in the spread of the Kingdom.

- How often we feel overwhelmed by the size of the task ahead of us, how often we feel like the results seem so small.

- This is a kingdom principle, God is making the seed grow, even seemingly small faith gets results, the light just needs to be allowed to shine.

- Many Christians are guilty of over thinking, over strategizing the seed of God's word, or the power of our testimony – if we will simply, with faith, allow the message to spread – God will guarantee good fruit.

- Be encouraged today – your efforts, your life, your testimony are having an impact – even if we *"(ourselves) do not know how"* (4:27). *"The earth yields crops by itself"*.

- It is the Lord's work to make the seed grow – let's be the ones planting seeds with lots of light added.

QUOTE OF THE DAY

"There is a living God. He has spoken His Word. He means just what He says, and will do all that He has promised."

J. Hudson Taylor (1832 – 1905)

DAY 199

📖 2 KINGS 4:8 – 37
📖 MARK 4:33 – 5:43

⊚ K E Y   T H O U G H T S

- Both our passages today show us the power of persistent faith, faith that does not give up, faith that pushes through barriers to the answer.

- **2 Kings 4** Both the Shunnamite woman and Elisha show considerable determination in seeing the little boy raised from the dead.

- The woman is confident in God "it is well", yet she will not be dissuaded from the urgency of the task by her husband's reasoning, or Elisha's attempt to have Gehazi deal with it.

- Elisha, does not always get his answer immediately, for God's own reasons, there is a process of asking, continuing in faith, asking again, continuing in faith and asking again.

- We do not understand all the avenues of faith, we do not know with precision how faith operates – clearly there are factors and forces involved that are beyond our perspective – the point is; confidence in God, persistence for the answer and, continuing in faith.

- **Mark 4:40** Jesus' question could be asked of all of us; *"why are you so fearful?"* (How are things in your 'little boat' – have you despaired to the point of thinking that He will let you perish?)
- Jesus is able to calm whatever storm is thrashing around your life, have faith today – it is going to be alright.
- 5:15 Jesus is more concerned with people than swine, the townsfolk on the other hand were mostly concerned with their pigs.
- The account of the woman with the issue of blood contains a similar instruction to the Shunnamite – she literally pushes through the crowds to get to Jesus, reaches out her hand and actually grasps the hem of His garment.
- (You have needs in your life, how faith-filled and persistent have you been? Are we convinced to the point of action?)
- Do we believe – *"if only I may touch (Him), I shall be made well?"* (5:28)
- Ask the Lord for your healing, ask Him with confident faith – He is able, He is willing – He has compassion upon your need.
- Our reading concludes with the repeated exhortation from Jesus: vs. 36 *"Do not be afraid; only believe."*

QUOTE OF THE DAY

"Man's extremity is God's opportunity. Jesus will come to deliver just when His needy ones shall sigh, as if all hope had gone forever."

Charles H. Spurgeon (1834 – 1892)

DAY 200

2 KINGS 4:38 – 5:27
MARK 6

KEY THOUGHTS

- **2 Kings 5:11** (How often have we resisted the Lord's simple instruction for our lives?) There are many people with much more knowledge than application in their lives.

- Perhaps this is what the phrase *"knowledge puffs up, but love edifies"* (1 Cor. 8:1), is referring to... a knowledge that puffs up our ego, to think that knowing is enough. Until Naaman actually accepted the word of the Lord and obeyed, he had no breakthrough.

- Gehazi – somehow through all of the association with the powerful ministry of Elisha, this man had not dealt with his own issues, his greed prompted him to lie for the silver and garments, then to cover up to Elisha.

- Isn't it true that once we have deceived ourselves sufficiently to sin, we lose track of who the offense is against? Like this particular prophet, (Elisha) was a good target to try to deceive with another lie?

- Covering up before the Holy Spirit is one of the surest signs that something is amiss in our heart – He already knows, He sees your heart – be open with the Lord, do not hide. He is waiting to restore you, waiting to forgive and release you from the burden of your sin.

- **Mark 6:6, 12, 13** – such a simple directive for what ministry should look like, vs. 12 *"so they went out... "*

- Both readings today have a miraculous multiplication of food – Jesus is certainly a prophet 'like' Elisha, and yet so much more than a prophet. Jesus lives a sinless life, dies on the cross and is resurrected from the dead for our salvation.

- Believe the Lord for your provision, He is able to multiply your supply, trust the Lord for your daily bread.

"Faith does not operate in the realm of the possible. There is no glory for God in that which is humanly possible. Faith begins where man's power ends."

George Meuller (1805 – 1898)

DAY 201

📖 2 KINGS 6:1 – 23
📖 MARK 6:45 – 7:37

◉ K E Y   T H O U G H T S

- **2 Kings 6:16** When we are faced with insurmountable odds against us, (an entire army against Elisha and his servant) – the Lord is always present even though His forces are unseen.

- Remember this promise: *"Do not fear, for those who are with us are more than those who are with them."*

- **Mark 6:52** This passage and those that follow speak a lot to "the heart". (What would your definition of a "hardened heart" be? What is it about a hardened heart that would have caused the disciples to "miss" or "not understand" about the loaves and fishes miracle? How would that be possible?)

- Our human nature has trouble building upon the miracles and faithfulness of the past, we are usually in doubt all over again, every time we need the Lord, regardless of His faithful presence in past situations.

- 7:2-7 Jesus is interested in our hearts, the dead legalism of ceremonial washings, certain foods etc… is not what Jesus is about – he is looking for people – whose hearts are not *"far from Me"* (vs. 7).

- 7:17-23 The heart. We will be tempted often to put stock in the externals, the presentation of a good exterior impression. Jesus is searching for hearts that seek Him, for a person whose "inside" man is true to Him.

- This is why the designation of David as a man after "God's own heart" is so significant. David was not perfect but the inside was continually seeking and returning to the Lord as His source.

- 7:28 Although we do not have the benefit of all the cultural nuances of this conversation – the key thought is that Jesus, in His response, is looking for faith in the woman, He does not refuse her. Don't miss that key point!
- Jesus is looking for people of faith, for people who will simply "believe".

QUOTE OF THE DAY

"A clear conscience is absolutely essential for distinguishing between the voice of God and the voice of the enemy. Unconfessed sin is a prime reason why many do not know God's will."

Winkie Pratney

DAY 202

📖 2 KINGS 6:24 – 7:20
📖 MARK 8

☉ K E Y   T H O U G H T S

- **2 Kings 6:24-7:20** Two interwoven stories: one of a lack of faith, another of the action of faith.
- The officer utters a negative view of God's "windows of heaven" – in other words, "even if God <u>had</u> windows, and if heaven <u>could</u> drop down all its bounty, there is no way that is happening here!" (7:2)
- The four lepers are good illustrations of those who, by faith take action, actually do something rather than just wait to die.
- When the miracle happens, (God is able to cause an entire army to run away based on His intervention), the man without faith – misses the miracle – it passes him by, not only that, it overwhelms and crushes him...
- Jesus says: *"do not be unbelieving but believing."* (John 20:27)

- **Mark 8:17** *"Is your heart still hardened?"* An unbelieving heart. The Lord is often at work right before our eyes, but if our heart is not "believing" we will miss what He is saying and miss what He is doing.
- Vss. 34 – 38 Spend some time today on the thought: *"deny himself and take up his cross and follow Me."*
- True followers of Jesus willingly accept the cross, the cost, of following Jesus.

DAY 203

📖 2 KINGS 8:1 – 6; 9:30 – 37; 10:28 – 31
📖 MARK 9

⊚ K E Y   T H O U G H T S

- **2 Kings 9: 36-37** Jezebel comes to a violent death as was prophesied by Elijah.
- 10:31 Even though Jehu did many good things, this phrase *"he did not depart from the sins of Jeroboam"* will be repeated often in the litany of kings who lived with compromise.
- **Mark 9:23, 24** Believing is the active ingredient that allows all the power of God to flow. This man is a blessing to us all, he articulates a desire to believe but also an honest confession of his struggle.
- Perhaps you can identify with this man – if you have the desire to believe that can be your first prayer – *"Lord help my unbelief"*. Jesus was more than willing to answer this prayer.
- Vs. 29 There will be certain obstacles that will present such a challenge that they will require "prayer and fasting" – the spiritual preparation of a season of purifying and spiritual focus. (Have you made prayer and fasting part of your spiritual life?)

- 9:34 This is hard to believe from our perspective, arguing about who would be the greatest. But perhaps our ambition or ego is just as present, just not as out in the open.

- Vs. 35 *"Last of all and servant of all"* – has this attitude been one that characterizes you?

- Vss. 42ff This passage is a dramatic way of teaching that nothing is more valuable or precious than our eternal soul. Jesus teaches by way of contrast – the loss of a hand or an eye would be nothing compared to spending eternity in "torment".

- Jesus is not teaching violent dismemberment, but rather that we are to be severe with the things that separate us from God. Temptation is to be anticipated, don't go to the places where it lurks, waiting to trap you.

- Set up safeguards for yourself, find someone to help with accountability – it is worth the effort to preserve your soul!

QUOTE OF THE DAY

"If God were not my friend, Satan would not be so much my enemy."

Thomas Brooks (1608 – 1680)

DAY 204

📖 2 KINGS 12
📖 MARK 10

⊙ K E Y   T H O U G H T S

- **2 Kings 12** Joash becomes king as a child – as long as he is under the direction of the godly priest Jehoida, there is spiritual renewal and a return to the worship of God.

- Once Jehoida dies, Joash drifts and does not continue in the path that he once walked. We can have an important influence on children and young people that are in our lives.

- Often with encouragement they will choose to follow the Lord, don't underestimate the power of encouragement and mentoring.

- (Who has the Lord put in your life that you could call on in the Lord?)
- **Mark 10** Those who have great wealth face the challenge of who they will serve – this rich young man could not bring himself to pay the price of setting Jesus on the throne of his life.
- It is not that the wealthy are unable to be saved, it is that once money has found its way to the throne of a heart it is a difficult god to dislodge.
- But, praise God, with God all things are possible!
- 10:45 Jesus came and set the example of what a great person looks like in the Kingdom of God. *"Even the Son of Man did not come to be served but to serve and to give His life a ransom for many."*
- Vss. 46ff Bartimaeus – this marvelous account of a man so desperate to meet Jesus that nothing is going to stop him.
- He makes a scene… calling loudly, continuing to call even after he has been scolded and told to stop!
- Then he throws off his cloak, (a garment that would represent his identity as a beggar) and runs to Jesus.
- Jesus says to him and He says to you and me today: *"what do you want ME to do for you?"*
- This is the heart of God, when faith is added to the desire of God – great things will happen.
- Throw aside anything that is hindering you from getting to Jesus – He is waiting to do wonderful things in your life!

QUOTE OF THE DAY

"We can stand affliction better than we can prosperity, for in prosperity we forget God."

Dwight L. Moody

DAY 205

📖 2 KINGS 13:14 – 21; 14:1-14
📖 MARK 11

◉ K E Y   T H O U G H T S

- **2 Kings** This prophetic incident of taking arrows and striking the ground was to give an indication of the heart of the king.
- His tepid response was lacking the enthusiasm that would have indicated faith – perhaps he was embarrassed at the simplicity of the prophetic act.
- How often it is that pride is a limitation to what the Lord wants to do in our lives, we are so worried about our image or about not feeling awkward that we miss God. It does seem that the Lord requires simple, obedient faith in all circumstances.
- **Mark 11:2-26** Faith and prayer:
- Meditate upon these verses and then ask the question of yourself – is my prayer life reflective of these promises?
- Vs. 24 Growing in prayer, growing in faith should mean that there is an increase of prayer activity in our lives.
- It is often true that our prayer life decreases as things go well – reducing our communion with the Lord.
- Prayer is so much more than just requests and petitions – it is about fellowship with the Holy Spirit, a closeness in spirit to the things of the Lord.
- Then there are the needs that we bring to Jesus. Asking in faith is a consistent instruction in Jesus teaching – the Lord is looking for faith!

QUOTE OF THE DAY

"There are two kinds of faith. There is the natural faith. But the supernatural faith is the gift of God."

Smith Wigglesworth (1859-1947)

DAY 206

2 KINGS 15:1 – 7; 32 – 37; 17:5 – 23

MARK 12:1 – 40

KEY THOUGHTS

- **2 Kings 17:5-23** is a summary of the rebellion and sin of the northern 10 tribes. The end result of their idolatry and rejection of God was conquest and captivity to Assyria.

- **Mark 12:14** The Pharisee's use a ploy of flattery to try to trick Jesus – they speak something that is true (*"You are true... teach the way of God in truth"*).

- Flattery is always dangerous to listen to, there is usually some hidden motive – Jesus affirms the lawful paying of taxes.

- Vss. 24-27 Jesus affirms life after death, a resurrection life where past people are known – *"He is the God of the living"*.

- Vss. 30, 31 Jesus confirms both the great commandment and the use of the OT to affirm timeless principles.

- He then adds the principle regarding neighbor, to love our neighbor as ourselves.

- In the parable of the good Samaritan someone asks "who is my neighbor?" trying to create technicalities for not wanting to love the wrong person.

- Jesus makes it clear that we are the neighbor, this commandment includes family, friends, acquaintances, business associates and strangers.

- For Jesus to say *"there is no other commandment greater than these"* is very significant.

- Vs. 40 These religious leaders were using religious loopholes and their position to take financial advantage of widows. Self-righteousness is a very devious condition – seek to walk humbly and authentically before the Lord.

"I want the whole Christ for my Saviour, the whole Bible for my book, the whole Church for my fellowship, and the whole world for my mission field."

John Wesley (1703-1791)

DAY 207

📖 2 KINGS 17:24 – 41
📖 MARK 12:41 – 13:37

⊛ K E Y   T H O U G H T S

- **2 Kings 17:24** This is the explanation for the people known in the NT as the Samaritans. They were a mixed race by design of a conquering king – part of the domination of one nation over another was the systematic destruction of the culture and religion of the conquered nation.

- Vs. 33 *"They feared the Lord, yet served their own gods."* Syncretism is the blending of religions, in this case adding idols to the worship of God – the idea that when it comes to gods – "more is better".

- Vs. 35b states God's instruction clearly – the legacy of this religious watering down was a form of religion with no heart, no soul and just the trappings of true relationship with God (vs. 41).

- **Mark 12:41ff** The widow's mite. Jesus honors this disadvantaged woman for her faith. Her giving is evidence of her complete trust in God for all of her needs. The principle to apply to our hearts is always – "how much is left over, not how much did I give?"

- Sacrifice is an integral part of the gospel.

- 13:10 This key indicator that Jesus gives has been and continues to be a deep motivator for renewed efforts to evangelize the world. This is where we get the idea of "speeding" the Lord's return.

- In prophetic passages there is usually a *"now and not yet"* perspective. There will be an application in the moment that the prophecy is given, as well as a future fulfillment yet to come.

- 13:32-37 This teaching that no one knows the day or the hour is consistently dismissed by people who like to set dates – Jesus says – *"don't do it!"*

- The strategy for believers living in the last days, (that is us right now) – is to *"watch"*. The worst scenario is to be unprepared.

- So Jesus summarized this whole teaching with one word – "WATCH".

- Take a few moments right now to think of what watching for the Lord's return would look like in your life. Perhaps there are some things that need to change.

QUOTE OF THE DAY

"No one has the right to hear the gospel twice, while there remains someone who has not heard it once."

Oswald J. Smith

DAY 208

📖 2 KINGS 18
📖 MARK 14:1 – 42

⊚ K E Y   T H O U G H T S

- **2 Kings 18** Hezekiah is another one the great revivalist kings of Judah. Revival always includes the removal of what is not godly and the restoration of what is godly.

- Vs. 4 Notice that the people had taken the bronze serpent used of God in the miracle in the wilderness and had turned it into an idol. The name Nehushtan means "unclean thing".

- The siege of Jerusalem is noteworthy because of the propaganda of the enemy. The essence of the psychological assault is this: your God is just like all the other gods and we beat them badly, you will also be beaten.

- *"Your God, told us to come and take your city!"*
- We must not listen to counsel or wisdom or mockery from those who are avowed enemies of the Lord – they will use intimidation, mockery, name calling and threats to move you off of your solid trust in the Lord. Listen to the voice of the Lord, listen to the word of God not to God haters who spout opinions on matters they know nothing about.
- **Mark 14:29** God bless Peter. He is such an encouragement to all of us who have ever been overconfident in ourselves. Peter even dismisses all the other disciples – saying that he will be the only one who will not betray Jesus.
- *"Could you not watch one hour?"* Our prayer life must be marked by specific times of prayer. (When do you pray? How often and how long do you pray?) These were significant questions for Jesus in teaching his disciples.
- 14:36 Jesus shows us how to lay our petitions before the Lord and then submit our will fully to His will – HE remains good and faithful even if the road ahead is difficult.

QUOTE OF THE DAY

"A revival of religion presupposes a decline."

Charles Finney

DAY 209

📖 2 KINGS 19
📖 MARK 14:43 – 73

✦ K E Y   T H O U G H T S

- **2 Kings 19:14** Hezekiah's action of petition before the Lord is a stirring sign of faith. The Lord does see, He does hear, HE does answer!
- There are times of desperation in all of our lives where we feel as Hezekiah did, perhaps you have a list of needs or a situation that requires a miracle – lay it before the Lord in prayer today.

(vs. 20) He hears.

- **Mark 14:50** Think of this…they all! After three years of eating and living together, experiencing all that they did – and all of them run. The only possible conclusion is that you and I would have run as well… sobering thought isn't it?

- (Have you ever run from a confrontation to your faith?) The good news is you can always run back as fast as you ran away! The Lord will receive your new humbled heart.

- Peter's famous denial: Peter is the picture of human inconsistency – he is you and me.

- Judgment of Peter is unwarranted. If you or I had all of our inconsistencies recorded for all of history to read in the volume of reading that Peter has had – we would be very quiet in our condemnation of this brother.

- Jesus knowing of Peter's weakness had tried to prepare him, tried to warn Him. By doing so Jesus was making it clear that even though Peter would fail, Jesus' heart was that he would overcome and not give in to temptation.

- And, that Jesus would still love him, still restore him, still use him mightily.

- Do not allow your struggles or failures to distance you from the Lord. The worst thing we can do is to isolate ourselves from Jesus out of guilt, we must run to Him immediately – make things right and then serve out the experience gained.

QUOTE OF THE DAY

"After grief for sin there should be joy for forgiveness."

A.W. Pink

DAY 210

📖 2 KINGS 20
📖 MARK 15

☀ KEY THOUGHTS

- **2 Kings 20** Hezekiah displays a determined heart of prayer – there is much to be learned from Hezekiah's prayer life. Even after the prophet has pronounced his death Hezekiah holds on in faith.

- He does not give up his faith because of the circumstances – he is willing to trust God! Notice that he is not in denial, he is not saying things that are not true, but rather, he is coming as a child to a loving father and presenting his need.

- The response of God through the prophet – *"I (the Lord), will heal you"*, is a marvelous miraculous answer to prayer.

- The use of medicine as the means does not diminish the supernatural cure – God is able to use medical/miraculous means to display His power.

- This is not a proof for medicine only or a lack of the miraculous – the sun dial moving back ten degrees is ample proof that this whole incident is God at work.

- Pride is a very destructive force in any life. This man of God, so mightily used and blessed, somehow gives in to proud displays.

- Perhaps late in life he forgot Who it was who had given all that he had, and Who had worked through Hezekiah to do all he had done.

- Just a warning, we're about to meet Manasseh – possibly the worst king of all Judah – Hezekiah's son, a tragic legacy.

- **Mark 15:2** There are a number of amazing statements of Christ's divinity in these passages – look back to 14:62, and ahead to 15:39 – there is no doubt in Jesus' mind or the minds of those witnessing the crucifixion who He was.

- Vs. 32 This continuous mocking, taunting cry – *"that we may see and then believe"* - is not the call of a sincere or searching heart – it is the sarcasm of a hardened opponent.

- Jesus says in Luke 16:31 *"…neither will they be persuaded though one rise from the dead."*

- The walk of faith is to "believe" first and then the "seeing" follows - we believe and then we see.

QUOTE OF THE DAY

"Faith does not grasp a doctrine, but a heart. The trust which Christ requires is the bond that unites souls with Him; and the very life of it is entire committal of myself to Him in all my relations and for all my needs, and absolute utter confidence in Him as all sufficient for everything that I can require."

Alexander MacLaren

DAY 211

2 KINGS 21:1 – 18
MARK 16

KEY THOUGHTS

- **2 Kings 21** Manasseh goes further into idolatry and syncretism than all who have gone before him.

- 2 Kings 21 lists 11 specific things that he brought into Judah. Notice how most of the idols and activity are brought to Jerusalem and even into the very temple of God!

- His violence and bloodshed accompanied the acceptance of foreign gods.

- Manasseh's son Amon reigns only two years and then he is murdered – remarkably Josiah, the greatest revivalist king of Judah is the grandson of Manasseh.

- **Mark 16** He is Risen – thinking back to Easter again, this most remarkable day of hope.

- Vs. 6 *"He is risen! He is not here."* The tomb is still empty, Jesus is alive today just as He was that first Easter Sunday morning.

- (What aspect of your life is needing a resurrection today? Has your faith been buried by the skepticism and doubts of the culture around you?)
- (Have your finances been buried by reversal or calamity?)
- "Lord Jesus bring Your resurrection power into my life today. Bring my faith to life again!"
- Why don't you speak the words today – "He is Risen, Christ is risen indeed."
- Mark notes that the angel included a special note to Peter, (vs. 7) *"and Peter"*. Heaven's plans for our lives are supported by the grace of God. All of heaven was pulling for Peter.
- All of heaven is on your side as well, allow the Lord to bring His hope and purpose to pass today as you follow Him.
- Vss. 15–18 A very clear commission – we are to go, to preach and bring the gospel to every creature, all must hear!
- Vs. 16 The formula of believing and baptism, indicating initial commitment and public confession. Baptism is not a means of salvation, but rather the public acknowledgement of what Christ has done in a heart.
- In most cultures baptism is the point of no return, it is the renouncing of a former religion and adopting of all that Jesus is – many people experience rejection and persecution only after baptism.
- We should expect all the promised signs and wonders with the proclamation of the gospel – the Lord will confirm His word to people's hearts.

QUOTE OF THE DAY

"You have nothing to do but to save souls. Therefore spend and be spent in this work. And go not only to those that need you, but to those that need you most. It is not your business to preach so many times, and to take care of this or that society; but to save as many souls as you can; to bring as many sinners as you possibly can to repentance."

John Wesley (1703 – 1791)

DAY 212

⊙ K E Y T H O U G H T S

- **2 Kings 22** This passage is such inspiration for those longing for revival.
- The need for revival presupposes a declension in true worship and holiness (Finney) – revival is when a person or people who once knew and once walked in the ways of the Lord have drifted away, or even willfully rebelled against God.
- Someone, comes upon the ways of the Lord, dedicates themselves fully and begins to take a stand. The Spirit of the Lord is drawn to such fervor and begins to bless – revival follows.
- Revival is marked by repentance, by purging and cleansing of all ungodly and worldly practices, and a return to passionate and singular worship of the Living God.
- Josiah undoes practices dating back to Solomon and notably to Jeroboam – the alternate altars.
- As you read through 2 Kings 23 – allow your heart to be transported to this time – imagine the turmoil, imagine the opposition by those who worshipped these idols,
- The families of those executed for their wickedness, all the people now unemployed because of the destruction of ungodly worship – revival has a very high price, it is very costly – it is not utopia.
- (Does your heart long for revival? Do you ache for a move of God – join me in calling on the Lord today.)
- And then, true revival begins in your heart and mine – it begins with me.
- Vs. 25 gives the description of why Josiah was such a wonderful reformer and revivalist – *".... Who turned to the Lord with all his heart, with all his soul, and with all his might."*
- "Oh God, bring a revival to my heart, cleanse me of my rebellious ways, restore the joy of my salvation, renew me in

Your Holy Spirit – bring Your fire Lord, bring Your fire to my heart."

DAY 213

📖 2 KINGS 23:26 – 30; 24
📖 JAMES 1

⊛ K E Y   T H O U G H T S

- **2 Kings** We are coming to the close of this particular season of Judah's history, the kings although under tribute still have a measure of autonomy.

- 24:13 is such a sad picture of the dismantling of all the images of the past glorious worship of Yahweh.

- Sin and rebellion have consequences in this life – the wickedness and idolatry of the previous kings was indeed carrying consequences into the future generations.

- **James 1:2** (Have you been able to come to this perspective in your life – 'joy in trials'?)

- Vs. 5 Ask today, He will give wisdom 'liberally'.

- Vs. 12 Endurance is called a blessing – endurance through (trial), temptation is one of the marks of a person with a deep walk with God, there will be a reward for those people.

- Vs. 22 It is so dangerous to grow in knowledge and not in practice. Knowledge, "been there done that" attitudes are very harmful to a dedicated walk with God – we must be 'doers' of the word.

- James has a lot to say about speech and the tongue, the power of words. He says here, quite strongly, that without evidence of Christ's Lordship over our speech – the 'religion' we profess is "useless!"

- Vs. 27 Consider what it would mean to be *"unspotted from the world".*

DAY 214

📖 2 KINGS 25:1 – 21
📖 JAMES 2

⊛ K E Y T H O U G H T S

- **2 Kings 25** The fall and captivity of Jerusalem – so tragic, such sorrow and heartache, all because of willful rebellion against God and His ways.
- God's heart was to bless, to provide, to protect – but by stepping outside of God's promises and seeking 'other' gods, the children of Israel eventually reaped the harvest of the sinful seeds they had been sowing.
- **James 2:9** Partiality to the rich or against the poor is sin.
- We are not saved by the law. (vs. 10)
- This powerful and very practical chapter is attacking a 'faith' that has no practical evidence in the person's life.
- The point of this teaching is that true faith is going to have evidence in the behavior of the believer.
- If the life does not change, the lifestyle is the same, if the character is not increasing in holiness – then what value is the so called faith?
- On vs. 24 "James and Paul do not contradict each other. Paul emphasizes that faith is not religious deeds without a born-

again heart; James stresses that faith is not a born-again heart without deeds. Neither would agree to the validity of an empty creedal faith." (SFLB)

- Vs. 26 summarizes the key thought of the chapter.

QUOTE OF THE DAY

"Faith is not an instinct. It certainly is not a feeling - feelings don't help much when you're in the lions' den or hanging on a wooden Cross. Faith is not inferred from the happy way things work. It is an act of will, a choice, based on the unbreakable Word of a God who cannot lie, and who showed us what love and obedience and sacrifice mean, in the person of Jesus Christ."

Elisabeth Elliot

DAY 215

📖 1 CHRONICLES 16
📖 JAMES 3

⊛ K E Y   T H O U G H T S

- **1 Chronicles 16** This significant event of the Ark of the Covenant being permanently placed in Jerusalem is marked by:

    a) great celebration for all the people including feasting

    b) a psalm of praise offered to God

- If you can, read this psalm out loud – put yourself in the midst of a great throng of people worshipping together.

- Vs. 36 *"Blessed be the Lord God … From everlasting to everlasting!"*

- **James 3:9-12** (What does an audit of your speech reveal? Is there blessing and cursing flowing from the same stream, has your tongue been sanctified along with your heart?)

- Jesus says: *"A good man out of the good treasure of his heart brings forth good; and an evil man out of the evil treasure of his heart brings forth evil. <u>For out of the abundance of the heart his mouth speaks.</u>"* Luke 6:45 (NKJV)

- Vs. 16 If there is confusion and evil in your immediate world, search to see if there is *"envy and self-seeking"* present. James teaches that the fruit of these things is confusion.

- Many times there are circumstances that don't add up, they don't make sense – there will be a motive in the back ground that explains the results.

- Vss. 17 & 18 These two verses provide a motto for godly living. Living in godly wisdom looks like this – we do not look to the world, or to godless voices to provide "self-help". We turn our attention to and look for our models from the scripture.

- (Does my life "sow in peace"? Are the results of the endeavors of my life, this type of harvest?)

QUOTE OF THE DAY

"God doesn't seek for golden vessels, and does not ask for silver ones, but He must have clean ones."

Dwight L. Moody

DAY 216

📖 1 CHRONICLES 28
📖 JAMES 4

✦ K E Y   T H O U G H T S

- **I Chronicles 28: 8-10** David's instructions to Solomon are solid and timeless principles of wisdom.

- Vs. 9 We are to serve the Lord with a "loyal heart" and a "willing mind". Examine your service to the Lord. (How would your life change if these characteristics were increased?)

- *"The Lord searches all hearts and understands all the intent of the thoughts."* We do not fool the Lord, we do not hide from Him, He truly knows what is inside of us.

- Knowing this brings two things to us:

    a) exposure of hidden sin and ungodly motives

b) encouragement, knowing that our hearts truly desire to serve the Lord, we long to be near to Him, but our flesh and our weaknesses display a different behavior

- It is a comfort to be able to go to the Lord when we struggle and be assured that He "knows my heart".

- Vs. 21 When the Lord is building something He prepares the skills and gifts of many people to contribute to the completion of the task. It takes all of the *"willing craftsmen"* to do the work of the Lord.

- **James 4:4** James uses the imagery of the OT, the adultery spoken of here is the unfaithfulness of the heart to be loyal and faithful to God alone. When the people of Israel worshipped idols, they were compared to adulterers, those who break their vows of loyalty.

- (How would you define *"friendship with the world"?*)

- James is very clear cut in his definitions, the NLT says it this way – *"if you want to be a friend of the world you make yourself and enemy of God."* It is impossible to have it both ways.

- 4:8 When we take a step toward the Lord, He is moving toward us at the same time, our initiation is always rewarded by His willingness.

- Vs. 10 Humility is always blessed by God's favor – this theme runs through the entire Bible – the Lord lifts up those who are humble – but He "resists" the proud.

- Think for a moment on the prospect of being "resisted" by God – being "lifted up" is much more desirable.

- Vs. 17 This powerful principle is such a help in those times when there is no clear cut command for a situation. An honest heart, a truthful mind, the inner witness of the Holy Spirit and the counsel of those who are godly will give us the guidance we need.

QUOTE OF THE DAY

"The greatness of a man's power is the measure of his surrender."

William Booth

DAY 217

📖 1 CHRONICLES 29
📖 JAMES 5

⊚ KEY THOUGHTS

- **1 Chronicles 29** David's personal generosity to the work of the building of the temple is a great example to his people.

- 29:5 "Who then is willing to consecrate himself this day to the Lord?"

- When we are willing to serve and to give, it is an indication of a consecrated or "set apart" heart to the Lord. Giving is always an indicator of the heart of the believer.

- Vs. 9 *"With a loyal heart they had offered willingly."* (Does this description fit our hearts?)

- Vs. 16 A key to a generous heart is the understanding of Who owns all that we have. Everything we have is from "the hand" of the Lord and is His own!

- **James 5** This chapter is an important guide for ministry and for prayer.

- Vs. 13-14 gives instruction for those suffering, cheerful, and sick.

- The practice of calling for elders, anointing with oil, laying on of hands and praying a prayer of (the) faith, (or the gift of faith), is a beautiful provision for the needs of those who are a sick among us.

- The person is saved from the sickness (not a connection to salvation), the oil is a symbol of the Holy Spirit and of the person's consecration to the process of God's healing power.

- 5:16-18 is one of the strongest, most encouraging passages on prayer.

- The summary of this section is that prayer makes a difference, prayer changes things. We are to be encouraged in prayer and to pray more.

- Elijah was no different than you and I, dear one. Pursue a fuller, deeper life of prayer.

- The final two verses of James' appeal for the body of Christ is to watch out for one another and to go after the ones who are stumbling. We are not to just let them wander off.
- This is powerful work in the church. We must care enough about one another to reach out, to challenge, to call one another on for God's glory.

DAY 218

📖 2 CHRONICLES 6 – 7

⊙ K E Y   T H O U G H T S

- **2 Chronicles 6-7** Interesting how at times when the Lord wants us to get a particular message across, that our Bible reading lines up on the same topic.
- This is the second day with a strong focus on prayer.
- In dedicating the temple Solomon offers a lengthy prayer in which he describes various scenarios that may occur.
- The prayer is summarized by the phrase *"then hear from heaven."* As you read this passage underline how many times Solomon says this... it is a remarkable reminder of how convinced we all must be that God is a prayer hearing and prayer answering God.
- The second major feature of his prayer is repentance.

- The assumption here is that God's heart is to bless. However, if the people rebel and willfully walk in sin there will need to be individual and corporate repentance.
- Vs. 40 *"Now, my God, I pray, let Your eyes be open and let Your ears be attentive to the prayer made in this place."*
- 7:12 – 22 is God's response to Solomon's prayer.
- 7:14 is perhaps the best known verse in the Bible on the subject of revival and prayer.
- The key components are:
  - Humble themselves
  - Pray
  - Seek My face
  - Turn from their wicked ways
  - THEN – the Lord will…
  - Hear from heaven
  - Forgive their sin
  - Heal their land
- Join with me: "Oh Lord God, we call upon You today. We are hungry for You to move in our lives and in our church, we turn to You today Lord, we humble ourselves before You. I repent of my sin, my wicked ways, I determine to turn from those ways. Now Lord, hear my prayer, forgive my sin – our sin, and heal our land."

QUOTE OF THE DAY

"Revival comes from heaven when heroic souls enter the conflict determined to win or die - or if need be, to win and die! The kingdom of heaven suffereth violence, and the violent take it by force."

Charles Finney

DAY 219

📖 2 CHRONICLES 20:1 – 30
📖 EPHESIANS 1

⊙ K E Y   T H O U G H T S

- **2 Chronicles 20** When we feel assailed by enemies with overwhelming numbers, we can follow the path that Jehoshaphat and the people took.

- Acknowledge that we do not have the answers and that we are looking to the Lord alone (vs. 12) *"our eyes are upon You."*

- Vs. 15 We are not to fear because the battle is not ours but "the Lord's".

- Vs. 17 *"Position yourself, stand still and see the salvation of the Lord, who is with you."* Be prepared for battle, get ready in heart, mind, soul – purify yourself. Do all that we know to do to be in a place where nothing in us will hinder the workings of God.

- The actual working part of this military campaign is praise! They lifted their voices *"loud and high".*

- *"Praise the Lord, For His mercy endures forever."*

- Vs. 22 Notice the sequence of victory – *"Now when they began to sing and to praise"* – *"the Lord set ambushes ...."*

- As we sing and praise there is spiritual power released in the heavens, there is a strategic power to singing, praise and worship. The presence of God dwells in the praises of His people (Psalm 22:3).

- Whatever you are facing today, begin to praise the Lord, to sing, to acknowledge Him in worship. This is an effective and strategic means of victory.

- **Ephesians 1:7** We have so many blessings in Christ;

  a) *"redemption through His blood"* redeemed out of debt, the debt of our sins, Jesus has paid the penalty/fines for us

  b) *"forgiveness of sins according to the riches of His grace".* What joy to know that the measure and availability of forgiveness is *"the riches of His grace"*.

- Vss. 17-19 list three blessings that Paul prays for the Ephesians – all are relating to wisdom that only God by His Spirit is able to give to us. So many blessings and resources are yours in Christ.

- Vss. 20-23 Jesus is the highest, above all, no other power, principality or foe can even compare with His authority and rule. His name is above EVERY name.

- All of these gifts and promises are for the church, that His fullness might be displayed to a lost and dying world.

- Give thanks and praise to the Lord today! Bring an offering of worship to Him. Allow your heart to be encouraged in these massive promises.

QUOTE OF THE DAY

"Unless God has raised you up for this very thing, you will be worn out by the opposition of men and devils. But if God be for you, who can be against you? Are all of them together stronger than God? O be not weary of well doing!"

John Wesley

DAY 220

📖 2 CHRONICLES 29
📖 EPHESIANS 2

⊚ K E Y   T H O U G H T S

- **2 Chronicles 29:5** This is a straightforward description of revival – the instruction to *"carry out the rubbish from the holy place"* is a fitting instruction for every one of us.

- We naturally accumulate rubbish in the place of our heart that should be devoted to God alone. Inspection of our life, every facet of our life, is vital to ongoing spiritual vitality.

- (Is there any rubbish in your life – anything that is not sanctified or consecrated to the Lord?)

- Vs. 16 describes it as "debris". If we don't clear out the debris then our worship will not be effective. Our relationship with God will be like trying to walk through a junk-filled room with the lights off – we end up stumbling and disoriented.

- Purity is about singleness of heart, it's about the ability to see clearly, to evaluate wisely, to walk near to the Lord.
- Vs. 36 When the Lord has prepared people's hearts, when He begins to move – things can happen *"suddenly"*.
- **Ephesians 2** This chapter is filled with so much depth and meat, what a blessing the Bible is!
- Vss. 8-10 These verses should be memorized by every believer – they are a solid anchor against much wrong doctrine.
- Vs. 13 As gentiles, our place in God seemed far off. As sinners we were far away because of our sin. And yet, Because of the blood of Jesus we have brought near! Praise God, drawn into a living relationship with the living God.
- Vs. 14 Jesus is our peace – our peace with God, settling the account, making a way for us, giving us the right to be His sons and daughters.
- Vs. 20 Jesus Himself is the chief cornerstone of the church and we all (vs. 22) are being built together to be a place where the Spirit of the Lord dwells – Hallelujah!
- We are God's building, we are being fitted together to grow into a holy temple in the Lord. What amazing grace is shown to us by the Lord!
- You and I are actually being shaped by the Master Builder, into something glorious, something for His glory. We are so privileged to be part of His plan. Choose to serve Him joyfully today.

QUOTE OF THE DAY

"We believe that to Christ belongs creative power--that "without Him was not anything made which was made." We believe that from Him came all life at first. He is the fountain of life. We believe that as no being comes into existence without His creative power, so none continues to exist without His sustaining energy. We believe that the history of the world is but the history of His influence, and that the center of the whole universe is the cross of Cavalry."

Alexander MacLaren (1826 – 1910)

DAY 221

📖 2 CHRONICLES 30
📖 EPHESIANS 3

🖋 K E Y   T H O U G H T S

- **2 Chronicles 30:6-11** In a season of spiritual revival there will be people who will laugh and mock at the call to "return to the Lord".

- Not everyone embraces a move of God, not everyone believes.

- But those who do push in to the moving of the Holy Spirit will find themselves filled with *"great gladness"* (vs. 21), *"rejoicing"* (vs. 25) and whole cities can be *"filled with joy"* (vs. 26).

- (Will you believe with me for a fresh season of the outpouring of God's power in our region?) How we long for days of refreshing, days of revival, where the things of God are of such preeminence in our lives that nothing else really matters.

- Souls coming to Christ, backsliders returning, people being baptized in the Holy Spirit, sick bodies healed, those in bondage delivered, the operation of all the gifts of the Holy Spirit, an unstoppable spirit of generosity and … the testimony of Christ spreading from one person to another all through the city.

- **Ephesians 3:10** God has placed such an important trust upon the church. Proving to principalities and powers the full wisdom of God. It is through the church, despite its blemishes, yet still through the church, the glory of God is made known to the entire world. Amazing!

- We must not disqualify, criticize, malign and gossip about Christ's church – we are those who labor for the building up and strengthening of this most valued body, Christ's body, called 'the church'.

- Vss. 16-19 describe four beautiful resources for the believer. Paul prays:

    1) *"That they may be strengthened with might through His Spirit in the inner man."*

2) *"That Christ may dwell in your hearts through faith."*

3) That they might know the massive dimensions of *"the love of Christ that passes knowledge",* and

4) *"That they may be filled with all the fullness of God."*

- Make those four things your request to the Lord today, right now... "Lord I ask that You would...." Make it personal, God bless you today in His riches.

QUOTE OF THE DAY

"The backslider likes the preaching that wouldn't hit the side of a house, while the real disciple is delighted when the truth brings him to his knees."

Billy Sunday (1862-1935)

DAY 222

📖 2 CHRONICLES 31:1 – 12, 20 – 21; 32:1 – 8, 20 – 26
📖 EPHESIANS 4:1 – 16

" WHEN YOU SEE A READING THAT IS MOVING QUICKLY THROUGH A COUPLE OF CHAPTERS, TAKE A MOMENT BEFORE YOU BEGIN, TO MARK THE CHOSEN PASSAGES FOR THE DAY IN THE MARGIN OF YOUR BIBLE. "

◉ K E Y   T H O U G H T S

- **2 Chronicles 31** This passage outlines the ground shaking transformation in the hearts of the people, evidenced by their overwhelming generosity in giving.

- They brought their first fruits, their tithes of everything plus freewill offerings, for the care and provision of the worship of God, for the priests and for the house of God.

- True revival shows true change in one of the most tightly held parts of our hearts; the money part. A generous, releasing spirit is truly an evidence of a move of God.

- 32:7, 8 These are great words of encouragement when you are facing opposition or enemies *"with him (the enemy), is the arm of flesh; but with us is the Lord our God, to help us and to fight our battles".*

- Vs. 25 gives us further insight into the matter of Hezekiah's later life – *"his heart was lifted up"*, pride was his downfall. After so much good, Hezekiah failed to give God glory and fell into the trap of pleasing people instead of the Lord.

- Even though he did humble himself, the consequence of his sin was visited upon the next generation.

- Let us live our lives so that the next generation is blessed beyond our blessings, advances beyond our advances, and is set up to conquer not to be put into bondage.

- **Ephesians 4:2** describes what a walk that is *"worthy of the calling with which you were called"*, looks like:

  - *"all lowliness and gentleness, with longsuffering, bearing with one another in love."*

  - The all-important endeavor to *"keep the unity of the Spirit in the bond of peace."*

- We are all called to live this way toward one another – the Lord will provide ample opportunities to grow in this regard, accept the challenge, grow in love, preserve the unity of the Spirit.

- Vss. 7-10 are variously interpreted and at times connected to 1 Peter 3:19 and or Acts 2:25-35, or Philippians 2:5-11. It is important not to go beyond the words of the text.

- The Spirit Filled Life Bible commentary says: "With reference to the view that He descended into hell, there is no biblical support for the notion that Jesus suffered in hell, only that He descended to Sheol to release the righteous dead into eternal glory, proclaiming the adequacy of the Atonement and validating the testimony of the prophets."

- 4:11 The five-fold gifts of Jesus for the ministry of the church make sense when we connect them with vs. 12 – *"for the equipping of the saints for the work of ministry, for the edifying of the body of Christ."*

- Vss. 13 - 16 describe a picture of a maturing, growing, loving church, every part being important, every part acknowledging the value of the others, all working together in harmony for God's glory!

- (Are you giving your ministry to the Lord's people... are you receiving ministry from the Lord's people?)

"Revival cannot be organized, but we can set our sails to catch the wind from heaven when God chooses to blow upon His people once again."

G. Campbell Morgan (1863-1945)

DAY 223

📖 2 CHRONICLES 34
📖 EPHESIANS 4:17 – 32

⊚ K E Y   T H O U G H T S

- **2 Chronicles 34:3** Josiah becomes king at a very young age. Notice that when he is sixteen he begins to seek the *"God of his father David."*

- The Lord is able to move powerfully in the hearts of children and young people, it appears that Josiah develops a heart for God, a heart that seeks the Lord. The results are the most sweeping and complete revival in all of Judah's history.

- Also noteworthy is the fact that Josiah's grandfather was the most notoriously evil king of Judah and his father was worse! (His father reigned only two years).

- God is able to raise up beauty out of ashes. He is able to resurrect people from the most unusual and least expected sources – God is bigger than a person's ancestry!

- Josiah's heart is for the Lord regardless of the reward. In spite of the revivals and reforms of Josiah's leadership, the judgment of God was still pending over Judah. This was because of the sins of the previous kings.

- Josiah seeks the Lord because it is right, he seeks the Lord because the Lord is good, he seeks the Lord because he loves the Lord – this is an example of a beautiful heart for God.

- **Ephesians 4:17 - 24** Being devoted followers of Jesus means that there will be tangible changes in our lifestyles. The old ways of living, *"given over to lewdness"*, the *"old man"* – those old ways of living – are to be decidedly *"put off"*.

- The image is of an old garment and a new garment – putting the old off, and putting the new on.
- We see a description of the old man from vs. 22.
- What is it that is to be renewed? (vs. 23)
- What does the *"new man"* look like? (vs. 24)
- Understanding the concept of grieving the Holy Spirit is to understand the Holy Spirit is a person who is faithful to convict and direct our steps toward godliness and holiness.
- If we continually snub and ignore the promptings of the Holy Spirit there is a grieving in the relationship. If this continues willfully there can be a *"searing"* or cauterizing of the conscience to the place where the voice of the Spirit is no longer in our frequency of hearing.
- This section contains very practical, specific behaviors and attitudes that are to have no place in the life of the believer.
- Our relationships with the other believers are also fully accountable to God (vs. 32).

QUOTE OF THE DAY

"What he needs is not increased spiritual teaching but an obedient heart which is willing to yield his life to the Holy Spirit and go the way of the cross according to the Spirit's command. Increased spiritual teaching will only strengthen his carnality and serve to deceive him into conceiving himself as spiritual."

Watchman Nee (1903-1972)

DAY 224

📖 2 CHRONICLES 36:11 – 23
📖 EPHESIANS 5:1 – 21

◉ K E Y   T H O U G H T S

- **2 Chronicles 36:11-23** This passage fills in the final gaps of the history of Judah prior to her captivity in Babylon.
- Vs. 36 states the three pronged attitudes of rebellion that had

characterized these people:

1) they mocked the messengers of God

2) despised His words

3) scoffed at His prophets…. *"till there was no remedy".*

- Vss. 22, 23 skip forward about 60 years to the season when permission is granted for a few of the Jews to begin returning from exile.

- The Lord moves upon the heart of a godless king (Cyrus), to bring fulfillment to the prophetic words of Jeremiah.

- **Ephesians 5:3** These sins and behaviors are not even to be named among believers – we are to have no part of them.

- Fornication – this refers to all forms of sexual immorality. There is no grey area with God on this matter, there is to be no sexual activity prior to or outside of marriage. So whether it is heterosexual, homosexual, consenting adults, common law partners, or any other man made exceptions… be clear.

- *"no fornicator"… "has any inheritance in the kingdom of Christ and God".*

- Meaning, any person, who willfully, continually, with no intent of turning away, stays in their sexual immorality, is not showing evidence of a transformed heart.

- The tense here is present, this is not referring to actions in the past that are under the blood, this is referring to those calling themselves a follower of Christ and yet refusing to bring the sexual area of their lives under the authority of the holiness of God.

- Vs. 18 Drunkenness is forbidden, the sinful behaviors that accompany it are what the apostle is trying to protect us from.

- The tense of being filled with the Spirit as opposed to drunk with wine, is present and continuous. Being filled with the Spirit is not a single, one time moment – but rather, an ongoing, continuing re-filling throughout our relationship with the Holy Spirit.

- *"keep on being filled with the Spirit"* – would be a good way of phrasing verse 18.

- Encouraging one another in fellowship is such an important part of why we gather together in the church – we are to serve each other with the ministry of encouragement, songs, hymns, and testimony.

QUOTE OF THE DAY

"People pay attention when they see that God actually changes persons and sets them free. When a new Christian stands up and tells how God has revolutionized his or her life, no one dozes off. When someone is healed or released from a life-controlling bondage, everyone takes notice."

Jim Cymbala

DAY 225

📖 JEREMIAH 1, 2
📖 EPHESIANS 5:22 – 33

☞ K E Y   T H O U G H T S

- **Jeremy 1** Jeremiah's call to ministry is encouraging to us in these ways:

    a) his calling was in the heart of God from when he was in the womb - God's love and knowledge of our lives is far beyond our understanding (1:5).

    b) Jeremiah is hesitant because of his youthfulness – when God calls someone and the call is affirmed by the Holy Spirit and by evident grace upon the life, age is not the primary qualification. God uses young people! (vss. 7, 8)

    c) When the Lord calls us to serve Him He will also provide the courage and the resources that we need to fulfill the task He has asked of us (vss. 17-19).

- Israel was looking to both other gods (idols, that are *"not gods"*), and to political and military alliances with foreign nations, instead of putting their trust entirely in the Lord (2:13).

- Our allies must be those that the Lord approves (vs. 37).

- **Ephesians 5** Christian marriage / Christ and His Church.

- The key to understanding this passage on marriage is to

keep the responsibility of the husband in balance with the responsibility of the wife – the two together make a great marriage.

- There is no "lording over" of the man's authority. The example is Jesus' love and sacrifice for His church. If men would follow Jesus' example, would give themselves to the good and betterment of their wives, there would be no issue with joyful submission and honor.

- 5:33 gives a succinct assignment to both husband and wife

    a) husbands love your wife as you love yourself

    b) wives, respect your husband

- Take care of your side of the assignment, this is not license to judge how well your partner is doing in their part – you do yours and trust the Lord to work in their heart.

- This type of mutual love and respect is the ground that good marriages grow in. If you are unsure of what to do, just go back to the example of Jesus – how did He love? How did He serve? Treat your spouse that way.

QUOTE OF THE DAY

"It is a masterpiece of the devil to make us believe that children cannot understand religion. Would Christ have made a child the standard of faith if He had known that it was not capable of understanding His words?"

Dwight L. Moody

DAY 226

📖 JEREMIAH 3:1 – 15, 22 – 25
📖 EPHESIANS 6

◉ K E Y   T H O U G H T S

- **Jeremiah 3** These passages give us understanding of the longing heart of God for the backslider.

- A backslider is someone who has drifted away from a previous position of loyalty and faithfulness in worship. They have neglected their first love, they have accepted other gods and put their affection on them.

- They were in a right position at one time, but like someone sliding backwards down a hill they have slidden away from God.
- This passage is an appeal, like the call of a father or mother to a wayward child to "come home". It is not a judgmental angry call.
- God affirms His commitment, like marriage to the backslider – He does not give up on them, He loves them, He is waiting for the joyful day of their return.
- Jesus picks up this theme in the parable of the prodigal son.
- If you know a backslider, do not give up on them, call them, invite them, offer to pray with them, they are precious to God's heart (3:22).
- **Ephesians 6:7, 8** As employees/employers, we are instructed about how we are to serve in our work. It is to be unto the Lord. We must ensure that all we do and the way we do it is honoring to God's name.
- The armor of God - each of these pieces has a function for our spiritual safety and advancement. The first instruction is to *"take up"* the armor of God – there is an intentional picking up of the armor – a decision, an action of faith.
- Vs. 16 *"above all"* – the role of the shield of faith is central to all the armor – extinguishing the enemy's lies and accusations with faith is a great skill to learn. This is the proactive role of faith.
- When the enemy lies – we counter with truth and faith in the truth. The practice of speaking the truth audibly in the face of doubt and fear is a powerful weapon for victory.
- Spirit Filled Life Bible commentary on vs. 18 – *"All prayer"* is literally "every order of praying," the specific method by which spiritual warfare is carried on. Prayer is to include supplication in the Spirit, a phrase that elucidates Rom.8:26, 27 and Jude 20, where Holy Spirit assisted prayer is taught and directed. In 1 Cor. 14:14, 15 Paul clearly shows that such praying may include prayer "in a tongue" not known to the person praying."

- Remember who it is that we are fighting (vs. 12). This is the reason that we need spiritual weapons that are equal and above the challenge of the enemy.
- There is victory in Christ Jesus' work on the cross, and in His provision of the Holy Spirit and the spiritual gifts that He gives.

QUOTE OF THE DAY

"We must not confide in the armour of God, but in the God of this armour, because all our weapons are only 'mighty through God.'"

William Gurnall (1617-1679)

DAY 227

📖 JEREMIAH 4:1 – 22
📖 COLOSSIANS 1

✪ K E Y   T H O U G H T S

- **Jeremiah 4** The plea of this 'weeping' prophet, Jeremiah, is to 'return'. Return to the Lord, return to His ways, return to having a loyal heart.
- Vs. 3b contains a familiar metaphor – the idea of breaking up 'fallow' ground.
- The most familiar verse on this theme is found in Hosea. It is a call to return to the Lord, to take personal inventory, to actually accept responsibility for the spiritual condition of our life. *"Sow for yourselves righteousness; reap in mercy, break up your fallow ground, for it is time to seek the LORD, till he comes and rains righteousness on you."* Hosea 10:12
- Fallow ground is unattended, hardened soil that grows no fruitful crops, but is over-run with weeds and thistles. Revival requires each individual to search their heart, to soften their ears to the call to repent and then to dig deeply into the things of God.
- Vs. 22 Notice what the people are wise to do. This is often the

case in a backslidden person, they become skilled at doing the things opposite to what is beneficial.

- **Colossians 1** There is so much in this one chapter – follow some of the highlights:
- Vs. 13 We are delivered from _____, and conveyed into _____ the Son of His _____. Praise the Lord!
- Vs. 14 In Christ we have _____, we've been bought back from the debt of our sins, by His _____ we have _____.

- Vs. 16 Christ's authority – never doubt, whether the Lord Jesus Christ has authority over the dark forces that seek to discourage and disrupt your life! He is the victor, He is triumphant – He is the creator of all that is.

- Vs. 21-23 Notice that apart from Christ we are alienated from God. His desire is to present us in a spectacular manner – His desire for you is good! Above reproach.

- Vs. 23 starts with a very big word – "IF", this is an important understanding – *"if you continue in the faith"*. An effective life for Jesus is an ongoing relationship, a continuance in the faith, not just an event of the past.

- Vs. 27 The hope we have of glory is *"Christ in you!"* The testimony of the believer is an assurance of the things yet to come in God's plan.

- Vs. 29 (Is your testimony the same?) *"His working which works in me mightily."* It is God's will that you experience His mighty power, and that His power work mightily in you. Might, strength, immense power are the dimensions of God's ability to equip and empower you! Receive more of Him today.

QUOTE OF THE DAY

"Take God into thy counsel. Heaven overlooks hell. God at any time can tell thee what plots are hatching there against thee."

William Gurnall, (1617-1679)

DAY 228

📖 JEREMIAH 5:18 – 31
📖 COLOSSIANS 2

⊙ K E Y   T H O U G H T S

- **Jeremiah 5:28** Characteristics of those who are in rebellion against God, treatment of the poor is a consistent indicator of the heart condition and one's nearness to God.

- As bad as the false ministry of the prophets and priests – is the desire of the people who *"love to have it so"*.

- There will always be people who like the sound of false teaching, usually because it give them justification to live in a self-ruled way, doing as they please, living as they choose rather than submitting to the Lordship of Christ's authority.

- **Colossians 2** Establishing and defending the supremacy, authority and rule of Jesus Christ is one of the primary objectives of the letter to the Colossians. Anything that undermines Jesus as the head of the body, the means of salvation, is a false doctrine.

- These people were falling victim to (or willfully adopting) two false means of relationship with God, Paul says they were being "<u>cheated</u>" by these things:
  a) "Philosophy and empty deceit", the ideas of man, basic principles of the world (vs. 8).
  b) The legalistic principles of Judaism, food laws, days and festivals etc... (vs. 16). Claims to higher spiritual revelation than Jesus.

- The word "<u>cheat</u>" is used again in vs. 18 – chasing these false teachings leaves you empty, feeling ripped off, confused.

- Jesus is the head of the body, the church. It is in Him that every gift flows in harmony and fruitfulness.

- Jesus is able, by the Holy Spirit, to give you strength against the indulgence of the flesh (vs. 23). To see God's power evident in our lives is the goal of Christ's Lordship.

- Jesus is most interested in transformed people, not endless arguments, opinions and debate.

DAY 229

📖 JEREMIAH 6:10 – 21; 7:1 – 27
📖 COLOSSIANS 3:1 – 17

☙ K E Y   T H O U G H T S

- **Jeremiah 6:13** The great sin identified here, and the indictment against the nation is that they as a whole were given over to covetousness, (to want somebody else's property, to yearn to have, greed, materialism).

- The picture of vss. 13 -15 is of a people who have lost their sensitivity to God's voice and have plunged head long into finding satisfaction in material and worldly things.

- 7:8-11 This is the hypocrite, the arrogant "Christian" – living a worldly, ungodly life and yet expecting answers to prayer, and proclaiming "special dispensations" of grace. In other words, "I am an exception to the rule, it's ok for me to disobey God and still have my relationship with Him".

- This is a bold and common deception that sin brings to the backslidden heart.

- **Colossians 3:2** An active, determined focus of the mind upon the things of God and the things "above". "Set your mind."

- The themes of "putting off" and "putting on" are repeated images in Scripture to help us understand the process of spiritual growth and godliness.

- The process is a cycle of growth, the putting off makes room for the putting on. Claims of spiritual vitality and position are of no value if the character of the believer is not being transformed in a way that is recognizable.

- Vs. 14 Whenever you see *"above all"* – this is to be highlighted in your heart. Love is the foundation of all character and growth.

- Meditate upon the idea of the *"word of God dwelling in you richly"* (vs. 16).

- As you go through your day, make the conscious decision to let all that you do and think be done in the Name of the Lord – see if there is a change in your attitude.

QUOTE OF THE DAY

"He shows much more of Himself to some people than to others-not because He has favourites, but because it is impossible for Him to show Himself to a man whose whole mind and character are in the wrong condition."

C.S. Lewis.

DAY 230

📖 JEREMIAH 8:18 – 22; 9:24; 10:10 – 16
📖 COLOSSIANS 3:18 – 4:18

☾ K E Y   T H O U G H T S

- **Jeremiah 8:18-22** Jeremiah is known as the weeping prophet. This paragraph gives us insight into the depth of his sorrow and intercession for the people of God.

- The people were glorying in idols and false hope. We are to look to the Lord alone for our strength and encouragement.

- The difference between the true God and false gods is that the Lord is the Living God! The Creator of all that is.

- **Colossians 3:18ff** Practical advice for wives, husbands, children, parents, employees, employers.

- Fathers especially, think through, and ask the Lord for wisdom on the concept of raising children without *"provoking to wrath"*, or causing hardness of heart through anger. Responding to children when we are angry is a sure way to frustrate them.

- Discipline is to be balanced and thoughtful, not tempestuous flare ups that will miss justice and love. Parents are also to be humble enough to admit fault when we have been unkind or have failed the kids.

- 4:2 Note the words *"continue, earnestly"* – this is a persevering, sincere heart that values prayer and makes a lifetime commitment to growing in it.

- Vs. 6 Our speech is to be a witness to the Lord who rules in our heart – out of the heart the mouth speaks.

- 4:7-18 gives us insight into how valuable relationships are in the body of Christ. These are actual individuals who are loved and valued as part of the working of Jesus in the church.

QUOTE OF THE DAY

"Parents provoke their children to anger by not practicing biblical love, not considering their children as more important than themselves, and not dying to self to become a servant of the Lord Jesus Christ."

John C. Broger

DAY 231

📖 JEREMIAH 12
📖 GALATIANS 1, 2

◉ K E Y   T H O U G H T S

- **Jeremiah 12:1-4** The question posed to God by Jeremiah, *"Why do the wicked prosper?"* is a common one in scripture and in our minds as well.

- The answer is never a clearly defined one, the explanations range from:

    a) The appearance of prosperity is temporary.

    b) The eternal prospects for the wicked are not good.

    c) God is still in control of all things, He does all things well, the wicked will answer before God.

d) Financial prosperity in this life is not a substitute for the blessings of God.

- Vs. 5 This is a great proverbial saying, in essence – "if your trust in Me wavers in this "easy" situation, how will you do when things get really tough?"

- The defining characteristic of godliness and relationship with God is "obedience". This is aligning ourselves joyfully with His authority.

- **Galatians 1, 2** Galatians is the clearest treatise in scripture regarding those who came to Christ through faith, then later, started adding on to the grace of Jesus. In this case, it was the ceremonial aspects of Jewish religious law.

- 2:16b *"for by the works of the law no flesh shall be justified."* There is no possible way around this verse, it is a helpful summarizing of the whole argument.

- Vss. 20, 21 Self must be crucified. Trusting in the flesh or in our own strength for any aspect of salvation is wrong thinking – our salvation, our relationship with God is based fully on faith in His grace, His mercy, His love.

- Do not let your behavior or attitudes make the death of Jesus a pointless sacrifice, by thinking that we could ever enhance His work by our own works (vs. 21).

QUOTE OF THE DAY

"Faith, which is trust, and fear are opposite poles. If a man has the one, he can scarcely have the other in vigorous operation. He that has his trust set upon God does not need to dread anything except the weakening or the paralyzing of that trust."

Alexander MacLaren (1826 – 1910)

DAY 232

📖 JEREMIAH 16
📖 GALATIANS 3 – 4:7

☞ K E Y   T H O U G H T S

- **Jeremiah 16** Although, because of Israel's unique relationship with God as His own special people, there is a judgment upon the people for the sins of the past (corporately). This is the real reason for their current situation is vs. 12.

- *"Each one follows the dictates of his own evil heart, so that no one listens to Me"* - hardness of spiritual hearing is the result of continual rebellion.

- **Galatians 3:2** The working of the Holy Spirit in the lives of the Galatians is one of the reasons that the writer urges them to "stick" with the Holy Spirit instead of going back to relying on the works of the law as their righteousness.

- Vss. 5 and 14 reference the ongoing experience with the Holy Spirit.

- "The language he (Paul) uses indicates an experience of the Spirit that extended beyond the Galatians initial reception. The verb "supplies" suggests a continual supplying in bountiful measure, while "works" indicates that God was continuing to perform miracles in their midst through Spirit-filled believers who had not slipped into legalism." (SFLB)

- The position and privilege of the believer as an heir with Abraham and a possessor of the promised blessings of Abraham through the *"promise of the Spirit"* – is such a great encouragement.

- In Christ, race, gender, social status, none of those exterior qualifiers make us right with God or give us standing with Him, it is Christ, and Christ alone – His work, His power, His love.

- 4:4 God has something called the *"fullness of time"*, the time when all of His conditions are right – He alone knows when it is the *"fullness of time"*, He will fulfill every promise when His time is right – depend upon it!

- Vs. 7 THEREFORE! Accept who you are in Jesus today, there

is great grace in this promise, you are not a slave or a hireling – but through Christ you are an heir and a son or daughter. Praise God.

QUOTE OF THE DAY

"Grieve not the Christ of God, who redeems us; and remember that we grieve Him most when we will not let Him pour His love upon us, but turn a sullen, unresponsive unbelief towards His pleading **grace**, as some glacier shuts out the sunshine from the mountainside with its thick-ribbed ice."

Alexander MacLaren

DAY 233

📖 JEREMIAH 17:5 – 18; 18:1 – 11
📖 GALATIANS 4:8 – 5:15

⊙ K E Y   T H O U G H T S

- **Jeremiah 17:8** The imagery of a tree planted by a living stream is a strong reminder of the heart of God for those who trust in Him.
- Freedom from anxiety, and fruitfulness when others are not. The Lord is able to do what no man can do to help and bless you.
- 17:9, 10 (Have you any experience with your heart being deceitful?) Those who have succumbed to temptation will know that in the midst of that struggle the heart can deceive.
- So many persuade themselves that "they can handle it", or "I won't go too far", or "I can quit whenever I want" – all the while the bondage is getting stronger.
- The Lord knows our hearts, He searches them to test them. Purify your heart before the Lord today. Have nothing hidden.
- There will be times when we will be in some desperate situation – in these times we can pray vs. 14 *"Heal me, O Lord, and I shall be healed; Save me, and I shall be saved, for You are my praise."*

- **Galatians 5:1** It is a common tendency in humans when faced with weakness, discouragement or temptation to consider going back to a former sin that you had once conquered.
- In this case the Galatians were going back to the law for their justification.
- *"Standing fast"* in the freedom you have found in Christ is a very helpful exhortation – notice the word *"entangled"* . It speaks of becoming snagged or trapped without expecting it – like a snare.
- If you have become entangled, the Holy Spirit is present to help you untie the knots and snares and to get you back to the freedom for which Christ has set you free!
- 5:13 This argument is still around today – "freedom means I can do whatever I want, live any way I want, sin whenever I want." Freedom or "liberty" is not for the purpose of fleshly indulgence, it is for the purpose of love and serving – freedom to serve.

QUOTE OF THE DAY

"He that puts the treasure into earthen vessels often allows the vessel to be chipped and broken that the excellency of the power may be of God and not of us."

Robert M. McCheyne (1813-1843)

DAY 234

📖 JEREMIAH 23:1 – 32
📖 GALATIANS 5:16 – 6:5

✺ K E Y   T H O U G H T S

- **Jeremiah 23:16-17** The nature of false prophecy is described in this chapter, particularly these verses. False prophecy will speak peace to those who "despise" the Lord, and to those who walk according to their own ways, (rebellion to the ways of the Lord). The false prophet reassures that no harm will come from it.

- False prophets, or those who speak their own thoughts, dreams, ideas – will not draw people to the Lord. They will draw people to themselves, they will also find ways to benefit personally from their manipulation of people.

- Contrasting the false words is vs. 29 – when there are words from the Lord they are *"like a fire, and a hammer that breaks the rock in pieces."*

- **Galatians 5:16** There is great hope for the believer, that when we walk in the Spirit, the flesh is brought under the authority of the Spirit, not the other way around – *"you will not fulfill the lust of the flesh."*

- This truly is a war, flesh against Spirit…"Who will deliver me from this body of death? I thank God - through Jesus Christ our Lord!" Romans 7:24b - 25 (NKJV)

- In case anyone wants to debate what is the flesh and what is not, vss. 20 and 21 give a list (not exhaustive) of examples of the flesh. Notice that those who "practice" such things, (live knowingly, willfully – continually), will not inherit the kingdom of God.

- So many people debate and argue about when you've crossed a line, or "how far you can go". This subject is about the heart of the true follower of Jesus.

- His or her heart is not trying to see how far away from Jesus they can get, but rather how near to Jesus we can walk.

- The fruit of the Spirit, the continual, incremental formation of the character of Christ in us, is evidence of His working, it looks like these things (vss. 23, 24).

- Vs. 25 This is the reference for the famous question, *"what would Jesus do?"* – also the reference for the little book 'In His Steps' (Charles Sheddon) - worth reading.

- So, today as you go through the day – ask the question when faced with a situation or temptation, *"what would Jesus do?"*

QUOTE OF THE DAY

"We must walk very close to a companion if we would have His shadow fall on us."

Mary Duncan – (1825 – 1865)

DAY 235

JEREMIAH 25:1 – 14; 26
GALATIANS 6:6 – 18

KEY THOUGHTS

- **Jeremiah 25** Jeremiah prophesies with precision – 70 years of captivity (recall the end of 2 Chronicles, Cyrus decree, was 70 years exactly).

- The life of the follower of Christ is never without threats and challenges – Jeremiah is threatened with death.

- The message of repentance (vs. 13) is often not popular – people prefer soft words of consolation to straight words of confrontation.

- *"Amend"*, change your ways – strong and clear instruction.

- Vs. 24 When you are in the will of the Lord there is complete safety knowing that our lives are in the hands of the Lord, He knows our days – we need not fear.

- **Galatians 6:6-10** "Paul applies the principle of sowing and reaping to a) support of those who teach/preach the word of God, (vs. 6), b) moral behavior (vs. 8), c) and to Christian service (vss. 9,10)." (SFLB)

- 6:9 This verse is truly one of the anchors of Christian behavior in the whole of scripture.

- (How often have you become weary? Lost heart?)

- The promise of God is that there will be a harvest, there will be a result for God's glory – we must continue to sow the good that the Lord has called us to.

- There must be someone reading this who is feeling like quitting, like giving up on the service, ministry, or kindness that you have been offering to the Lord – be encouraged today.

- The Lord sees your life, is keeping track of your sacrifice and the things that no one else sees.

- *"In due time"* – in God's time, in His way there will be a reaping … encourage yourself in the Lord today, do not lose heart, keep going! Bless you today, dear fellow servant.

QUOTE OF THE DAY

"God will neither expect nor desire His blessing without exertion; for it has always been God's way to crown only those that run the race that is set before them, and fight the good fight of faith."

William Jay (1769-1853)

DAY 236

📖 JEREMIAH 29:1 – 23; 30:1 – 3, 23, 24
📖 1 THESSALONIANS 1, 2

⊛ K E Y   T H O U G H T S

- **Jeremiah 29:11-14** These four verses are wonderful promises of the ongoing care and love of God for His people, His children.
- The heart of God for you is revealed in these statements:
  - *"thoughts of peace and not of evil."*
  - *"give you a future and a hope."*
  - *"pray… and I will listen to you."*
  - *"seek Me and you will find Me."*
- The Lord is full of goodness toward us, His heart is to bless us, to be intimately close to us, for our good.
- Our tendency is always toward independence rather than dependence – if we could only come to peace with the principle that <u>the nearer we are to the Lord the better we are, in every part of our lives</u>.
- Vs. 23 The Lord is the witness to lies and adultery. How often does the liar deny his lies, and the adulterer shift the blame, saying "it's not really like that".
- God is a perfect witness, He knows what is really happening, every person will answer for their actions before God.
- **1 Thessalonians 2:13** What is the gospel? Not the words of men, but… *"the word of God, which effectively works in you who believe".*

- Vs. 19, 20 When we have the privilege of bringing someone to Jesus, or we have the joy of discipling a new believer – they become the *"crown of rejoicing"* in our lives.

- It is such an amazing experience to help someone grow in the Lord, to walk with them into a fuller understanding of the goodness of the Lord, to coach them through hard times and to stand with them in trials.

- The things of greatest value in this life are those things that have the most value in the next life – love, relationships, expanding the kingdom of God.

QUOTE OF THE DAY

"Use a few spare half-hours in seeking after the lambs on the week days. This will prove to the parents that you are in earnest. To bring one child to the bosom of Christ would be reward for all our pains in eternity." (to Sunday school teachers)

Robert M. McCheyne (1813-1843)

DAY 237

📖 JEREMIAH 31:1 – 15, 31 – 34
📖 1 THESSALONIANS 3 – 4:8

☉ K E Y   T H O U G H T S

- **Jeremiah 31:3** Stop and think for a few moments of what it means that Lord has loved you with an *"everlasting"* love.

- His *"drawing"* is evidence of His lovingkindness – when we wander or stray, the Lord's kindness is what pulls us back to Him. We ought to welcome His conviction, His wooing of our hearts.

- So often we resist, feeling ashamed or disconnected, if we would only run to return to the Lord we would find comfort, restoration and a hopeful future.

- Vs. 12 What a beautiful picture of people returning to the Lord – *"streaming to the goodness of the Lord"*.

- "Lord may it be so in our church, in our town – people streaming to the goodness of the Lord."

- Vss. 13, 14 Depict the type of joyful display that those who return to God will have, enthusiastic joyful expressions of gratitude.
- The key words are "satisfy", "satiate" – only in the presence of the Lord is there true satisfaction, only in His goodness!
- Vs. 15 is a prophetic foreshadowing of the distress of the mothers in Israel when Herod killed the male children under two years of age in the search for the Christ child (Matt. 2:17).
- **1 Thessalonians 3:12** The relationship with brothers and sisters in the body of Christ is a deep and meaningful aspect of the Christian life. We are made to be in fellowship, made to know and be known.
- (Are you in a small group of believers that meet regularly to learn from the word, pray and encourage one another?) We all need a corporate celebration (church service), and a small group to connect us in fellowship. Make those things a practice of your life.
- 4:1-8 Practical sanctification (vs. 3), *"abstain from sexual immorality".* This is not a suggestion, neither is it debatable. This encompasses every manner of sexual immorality and is a strong exhortation to our culture today!
- Vs. 6 is a straightforward reason why single Christian men and women are not to be engaged in sexual activity before marriage – as brothers and sisters; we are not to *"defraud, or take advantage"* of one another.
- When a person (outside of God's prescribed plan for sexual relations - outside of marriage) uses another person's body for their own gratification – they are treating a brother or sister in Christ in a shameful way.
- God's love does not manifest itself in the mistreatment of others, or in taking what is not rightfully ours. Without the commitment of marriage a person has no right before God to any sexual aspect of another person's body.
- Notice the strength of vs. 8 – *"he/she who rejects this does not reject man, but God, who has also given us His Holy Spirit."* The writer speaks from an authoritative position in the Holy Spirit.

"Premarital sex defrauds the future marriage partner of the person with whom you are involved. You are robbing that person of the virginity and single-minded intimacy that ought to be brought into a marriage. Thus, sexual impurity is as much a social injustice against others as it is a personal sin against God."

Sam Storms

DAY 238

☐ JEREMIAH 32:16 – 44
☐ 1 THESSALONIANS 4:9 – 5:28

☺ K E Y   T H O U G H T S

- **Jeremiah 32:17** When we have doubts about the power and ability of God to respond to our needs, we should do what Jeremiah did, recall the great power of the Lord and then declare with faith – *"There is nothing too hard for You"*.

- Vs. 27 puts the same fact in God's voice – *"Is there anything too hard for Me?"*

- Vs. 33 The description of people who will not listen. (Have you ever had someone turn their back to you and walk away?) Imagine people doing that to the Lord's instruction.

- Vs. 40, 41 Very important scripture declaring the nature of God's commitment to the people of Israel – His covenant to bring them back to the land is everlasting. In other words it still applies today!

- Think of our God actually "rejoicing" over His people to do them good! God's heart is so for you, so deeply committed to your blessing and the prosperity of your soul.

- **I Thessalonians 5** *"The day of the Lord"* – this promise is a high profile part of the daily life of the believer in the times of this writing.

- They were living in expectation of the return of Christ, of being delivered from the hardships and persecutions that they were enduring.

- There are a number of key characteristics regarding the day of the Lord:
  - It will come as a thief, unexpected, suddenly (5:2).
  - We are to be watchful and prepared (5:6).
  - We are not appointed to "wrath", perhaps referring to the wrath of the tribulation (5:9).
- 1 Thess. ends with a practical list of exhortations all the way from honoring those who *"labor among you and are over you in the Lord"*, spiritual leaders
- to not despising prophecy, to prayer and rejoicing…
- Vs. 22 sums up the teaching on morals – *"Abstain from every form of evil"*.

QUOTE OF THE DAY

"Our greatest fear as individuals and as a church should not be of failure but of succeeding at things in life that don't really matter."

Francis Chan

DAY 239

📖 JEREMIAH 33
📖 2 THESSALONIANS 1, 2

⊛ K E Y   T H O U G H T S

- **Jeremiah 33:3** Make this promise one of the life verses that you build your faith upon: *"Call to Me, and I will answer you, and show you great and mighty things, which you do not know."*
- When we call upon the Lord, He has blessings that surpass our asking, blessings that are in His wisdom and perspective and blessings that will astound us for their greatness!
- The covenant plan of God to bring restoration from the "desolation" is a beautiful picture of what God can do with a life, or a family.

- Cleansing, pardon – His Name will be a joy, a praise and an honor! (vss. 8, 9)
- Vss. 19-21 The permanence of God's covenant with His own people, is as secure as the daily rising and setting of the sun.
- **1 Thessalonians 1:8, 9** There have always been those who teach a universalist view of the salvation of people, that everyone will eventually be saved. This view pits God's love over His justice.
- These two verses are about as clear a denouncement of that view as possible. Notice, that it is an everlasting destruction!
- There is no avoiding of individual responsibility to surrender to the authority of Jesus and to live in ongoing obedience to His commands.
- Christ's return is certain, part of the indication of His coming will be the apostasy of many, false and lying miracles, signs and wonders.
- 1 Thess. 2:15 Stand fast! Do not move from the *"traditions"* that you were taught. Not all traditions are bad when they are the apostolic foundations of doctrine taught in the scripture – hold firm to the essential truths that you were first taught.
- Do not be easily moved by "new" revelation, or quickly discard the things you were taught by those who brought you to Christ.

QUOTE OF THE DAY

"Faith, which is trust, and fear are opposite poles. If a man has the one, he can scarcely have the other in vigorous operation. He that has his trust set upon God does not need to dread anything except the weakening or the paralyzing of that trust."

Alexander MacLaren.

DAY 240

📖 JEREMIAH 37:11; 38
📖 2 THESSALONIANS 3, 1 TIMOTHY 1

⊙ K E Y T H O U G H T S

- **Jeremiah 37** Put yourself in Jeremiah's place, the life of this prophet is far from glamorous.

- (If you were suffering the same kind of persecution for your obedience to the Lord's call on your life, at this point in your spiritual growth, how do you think you would be responding?)

- In the midst of the impending doom, there is always mercy for those who are contrite before the Lord – His ear is always open to those with a humble, obedient heart.

- 38:28 *"He was there when Jerusalem was taken."* We do not know sorrow like these people suffered. There is always someone who is enduring deeper pain than we are… there have been many through time who have endured greater suffering than I have… for the sake of the Lord. Take courage friend.

- **2 Thessalonians 3:13** This encouragement is found many times in the NT – do not grow weary in doing good! In other words, do not become discouraged in serving the Lord, do not give up when things get difficult, do not drift away from the call of God. Continue, be faithful to His call, and serve another day.

- 1 Tim. 1:4 Some people love to debate and argue, finding entertainment and value in *"endless genealogies and fables"*.

- Paul is exhorting his son in the faith, to pursue love and godly edification.

- The gospel is straightforward, clear, simple, powerful - stick with the commandment (gospel) that produces love and good fruit instead of that which leads to "idle talk".

- Vs. 15 (Why did Christ Jesus come into the world?)

- Paul is a pattern of encouragement to those coming later. No one is beyond the reach of the gospel, God is longsuffering (patient) toward them all!

- Life in the kingdom is a fight, it is warfare (vs. 18) – we are to *"wage the good warfare"*.

- Those who do not may suffer the *"shipwreck"* of their faith - Paul names two men who have gone this way.

- Our faith must be current, active, growing – it is a living relationship with the living God, not just an historical event that has no bearing on the way we live our lives.

QUOTE OF THE DAY

"He wants all or nothing. The thought of a person calling himself a 'Christian' without being a devoted follower of Christ is absurd."

Francis Chan, 'Crazy Love'

DAY 241

📖 JEREMIAH 42, 43
📖 1 TIMOTHY 2

◉ K E Y   T H O U G H T S

- **Jeremiah 42** Even in the midst of exile and political domination by foreign powers, the people have opportunity to either obey the Lord or to rebel against His ways.

- You would think after all that has happened there would be an automatic response of obedience, and yet...

- 43:4, 7 *"the people would not obey the voice of the Lord."*

- When we are in a season of discipline, or in a desert because of disobedience, we will always have an opportunity to turn it around by current obedience. The Lord is forgiving and gracious – there are references to Him *"relenting"* from the severe discipline first intended (42:10).

- There is no substitute for a submitted, obedient heart if we are to truly follow the Lord.

- **1 Timothy 2** Prayer for those in authority, for all men, for those who are in authority.

- The authorities of these times were not godly, it was an extremely pagan, immoral and idolatrous culture. We are commanded to pray for leaders, regardless of their spiritual condition.
- A particular exhortation to the men (vs. 8). Pray.
- Vs. 11-12 "Positively, Paul exhorts women to be disciples and to maintain a conduct that would not discredit the church. The prohibition of vs.12 refers to the authoritative office of apostolic teacher in the church. It does not forbid women to educate, proclaim truth or exhort (prophesy). See Acts 2:17; 18:26; 21:9; 1 Cor. 11:5; Phil 4:3; 2 Tim. 1:5; 3:14,15; Titus 2:3-5." (SFLB)

QUOTE OF THE DAY

"By the beginning of the twentieth century there were forty evangelical missionary organizations led by women. Armies of women missionaries went out, not only evangelizing but also starting hospitals and schools... Women missionaries were the first to translate the Bible for hundreds of language groups. And they did it in the most rugged and remote places. As one writer said: "The more difficult and dangerous the work the higher the ratio of women to men."

Loren Cunningham 'Why Not Women'

DAY 242

 JEREMIAH 44
 1 TIMOTHY 3

 K E Y   T H O U G H T S

- **Jeremiah 44:16, 17** This response is clear evidence that the people had lost touch completely with the Lord, the rule becomes *"whatever has gone out of our own mouth".*
- In other words, "We will do whatever we want, not what God wants, or what you, his prophet (Jeremiah), speaks."
- The people were mistakenly blaming God for their problems, they were choosing an Egyptian goddess instead, saying that

while they sacrificed to her all things were well.

- Amazing that people will blame the Lord rather than their own rebellion for their problems.

- **1 Timothy 3** Bishops (overseers, those with local authority, for example a pastor) must show proven character as qualification for leadership.

- The same is true for deacons, or those who would serve in the church.

- The important thing is to take the character, reputation and record of serving as a whole, without blame does not mean perfection, but that no evil charge can be proved.

- Both husbands and wives in leadership roles must exhibit God honoring characteristics and moderation.

- Vs. 15 The house of God, the church of the living God is: *"the pillar and ground of the truth"*.

- The Bible writers had a high view of Christ's church and its leaders. It has been fashionable to discredit His church. Let us instead love His bride, love His body, build His church!

QUOTE OF THE DAY

"Revivals begin with God's own people; the Holy Spirit touches their heart anew, and gives them new fervor and compassion, and zeal, new light and life, and when He has thus come to you, He next goes forth to the valley of dry bones... Oh, what responsibility this lays on the Church of God! If you grieve Him away from yourselves, or hinder His visit, then the poor perishing world suffers sorely!"

Andrew Bonar

DAY 243

📖 JEREMIAH 52
📖 1 TIMOTHY 4, 5

⊛ K E Y   T H O U G H T S

- **Jeremiah 52** The judgment that comes upon Israel, because of disobedience and idolatry, is very sobering.

- There will always be consequences to our sins, the ways of the Lord are always better and always provide a more sure inheritance.
- **1 Timothy 4:2** If a person continually discounts the voice of the Holy Spirit through their conscience, it has a cauterizing effect upon the conscience – it no longer functions properly.
- Vs. 12 The example that young leaders are to show is in their character and behavior – *"reading, exhortation and doctrine"* are to be the areas of Timothy's focus. *"Continue"*, or keep going, is a common encouragement.
- Be faithful to the doctrine you have been taught by your spiritual parents.
- We are to honor spiritual leaders, to correct those who sin, and to keep pure (5:22).
- The eventual reward for those who are sinning and those who are living righteously, will be made known.
- There are often people in life who seem to be getting away with things that are not right, or presenting a godly exterior when on the inside things are not right.
- They will be exposed, they will be disciplined/judged, in God's time and God's way.
- We all are in need of the reminder to stir up the gifts of the Spirit for ministry that are within us – it is common for those gifts to fall into disrepair or to become rusty with a lack of use.
- We are called to serve the Lord, He is faithful to equip us for that service.

QUOTE OF THE DAY

"Look! Don't be deceived by appearances - men and things are not what they seem. All who are not on the rock are in the sea!"

William Booth

DAY 244

📖 EZRA 1; 3:8 – 13
📖 1 TIMOTHY 6

⊙ K E Y   T H O U G H T S

- **Ezra 1:5** The Spirit moves the heart of people to specific tasks.
- 42,360 people returned to Jerusalem in this re-establishing of the city.
- 3:10, 11 A marvelous picture - when the foundation was laid there was great celebration and worship. The rebuilding of the temple symbolizes the rebuilding of the spiritual life of the nation.
- Even though there was great rejoicing, those who could remember the former temple of Solomon couldn't help weeping.
- Let us be those people who are truly able to rejoice in what God is doing now. Let's keep our perspective forward looking.
- **1 Timothy 6:7-10** If there were no other passages on money in the scripture, these four verses would be enough wisdom to keep us going in the right direction.
- Think of a few 'evils' that the love of the money keeps fueling.
- Vs. 12 Fight! The life of faith is likened to an actual battle, there will be struggles, hardships and conflict.
- We are to keep the commands of Jesus, and the commissions of the gospel – *"without spot"*.
- Vs. 20 Notice the emotion in Paul's writing, *"O Timothy"*. The elder is concerned that the young pastor will guard what has been given to him in trust.
- It is our responsibility to be faithful to the spreading of the gospel, to stick to the main and the plain.

"If a person gets his attitude toward money straight, it will help straighten out almost every other area in his life."

Billy Graham

DAY 245

📖 EZRA 4:1 – 5, 23, 24; 5:1 – 5; 6:1, 6 – 12
📖 2 TIMOTHY 1, 2

☾ K E Y   T H O U G H T S

- **Ezra 4-6** these passages give insight into the battle that is inevitable whenever we attempt to do anything for the Lord.
- Even though they have permission from one king, those who opposed the nation politicked to stop the revival.
- But God! He is at work in the hearts of leaders, the work continues with the provision and blessing of the new government.
- We should take courage when we are following the leading of the Lord. He will provide, He will fight for you, He will keep His promise.
- Our part is to obey, to be faithful and to persevere.
- **2 Timothy 1:6, 7** Whenever we accept ministry responsibility there will be doubts and questions that will come. In those times we are to remember our calling and the affirmation of the leaders who appointed us to the task.
- Fear is not of the Lord, fear is not productive or helpful. We have been given a different spirit – *"power, love and a sound mind"*.
- Focus on the sound mind part for a moment – in other words "keep your head" – do not be overcome with irrational emotions or speculation stay focused on the Promise giver.
- 2 Tim. 2:1, 3 Exhortations to "be strong", and "endure hardship". The road of spiritual life and leadership does have difficult times – we are called soldiers and there is no avoiding the times in the trenches.

- Vs. 11-13 Regardless of our failings or weaknesses, the Lord remains faithful – *"He cannot deny Himself"*.

- Vs. 22 The action we are to take when dealing with youthful lusts is to "flee". There is no shame in running away from things that will entrap you in lust. Take action, do not be passive in this area.

- Vss. 23-26 gives us a manual for how to deal with those who are contentious or who love to quarrel over doctrine and controversy. It is not a fitting characteristic for the man or woman of God to "quarrel".

- There is a place for correction done in humility (vs. 25), but then we are to commit those people to the Lord, for His discipline and correcting.

QUOTE OF THE DAY

"Contention is the devil's forge, in which, if he can but give a Christian a heat or two, he will not doubt but to soften him for his hammer of temptation."

William Gurnall (1617-1679)

DAY 246

📖 EZRA 6:13 – 22; 7
📖 2 TIMOTHY 3

⊙ K E Y   T H O U G H T S

- **Ezra 6, 7** The reading in Ezra gives us a miraculous picture of God's favor coming upon a people through an ungodly king/ leader.

- God is able to prosper and provide for His blessed sons and daughters even when all of the usual sources seem to have dried up. He is able to provide for you!

- **2 Timothy 3:7** There are people who have increased learning but the fruit of their lives gives no evidence of an advantage. It would be logical to think that increased learning automatically means increased godliness – this is often not the case.

- Coming to "the knowledge of the truth", means the full application of the truth and the changing from a life of sin and rebellion, to a life of devotion to Christ's commands and instruction.
- 2 Timothy 3:16 This is a key verse on the inspiration of the scripture in the whole of the Bible. Another complimentary passage is, 2 Peter 1:20-21 (NKJV) *"Knowing this first, that no prophecy of scripture is of any private interpretation, for prophecy never came by the will of man, but holy men of God spoke as they were moved by the Holy Spirit."*
- A biblical view of the inspiration of the Scripture is that the whole, (all), of the Scripture is inspired by the Holy Spirit and that the very words themselves are inspired by God.
- More than concepts or generalities, Scripture asserts a high view, a supernatural view – the technical term is "the plenary verbal" inspiration of the Bible, (full, every word).
- Another way of expressing this view is that the scripture is "God breathed". Flowing through human instruments whose personalities and writing styles differ, and yet the master themes and even the details agree.
- 66 books
- Written over a span 1600 years – miraculous preservation
- 40 different authors
- One theme!
- John 3:16 *"For God so loved the world that He gave His only begotten Son that whosoever believes in Him shall not perish but have everlasting life."*

QUOTE OF THE DAY

"The Bible will always be full of things you cannot understand, as long as you will not live according to those you can understand."

Billy Sunday

DAY 247

📖 EZRA 9
📖 2 TIMOTHY 4

◉ K E Y   T H O U G H T S

- **Ezra 9** Even after having been in exile for their compromise with pagan nations around Israel, the remnant people who returned to Jerusalem were intermarrying with the nations around them.

- This sin is about compromise and the influence of pagan religions – God is holy, pure, without equal – the blending of religious practice and devotion is strictly, unequivocally forbidden.

- 9:8 is an important verse – how often have we only experienced "a measure of revival", when God's heart is to bring complete revival and renewal?

- "Oh Lord, bring our people, in this time, into a surging, fiery revival of passion for Your Name and for Your ways."

- **2 Timothy 4:1-5** Paul's charge to Timothy – we all should receive this charge to our spirits.

- Vs. 2 The work of spiritual leadership and discipling of others requires these things: *"preaching, readiness, convincing, rebuke, exhortation ... WITH patience and teaching."*

- Leadership is more than just having a nice personality – it takes diligence and investment in people over time.

- Many will falter and fail, many winds of doctrine and fads of ministry will come and go – but YOU! Vs. 5 – *"be watchful in all things, endure afflictions..."*

- And, *"DO the work of an evangelist"!* Evangelism is work, it requires a strategic decision to actually do something, it takes a making up of the mind, and a plan of action to deliver the work.

- Many people remain idle behind the myth that when people are properly discipled they will automatically bring people to Jesus. This is a tidy thought but experience and observation prove that evangelism does not automatically accompany "maturity" in the Lord.

- (Receive this exhortation today – who is in your life that does not know Jesus, who are you praying for to receive Christ? Who are you reaching out to, who have you invited lately?)
- Do the work of an evangelist today!

QUOTE OF THE DAY

"Any method of evangelism will work—if God is in it."
Leonard Ravenhill

DAY 248

📖 EZRA 10
📖 TITUS 1, 2

⊙ K E Y   T H O U G H T S

- **Ezra 10** Characteristics of a national revival.
- In this chapter the people are brought before the Lord to answer for their blatant transgressions – intermarriage with people from the surrounding nations.
- This was an issue primarily because God had forbidden it, secondly because of the issue of religious purity. The foreign wives brought foreign gods with them.
- This was the ongoing issue for Israel. For us the application is the same, without a living, personal relationship with Jesus, we too will be tempted to try the high sounding promises of "other" gods.
- Materialism, entertainment, self-will, immorality, ambition, all vie for our affections.
- Ezra 10:15 Even though the whole nation was convicted in their hearts and began to repent and make restitution for their sins, there were those who opposed the revival.
- There will always be those who oppose revival for one reason or another. Revival never functions with unanimity – someone

is not going to like it. Popularity is not one of the hallmarks of true revival.

- **Titus 1, 2** this little book is very focused on setting up the church with leaders who are well trained in doctrine and in character.
- The elders were appointed in "every city". (1:5) This biblical pattern is based on the recognition and affirmation of ministry giftings and character in a person's life. It is not based on popularity or profile. Titus was to "appoint".
- Democracy is not the NT church pattern for the selection of those who are to lead in the church.
- Whether you are considered an elder in the church or not, why not apply these lists to yourself as a checklist of things that could be worked on in God – ways to grow.
- 1:6-9; 2:1-10
- 2:8 Our speech is a vital indicator of the godliness in our heart. It is directly connected to our testimony among those who might oppose the gospel.

QUOTE OF THE DAY

"The greatest test of whether the holiness we profess to seek or to attain is truth and life will be whether it produces an increasing humility in us. In man, humility is the one thing needed to allow God's holiness to dwell in him and shine through him. The chief mark of counterfeit holiness is lack of humility. The holiest will be the humblest."

Andrew Murray, 1828-1917

DAY 249

☐ NEHEMIAH 1 – 2:10
☐ TITUS 3

 KEY THOUGHTS

- **Nehemiah 1** As we start the book of Nehemiah, read this helpful summary of the times and events of the books of Ezra/ Nehemiah.

- Spirit Filled Life Bible: "The historical period covered by the books of Ezra and Nehemiah is about 110 years. The period of rebuilding the temple under Zerubbabel, inspired by the preaching of Zechariah and Haggai, was twenty one (21) years. Sixty (60) years later Ezra brought a revival and proper teaching on temple worship. After thirteen (13) years Nehemiah came to work on the walls. Nehemiah and Malachi worked together to eradicate the evil of the worship of many gods, and they attacked the evil of compromise with the peoples (of the surrounding nations)."
- Nehemiah is a study in character and prayer – notice how he prays before his request to the king, how during his meeting with the king he prays for wisdom (just a thought prayer)?
- This is also a challenging example of someone who sees a need and is willing to personally step up to the challenge to see the need met.
- Most of us will not have the opportunity to affect national change through high level governmental influence (some will), but all of us have daily moments of decision.
- (Will I, will you be the one to help, to serve, to step up, to shoulder the load?)
- 2:10 Meet Sanballat and Tobiah – these guys are very interesting characters – you'll get to know them in this very intriguing little book.
- They may be ungodly but they are consistent – always opposing!
- **Titus 3:5** This verse should be memorized – it is a foundational verse on the means of our salvation – *"not by works"*.
- The phrase – *"be careful to maintain good works"* is repeated twice – a claim to religion without practical evidence is a faulty claim – Titus does not want us to be *"unfruitful"*.
- 3:9 is a powerful directive that will save you much anxiety and energy.

DAY 250

📖 NEHEMIAH 2:11 – 20; 4
📖 PHILEMON

☀ K E Y   T H O U G H T S

- **Nehemiah 2** Notice how a word from the Lord can cause encouragement to take on a task together? *"Let us rise up and build!"*

- Sanballat, Tobiah and Geshem could easily represent the enemies in our lives, take note of the tactics they employ.

- Mockery, ridicule, threats, false rumors …

- When we are opposed by people or by the enemy himself the tactics are never fair or above board – it's not like warfare in the "good old days" of honor.

- In spiritual battle our enemy will always attack unexpectedly and always attack at our weakest point.

- Nehemiah uses wisdom in rallying his people to the task – they fought for the right reasons.

- As you seek to be a spiritually growing follower of Christ, be certain that the spiritual battles that you are fighting will have a great effect on your "sons, your daughters, your spouse and your little ones."

- **Philemon** Onesimus is a runaway slave who has come to Jesus through the ministry of Paul.

- This little book is a wonderful study in the transforming power of Christ – notice what Jesus produces in the relationship between slave and master.

- Notice also that slavery of any sort does not have a place in the heart of Christ. One people dominating or one person owning another person(s) is not God's heart.
- In Christ ..."There is neither Jew nor Greek, there is neither slave nor free, there is neither male nor female; for you are all one in Christ Jesus." Galatians 3:28
- (Is there someone from your past who has since come to faith in Christ that you should release and forgive?)
- Ask yourself, "If Jesus will forgive them, if Jesus will give them eternal life by His blood, just the same as me, would I place myself above His judgment and refuse to forgive?"

QUOTE OF THE DAY

"If God's love is for anybody anywhere, it is for everybody everywhere."

Edward Lawlor

DAY 251

📖 NEHEMIAH 5
📖 HEBREWS 1

◉ K E Y T H O U G H T S

- **Nehemiah 5** How we treat our brothers and sisters in Christ is such a telling indicator of our true relationship with the Lord.
- A revival of true worship of God affects our character, the deep, motivating places of integrity, honesty, and compassion.
- Oppression of the weak, or taking advantage of the simple, mistreating the vulnerable are all forbidden by the Spirit of Jesus.
- **Hebrews 1, 2** This book can be a little intimidating with all of its references to Judaism and the OT. Without taking away from the magnificence of the writing – it is really all about the supremacy of Christ. He alone is the highest, the exalted, unique provision of God for all our sins.
- 1:1-4 It is Jesus who is the spoken revelation of God,

- Jesus who is the heir of all things.
- Jesus who made the worlds.
- Jesus is the brightness of His glory and the express image of His person.
- Jesus upholds all things by His power.
- Jesus by Himself has purged our sins.
- Jesus is seated at the right hand of the Majesty on High.
- Jesus is "so much better"… than the angels (a key phrase).
- Jesus has a more excellent Name!
- Vs. 8 *"…but to the Son!"*… another key phrase.
- An everlasting throne, anointed with the oil of gladness.
- The Son… *"laid the foundation of the earth…the heavens".*
- All His enemies will be His footstool.
- Ill-informed people in our world will call Jesus a great teacher, compare him to other respected earthly leaders or religious founders.
- Dear ones - there is no one like Jesus, He has no equal, no comparisons are even close, He alone is "mighty to save".
- To live fully in all the blessings of God we must have the highest view of who Jesus is. Satan and all of hell have been trying to diminish Him since He walked the earth.
- Exalt the Lord Jesus in your heart right now, confess that He is all that the Bible says He is, set aside all other affections and worship this one and only, this marvelous, matchless Jesus!
- Let your faith come into the fullness of joy that can only be found in a revelation of Jesus Christ of Nazareth.

QUOTE OF THE DAY

"Likewise today, some Christians are content to merely exist until   they die. They don't want to risk anything, to believe God, to grow or mature. They refuse to believe his Word, and have become hardened in their unbelief. Now they're living just to die."

David Wilkerson

DAY 252

📖 NEHEMIAH 6
📖 HEBREWS 2

◉ K E Y   T H O U G H T S

- **Nehemiah 6** is a classic chapter on leadership. Every type of leadership has these same challenges, from the home, neighborhood, school, community, work, nation – all leadership faces these obstacles.

- The opponents use various tactics to get Nehemiah off track, they try to distract him with meetings on the "plains of Ono". Remember that phrase for those things that are a distraction, not necessarily wrong – but just get us off task.

- They accuse him of ambitious and seditious motives – Nehemiah's response in 5:8 is a life verse for those endeavoring to lead for God's glory – pray with Nehemiah right now: "<u>Now therefore, O God, strengthen my hands</u>."

- Vs. 12 The Holy Spirit will help us to be able to discern what is of God and what is not.

- The great task of rebuilding the walls was completed in 52 days – the surrounding people had to concede that "this work was done by God".

- The last challenge in this passage is family connection pressure – Tobiah was an enemy, and yet through intermarriage many of the people were appealing on his behalf. Nehemiah stands firm and is not frightened into retreating by the pressure of family clans.

- **Hebrews 2** Two warnings summarize this chapter, vss. 1 and 3.

- Dig in, study, be serious about the gospel, and the word of God, *"give more earnest heed"*… if we do not we are in danger!

- The danger is "<u>drifting away</u>". Like a boat that comes untied on a fast flowing river - like a little piece of wood carried out by the retreating tide. (How many people do you know who have just "drifted" - now where are they?)

- The second warning is to those who "<u>neglect</u>" this great salvation – carelessness, indifference like a vegetable garden that is uncared for – eventually the weeds overtake it. Like a fruit tree that is not pruned or husbanded... it will eventually bear little or no fruit.

- (Have you been drifting? Have you been neglecting the care and nurture of this great salvation?)

- Vs. 18 Jesus is able to aid you when are tempted, because He Himself suffered – temptation is called suffering! To win a battle with temptation is to win against the suffering of the soul.

- A physical trial or pain is also a temptation to doubt, to accuse God of evil... Jesus is the One who is able to understand and help – reach out to Him when you suffer, draw close to the One who truly, knows what you are going through.

QUOTE OF THE DAY

"The church is not a dormitory for sleepers, it is an institution for workers; it is not a rest camp, it is a front line trench."

Billy Sunday

DAY 253

📖 NEHEMIAH 8 – 9:3
📖 HEBREWS 3 – 4:10

✪ K E Y   T H O U G H T S

- **Nehemiah 8** This scene of the people gathered together, the leaders explaining, the praise unified and passionate... revival is a magnificent thing!

- 8:10 *"The joy of the Lord is your strength."* When we are right with God, there is an inner joy, a strength that comes from the freedom of being clean before the Lord, right with the Lord and near to Him in fellowship.

- We are free to worship, free to trust Him, free to serve with all our heart, because there is nothing between us.

- The pattern of 9:1-3 is a good example to follow:
  - a) reading the Word
  - b) confession of sin
  - c) worship!
- **Hebrews 3:12-14** "Unbelief is caused by a hardened heart, which is caused by the deceitfulness of sin. The result is apostasy, departing from the living God. The writer views the abandonment of the Christian faith as turning away from God. Constant encouragement in the midst of a caring fellowship will help believers remain faithful." (SFLB)
- Vs. 19 *"Entering in"*, for the believer, just as in the case of the Israelites heading to Canaan, requires belief and obedience.
- The journey into God's blessing in this life and the promised "rest" of heaven requires steadfastness and perseverance.
- There were a lot of people who received the promise of Canaan who never got there. They disobeyed, they were filled with unbelief and they were rebellious to the Lord.
- We should all heed the dire warning of 3:12, we must not allow *"an evil heart of unbelief, departing from the living God."*
- And let us "fear lest any of you seem to have come short of it, (God's rest)". (4:1)

QUOTE OF THE DAY

"The Bible will keep you from sin, or sin will keep you from the Bible."

Dwight L. Moody

DAY 254

📖 NEHEMIAH 10:28 – 29
📖 HEBREWS 4:11 – 5:14

☾ K E Y   T H O U G H T S

- **Nehemiah 10** In this phase of the revival the people return to proper principles of giving, the timeless principles of "the firstfruits" and the "tithe" are developed and re-established.

- The truth that is imbedded in these practices is the acknowledgement that; everything belongs to the Lord and all that we have is a trust from Him. The tithe belongs to the Lord, it is holy, it is to be brought to the *"House of God."*

- In all this we, the people of God are not to *"neglect the house of God".* (10:39)

- There are many people today who are shouting loudly that the house of God is not important, and as such, should be neglected. True revival includes a renewed love for God's house, a renewed desire to be in the house of God with the people of God. It includes a respect and honor for the leaders in the house, appointed by God.

- **Hebrews 4:11** We are to be diligent, so that we avoid a fall, like the examples just given of the children of Israel's disobedience.

- 4:12, 13 God's word is the standard of all evaluation. No one can hide from His gaze, His penetrating knowledge of all things – we will all give an account to Him.

- (If today was your day to give an account, would you be ready?)

- 4:14 Hold fast, hold on tight to Jesus, grip your salvation tightly – it is precious.

- There is no other priest, or mediator who is qualified, other than Jesus. He is our great High Priest – the one who can truly carry our sins.

- 5:7 The "godly fear" spoken of here is a "reverent submission to the will of God". (SFLB)

- 5:9 Jesus is the "author of eternal salvation to all who obey Him".

- Vs. 14 Reading the Word, studying, thinking and grappling with spiritual truth is required to "exercise our spiritual senses" to be able to tell the difference between good and evil!

- Growth in the Lord, spiritual maturity requires effort. Many have been lazy with God's Word and are then easily led into error and extremes – bless you for your diligence in reading and studying the living word of God!

"He (Jesus) is the image of the invisible God, the firstborn over all creation. For by Him all things were created that are in heaven and that are on earth, visible and invisible, whether thrones or dominions or principalities or powers. All things were created through Him and for Him. And He is before all things, and in Him all things consist. And He is the head of the body, the church, who is the beginning, the firstborn from the dead, that in all things He may have the preeminence. For it pleased the Father that in Him (Jesus) all the fullness should dwell."

Colossians 1:15-19

DAY 255

📖 NEHEMIAH 13
📖 HEBREWS 6

☺ K E Y   T H O U G H T S

- **Nehemiah 13** An alliance had been made with Tobiah, he had actually obtained a room in the house of God that had formerly been used for the offerings and tithes of God.

- Apart from the drama of the context, this incident is a powerful illustration of the effect of spiritual compromise.

- There are times in every life where we need to *"grieve bitterly... and throw all the household goods of Tobiah out of the room"* (vs. 8).

- This is a picture of a purging, repentant heart, a heart that has come to realize that inroads have been made by the enemy. There can be no compromise or fellowship with the enemy *"in the courts of the Lord"*.

- Those places in our heart that are to be devoted entirely to the Lord must not be contaminated with the "household goods" of the enemy.

- In vs. 27 one of the sons of the priest had married Sanballat's daughter – the description of Solomon in vs. 26 *"Nevertheless pagan women caused even him to sin"*, is a strong warning of the dangers of ungodly relationships.

- Many, many people lose their faith over a woman or a man. If you are in an ungodly relationship follow Nehemiah's example, allow the Lord to honor you, to provide for you, to bless you.

- **Hebrews 6:4-6** "The language of vss.4 and 5 clearly describes those who have experienced the saving grace of God, and the language of v.6 denotes a complete disowning of Christ. It is a deliberate and decisive abandonment of the Christian faith. The people described are not backsliders but apostates. They have not merely fallen into sin but have denounced Christ. They have become as those who crucified Jesus." (SFLB)

- Only God knows the condition of a person's heart, anyone who will repent will be forgiven. These people however, have become so hardened, so consumed in sin, so angry toward God that they will refuse to ask for forgiveness.

- Their own stubborn denial of God is the basis of their apostate condition. Their own refusal to believe and obey is their demise.

- God has made a promise, and confirmed it with an oath – He cannot lie, it will come to pass. (Vss. 13-20)

- This hope, based on the character of God, is our anchor. The Anchor is secured to Christ Jesus who is "within" the veil. Hallelujah, the very "presence" of God.

QUOTE OF THE DAY

"His oath, His covenant, His blood, support me in the whelming flood…..In every high and stormy gale, my anchor holds within the veil. On Christ the solid Rock I stand, all other ground is sinking sand, all other ground is sinking sand."

Edward Mote (1834)

DAY 256

📖 ESTHER 1 – 2:18
📖 HEBREWS 7

◉ K E Y   T H O U G H T S

- **Esther 1, 2** The story of Esther is a fantastic drama, showing the purposes of God for individuals and nations as the themes.

- Esther is an example of someone who has the favor of the Lord upon their life, who is willing to follow the Lord's leading and has the spiritual depth to respond well to the challenge of leadership laid before her.

- **Hebrews 7** Melchizedek is a mysterious figure in the Bible, the best way to view this "priest forever" is to see him as a foreshadowing revelation of Jesus or, theophany. Jesus revealing Himself in the OT.

- For the Hebrews, Melchizedek is a priest of a different order, Jesus being the great High Priest.

- Vss. 4-9 An interesting passage on the place and significance of tithes prior to any Mosaic law.

- 7:25 *"Save to the uttermost"*. What an amazing thought, Jesus is able to save… "all the way", the availability of His mercy and forgiveness is complete, full, sufficient.

- Vs. 27 Jesus offered Himself "once" for all, praise God.

- Vs. 28 Jesus has been perfected forever, He alone is fully and completely qualified as our High Priest.

- Jesus alone is the One who is able to reconcile us to God.

QUOTE OF THE DAY

"Oh, when we are journeying through the murky night and the dark woods of affliction and sorrow, it is something to find here and there a spray broken, or a leafy stem bent down with the tread of His foot and the brush of His hand as He passed; and to remember that the path He trod He has hallowed, and thus to find lingering fragrance and hidden strength in the remembrance of Him as "in all points tempted like as we are," bearing grief for us, bearing grief with us, bearing grief like us."

Alexander MacLaren (1826-1910)

DAY 257

📖 ESTHER 3
📖 HEBREWS 8, 9

🔅 K E Y   T H O U G H T S

- **Esther 3** Anti-Semitism has been present in our world since the time of Isaac and Ishmael.

- God appointed Esther to intervene on behalf of the Jews.

- As followers of Christ we must do all we can to defend His people, to love the Jews, to pray for the peace of Jerusalem.

- There must be no anti-Semitism in our hearts.

- Haman's plan is a diabolical and ruthless scheme to annihilate the Jews, on one day - rewarding those who are willing to be the executioners.

- **Hebrews 9:12** The blood of Jesus has replaced the blood sacrifices of animals, Jesus blood has obtained *"eternal redemption"*.

- 9:14 Whenever we see the words *"how much more?"* we should take note that a comparison is being drawn.

- Jesus is so much higher than any other sacrifice or provision.

- In fact there is not comparison – He is unique.

- Vs. 15 *"He is the mediator"*. This is one of His titles. Mary is not our mediatrix, a priest is not our mediator, angels are not our mediators, saints are not our mediators, Jesus alone is our Mediator, our go between – the bridge to God.

- Vs. 28 (Are we those who are eagerly waiting for Him?)

- He is going to appear a second time, *"for salvation"*.

- Vs. 27 This summary verse is a powerful help in sharing the urgency of a decision with people you are witnessing to.

- Every one of us will die, every one of us will face the judgment. For believers it is the judgment seat of Christ, for unbelievers, the Great White Throne judgment.

- But, we all will die… we all will face the judgment.

DAY 258

📖 ESTHER 4, 5
📖 HEBREWS 10

⊛ K E Y   T H O U G H T S

- **Esther 4** This situation is a perfect example of something that seems impossible. It is a national issue, the momentum is all in Haman's favor, it appears from every indicator that the wicked will have their day and their way.

- It looks like all hope is lost – but God has other things in His heart.

- 4:13,14 One of the great prophetic exhortations in history, God has a desire for His kingdom to come and His will to be done on the earth.

- There will always be a need for specific people who are willing to use their influence for God's glory. People who are willing to stand against the tide of evil, people willing to stand and be counted against all the odds of wickedness.

- Esther is that person! She rises to the occasion.

- Notice the preparation she makes? Fasting and prayer – corporate intercession, and then action. Her strategy blends action with abandon to the will and purpose of God.

- Every person has opportunities for greatness throughout their lives. (They won't all be nation changing, but it could well be that you will have a moment like Esther - will you step up? Will you rise and be counted?)

- The preparation for the big moments will be the small moments of conscience, compassion, obedience. Character is <u>developed</u>, not inherited or deposited.

- **Hebrews 10:22-24** These verses followed by the *"therefore"* of vs. 19 give us very practical applications to the majestic theology being presented. We are to:

a) Draw near

b) Hold fast

c) Consider one another

d) Not neglect or forsake gathering together (be faithful in church and small group attendance)

e) Exhort one another

- **Vss. 26ff** Keep in mind that the context of this book is to challenge those who were going back to the old ceremonial system of religion – they were, by their return to the ceremonial/ sacrificial system – trampling under-foot the very precious blood of Jesus.

- This passage gives clear indication that apostasy is indeed possible, and that those who willfully deny the blood of Jesus as the sole means of cleansing, will be lost.

- Finally in vs. 39 we are to resolve, we will not be those who "draw back", or shrink back! We will be those who *"believe to the saving of the soul"*.

QUOTE OF THE DAY

"So enormous, so dreadful, so irremediable did the Trade's wickedness appear that my own mind was completely made up for Abolition. Let the consequences be what they would, I from this time determined that I would never rest until I had effected its abolition."

William Wilberforce (1759 – 1833) (He was the leading voice against the slave trade in England. His labor against this injustice took over 50 years of effort, three days before his death, and largely because of his tireless efforts, slavery was abolished in most of the British Empire in 1833.)

DAY 259

📖 ESTHER 6, 7
📖 HEBREWS 11:1 – 5

◉ K E Y   T H O U G H T S

- **Esther 6-7** Take note of all the factors in this incredible drama.
- God's involvement (6:1).
- Mordecai's previous loyalty.
- Esther's obedience and wisdom.
- Haman's pride, ambition and hatred.
- God is always at work, He will never be thwarted by the enemy's schemes.
- Take heart brother or sister, stay in the battle – the Lord is on your side. And if the Lord is on our side, who can be against us!
- **Hebrews 11** One of the great chapters of the whole Bible.
- Take time to meditate on the key verses on faith.
- 11:1 Faith is substance!
- What is understood by faith? (vs. 3)
- Vs. 6 What is impossible without faith?
- Faith is the like the ignition or power button on any vehicle or technology – without faith (ignition/power) nothing happens.
- With faith (ignition/power) everything starts working, every system begins to function.
- Jesus said to Thomas *"Do not be unbelieving, but believing"*. (John 20:27)

QUOTE OF THE DAY

"Seek not to understand that thou mayest believe, but believe that
thou mayest understand."

Augustine

DAY 260

◉ K E Y   T H O U G H T S

- **Esther 8** The law of Haman, having been established by the King was irreversible – even though Haman had been exposed and hanged, there was the matter of the legal day of slaughter of the Jews.

- Mordecai's law gave the Jews the legal right to arm themselves and defend themselves.

- They were legally allowed to fight back if assaulted.

- The result is an amazing reversal, instead of the Jews being annihilated, they inflicted defeat upon their enemies.

- Esther and Mordecai are exalted in the Kingdom, the Jewish feast of Purim is established, and God is glorified.

- If you are facing insurmountable obstacles and your enemies have aligned against you, remember, it is the Lord who delivers.

- It is the Lord who has a way through for you – trust Him.

- Esther on two occasions, risks her life for the cause before her – she was a courageous and humble leader willing to lay it all on the line for her calling.

QUOTE OF THE DAY

"There is some task which the God of all the universe, the great Creator, your redeemer in Jesus Christ has for you to do, and which will remain undone and incomplete until by faith and obedience you step into the will of God."

Allan Redpath

DAY 261

📖 PSALM 73
📖 HEBREWS 11:7 – 40

◉ K E Y   T H O U G H T S

- **Psalm 73:2, 3** Take note of what it is that has caused the writer's steps to nearly slip.
- Vss. 25, 26 Complete resignation to the goodness and authority of God, *"God is the strength of my heart"*.
- Vs. 28 It is good to draw near to the Lord, to intentionally move yourself into the presence of God, to make changes in your life to get closer to the Lord – it is good!
- A summary statement of all living relationship with the Lord, *"I have put my trust in the Lord God"*.
- **Hebrews 11:7ff** This passage is so strong, so pointed and challenging – notice in particular that the faith of these heroes brings action!
- Faith, true faith, is seen by the action of the one with the faith. It is more than feelings, more than thinking/understanding – these people did stuff through faith!
- Recounting all the struggles and trials that these people went through (who are commended for their faith, not their lack of faith), brings us a helpful balance in the study of faith. (vss. 35-38)
- "The same faith that enables some to escape trouble enables others to endure it. The same faith that delivers some from death enables others to die victoriously. Faith is not a bridge over troubled waters, but is a pathway through them. Discerning the pathway and the source of any hardships encountered requires aggressive prayer and worship. Through these means, God's perspective becomes focused." (SFLB)

"Enter into the promises of God. It is your inheritance. You will do more in one year if you are really filled with the Holy Ghost than you could do in fifty years apart from Him."

Smith Wigglesworth

DAY 262

📖 PSALM 77
📖 HEBREWS 12

◉ K E Y   T H O U G H T S

- **Psalm 77** In times of trouble, call upon the Lord, make your requests and questions known to Him.

- Vss. 11, 12 Once we have unloaded all our concerns and questions, unburdened our heart – we must always come back to remembering:

  - *"The years of His power"* (right hand)

  - *"the works of the Lord, and wonders of old"*

  - Vs. 14 *"You are the God who does wonders"*

- **Hebrews 12** Another high point in the NT.

- Vs. 1 (What "weights" or "hindrances" are you carrying right now?) We are instructed to lay them aside!

- Running requires endurance!

- Vs. 2 Our motivation and focus is to be Jesus, not people, not activity – "looking to Him" is the secret to the endurance that is needed.

- He is our example, He is our encouragement, He is our strength.

- Considering Jesus and all that He went through for our redemption will preserve you from becoming *"weary and discouraged in your soul".*

- (Are you feeling weary or discouraged?) Take some time right now, look to Jesus, meditate on His amazing sacrifice and love for you – be strengthened in your spirit.

- Vss. 5-11 We all, at times, require chastening from the Lord. (How do you respond to the thought of the God of the universe loving you so much that He is willing to bring correction to your life?)
- Only an unloving, selfish parent places their own feelings above the need to chasten/discipline/prune a precious child.
- The whole point is found in vs. 11 – our loving Father in heaven is unflinchingly committed to see that our lives *"yield the peaceable fruit of righteousness"*.
- Vs. 15 *"Root of bitterness"* – roots are underground, roots have many offshoots and branches, roots cover a lot of ground – roots are strong enough to break concrete.
- Bitterness will destroy the one who lets it grow.
- Vs. 28 Here is our goal – *"serve God acceptably with reverence and godly fear"*.

QUOTE OF THE DAY

"Transiency is stamped on all our possessions, occupations, and delights. We have the hunger for eternity in our souls, the thought of eternity in our hearts, the destination for eternity written on our inmost being, and the need to ally ourselves with eternity proclaimed by the most short-lived trifles of time. Either these things will be the blessing or the curse of our lives. Which do you mean that they shall be for you?"

Alexander MacLaren

DAY 263

📖 PSALM 78:1 – 41
📖 HEBREWS 13

⊙ K E Y   T H O U G H T S

- **Psalm 78:14** The Lord leads us by day and by night if we are willing to be led!
- *"In spite of this"* - it is difficult to fathom how a people who had seen so much would choose not to believe *"in His wondrous works"*.

- (Am I like those people? Are you? Does our faith rise and fall on the momentary feelings caused by our circumstances?)
- Let us not be like this (vs. 41), let us learn from the examples of scripture and put our trust and faith in Him fully, in every situation.
- **Hebrews 13:4** Freedom within marriage in sexual expression – that couples in a loving covenant relationship can grow in the physical aspect of their love by communication and patience.
- Extra marital and pre-marital sexual activities are strictly prohibited. God's plan and place for sexual relations are very defined, one man, one woman – in marriage.
- Believe in the Creator, believe Him in this regard – His way is the best possible pathway to fullness and happiness.
- Vs. 5 The famous statement, *"I will never leave you nor forsake you"* is preceded by the instruction to live without covetousness! This promise relates to our finances!
- Vs. 6 Declare it with your mouth out loud! "THE LORD IS MY HELPER; I WILL NOT FEAR. WHAT CAN MAN DO TO ME?"
- 13:8 Memorize this verse – it provides valuable context to all that we do and believe, especially regarding the operation of the supernatural today, as it was in the times of Jesus.
- As you bring your time in the Word to a close today – take a few minutes now and throughout your day to follow the instruction of vs. 15, *"Let us continually offer the sacrifice of praise… the fruit of our lips giving thanks in His Name"*.

QUOTE OF THE DAY

"Receive every day as a resurrection from death, as a new enjoyment of life; meet every rising sun with such sentiments of God's goodness, as if you had seen it, and all things, new-created upon your account: and under the sense of so great a blessing, let your joyful heart praise and magnify so good and glorious a Creator."

William Law.

DAY 264

📖 PSALM 80
📖 1 PETER 1

⊙ K E Y   T H O U G H T S

- **Psalm 80:3,7,19** Repeat the phrase – "Restore us, O God". The cry of our hearts for restoration is a common one – how we long for the Lord's restoration and revival (vs. 18).

- Pray verses 14 and 15 for your church. When the Lord looks down and visits us, amazing things happen.

- **1 Peter 1:7** Faith must be genuine, testing helps to bring a purifying and a clarity to our faith, even though the "fires" are unpleasant.

- Vs. 13 Soberness, clear-minded thinking takes effort and a commitment to steadfastness. There will always be a "latest and greatest" thought or wind of doctrine – stand firm in the grace of God.

- Reject teachings that mock holiness, encouraging fleshly indulgences and worldliness, as indicators of liberty.

- Vs. 15 There is a very good reason to be holy - because "He is Holy"!

- The practical result of purity and obedience is going to be "fervent" love for one another with a pure heart.

- God's word lives and abides forever! Fads and guru's come and go, various teachers will rise and gain popularity and then fade from the scene. Ground yourself in the Word of God.

- "God's will to save us (2 Peter 3:9) has been effectively expressed in His Word, which accomplishes that work (John 1:13)." (SFLB)

QUOTE OF THE DAY

"Nowhere can we get to know the **holiness** of God, and come under His influence and power, except in the inner chamber. It has been well said: "No man can expect to make progress in holiness who is not often and long alone with God.""

Andrew Murray

DAY 265

📖 PSALM 81, 82
📖 1 PETER 2

☕ K E Y   T H O U G H T S

- **Psalm 81:10** This is a powerful picture of God's intention for us. All of His blessings and provisions are available to be poured into our hearts, satisfying the hunger and longings of our lives.

- (How often do we, like His own chosen people, close our mouths – refusing to receive – and go our own ways, following our own stubborn heart instead?)

- Vs. 16 The Lord is the One who has the provision of the finest delicacies for us! His ways result in the best, most satisfying supply of food for our souls.

- We also have the promise of His physical provision.

- Ps. 82:3, 4 This declaration of justice to the poor and fatherless is a timeless principle that should operate in the heart and through the practical action of every believer!

- What have you done lately to fulfill this command? It takes thought and a prepared heart.

- **1 Peter 2:3** If we have "tasted" the Lord's graciousness, it should result in character-evidence and a desire for more of God's word – just as a new born baby craves its mother's milk.

- 2:9 This is who we are in Christ! The benefits and blessings of God ought to cause praise to burst from our lips! He has taken us from so many bad places and put us in so many good places – thank you Lord.

- 1 Peter 2:11, 12 Two reasons to abstain from fleshly lusts:

    1) We are travelers and pilgrims... this life is temporary and passing – we must live in preparation for the permanent.

    2) Fleshly lusts make war against our soul, they trouble our inner man, cause unrest, uncertainty and fear.

- War means instability and danger - allowing fleshly lusts to reign in our lives will inevitably lead to spiritual casualties.

- Vs. 25 Take courage and comfort in these two titles for Jesus: "Shepherd and Overseer". He is far more than a tragic figure on a cross – He is the living, powerful God of all, able to help and bring change to our daily living!

QUOTE OF THE DAY

"It is the heart which perceives God and not the reason. That is what faith is: God perceived by the heart, not by the reason."

Blaise Pascal (1623 – 1662)

DAY 266

📖 PSALM 84, 85
📖 1 PETER 3

⊛ K E Y   T H O U G H T S

- **Psalm 84** The Psalmist expresses a longing heart for the house of God and the presence of God. What a blessing to meet with brothers and sisters, to worship and be strengthened in God's word.

- Vs. 4 "Dwelling" for believers does not depend entirely upon being in the physical house of God. We must highly value and make it a non-negotiable to attend church. We also have the joy of a personal relationship with the Holy Spirit that continues no matter our location.

- Vs. 10 The powerful beauty of being in the presence of the Lord - so much can happen so quickly.

- Vs. 11 *"Sun and shield"* - warmth and protection.

- Receive this promise today (vs. 11b), *"no good thing will He withhold from those who walk uprightly"*.

- **1 Peter 3** Wisdom for both husbands and wives. The keys to proper interpretation of this passage are:

    a) Wives: grow in godliness and the *"incorruptible beauty of a gentle and quiet spirit"* (vs. 4).

b) Husbands dwell with your wives *"with understanding, giving honor to the wife".*

- Do not bog down on a word or difficult concept in this passage – apply the overall principles and the result will be a blessed marriage.

- Vss. 10-12 are a combination of teachings from Psalm 34 and James 1. This is a wonderful maxim for *"inheriting a blessing".*

- Vs. 15 *"Always be ready!"* Never be reluctant to testify to the Lord's goodness, be prepared to take the time in the most unexpected circumstances.

- Vss. 18-22 This is a challenging passage that has been used by some to teach a second chance for salvation – this is not consistent with the whole of the scripture, and in particular Jesus' own teachings.

- The key principle to take a hold of is in vs. 22 – that all *"angels and authorities and powers"* have been made subject to Christ. He is Lord of all, Lord over all, Jesus is Lord!

QUOTE OF THE DAY

"A true revival means nothing less than a revolution, casting out the spirit of worldliness and selfishness, and making God and His love triumph in the heart and life."

Andrew Murray

DAY 267

📖 PSALM 86, 87
📖 1 PETER 4

🌀 K E Y   T H O U G H T S

- **Psalm 86** There is a preparation for the *"day of trouble".* When we come to that day we must *"call upon the Lord".* He will help and answer (vs. 7).

- Ps. 86:11 contains the phrase *"unite my heart".* This frequently used thought points out the tendency of our hearts to be distracted and wander after other suitors.

- Singleness of heart and mind, a united commitment to the Lord is what is required.

- 87:7 *"All my springs are in you."* The metaphor of a spring of water as a fountain of life – the life of the inner man is found in Christ and Him alone.

- Springs are also referred to as a man's seed or fruitfulness – or, the efforts of his life. This thought also applies to a faithfulness of purpose, strategically sowing the seed of our life and energy into the things of God.

- **1 Peter 4:6** "Those who are dead are people who heard the gospel preached while alive and thus were given an opportunity to live according to God in the spirit. "In the spirit" here refers to the realm of the Spirit, with eternal life especially in view (see 3:18, where Christ was made alive, "by" or "in" the Spirit. The opportunity also meant they were judged according to men "in the flesh", meaning that the issue of eternal judgment is determined by one's response to the gospel while alive. (See Heb.9:27) (SFLB)

- 4:10 Each person is a steward of the "gift" of ministry that we provide to the body of Christ. We are to minister it in light of the grace of God.

- Involvement in the lives of others for the sake of their good and their growth is a responsibility we all must share. Every contribution is valuable and necessary.

- Suffering for Christ's sake is honorable, suffering for the things listed in vs. 15 is not.

- Notice how Peter includes *"a busybody in other people's matters"* in this list, along with murderers, thieves etc.

- We are to continue to do good even in the midst of suffering – it is a prophetic act of faith in the "faithful Creator".

QUOTE OF THE DAY

"When the Christians, upon these occasions, received martyrdom, they were ornamented, and crowned with garlands of flowers; for which they, in heaven, received eternal crowns of glory."

John Foxe (1517-1587)

DAY 268

📖 PSALM 88, 89
📖 1 PETER 5

⊙ K E Y   T H O U G H T S

- **Psalm 89:13-15** Descriptions of the capacity and the character of God are intended to encourage us in God.

- The world and the devil will continually accuse and malign our God. The scripture is a great defender of the holiness and love of the Lord.

- These are not just observations of occasions where the Lord shows these qualities – He IS all of these things!

- **1 Peter 5:6, 7** The progression of personal development to experience being lifted up is to first humble yourself, then cast your care upon Him (because He cares for you).

- The result is the *"lifting"* up of the Lord. When He elevates you in any way it is a true and right blessing.

- Not personal ambition or striving, but a true blessing from God.

- We are to be *"sober and vigilant"* - because there is an enemy of our souls who is prowling around seeking our destruction.

- Resistance is accomplished through "faith"!

- It is our faith that extinguishes the enemy's fiery arrows of accusation and intimidation (Eph. 6:16).

- Notice the four benefits that Christ Jesus brings in vs. 10
  - Perfect you
  - Establish you
  - Strengthen you
  - Settle you

"I'm against sin. I'll kick it as long as I've got a foot, and I'll fight it as long as I've got a fist. I'll butt it as long as I've got a head. I'll bite it as long as I've got a tooth. And when I'm old and fistless and footless and toothless, I'll gum it till I go home to Glory and it goes home to perdition!"

Billy Sunday

DAY 269

📖 PSALM 90, 91
📖 2 PETER 1

⊕ K E Y   T H O U G H T S

- **Psalm 90:4-11** is a build-up to vs. 12. Our lives are brief and fragile. We do not have guarantees of decades or years to sort things out or procrastinate on obedience to the will and ways of God.

- Vs. 12 A great principle to live by is to see each day as a gift, a treasure. Think of maximizing every day's potential for God's glory, rather than wasting time. Put prayer into what good purpose God has for each and every day!

- Like compounding interest in a savings account, the incremental investment of Spirit-filled people serving daily the Kingdom of God becomes a great treasure in this life and in the life to come.

- Ps. 91 Read this marvelous signature Psalm out loud – this is a Psalm that you should return to often.

- This Psalm is a wonderful chapter to read to someone who is sick or in hospital – such comfort!

- The latter verses give us insight into Jesus' tender relationship with the Father. This type of intimacy - *"He has set His love upon Me"* - is the Father's heart to you today.

- Think of it. The Creator of the entire universe, has set His love upon you today!

- **2 Peter 1:5-8** Consider what it means to *"give all diligence"*.

- These couplets are an amazing picture of spiritual growth. We often make the mistake of picking a particular aspect of spiritual growth and focusing too much on that one part, rather than building a balanced and accountable spiritual life – where each characteristic modifies and enhances the others. Add:
  - Virtue/character/integrity to faith
  - Knowledge to virtue
  - Self-control to knowledge
  - Perseverance to self-control
  - Godliness to perseverance
  - Brotherly kindness to godliness
  - Love to brotherly kindness
- The goal or purpose of following this pattern for life is to be fruitful and fertile, rather than unfruitful and barren (vs. 10).
- How sad to see a believer whose life is unfruitful. It is not God's will for you to live a dry, dead, barren life.
- The Apostles were *"eye witnesses"*. This is important!
- Vs. 20 and 21, along with 2 Timothy 3:16 – two excellent descriptions of the inspiration of the scripture – this is a miraculous, spiritual book, given by God through the Holy Spirit.
- The Bible is no ordinary book, the power of God's word is still transforming lives and peoples all over the world.

QUOTE OF THE DAY

"A readiness to believe every promise implicitly, to obey every command unhesitatingly, to stand perfect and complete in all the will of God, is the only true spirit of Bible study."

Andrew Murray

DAY 270

📖 PSALM 92, 93
📖 2 PETER 2

⊚ K E Y   T H O U G H T S

- **Psalm 92:10** The term "horn" is used metaphorically for "strength". The image is of a great, strong beast, (ox, buffalo, rhino) whose strength is characterized by the horn on their head.

- *"Fresh oil"* – the anointing oil of the day was fragrant, freshly made and had both penetrating and healing properties. The Holy Spirit has fresh oil of anointing for you today, ask Him now for a "fresh" anointing of the Spirit.

- 92:13-15 This is a beautiful image that comes out of the instruction to be "planted" in the house of the Lord. Many people are a long ways from being "planted". They are more like tumbleweeds, that are blown here and there where ever the wind takes them… never settling down, never committing, never serving.

- The result of this planting in the house of the Lord, will be: Flourishing, bountiful healthy growth

- Still bearing fruit in old age, still fresh in old age, still growing in old age!

- What a great picture – to be old and still ministering, still sweet, still growing - wow!

- **2 Peter 2** is a description of false teachers and a very stern warning against them.

- The focus is more upon false lifestyle and motives than false doctrine.

- Two of the characteristics are: covetousness and fleshly lusts; and great promises but no delivery. Often these false teachers have extremes to their ministry, some very positive results (and testimony) accompanied by many contrasting, confusing, hurtful results.

- Peter does not mince words about the destiny of these deceivers.

- Vss. 20-22 are about as clear as you can get that those who have known Christ and turn away are indeed very lost.
- "The false teachers, having experienced the cleansing power of Christ, are now rejecting Him. Hence, they have returned to their former corrupt life-style and are worse off than they were before. Believers who fall into apostasy by deliberately rejecting the death and resurrection of Jesus Christ are in a more tragic position than unconverted pagans." (see Heb. 6:4-6; 10:26) (SFLB)

QUOTE OF THE DAY

"Yes, apostasy happens. Sometimes the catalyst is flagrant sin. The pain of conviction and repentance is refused, and the only alternative to it is wholesale rejection of Christ. But sometimes the catalyst is a thorn growing quietly in the heart, an indifference to the way of the Cross, a drifting that is not reversed by the knowledge of biblical warnings."

Sinclair B. Ferguson

DAY 271

☐ PSALM 94, 95
☐ 2 PETER 3

☾ K E Y   T H O U G H T S

- **Psalm 94:17-19** Times of anxiety, a sense of slipping from a secure place, a need for help... the LORD is sufficient to provide for all our needs in these trying times.
- The Lord is our help, He will help you! Stand firm!
- 95:6 Take the time right now to actually kneel before the Lord and worship Him. There is a powerful significance to the humble posture of bowing down.
- This is a valuable practice for all believers – to kneel before the Lord.
- Vs. 8 Hardening of the heart happens when we close our ears to the voice of the Lord. He is speaking but we are choosing to

not hear. The result is an increasingly hardened heart.

- **2 Peter 3:8** God has a timetable that is vastly different than ours. Do not make the mistake of insisting that God time His efforts with our ideas of the right time for something to happen. He knows the right time.
- Many have testified to this: "the Lord is seldom early, but He is never late".
- Vs. 9 clearly describes the heart of God – His saving grace is expansive enough to welcome every person. His heart is that none should perish.
- God would not predestine anyone to hell! We are all free to choose. His great heart is that all would know salvation and have eternal life.
- Vs. 11 There is a holy conduct that is characteristic of true followers of Jesus, this includes an anticipation of His returning.
- Our faith will affect the way we live our lives – or it is not faith at all!
- Vs. 17 There is always a prevalent danger for believers to listen to the errors of the wicked and be shaken from their own steadfastness – listen to the godly, listen to the faithful, do not be moved by the shouting of the wicked!

QUOTE OF THE DAY

"If a thing is free to be good it is also free to be bad. And free will is what has made evil possible. Why, then, did God give them free will? Because free will, though it makes evil possible, is also the only thing that makes possible any love or goodness or joy worth having."

C.S. Lewis

DAY 272

📖 PSALM 96, 97
📖 1 JOHN 1

⊙ K E Y   T H O U G H T S

- **Psalm 96** We have been created by God to sing, to worship and exalt the Lord. Growth in praise and worship is critical for growth in the Lord.

- Vss. 4ff Declaring the characteristics and works of the Lord in our worship is a faith building and strengthening practice.

- Vss. 11-13 Many in our world have perverted the admiration of nature into the worship of nature. The believer's appreciation of nature comes from the awareness that nature by its beauty and activity is offering praise and worship to God.

- Nature's wonders testify to the wonder-working power of God, not to nature itself.

- 97:10 A very plain instruction to those who love the Lord. The nearer we draw to Jesus the more we are repulsed by evil and have no desire to fellowship with it.

- **1 John 1:5** *"God is light"* – there is enough truth and depth in these three words to provide tremendous guidance and stability – there is no darkness in Him, none at all!

- The enemy is continually trying to convince us that the Lord is not who He says He is. Most sin comes from the doubting of God's goodness, doubting His promises, doubting His character.

- Vs. 6 What does John indicate is evidence of the "practice" of the truth? Note that it is more than the knowledge of the truth.

- Vs. 7 Nearness to the light of God results in nearness to one another, how fantastic! If you want to be near to other people, draw near to the Lord. His presence and work in you will result in deeper and multiplied relationships with other kindred hearted people.

- Vs. 9 A bedrock scripture of hope and confidence. This verse should be memorized as a reference point for our lives.

- Vs. 10 Prideful denial of sin is akin to calling God a liar, a very foolish accusation. He does not lie!

DAY 273

📖 PSALM 98, 99
📖 1 JOHN 2

◉ K E Y   T H O U G H T S

- **Psalm 98** Continued encouragement to shout and praise the Lord!

- Ps. 99:8 God is given the name/title *"God-who-forgives"*. It is one of the actual names of our God.

- But it is important to remember that there are always earthly consequences to our sin, even though our sins are forgiven, a seed sown will produce fruit after its own kind.

- A lie will reap a harvest of the loss of integrity. A theft will reap a harvest of the loss of employment or incarceration – sin, though forgiven has a splash to it you will always get some on you. The Lord will strengthen you through it.

- **1 John 2** This chapter is filled with great truth for us.

- Vs. 1 As in Psalm 99, we have another name for our God – Jesus is our "Advocate" with the Father – He is our go-between, His blood and His sacrifice for us are the advocacy of heaven!

- Vs. 3 There are specific ways that we can "know" that we know Him.

- Vs. 5 by keeping His word, the Lord's purposes are in a

continual process of being perfected in us.

- Vss. 9-11 The practical walk of reconciliation must be a part of the life of every true believer – hatred of brothers and sisters in Christ is incompatible with a dedicated life to Christ.

- The world is characterized by three things in vs. 16:

    1) the lust of the flesh

    2) the lust of the eyes

    3) the pride of life (self-sufficiency, arrogance)

- Vs. 18"We do affirm these things: 1) God is the Sovereign of the Universe and the God of history. Which is His-Story. 2) As such, He knows the end from the beginning and at the end of history will have been verified as All-Wise and vindicated as All-Just. 3) His Son, Jesus Christ, shall come to earth again for His church (John 14:1-3; Acts 1:11; 1 Cor. 15:5-58; 1 Thess. 4:16, 17), and shall rule on earth (Is. 9:7; 11:6-9); Rev.20:1-6). 4) There is a final judgment, with the reward of eternal life in heaven promised to the redeemed and the judgment of eternal loss in hell for those who remain un-regenerate (Rev. 20:11-15; 21:22 – 22:5)." (SFLB)

- Vs. 27 The Holy Spirit is able to anoint us. He is our teacher! Beware of teachers who by their teaching, create a dependency upon themselves.

- If you find that you are unable to be free to receive from the Word, understand it and have the Holy spirit apply it to your life, and you feel bound to hear from some teacher before you will feel edified, or certain that you are right – you have lost the joy of this promise of God.

- You can understand the Bible! You can receive insights from God to your spirit from the Holy Spirit – teachers are helpful, but our dependency needs to be on the Spirit of truth, not on the words of a teacher interpreting the Spirit's truth.

- Read your Bible, receive the anointing of the Spirit to bring it to life to your heart – the Holy Spirit will teach you all things!

"The vigor of our spiritual life will be in exact proportion to the place held by the Bible in our life and thoughts."

George Mueller

DAY 274

📖 PSALM 100
📖 1 JOHN 3

☮ K E Y T H O U G H T S

- **Psalm 100** Five little verses that contain a heart-lifting expression of praise to God.

- Read this Psalm out loud. Make it an expression of your praise to the Lord.

- Ps 101:3 We need to make strategic decisions regarding what we deliberately put before our eyes. Nothing wicked!

- Be very cautious about spending too much time or energy studying the work of the wicked.

- If you have ever experienced the sense of having been polluted by some person's wickedness you understand this. It's a bit like walking through a barnyard – you can't help getting some on you.

- Slander has no place in the life of the believer.

- **1 John 3:8** Sin must always be connected to its author – there are no harmless sins – those who sin are "of the Devil".

- John is defending believers against false teachers who were telling the believers that their spirit and their flesh were disconnected. They were saying in essence "you are free to indulge your flesh, sin freely, it does not impact your spirit".

- Vs.9 "Sin is natural to the children of the Devil, who 'has sinned from the beginning', but unnatural to children of God, who cannot sin without the Spirit's conviction. A constant indulgence in sin contradicts the claim to have a personal knowledge of Christ." (SFLB)

- Vss. 14-15 A beautiful evidence of new life – love for the brethren. (Vss. 16-19) Practical evidence of heart transformation – not just "in word or in tongue" but in actual action!
- The next practical evidence of Christ in us: we live "by the Spirit" whom He (Jesus) has given us. The inner witness of the Holy Spirit.

DAY 275

📖 PSALM 102
📖 I JOHN 4

☉ K E Y   T H O U G H T S

- **Psalm 102** During a time of trial or struggle we must be free to pour out our hearts and our anguish to the Lord. He is able to hear the cry of our hearts.
- The Psalmists were experts at 'pouring' out their troubles to God.
- Vss. 12 and 27 highlight the key perspective to have in difficult times: the Lord *"endures forever"* and *"You are the same and Your years will have no end"*.
- **I John 4** This chapter is almost one continuous highlight.
- How to identify false prophets (vss. 2-3).
- The key to overcoming – verse 4. Say it loudly and personalize this great verse *"He that is in me is greater…"*.
- Vs. 7 Love must be manifested through us to other people.
- Vs. 10 This is the second time we come across the word "propitiation". It refers to Jesus bearing the wrath of God against our sins. The wrath of God flows from His holiness, sin must be punished. Jesus was our substitute.

- Vs. 13 Another recurring theme – the indwelling relationship with the Holy Spirit.
- Vs. 14 Our confession is so very important, the central test of Christian orthodoxy is the nature of the confession of Christ – "who do you say that He is?"
- Vs. 18 There is a good reason to have "no fear". It is that the magnificent love of God has cast it out. Accepting the love of God fully, delivers from fear. It is His nature to love. His love is not based on our being worthy or qualified – the fear of rejection is cast out by undeserved and abundant love.
- Vs. 21 This is a commandment! "Must love". The love of God in our hearts makes hatred and bitterness impossible – they cannot mix.
- The presence of one cancels the other. Either love will cancel hatred or hatred will cancel love!
- *"Let us love one another, for love is of God."*

QUOTE OF THE DAY

"Hating people is like burning down your own house to get rid of a rat."

Harry Emerson Fosdick

DAY 276

📖 PSALM 103
📖 I JOHN 5

◉ K E Y   T H O U G H T S

- **Psalm 103** To bless the Lord, to praise Him and recount His blessings is a vital part of a growing and faith-filled life.
- We too easily forget His "benefits" - two are listed here.
    a) Forgives all your iniquities.
    b) Heals all your diseases.
- Vs. 3 Healing of the body is contained in both the old and the new covenants.

- Believing and asking for healing is one of the blessed privileges of following Jesus. Do not hesitate or be afraid to ask.

- Vs. 12 What a blessing to know how far the Lord has removed our sins from us! He never brings them up again – they are gone.

- Vs. 13 There is comfort in our weakness and failures. He knows that we are flesh. He is not a severe, uncompassionate drill sergeant – He knows our frame.

- Take some time right now to "bless the Lord!"

- **1 John 5** John is addressing various heresies concerning the divinity of Jesus and the place of the Holy Spirit in the Trinity.

- Most heresy has to do with some aspect of Jesus' Divine fullness and His humanity.

- Father and Son are One (vs. 1), Father, Son and Holy Spirit are One (vs. 7).

- Faith overcomes the world – faith is powerful. Faith has conquering power.

- 1 John 5:12 One of the simplest, most straight forward statements of the news of salvation in all of scripture.

- Vs. 13 You can "know" that you have eternal life. Doctrines that leave you uncertain and questioning are not being true to the Word. Stick to the "main and the plain" teaching of scripture.

- Vss. 14 – 15 Our confidence in prayer: "we know" He hears us. We know "we have" the petitions we have asked for.

- Be encouraged! Continue in prayer. Do not give up! He hears and He answers.

QUOTE OF THE DAY

"And this is the testimony: that God has given us eternal life, and this life is in His Son. He who has the Son has life; he who does not have the Son of God does not have life."

1 John 5:11-12 (NKJV)

DAY 277

📖 PSALM 104
📖 II JOHN
📖 III JOHN

⊙ K E Y   T H O U G H T S

- **Psalm 104** All creation is a testimony to the power of the Creator!

- Notice all the action statements: *"He sends...", "He waters...", "He causes..."*

- Verse 24 summarizes *"... the earth is full of Your possessions".*

- Vs. 33 Make the determination today to *"sing to the Lord as long as I live".*

- **II John: 8, 9** These are definitive verses to test orthodoxy

  a) the confession of Christ must not be diminished in any way. He was at once fully God and fully man!

  b) There are those who do "abide" in the doctrine of Christ.

- John is very straightforward. Those who do not "abide" do not have God.

- The tension is obvious, false teachers were trying to take advantage of this gracious lady's hospitality. She was to resist the false teachers and not receive them.

- **III John** Three individuals present in the church. Two are positive and are commended. One is exposed as a divisive manipulator.

- Diotrophes is a real person at the time of writing. He could also be a character profile for us to recognize in the church today.

- Church unity, humility and love for the brethren are high values and worthy of defending.

- Diotrophes is a modern day power broker or bully in the church.

- Do not be intimidated – choose to have the commendable character of Demitrius instead.

"Beloved, have you ever thought that someday you will not have anything to try you, or anyone to vex you again? There will be no opportunity in heaven to learn or to show the spirit of patience, forbearance, and longsuffering. If you are to practice these things, it must be now."

A.B. Simpson

DAY 278

📖 PSALM 107
📖 JUDE

⊚ K E Y   T H O U G H T S

- **Psalm 107** This Psalm has a number of stanzas all prefaced by the phrase: *"Oh that men would give thanks to the Lord for His goodness and for the wonderful works to the children of men."*

- Vs. 9 describes the primary characteristics of our God, as they relate to our souls.

    a) "He satisfies the longing soul"

    b) and "fills the hungry soul with goodness".

- Vs. 43 The wise observation of "the things" will bring us to experience and understand the loving kindness of the Lord.

- **Jude** *"Contend for the faith".* Stand up and defend the faith that was originally delivered by the Apostles.

- "The corruption of the faith is found in self-centered and unloving behavior, immoral or sensual lifestyles and in distorted or deceitful teachings." (SFLB)

- Vs. 16 Note carefully these characteristics of false teachers (vs. 19).

- Vs. 20 One of the proven and recommended ways of building yourself up in your most holy faith is to "pray in the Spirit".

- Our prayer language edifies the inner spirit. When we commune in the Spirit we are strengthened in our inner man.

- The Spirit witnesses to the truth, guides with discernment and strengthens hope.
- We are to seek to rescue those who are nearing the fires of judgment by losing sight of the truth.
- Snatching someone from the fire (vs. 23) is a strong metaphor for reaching out to those who are being drawn in by false teaching.
- 12 characteristics of a false teacher... (vss. 8-19)"1) teaches things one cannot apply 2) practices licentious behavior 3) speaks disrespectfully of authority 4) rejects established authority 5) is more worried about money than the welfare of those to whom he ministers 6) promises things he cannot and does not produce 7) constantly changes his message: always teaches "some new thing" 8) shows no enduring fruit 9) complains and criticizes others 10) is motivated by personal gain 11) is a self-promoter 12) flatters others when it is to his advantage." (SFLB)

QUOTE OF THE DAY

"This man is like a burning stick that has been snatched from the fire."

Zechariah 3:2b (NLT) (When John Wesley was five years old the rectory caught fire. So it was that in future years John Wesley frequently referred to himself as "a brand from the burning" – someone plucked by God from the flames.)

DAY 279

📖 PSALMS 108, 109
📖 REVELATION 1

☞ K E Y   T H O U G H T S

- **Psalms 108, 109** These two Psalms present the pleas of someone with enemies and someone falsely accused.
- Praise, worship and remembrance of the goodness and faithfulness of God are vital attitudes in the midst of conflict. These attitudes keep our perspective right.

- 108:13 It's always God, if any "treading" down of enemies is going to happen, who does the treading.
- 109:4 The appropriate response to accusations is to give ourselves to prayer!
- After a long list of things asked for toward his enemies (nothing wrong with pouring out our hearts to God) then the psalmist changes gears to praise and petition.
- Vs. 25 *"Help me…" "save me…"* David is confident in the Lord. This is where our confidence must be.
- **Revelation 1:3** We are instructed by the Holy Spirit that there is a blessing promised those who will read and hear the words of this prophesy.
- Not only read and hear but "keep" the warnings and instructions contained in these chapters.
- Vss. 8, 11, 17, 18 All identify the speaker of the prophecy as Jesus Christ.
- The First and Last, the Almighty, The Eternal One, possessing the keys of hell and death.
- He is the One with all authority. He is alive forevermore.
- We too would do well to worship Him as John does (vs. 17) but we are not to be afraid. Praise God.
- All this magnificence and power and we are allowed to know Him without fear.

QUOTE OF THE DAY

"A readiness to believe every promise implicitly, to obey every command unhesitatingly, to stand perfect and complete in all the will of God, is the only true spirit of Bible study."

Andrew Murray

DAY 280

📖 REVELATION 2, 3, 4

⊕ K E Y   T H O U G H T S

- **Revelation 2-4** We will focus our reading in Revelation for the next seven days.

- Reading Revelation in one sitting is the best way to get a feel for the larger themes.

- By getting some traction through this book we will try to understand some practical themes for our lives. We will not delve into all the varied eschatological nuances (there are good study resources available).

- As an intro let me quote the Spirit-Filled Life Bible:

- "Both the Rapture of the church (including the second coming of Christ) and the Millennium (1000 year reign of Christ on the earth) are center pieces in the prophetic future."

- Both events are absolutely certain in scripture. What is less certain is precise timing and sequence of these events.

- "The mainspring of Christian hope and courage is the certainty that the Enemy has been defeated and is doomed and that followers of the Lamb are not fighting a losing cause. He has already overcome and therefore they can and will be overcomers." (SFLB)

- Revelation 2, 3, and 4 contain the messages of Jesus to seven churches.

- The instruction to each of these churches is as follows:

    1) Ephesus: "You have left your first love – do the works you did at first."

    2) Smyrna: "Be faithful until death."

    3) Pergamos: "Repent."

    4) Thyatira: "Judgment is coming, keep the faith."

    5) Sardis: "Repent and strengthen what remains."

    6) Philadelphia: "Keep the faith."

    7) Laodicea: they were lukewarm, neither hot nor cold – "Be

zealous and repent."

- Rev 3:20 Jesus is always knocking at our heart's door. A beautiful image of fellowship with the Lord. Open the door today! Right now.
- If you see yourself described in any of these churches, take the steps of restoration that are prescribed.

QUOTES OF THE DAY

"Nevertheless I have this against you, that you have left your first love."

Revelation 2:4 (NKJV)

"Look how far you have fallen! Turn back to me and do the works you did at first."

Revelation 2:5 (NLT)

DAY 281

📖 REVELATION 5, 6, 7

⊙ K E Y   T H O U G H T S

- **Revelation 5:5** A number of the names of Jesus – the Revelation in its prophetic glory has a number of overarching themes. The exaltation and supremacy of Christ, His glory, His victory is one of the main themes.
- Vs. 5:8 The value of the prayers of the saints – our prayers are never lost. The prayer of a righteous man or woman is highly valued in heaven.
- (How does your worship reflect upon the greatness of our God? Is it suited to the immensity and power of the Lamb?)
- Vss. 13 – 14 A picture of the absolute submission of all creation "every creature", to the authority of the Lord.
- (SFLB) "All history is moving toward the predestined goal of the eventual and ultimate universal recognition of the Lordship of Jesus Christ." AMEN!
- 7:1-8 Israel has a permanent covenant place in the heart of

God. He himself will seal 144,000 for His own glory and in keeping with His promise.

- 7:17 A beautiful promise and picture of the healing, restoring role of the Lamb. Imagine a day when *"God will wipe away every tear from their eyes".*

- One of the great promises of heaven, one of the marvelous miracles of being in the presence and light of God forever is that all regrets, all pain, all remembrance of evil will no longer cause sadness or tears.

- Perhaps, because of *"knowing even as we are known"*, our understanding and capacity being so expanded we will be able to see the whole picture.

- Heaven will not be diminished by earth's sorrows!

QUOTE OF THE DAY

"Heaven is not here, it's there. If we were given all we wanted here, our hearts would settle for this world rather than the next. God is forever luring us up and away from this one, wooing us to Himself and His still invisible Kingdom, where we will certainly find what we so keenly long for."

Elisabeth Elliot

DAY 282

📖 REVELATION 8, 9, 10

⊛ K E Y   T H O U G H T S

- **Revelation 8-10** The believers' great hope is in being preserved from these days of wrath and judgment.

- Christ's second coming and the rapture of the church prior to all these horrors, is often called the "blessed hope".

- The purpose of these judgments continues to be the hope of God that the people left behind would repent and lay down their lives for Him!

- 9:20 - 21 Murders, sorceries, theft and sexual immorality are not repented of!

- A hardened, rebellious heart is a fearful thing.
- 10:8-11 The little book represents the gospel message that John and the witnesses are to declare.
- The gospel contains both sweet and bitter components.
- Sweet to those who respond humbly and totally to the grace of God.
- Bitter to those who persist in sinful ways, being offended by the gospel as it points to their error and the certainty of judgment.

QUOTE OF THE DAY

"The beginning of men's **rebellion** against God was, and is, the lack of a thankful heart."

Francis Schaeffer

DAY 283

📖 REVELATION 11, 12, 13

💮 K E Y   T H O U G H T S

- **Revelation 11-13** We meet a number of key figures in these chapters.
- Our purpose in this reading guide is not to provide an extensive study of end times.
- There are those who have devoted great study to end times – our purpose is to read it, as John instructed us and to identity the larger themes within the prophetic imagery.
- The two witnesses: God is always reaching out to humankind – He is always preparing a witness to His Name. After an earthquake (vs. 13) there are those who give glory to God.
- 12:9-11 give some insights into some of the character and work of Satan. He is, always has been and always will be:

  a) a deceiver

  b) the accuser of the brethren
- There are many in our world unwilling to admit that there is

an entity who is evil. Satan is absolutely sold to wickedness, hatred and evil, the father of lies. Revelation gives us such a clear picture of this. 11:11 Those who overcome have victory through two things:

a) the blood of the Lamb

b) the word of their testimony

- Those are effective weapons for victory today. There is spiritual authority over the enemy! Use these resources today.

- The Anti-Christ or the beast is introduced in this passage. Much speculation has flown over the years as to who this will be. All that is certain is that he will appear at a certain point in the tribulation.

- It is not hard to conceive of one world ruler, global currencies or "marks". We are living in the last times. Our task is to live ready, diligent in the work of the Lord.

QUOTE OF THE DAY

"We overcome the accuser of our brothers and sisters, we overcome our consciences, we overcome our bad tempers, we overcome our defeats, we overcome our lusts, we overcome our fears, we overcome our pettiness on the basis of the blood of the Lamb."

D. A. Carson

DAY 284

📖 REVELATION 14, 15, 16

◉ K E Y   T H O U G H T S

- **Revelation 14** Be encouraged dear ones! All of the pain and sorrow described in the passages is intended to make clear in a final sense – God will not be mocked, blasphemed or defeated!

- 14:9-11 The consequence of worshipping the beast is a fearsome judgment.

- 14:12 Notice the description of saints - "patience".

- The segment, Rev. 15 & 16, is the "wrath" passage.

- Jesus interjects in 16:15. This is something sure and directly applicable to our lives and our preparation for the day of the Lord.
- There is great strength in knowing the extent of the horror of these days.
- Dear brother, dear sister – do all you can to live holy, to be ready, to be among those who are caught away in the clouds.
- Live near to Jesus today, consecrate your life – do not risk or gamble with your soul.

QUOTE OF THE DAY

"But of that day and hour no one knows, not even the angels in heaven, nor the Son, but only the Father. Take heed, watch and pray; for you do not know when the time is. . . . Watch therefore, for you do not know when the master of the house is coming--in the evening, at midnight, at the crowing of the rooster, or in the morning--lest, coming suddenly, he find you sleeping. And what I say to you, I say to all: Watch!"

Mark 13:32-35, 36, 37

DAY 285

📖 REVELATION 17, 18, 19

✺ K E Y   T H O U G H T S

- **Revelation 17** You will start to feel the momentum shift in our reading today – stand firm, this saga of end times has a magnificent ending!
- 17:8 "The book of Life" is a recurring theme in Revelation. Those who are born again and those who have been washed of their sins by the blood of Jesus are those whose "names are written in the book of Life".
- 17:14 A burst of praise and a wonderful designation for those who *"are with Him" – "chosen and faithful".*
- What an insightful description of our standing in Christ, chosen by Him and then faithful to Him, the balance of grace and free will.

- 18:20 Much of the sense of the apocalyptic scenes has to do with the ultimate retribution of God against the wickedness of this world. It is the Lord who vindicates in perfect justice.
- 19:6, 7 The marriage supper of the Lamb – loud enthusiastic outbursts of praise. Put yourself in the midst of this awesome time of worship – what a celebration. What a feast of blessings.
- 19:11ff Here comes the triumphant Jesus Christ. *"King of kings and Lord of lords"*.
- 19:20b One of the best verses in the Bible! More to come… tomorrow.

QUOTES OF THE DAY

"God's wrath arises from His intense, settled hatred of all sin and is the tangible expression of His inflexible determination to punish it. We might say God's wrath is His justice in action, rendering to everyone his just due, which, because of our sin, is always judgment."

Jerry Bridges

"Faith, which is trust, and fear are opposite poles. If a man has the one, he can scarcely have the other in vigorous operation. He that has his trust set upon God does not need to dread anything except the weakening or the paralyzing of that trust."

Alexander MacLaren

DAY 286

📖 REVELATION 20, 21, 22

◉ K E Y   T H O U G H T S

- **Revelation 20, 21, 22** What a blessing to come to the end of the story and see the triumph, the blessing and the joy of the heavenly vision!
- The struggle of the middle chapters is wiped away as the events of the end of time and the beginning of a New Day is unveiled.

- 20:10 This is the judgment and the final appearance of the Enemy! He will never tempt again, never accuse again, never lie again! Hallelujah!

- 21:4 Allow yourself to meditate and rejoice in these magnificent promises. This place called heaven will be unlike anything we've ever experienced before. The removal of all these negative factors will turn everything currently wrong into being right.

- The new Jerusalem is an actual place - approximately 1400 – 1500 miles (2400 km) square. It is described as a cube with these dimensions – lots of room for everyone who has responded to Christ's invitation of salvation.

- 21:22-27 describes the magnificent glory of this new Jerusalem – all the best of the first creation with the glory of a new creation added to it!

- 22:3 Consider the depth of impact when there is "no more curse", everything from sickness, death and hatred to thorns and plagues will be gone!

- 22:7, 12, 20 Jesus emphasizes the imminence of His return. From our limited view these events may seem to be in the distant future, but in God's time table events are moving as planned and at a rapid pace.

- There is no room for gambling with the timing of our devotion to Christ – it must be all out at all times! No one knows the day or the hour, the consistent instruction for those desiring godliness is to be ready, and ready now!

- 22:17 The last record of an invitation, the vast and loving heart of God extends His desire to us once again. There is satisfaction for the soul, there is a place where our spiritual thirst will be satisfied...

- *"Whoever desires... take freely."* There is no rationing of God's grace or love, there is only the sorting out of our values to choose blessing and fulfillment, over selfishness and sin. If we will, He will!

DAY 287

📖 PSALMS 110 – 113

◉ K E Y   T H O U G H T S

- **Psalm 110:3** An indicator of the moving of the Lord in the hearts of the people of God is when "the people" are willing volunteers. The Holy Spirit moves people's hearts to engage, to help, to pull the load together.

- (Is there a need that you see in the church? Would you be a "willing volunteer"?) Taking steps to involvement will always cause you to feel connected, to feel that you are contributing and to experience the joy of sharing a vision with people who are like minded.

- 111:1 There is value to gathering in the assembly and the congregation. This is where together, our spirits are lifted in praise to the Lord, with our whole heart, enthusiastically.

- 112:1 *"The fear of the Lord"* - this frequently mentioned principle brings so many benefits to our lives. The fear of the Lord is a reverence for God's holiness and greatness, a submissive heart to His commandments and ways and a willing heart that continually leans toward trusting the Lord and His character of goodness.

- The benefit is "blessing" – blessed is the man/woman who fears the Lord!

- 113:3 Our praise is to be a continuous flow from morning to evening. Think what it would do to your perspective if all day long you were giving praise to the Lord – we are instructed in other places to give thanks in everything. (1 Thess. 5:16)

- We have the blessing of a relationship with the living God, which is not conformity to religious limitations. Be a friend of

God, commune with Him throughout your day, as friend with friend.

- 113:9 We want to pray today for those whose hearts ache for children and yet there is barrenness in their lives. This verse says the Lord grants the barren a home.
- "Lord we are asking today that you would bring fruitfulness and Your blessing of children, into the homes of those couples whose hearts are longing for children. In the name of Jesus, we call upon You Lord, for the blessing of many children."

QUOTE OF THE DAY

"Worship is a meeting at the centre so that our lives are centred in God and not lived eccentrically. We worship so that we live in response to and from this centre, the living God. Failure to worship consigns us to a life of spasms and jerks, at the mercy of every advertisement, every seduction, every siren. Without worship we live manipulated and manipulating lives. We move in either frightened panic or deluded lethargy as we are, in turn, alarmed by spectres and soothed by placebos. If there is no centre, there is no circumference."

Edmund Clowney

DAY 288

📖 PSALMS 115, 116, 118

👉 K E Y   T H O U G H T S

- **Psalm 115** The contrast between the living God and idols is presented here. Although an idol has the appearance of ears, eyes etc... they are inanimate, dead objects with no personhood.
- But the Lord is our *"help and our shield"* (vss. 9, 11), and He has been "mindful" of us.
- Vss. 14, 15 The desire of the author for God's blessing upon His people. It is a blessing of increase that is described as "more and more".
- Vs. 18 Our responsibility is to bless the Lord – continually.

- Chapter 116 *"He has heard my voice"* – think of that... the Lord actually hears your voice when you call upon Him.
- This is one of the keys to persevering prayer – we are heard when we pray. Add to that truth the fact of God's goodness, faithfulness and mercy and we have a powerful motivator to continue in passionate prayer.
- Vs. 4 In times of trouble and sorrow the action we must take is to *"call upon the name of the Lord"*.
- And then...vs. 7 – we are called to rest in the Lord, to not allow anxiety and worry to rule our lives. We call, He hears, we rest.
- Chapter 118 has a number of wonderful promises of encouragement:
- Vs. 6 The Lord is *"on your side"* do not fear.
- Vs. 8 It is better to trust in the Lord than to put *"confidence in man"*.
- Vs. 14 The Lord is your "strength and song".
- Vs. 24 This is the day that the "Lord has made".
- Vss. 22-24 This prophetic stanza refers to Jesus. It is quoted by Jesus in Matthew 21:42.
- Our reading concludes today with another exhortation to give thanks to the Lord – for *"He is good"*!

QUOTE OF THE DAY

"The very first temptation in the history of mankind was the temptation to be discontent... that is exactly what discontent(ment) is - a questioning of the goodness of God."

Jerry Bridges

DAY 289

📖 PSALM 119:1 – 88

⊙ K E Y   T H O U G H T S

- **Psalm 119** We have come to one of the great chapters of the Bible. Although the language used by the psalmist refers to the law, the subject is the word of God, the written word.

- The Bible, His inspired word, is a precious commodity that must be central to all of our thinking and living – the word cannot be a casual add on to other ideologies.

- Learning to love the word of God is a key to being stable and mature in the Lord, knowing His word will mean you will not be easily shaken.

- Vs. 2 Seeking the Lord in order to receive blessing requires the "whole heart". This means a heart that is undivided by other affections or "idols" - a heart that is transparent without attempts to hide or deceive – a heart that is quick to repent, willing to admit need, eager to trust!

- Whenever you come to words with the root word of "revive" (revived, revival, revives) circle them in your Bible. It is comforting to know that even the great men and women of Bible times were aware of their need for reviving! (vss. 25, 40…etc.)

- Vss. 23, 24 When we face opposition our refuge is the word of God, the testimonies of God's past faithfulness and works. His word will restore your joy.

- Vss. 36, 37 Covetousness is one of the things that will turn our hearts from the Lord.

- Vs. 37 is a fantastic motto for victory – "Turn away my eyes from looking at worthless things." Wow!

- When you struggle or enter a dry season you will find your heart beginning to long for the truth of the word. Do not deny the craving of your soul for the Lord, He is the only one who can satisfy (vs. 40).

- His word gives us life (vs. 50).

- Vss. 67, 71 Affliction processed properly brings us back to the precepts and statutes of the Lord. In that regard affliction is good.
- Vs. 72 (Could it be said of you or of me, that the word of God is worth more to us than thousands of coins of gold?)
- Vs. 87, 88 Again, enemies and hardship almost make "an end" of us – but we are those who do not forsake the word of God.
- We are those asking and seeking to be revived!

QUOTE OF THE DAY

"The coming revival must begin with a great revival of prayer. It is in the closet, with the door shut, that the sound of abundance of rain will first be heard. An increase of secret prayer with ministers will be the sure harbinger of blessing."

Andrew Murray

DAY 290

📖 PSALM 119:89 – 176

⊛ K E Y T H O U G H T S

- **Psalm 119:89** The word of the Lord is not in a state of flux, His character, wisdom and precepts do not change with time.
- The ordinances of God (all these are the ordinary or evident aspects of His character), does not change.
- Vss. 97-100 Wisdom and understanding flow from walking in the commandments, testimonies and precepts of the land.
- Vs. 105 God's word is like having a bright light to illuminate the path of life. The word of the Lord is like having a strong flashlight in the woods – it will keep you from stumbling, keep you from falling off a cliff, and light your way when all around is darkness.
- *"Revive me"* – the psalmist uses this phrase repeatedly throughout the remainder of the Psalm.
- Make this your prayer today – "revive me" (vss. 107, 154,156,159).

- According to: "Your word, Your judgments, Your precepts, Your lovingkindness".
- Vs. 136 (Are we grieved for the lack of keeping of God's word around us? Does the drift of our culture and people we know move us to prayer? To intercession?)
- Vs. 160 Mark this verse well - *"the entirety of Your word",* endures forever!
- Vs. 176 When we wander, we can be confident that the Lord will seek us out. Jesus picks up this theme in the parable of the one sheep that was lost (Luke 15:4).

QUOTE OF THE DAY

"How we have prayed for a revival - we did not care whether it was old-fashioned or not - what we asked for was that it should be such that would cleanse and revive His children and set them on fire to win others."

Mary Booth

DAY 291

📖 PSALM 120 – 126

☉ K E Y   T H O U G H T S

- **Psalm 120** (What do you do when you are in distress?) Our default should be to "cry out" to the Lord, let Him hear our cause, bring our burdens to Him first.
- 121:1, 2 The "hills", in the writer's view, represents the dwelling place of the presence of the Lord, "Mount Zion", the place of the temple.
- The Lord is our help, He is the One who creates, who "makes" all things.
- Vss. 5, 6 He will keep us, He will shade us from the burning rays of the sun, (persecution, struggle).
- 122:6 It is a clear instruction of scripture that we are to pray for the peace of Jerusalem. Jerusalem is one of the most contested cities in the world. Sorting out all the religious and

political perspectives is almost impossible. Pray for Jerusalem's peace!

- 123:1 Look to the Lord during difficult times, look to the Lord, not the circumstances, not the obstacles – look to Him!
- 124:1, 8 Without the Lord… how could we have even carried on. He is the One who is our help, our strength. He is the One who created all that is.
- 126:5, 6 This beautiful picture is taken from the agricultural practices of the day. The seed that is to be sown is the last of the food for the farmer and his family. It appears to be a sad end to the story, however, there is a harvest coming for those who faithfully sow in faith.
- The seasons of God are consistent and reliable. You may have a garden of sorrows in your life - sow seeds of faith in God, sow seeds of prayer and trust in Him.
- Prayer, prayer with tears and passion, brings a harvest of blessing. Be encouraged, the Lord hears your prayers, He sees your tears.

QUOTE OF THE DAY

"Whether we like it or not, asking is the rule of the Kingdom. If you may have everything by asking in His Name, and nothing without asking, I beg you to see how absolutely vital prayer is."

Charles Spurgeon

DAY 292

📖 PSALMS 127 – 132

◉ K E Y T H O U G H T S

- **Psalm 127:1** It is only in the strength of the Lord and in the will of God that a "house" can be built, be it a church or a personal household. When the Lord is doing the building, it will be a lasting structure – when we do things in our own strength, they will come to nothing.

- Vs. 2 Worry and anxiety do not bear good fruit. What a blessed promise that those in an intimate relationship with the Lord will be able to sleep – casting our cares upon Him!
- 127:4 – 128:6 The joys, beauty and strength of family and hard work.
- A few thoughts on these themes:
    a) If you are able, have children. Follow the biblical instruction. We were created to procreate - it is a good thing.
- This life is unstable and shifting. Children and family are one of a very few things that can be relied upon to bring richness and depth to our lives.
- A family, a hard working father – the traditional family unit, allows the Lord to bring His goodness to your life through these unchanging values.
- b) If you are unable to have children, rejoice in the family that God has given you, be it extended family, spouse, or the family of God. Continue to believe God that He will enable your ability to have children – if it is a physical limitation, that you will be healed.
- Ps. 130:3, 4 Praise God, there is forgiveness in the Lord!
- Ps. 131 The simple, explicit trust in the Lord brings a grounded strength to life.
- (Are we humble enough to not "concern ourselves with great matters", or things "too profound for us"?)
- We often wind ourselves up with concerns that are not ours to be concerned about. Let's put our trust in the Lord, He will judge, He will vindicate, He will restore and care.

QUOTE OF THE DAY

"The family is the test of freedom; because the family is the only thing that the free man makes for himself and by himself."

G.K. Chesterton

DAY 293

📖 PSALM 133, 134, 136, 137, 138

◉ K E Y   T H O U G H T S

- **Psalm 133:1** Unity is *"good and pleasant"*. Our challenge is to prepare our hearts for times and seasons when unity is under stress.

- (When things go wrong in our relationships, when something happens that we do not understand, how do we respond?)

- Paul exhorts the Ephesian church: 4:1-3 *"I, therefore, the prisoner of the Lord, beseech you to walk worthy of the calling with which you were called, with all lowliness and gentleness, with longsuffering, bearing with one another in love, endeavoring to keep the unity of the Spirit in the bond of peace."*

- 133:3 It is in that place of unity that the Lord "commands" the blessing. Blessing in our lives flows from a steadfast commitment to unity as a value – it does not happen without effort and without sacrifice on our part... another translation says *"make every effort"* (Eph. 4:1 NLT).

- Ps. 136 is a responsive hymn. The format would have the leader read or sing the first line of every verse and then the congregation would respond with the second line *"For His mercy endures forever"*. Follow this method, read the first line out loud, read the second line silently.

- Mercy is also translated – "lovingkindness", "unfailing love", "steadfast covenant". The NT equivalent word is "grace".

- Undeserved and yet abundant grace is the hope and comfort of each of His children. Thank you Lord.

- Ps. 137 While in exile, the Babylonians wanted to hear the Hebrew songs of Zion for entertainment. The hearts of the people were broken for the presence of God in Jerusalem, they longed to worship together in the Lord's house.

- 137:9 This is what had happened to the children of the Jewish exiles, they were advocating an *"eye for an eye"*. It is very difficult to even imagine the depth of the atrocities committed in those days. Our only hope when we are unjustly treated is to forgive and allow the Lord to vindicate.

- 138:1 (Can you say, truthfully, "I will praise You with my whole heart"?)

- 138:8 What a hope filled promise: *"the Lord will* perfect *that which concerns me."* Think today, that the Creator of the universe is at work to perfect (or bring to fulfillment) the things that relate to your life. His personal care for us is that specific, His love that far reaching! Praise God.

QUOTE OF THE DAY

"I am not a theologian or a scholar, but I am very aware of the fact that pain is necessary to all of us. In my own life, I think I can honestly say that out of the deepest pain has come the strongest conviction of the presence of God and the love of God."

Elisabeth Elliot

DAY 294

📖 PSALM 139

✒ K E Y   T H O U G H T S

- **Psalm 139** is another of the benchmark chapters of the Bible.

- Just about every verse deserves comment.

- Vs. 1 The Lord truly knows our innermost being, He knows the thoughts and intents of our hearts. Take this in a positive light, so often our intentions are good but our behavior, not so much.

- We can lean upon the Lord's knowledge of our heart, He knows our "frame", or the weakness of our flesh – He understands the frailty of being human.

- He formed us. He covered us while we were still in the womb! The unborn child is a precious and valued possession of the Lord, every life from conception to natural death is in the Lord's hand.

- Vs. 16 There is a purpose of God for your life. A phrase used when deciding what to do with a particular piece of property: *"what is the highest and best use?"*

- Our Lord has a "highest and best" plan for our lives. As we follow Him, and allow Him to lead us, the best life, the life with the most good, the most joy, the most fulfillment will be found in His ways, not our own.

- Vs. 18 Even when we "awake" in the next life, we are still with Him. Eternal life is a blessed promise of being in the presence of God, the One who has endless thoughts toward us.

- Vss. 19-22 There are evil people in the world, they spoil the beauty of God's intentions for man with their wickedness.

- Vss. 23, 24 Make this your prayer today, *"search me ... know my heart."* Allow the Lord to search every part of your heart and mind. Trying to cover and hide is futile – embrace His gracious love and knowledge of your heart.

- If there is any wicked way in us, make it right quickly – and then continue in His way, the "everlasting" way!

QUOTE OF THE DAY

"Receive every day as a resurrection from death, as a new enjoyment of life; meet every rising sun with such sentiments of God's goodness, as if you had seen it, and all things, new-created upon your account: and under the sense of so great a blessing, let your joyful heart praise and magnify so good and glorious a Creator."

William Law

DAY 295

PSALM 141 – 143

KEY THOUGHTS

- **Psalm 141:3** It is so important to learn the discipline of when to speak and when to not speak. James says:

- *"And the tongue is a fire, a world of iniquity."* James 3:6 (NKJV)

- Invite the Lord to be the doorkeeper over your mouth and your speech. If you need some motivation, just remember all the times you have had to repent for something spoken carelessly, in anger or without all the information.

- 141:5 We ought to welcome the correction and input of those who are godly in our lives. A key question for anyone desiring to be mature in Christ is, "Am I teachable?" When last did I receive the "teaching" or rebuke from a brother or sister?

- This rarely happens unless we invite it. Find someone you trust, ask them to speak into your life – it will be the same as a blessed anointing with God's oil of blessing.

- Ps. 142 Notice how often the phrase, *"I cry out to the Lord"*, is used? We have such a privilege to be in this type of relationship with the Lord, this is a picture of a person of prayer.

- 143:1 *"Hear my prayer, O Lord."* This is a psalm of David. (Are you willing to grow in your prayer life? Do you desire to pray more? Is the Lord increasingly your source and your confidant?)

- Vs. 6 This expresses the desire of someone drawing near to the Lord, longing for more of Him.

- Vss. 7 – 11 A list of requests for growth in our lives:
  - "Answer me."
  - "Cause me to hear."
  - "Cause me to know the way."
  - "Deliver me, O Lord."
  - "Teach me to do Your will."
  - "Lead me."
  - "Revive me, O Lord, for Your name's sake."

QUOTE OF THE DAY

"Do not strive in your own strength; cast yourself at the feet of the Lord Jesus, and wait upon Him in the sure confidence that He is with you, and works in you. Strive in prayer; let faith fill your heart-so will you be strong in the Lord, and in the power of His might."

Andrew Murray

DAY 296

📖 JOB 1, 2
📖 PSALM 144

◉ K E Y   T H O U G H T S

- **Job 1** Job is a man identified by God as: *"blameless and upright"* and *"one who feared God and shunned evil."*
- 1:6 – 2:7 gives us helpful insight in the nature and character of Satan.
- "(SFLB) 1) Satan is accountable to God (1:6), since he came to present himself to God; 2) Satan's mind is an open book to God – God's questions are asked to compel Satan to confess; 3) Satan is behind the evils that curse the earth (2:7); 4) he is neither omnipresent nor omniscient (all knowing); 5) he can do nothing without divine permission (1:10); 6) when God gives permission to Satan, He sets definite limits on his power."
- 1:21, 22 Job shows a steadfast example of the perspective of a godly man – we enter this life with nothing, we leave this life with nothing. The Lord's goodness does not change.
- Job does not *"charge God with wrong"*. This is a huge lesson to learn! Satan has forever been charging God with injustice, unfairness, favoritism, spite, cruelty, indifference ….
- Learn this lesson and you will have a deep and lasting relationship with the living God – Job, in spite of all his sorrow and calamity does not move from questions to accusation of wrong (there is a big difference!)
- Satan is behind all suspicion of accusation against God – do not fall for his ancient ploy.
- 1:10 Not only does Job not sin in his heart, he does not sin with his lips.
- 1:11 The initial motivation of Job's three friends is admirable, their methods, as you will see are far from helpful.
- **Psalm 144** Singing and worship are absolutely necessary and beneficial to the spiritual well-being of every believer.
- The blessing of the Lord, *"happy are the people",* follows

those who live in the confidence that the Lord has knowledge of them, that the Lord is the One who blesses and provides for them, that the Lord is their protector.

- The blessing of God is described in abundant terms, from physical provision to family blessing.
- This is God's heart for all His children.

QUOTE OF THE DAY

"When we lose one blessing, another is often most unexpectedly given in its place."

C.S. Lewis

DAY 297

📖 JOB 3, 38

⟳ K E Y   T H O U G H T S

- **Job 3** Job laments the day of his birth, he fully pours out his grief over the loss of his family, over his health and deplorable unexplainable condition.
- He does not, however, blame God or curse Him, as Satan had predicted he would.
- The chapters following Job 3 record three sets of dialogue between Job and his "friends". A younger man, Eliphaz, then pontificates at length with his own wisdom.
- It is good at some point in your development of Bible knowledge and classic ancient literature to read the book of Job in its entirety.
- There are many valuable "proverb type" statements in these speeches – however the bulk of the reasoning is wrong, and presents a human perspective on God that is incorrect. This does not diminish the inspiration of these passages, as a record provided by the Holy Spirit within the whole of the scripture as perspective for life, especially how "not" to view hardship.
- "The four men seek to answer the question, "why does Job suffer?"

- "The three men come to the same basic conclusion: suffering is the direct outcome of sin, and wickedness is always punished. They argue that one can ascertain God's favor or disfavor toward a person by looking at his material prosperity or adversity. They falsely make the assumption that people can comprehend the ways of God without taking into account the fact that divine retribution and blessing extend beyond this present life." (SFLB)
- In God's response to Job in the whirlwind (chapter 38ff), there are three conclusions:
- "1) Job was not meant to know the explanation of his sufferings. Some things about human suffering God cannot possibly explain to us at the time without destroying the very purpose they were designed to fulfill. 2) God is involved in human affairs: Job and his grief meant enough to God to cause Him to speak. 3) God's purpose also was to bring Job to the end of his own self-righteousness, self-vindication, and self-wisdom, so he could find his all in God." (SFLB)

QUOTE OF THE DAY

"I have made a covenant with my eyes: Why then should I look upon a young woman?"

Job 31:1

DAY 298

📖 JOB 40, 4
📖 PSALM 145

⊛ K E Y   T H O U G H T S

- **Job 40:7-14** The Lord presents the absurdity of a man questioning and judging God – in essence to accuse God is to boast that:
- we can do it ourselves, we don't need His help, our "own right hand" is able.
- All these human sentiments are incorrect.

- Animals: possibly, hippo, crocodile, whale/shark...
- 42:5, 6 Job is very willing to repent and humble himself before the awesome majesty of God.
- The four friends are humbled before God – their position is summarized this way in vs. 8: *"you have not spoken of Me what is right, as My servant Job has."*
- Vs. 10 This significant verse gives us insight into the power of forgiveness and the releasing of bitterness.
- Job is restored – twice as much <u>when he prays</u> for his friends!
- Job would have had no restoration if he had harbored bitterness. Unforgiveness is not the soil that God seeks to plant His seeds of blessing in.
- A hardened, bitter heart is not equipped for the responsibility and humility required in one who is blessed by God. The two do not go together, bitterness and blessing do not mix.

QUOTE OF THE DAY

"I wish, brothers and sisters, that we could all imitate "the pearl oyster"--A hurtful particle intrudes itself into its shell, and this vexes and grieves it. It cannot reject the evil, but what does it do but "cover" it with a precious substance extracted out of its own life, by which it turns the intruder into a pearl! Oh, that we could do so with the provocations we receive from our fellow Christians, so that pearls of patience, gentleness, and forgiveness might be bred within us by that which otherwise would have harmed us."

Charles Spurgeon

DAY 299

📖 ECCLESIASTES 1 – 4

✪ K E Y   T H O U G H T S

- **Ecclesiastes 1-4** Solomon contributes some amazing "wisdom" literature to the scripture: Proverbs, Ecclesiastes and Song of Solomon.

- This book is the chronicle of the wisest man to ever live trying to find meaning in this life alone.

- The lessons we learn from his search will preserve us from trouble and sorrow, if we will learn from his example.

- This is another of the books in the Bible that presents challenges in its reading, but fortunately they end well!

- Solomon misses the one great perspective that gives this life meaning – this life is not all that there is! Hallelujah.

- We will try to cover Ecclesiastes in three days reading.

- 1:3 and 12:8 provide the summation of the purpose of this writing, these bookends give us the right perspective on the content in between.

- 1:18 Our world believes the faulty notion that increased knowledge is the solution to everything. "The preacher" (Solomon) concludes that knowledge and even wisdom (although they have some value), contribute to sorrow.

- If your whole life is spent in the pursuit of knowledge you will be greatly disappointed.

- Chapter two is a list of every imaginable pleasure and accomplishment in this life – vs. 10 gives a snapshot of the level of indulgence that Solomon explored. *"Whatever my eyes desired I did not keep from them. I did not withhold my heart from any pleasure."*

- The conclusion is the same as before - "vanity" (that which is mortal, transitory, and of no permanence), and grasping for the wind. The next time you are in a strong breeze try to grasp it in your hand, do not let the illustration be lost on you.

- 2:18-21 A discourse on the frustrating prospect of leaving an inheritance of your labor to those who follow. (Do you have a will? Have you considered God's house and His work as a legacy? Consider making the Lord's work, eternal work, one of your beneficiaries.)

- 3:11 A beautiful verse – we can never fully know all the work that God does. One day we will *"know as we are known"*.

- 3:13 Enjoying the good things of God in this life has value. Every good and perfect gift is from Him. There are things in this life that are good and bring joy – do not withhold your soul from embracing and enjoying the blessings of God.

- 4:6 This simple statement could save us so much grief!

- 4:9 -12 The value of friendship and relationships – pursue godly friendships, be a godly friend. Call one another on in the things of God, serve together, minister together.

- Great leaders are found to have someone with them, learning, at all times.

- 4:13 Note well the description of a king who is old and foolish - the reason? He *"will be admonished no more"*. He has crossed into the realm of the unteachable. No one has permission to speak into his life anymore. He will hear no rebuke…what a sad epitaph, "old and foolish".

QUOTE OF THE DAY

"There is a difference between happiness and wisdom: he that thinks himself the happiest man is really so; but he that thinks himself the wisest is generally the greatest fool."

Francis Bacon

DAY 300

📖 ECCLESIASTES 5 – 8

☉ K E Y   T H O U G H T S

- **Ecclesiastes 5:2b** *"Let your words be few."* We live in a time when words are not few, everyone expresses their opinions freely seeing this as their entitlement.

- Wisdom understands that God is higher, wiser, greater - from that foundation there are many times we should be silent and allow Him to sort things out, without our words.

- 5:10 Riches do not satisfy, riches do not guarantee health or a happy family, and riches are a deceptive and fleeting pursuit.

- 6:6 All go to the grave.

- 7:21, 22 This is very valuable wisdom. Learning that people will most often say more than they mean, say it with more emotion than they intend, and say it more freely away from you than face to face, will save you many offenses.

- The standard of recalling things you have said about others, and quickly regretted or recanted what you said will help you when you hear what someone has said about you.

- Learning the maturity of not being easily offended is one of life's great goals.

- 8:8 Solomon is coming to true conclusions about the spirit, death and a man's inability to control these events. All people are the same in death, wealth, power, reputation do not chase death away.

- What Solomon does not know is the power of a personal relationship with Jesus Christ! He does not know the deep assurance of salvation that comes from the witness of the Holy Spirit.

- He is missing the greatest hope and comfort by focusing only on this life (although that is most likely the point of this particular book).

- This life is not the end, this life is not all there is – there are many streams of wisdom that if followed will bring greater blessing to this life. We are travelers, pilgrims on our way to a better land.

- In that land there will be justice, there will be comfort, there will be reward and joy forever!

- Thank God for our hope and confidence.

QUOTE OF THE DAY

"Let not your heart be troubled; you believe in God, believe also in Me. In My Father's house are many mansions; if it were not so, I would have told you. I go to prepare a place for you. And if I go and prepare a place for you, I will come again and receive you to Myself; that where I am, there you may be also."

John 14:1-3 (NKJV)

DAY 301

📖 ECCLESIASTES 9 – 12

⊛ K E Y T H O U G H T S

- **Ecclesiastes 9:4** The value of life; when there is life there is hope! Life is precious, it is God's to grant and God's timing to end. It is wrong for man to think himself wise enough to determine when a person's life should end.

- For every current euphemism; euthanasia, assisted suicide, etc., the Bible has an answer. Life is only properly valued when it is left in God's hands, from conception to death.

- When people begin to make themselves God, choosing who has quality of life and who does not, it is a huge indicator of the godlessness of that people.

- 9:11, 12 Proverbs that point to readiness at all times.

- 10:1 The key words are *"a little folly"* – it is the small indulgences of the flesh, the little breaches of integrity that become the eventual downfall of leaders.

- This is referring to those "respected for wisdom and honor".

- 10:20 (How often have you said something that comes back to you later in a form you never intended?) The rule should be, if it cannot be spoken in public, be very careful speaking it in private. Words have a way of "flying" around.

- 11:5 God's ways are beyond our ways - this is a perspective that is fundamental to a healthy faith in God.

- 12:13, 14 Praise God, Solomon comes around with the bookend on all of his pursuits to find meaning.

- *"This is man's all."* Contrasted with all the "vanity" that has gone before.

- *"Fear God and keep His commandments"* – this is wisdom, this is blessing, this is the pathway to fulfillment in this life and the life to come!

- He will judge every work, including every secret thing.

"I can know if I truly fear God by determining if I have a genuine hatred of evil and an earnest desire to obey His commands."

Jerry Bridges

DAY 302

📖 SONG OF SOLOMON 1 – 4

⊛ K E Y   T H O U G H T S

- **Song of Solomon 1-4** There are two appropriate streams of interpretation for the Song of Solomon:
  1) A prophetic picture of God's relationship with His covenant people over the years, a love relationship that when fully engaged is completely fulfilling.
  2) A marriage relationship between a man and a woman – all of the imagery of physical, emotional and spiritual love provides the picture of God's highest and best intentions for His gift of love.
- Romantics, musicians, preachers, poets should be very cautious to translate the imagery of Song of Solomon into personal expressions of relationship with Christ.
- Some have erred in a desire for intimacy with Christ, by drawing to near to physical analogy, and losing a proper reverence for who Jesus is as King, Lord, Creator.
- Jesus is the *"Lover of our souls"* – but He is also the Majestic, triumphant, Omnipotent ruler of all that is and ever will be.
- There is much value in seeing ourselves loved and accepted as the Shulamite is, but there is danger in defining the fullness of our relationship with Christ in these terms.
- Keep reminding yourself, as you read, of the two main interpretive foundations for the book. Israel and the marriage relationship between one man and one woman.
- *"Do not stir up nor awaken love until it pleases"*, occurs four times (1:7; 3:5; 5:8; 8:4).

- This phrase provides a very practical guide for parents and young people. Our culture is driving the exposure and information about sexual relations to children younger and younger.

- <u>Parents</u> – be the primary source, the most open and reliable source of information to your children regarding God's design in their sexuality – but do not stimulate their curiosity by too much information too soon.

- <u>Youth</u> – dating too young awakens love in a manner that has many harmful results:

  1) frustration; you are too young to do anything about it, fourteen year olds are not thinking marriage.

  2) Sexual experimentation; starting young to explore the physical aspects of relationship that belong strictly within the framework of marriage.

  3) Hurt and isolation. When the "too young love" is awakened, inevitably the young dating couple breaks up... now you have a teenaged youth, carrying around the emotional wounds and hurts of betrayal, rejection and sexual sin. All unnecessary!

- Grow in your personality and character by having many friends, observe and develop friendships with the opposite sex in group settings and ministry settings. Do not awaken love before its time. To ignore this wisdom, is to guarantee many pains and hardships that God's heart and purpose would love to preserve you from.

QUOTE OF THE DAY

"The monstrosity of sexual intercourse outside marriage is that those who indulge in it are trying to isolate one kind of union (the sexual) from all the other kinds of union which were intended to go along with it and make up the total union."

C.S. Lewis

DAY 303

📖 SONG OF SOLOMON 5 – 8

☉ K E Y   T H O U G H T S

- **Song of Solomon 5-8** "The song of Solomon is often interpreted as an allegory of the love of Yahweh for Israel or of Jesus for His bride, the church. However, the grammatical-historical approach to exegesis interprets the Song simply as one of the finest examples of ancient, Oriental love poetry. The Hebrew culture celebrated the sexual relationship experienced between a man and a woman within the sanctity of marriage as an exquisitely beautiful gift from our Creator." (SFLB)

QUOTE OF THE DAY

"Many waters cannot quench love, nor can the floods drown it. If a man would give for love all the wealth of his house, it would be utterly despised."

Song of Solomon 8:7

DAY 304

📖 ISAIAH 1, 2

☉ K E Y   T H O U G H T S

- **Isaiah 1:5** The result of rebellion and unfaithfulness to the Lord is that the soul is beaten, stricken with all the ill effects of sin and separation from God.
- The result is that the "*whole head is sick, and the whole heart faints*".
- Vs. 13 "Isaiah is not opposing sacrifice, prayer, corporate worship, and blood atonement. He is only condemning their empty-hearted sacrifice and soul-less worship, which was not accompanied with social justice and true devotion." (SFLB)
- Vss. 18-20 This is a marvelous and classic passage on repentance, forgiveness and restoration – the options of eating

the good of the land or being devoured by the sword are so clear, so easy to understand – and yet...

- Vs. 23 One of the certain indicators of a person's or a nation's moral decay is shown in the way that they treat the fatherless and the widow.

- 2:12 The phrase *"the day of the Lord"*, is used often by Isaiah to describe the coming of God's justice upon those who are rebellious or lifted up in pride.

- Those who are arrogant, haughty (prideful), lifted up or unwilling to receive direction or correction, will be brought low.

- Pride comes before a fall. *"First pride, then the crash— the bigger the ego, the harder the fall."* (Prov. 16:16 MSG)

- Idols are not the answer for the needs of the soul, they cannot answer prayer, they do not have life to give.

- How tempted man is to defer to something he can see, (an idol) rather than to have faith in God.

QUOTE OF THE DAY

"The greatest enemy to human souls is the self-righteous spirit which makes men look to themselves for salvation."

Charles Spurgeon

DAY 305

📖 ISAIAH 5, 6

◉ K E Y   T H O U G H T S

- **Isaiah 5** is a wonderful, poetic picture of the relationship between Yahweh and His vineyard Israel.

- The descriptions are amazingly colorful and articulate – enjoy some of ancient literature's greatest writings.

- Woes characterize the second half of the chapter.

- Vss. 11, 12 and 22, 23 warn against all forms of drunkenness. The vices that accompany a drunken leader usually include injustice and oppression of the poor.

- The primary offense is that Israel and Jerusalem have rejected the "law" or commandments of the Lord and gone their own way.

- 6:5 The holiness of God will cause us to be aware of our own "uncleanness". Drawing near to the presence and holiness of God is vital for proper perspective on our own self-righteousness. None can stand in His presence.

- 6:7 gives us the hope of the Lord's purifying. Through Christ we know that we have the forgiveness of sins, and cleansing from all sin.

- *"But when the kindness and the love of God our Savior toward man appeared, not by works of righteousness which we have done, but according to His mercy He saved us, through the washing of regeneration and renewing of the Holy Spirit, whom He poured out on us abundantly through Jesus Christ our Savior."* Titus 3:4-6

- 6:8 Isaiah's call. The Lord is still looking for those that He can "send". (Isaiah's answer is such an inspiration – will you answer as he did? *"Here am I, send me."*)

- One of the cries of every intercessor is "how long?"

- (As you see the ways of the world unfolding around you, is there a cry in your heart? "How long Lord? How long will the wicked have their way, will injustice continue without correction? How long will the lost be oppressed by the enemy, captive to sin, bound in darkness?")

- Join me today in prayer for the Lord to visit our land, our cities.

- "Lord we call upon You today, have mercy upon our land, we ask You, pour out Your Holy Spirit in conviction and love. Help us Lord, fill us Holy Spirit, come Lord Jesus, make your glory known in this city!

QUOTE OF THE DAY

"Jesus Christ carries on intercession for us in heaven; the Holy Ghost carries on intercession in us on earth; and we the saints have to carry on intercession for all men."

Oswald Chambers

DAY 306

📖 ISAIAH 7, 9:1 – 7
📖 PSALM 146

☞ K E Y   T H O U G H T S

- **Isaiah 7:4** Isaiah's introduction to his word to Ahaz is so good, *"Take heed, and be quiet; do not fear or be faint hearted."*

- We should all take heed and be quiet!

- 7:9b *"if you will not believe, surely you shall not be established."*

- Believing is the foundation for all works of God. Believing establishes the active working of His power in our lives.

- *"But without faith it is impossible to please Him, for he who comes to God must believe that He is, and that He is a rewarder of those who diligently seek Him."*

- 7:14 "This prophetic sign was given to Ahaz as an assurance of Judah's hope in the midst of adversity. It therefore had an immediate, historical fulfillment. It's usage in the NT shows that it also has a messianic fulfillment." (SFLB)

- The incarnation of Jesus Christ is a supernatural miracle, never imagined by man.

- The Messiah, "Immanuel", (God with us) would have no earthly biological father. He would be the result of a miraculous conception by the Holy Spirit.

- That a virgin would conceive without a man's involvement guaranteed the sinlessness of Christ, thus making Him qualified to offer Himself as the sacrifice for the sins of the world.

- *"God with us"* – our God is not far away. He lived among men, He understands our weaknesses and our needs.

- He is not only "with us" – He is "for us".

- Romans 8:11 *"What then shall we say to these things? If God is for us, who can be against us?"*

- 9:2 Jesus is the great Light. He brings light to lives that are in the shadow of death.

- 9:6 Take a few moments to meditate on these powerful descriptive names for Jesus. Each of them contains a promise of the blessings of the Lord in our lives.
- Beyond the personal application is the promise of a governmental authority that will right the wrongs of the godless rulership of this world.
- **Psalm 146:5** *"Happy is he…"*
- (Are you able to testify, "I am happy in the Lord"?)
- 146:8, 9 Incredible promises to those who trust in the Lord.

QUOTE OF THE DAY

"True faith, by a mighty effort of the will, fixes its gaze on our Divine Helper, and there finds it possible and wise to lose its fears. It is madness to say, "I will not be afraid;" it is wisdom and peace to say, "I will trust and not be afraid.""

Alexander MacLaren

DAY 307

ISAIAH 11, 12
PSALMS 147, 148

KEY THOUGHTS

- **Isaiah 11:11-5** This is a marvelous prophetic description of the coming Messiah. It also contains more of the names of Christ.
- Rev. 5:5 calls Jesus the *"root of David"*.
- 11:2 What a beautiful picture of the anointing upon Jesus' life, it is the Holy Spirit who brings the same blessings to our lives.
- Wisdom, understanding, counsel and might, knowledge and the fear of the Lord, are all available to you as you seek to be filled with the Spirit daily.
- 11:6-9 A picture of the millennial kingdom, when the order of things is restored to the original state (prior to the fall).
- The key to understanding this season is that it is a time when

"the earth shall be full of the knowledge of the Lord."

- 12:2 It is in trusting that we are able to overcome fear.

- 12:3 There is an abundant supply of refreshing blessing that springs into our lives as we enter into and live in the "salvation" of the Lord.

- There is joy in our salvation, a great celebration to know we are redeemed, accepted, loved. Draw the water of salvation from the wells of the Lord, there is no true satisfaction for the soul, anywhere else.

- **Psalm 147:6** Humility is highly valued by the Lord, this is a consistent theme through the Bible. The Lord "lifts" up the humble.

- The picture here is of a humble servant who bows down to the ground in submission, knowing his/her true place. And yet the master bends toward his servant, lifting them up, turning their face to His, and blessing them.

- Only the humble have the character necessary for the advancement of the Lord – otherwise pride and self-sufficiency ruin the sweetness of the soul. God must receive all the glory!

- 147:11 There is a way to know that the Lord takes pleasure in us, *"those who fear Him, who hope in His mercy."*

- Ps. 148 We are to join all creation and praise the Lord! We are not to withhold our praise, be stingy with it, measured or cautious. Rather, we are to be extravagantly enthusiastic with our praise. He is worthy!

- We are fulfilling one of our God given purposes in this life. When we praise Him – it is right to do, it is good to do.

- Make praise the perspective of this day! Praise the Lord!

QUOTE OF THE DAY

"Every good gift that we have had from the cradle up has come from God. If a man just stops to think what he has to praise God for, he will find there is enough to keep him singing praises for a week."

D.L. Moody

DAY 308

📖 ISAIAH 14
📖 PSALMS 149, 150

◉ K E Y   T H O U G H T S

- **Isaiah 14** The prophetic ministry of Isaiah has a very clear *"now and not yet"* component. Prophecies that were for that day also had a future component or a broader prophetic message.

- Babylon (the historical nation) and its king (a specific individual) are intended in chapter 14. There are, in addition to those specifics, broader meanings in this passage.

- Babylon and its king are often used through the Scripture to represent evil in general, or a system of evil. Its king or ruler is often a reference to the trouble and evil of Satan himself.

- 14:9 is an interesting reference to the awareness of hell of the arrival of a new evil prisoner. Hell is not annihilation, it is the fullness and consciousness of all evil, the exact opposite of all that heaven is.

- Vss. 12-21 Keeping in mind this dual aspect of the prophetic; this is a reference to the king of Babylon during Isaiah's time, but also to Lucifer himself in the greater prophetic view.

- "Lucifer means "Light Bearer." The basic sin was that of unchecked personal ambition, desiring to be equal to or above God." (SFLB)

- "'I will' occurs five times. Satan's fall was occasioned by two things: pride that presumed to supplant God's rule with his own, and self-will that asserted independence from the Most High." (SFLB)

- Vss. 15-21 reveal five judgments against Lucifer as God makes it clear that every evil, every wicked act and lie will have its just judgment.

- Vs. 20 One of the most tragic thoughts presented is that those who die in a state of rebellion against the Lord, die alone.

- Life outside of Christ, life devoted to the ways of evil, ends up being a lonely, isolated path of sorrow.

- **Psalms 149, 150** The two final chapters of the mighty book of Psalms. The refrain is familiar – praise the Lord!
- *"Let everything that has breath, praise the Lord!"*
- The Lord is worthy of praise today, regardless of the circumstances of life. He is the same, He is high above all the petty annoyances of this life – Jesus is Lord, He is to be unreservedly, unendingly praised.

QUOTE OF THE DAY

"How divinely full of glory and pleasure shall that hour be when all the millions of mankind that have been redeemed by the blood of the Lamb of God shall meet together and stand around Him, with every tongue and every heart full of joy and praise! How astonishing will be the glory and the joy of that day when all the saints shall join together in one common song of gratitude and love, and of everlasting thankfulness to this Redeemer! With that unknown delight, and inexpressible satisfaction, shall all that are saved from the ruins of sin and hell address the Lamb that was slain, and rejoice in His presence!"

Isaac Watts

DAY 309

📖 ISAIAH 22, 25
📖 DANIEL 1

 K E Y   T H O U G H T S

- **Isaiah 22** The principle issue in the waywardness of Jerusalem is an independent spirit. The people of Jerusalem abandoned the ways of God for their own ways. They looked to other 'gods', they trusted in themselves or other flesh instead of trusting solely in the Lord.
- Vss. 12-14 Instead of repentance at the impending conquest and doom, the people took an attitude of "party hard" because tomorrow we will die. Forgetting that the Lord is able to deliver, they resigned themselves to a frivolous anticipation of doom.

- Vs. 19 It is the Lord who exalts leaders, and the Lord who removes them in His time.
- Vss. 20-23 Eliakim is a type of Christ – one of the interesting names for Jesus in the scripture is *"the peg fastened in a secure place"*.
- Vs. 24 *"On Him will hang all the glory"* – the Lord Jesus is a strong and secure "peg".
- The image presents a picture of the robes of the priestly office, the sacrifice, everything relating to the worship of God, and the office of prophet, priest and King – hanging upon Jesus.
- He is able to carry it - He is reliable, secure, trustworthy and unchanging! When you lean on Him, put your weight of trust upon Him He will carry you!
- Isaiah 25:7, 8 A sparkling picture of the future glory of heaven and the reign of the Messiah King, Jesus.
- **Daniel 1:8, 9** Daniel is one the Bible's greatest examples of a man completely committed to the ways of the Lord. He purposed in his heart *"not to be defiled"*.
- (Have you made that purpose? In Daniel's case it was relating to food, what is the defiling thing that the Lord would prompt you to remove from your life?)
- Vs. 9 It is the Lord who is able to bring "favor and goodwill" upon your life. It is the Lord who opens doors, who gives us favor with people, employers, government.
- Vs. 17 God gives "knowledge and skill", as well as the charismatic insight into the prophetic realm.
- Seek the fullness of the Holy Spirit. Invite the Holy Spirit to flow and operate in your life so that you would have Spirit inspired insights and discernment.
- Vs. 20 Such favor rested upon these young men that they were ten times "better" than the wisest of the worldly men.
- "Lord grant to us, that anointing of favor and wisdom, that in our world, for Your glory, we might advance ten times beyond the best the world has to offer."

"The Holy Spirit is the gift of the Risen Christ. His anointing filling, empowering work is a baptism of love that gives power to make Jesus real to you and known to others."

Winkie Pratney

DAY 310

📖 ISAIAH 26
📖 DANIEL 2

☙ K E Y   T H O U G H T S

- **Isaiah 26:3** Perfect peace. What a thought - perfect peace! The way to this place is to keep our minds fixed, stayed, focused on the Lord.

- Not on the troubles, not on the wicked or what they say, not on the uncertainty of the future but fixed on the greatness and goodness of the Lord – peace follows.

- Vs. 9 The expression of someone desperate and longing for more of the Lord – even in the night, or early in the morning this longing heart is seeking the Lord.

- The Scripture promises that those who seek the Lord will *find Him.*

- "Then you will call upon Me and go and prayer to Me, and I will listen to you. And you will seek Me and find Me, when you search for Me with all your heart. I will be found by you, says the Lord." Jer. 29:12-14

- Isaiah 26:18 This verse always stands out to me. It expresses the anticipation of childbirth, and yet in the end no child is born.

- There is a prophetic frustration presented here and a repentant heart. So often we have anticipation in our hearts that the Lord is about to do something special, or that we are to press into His promises or His work.

- And then, distractions come, or difficulties come and we fail to push through to the actual delivery of the promises that the

Lord has put inside of us.

- (What has the Lord drawn you to in the past, what has He stirred in your heart for vision, obedience or calling?) Do not give up on the "delivery table" – continue to focus on the promise, push through to the "full delivery" of His blessings.
- **Daniel 2** The Babylonian king, Nebuchadnezzar, is a major figure in the Bible - his influence in the affairs of Israel (in exile) is significant.
- We see in vss. 1-13, this King was weary of empty promises and occultic patronizing. He was looking for something genuine and supernatural. As you pray for the leaders of our nation remember Nebuchadnezzar, a great leader sincerely searching for spiritual truth.
- Pray that God would put "Daniels" in the path of our business, educational and political leadership.
- The dream and its interpretation have significant political and national meaning. The *"Stone... cut out without hands"* is a type of the sovereign rulership of God.
- Vss. 34, 35 (SFLB) ". . . represents God's sovereign power over history, a sovereignty that is implemented through human rulers. To Daniel's immediate readers this "stone" would have been King Cyrus who invaded Babylon, brought it under the dominion of the Medes, and was used by God to release the Hebrews to return to Jerusalem. The face that it is described as ultimately becoming a great mountain that filled the whole earth shows the long-range development of the stone imagery. ... Hence, the stone ultimately prefigures Jesus Christ, God's consummate Ruler over all governments and all history. Upon His return, He shall "set up a kingdom which shall never be destroyed... and consume all these kingdoms" (vs. 44).
- There are many indicators of Daniel's godly character - in vs. 49 Daniel remembers his friends! Even though the Lord has promoted him, and given him a new life, Daniel is faithful to his earthly relationships and is not focused solely on himself.

QUOTE OF THE DAY

"You will keep him in perfect peace, whose mind is stayed on You, Because he trusts in You."

Isaiah 26:3 (NKJV)

DAY 311

📖 ISAIAH 28
📖 DANIEL 3

◉ K E Y   T H O U G H T S

- **Isaiah 28** Warnings to people filled with pride, people obsessed with pleasure and drunkenness.

- 28:7, 8 Particularly strong rebuke to leaders, priests and prophets, who have been overcome by wine and "intoxicating" drink.

- There is no gray area in Scripture when it comes to drunkenness, it is strictly and clearly forbidden and included in various lists of sins. (Luke 21:34; Romans 13:13; Galatians 5:21; 1 Peter 4:3)

- Leadership needs to carefully consider any consumption of alcohol, from a position of love, and from a position of reflective judgment – leaders are free to abstain. Liberty does not only mean indulgence, it also releases people to choose lovingly, humbly not to imbibe.

- Vs. 11 Paul quotes this verse in 1 Cor. 14:21, "to explain that one use of the NT gifts of tongues and interpretation is that of a sign of warning to unbelievers." (SFLB).

- Vs. 16 A prophecy (as in many of Isaiah's prophetic words), with a contemporary fulfillment and application, as well as a distant hope – to be fulfilled in Jesus Christ.

- Vs. 16b *"a tried stone, a precious cornerstone, a sure foundation"* - this is fulfilled in Christ. (2 Peter 2:4-9)

- Therefore it is also contained in the Scripture, *"Behold, I lay in Zion a chief cornerstone, elect, precious, and he who believes on Him will by no means be put to shame." Therefore, to you who believe, He is precious; but to those who are disobedient, "the stone which the builders rejected has become the chief cornerstone. (Ps. 118:22) and a stone of stumbling and a rock of offense." (Is 8:14). They stumble, being disobedient to the word, to which they also were appointed. "But you are a chosen generation, a royal priesthood, a holy nation, His own special people, that you may proclaim the praises of Him who called you out of darkness into His marvelous light."* (1 Pet. 2:6-9)

- **Daniel 3** The famous account of Shadrach, Meshach and Abed-Nego, "the three Hebrew children and the fiery furnace".
- 3:17, 18 This is a timeless and classic statement of faith in God and fearlessness of witness in the face of certain death.
- It shows trust in God's miraculous power to deliver, to the point of being thrown in the furnace.
- While at the same time there was complete trust and resignation to the goodness of God and his will. They knew God had the freedom to act or to not act as He choose. Their loyalty to God was not going to waiver whether they lived or died.
- Vs. 25 The appearance of Jesus in the furnace is called a Theophany, a pre-incarnate appearance of Christ.
- Vss. 29, 30 Although Nebuchadnezzar acknowledges God in various ways, there is nothing but faint indication of a personal surrender to the authority of Yahweh as the one true God.
- He is not one among many, but *"the Way, the Truth, the Life"*.

QUOTE OF THE DAY

"But if not, let it be known to you, O king, that we do not serve your gods, nor will we worship the gold image which you have set up."

Daniel 3:18

DAY 312

📖 ISAIAH 29
📖 DANIEL 4

◉ K E Y   T H O U G H T S

- **Isaiah 29** These prophecies are meaningful when understood in the context that they are given. This was a time in Israel's history preceding the invasion of Jerusalem by Sennacharib.

- The people were rebellious, unwilling to hear. The prophets had become hirelings and the spiritual condition of the nation was terribly backslidden.

- 29:13 This verse is a powerfully accurate description of a religious people with no spiritual vitality, where only the form remains. The heart is what God is interested in, not the appearances of religious correctness.

- *"Their hearts are far from Me."*

- People in this condition also become confused enough to believe that their thoughts and actions can be hidden from the Lord… vs. 15b, *"Who sees us?"* and *"Who knows us?"*

- Vs. 16 How true in our time as well. Man elevates himself above God his Creator. We must always remember that God, our Creator, is all wise, all knowing and worthy of all submission and honor!

- Vs. 14 is a promise that we can take hold of – *"I will again do a marvelous work among this people."*

- That is our prayer Lord! Do Your marvelous work among us.

- **Daniel 4** The humbling of a great king.

- Even though God gave Nebuchadnezzar a prophetic warning and an opportunity to humble himself and repent – he ignores this, believing his own press and so, he is humbled by the Lord.

- It is true wisdom to humble ourselves first rather than to have the Lord humble us.

- Nebuchadnezzar fails to give credit and honor to God, in spite of all the revelation that had been granted to him through Daniel and through the three godly young men at the furnace… still he is full of pride.

- He loses his mind. He is so far gone that he lives outdoors like an ox, eating grass. He lives without any grooming at all, (nails, hair), and becomes just as an animal. This condition has been documented as an actual disease – called "bo-anthropy".

- After the Lord restores him, there is indication of a change of heart, but to what extent we do not really know.

- Vs. 37b *"Those who walk in pride He is able to put down."*

"I believe firmly that the moment our hearts are emptied of pride and selfishness and ambition and everything that is contrary to God's law, the Holy Spirit will fill every corner of our hearts. But if we are full of pride and conceit and ambition and the world, there is no room for the Spirit of God. We must be emptied before we can be filled."

D. L Moody

DAY 313

📖 ISAIAH 30:15 – 26; 31:1 – 3
📖 DANIEL 5

⊛ K E Y   T H O U G H T S

- **Isaiah 30:15** Returning and resting, quietness and confidence - these characterize the person who is in a faithful and trusting relationship with God.

- The Lord's desire for His people and for you and me is that He would be all that we need, He would be the one Who we trust, He would be sufficient for us.

- Our impatience and short sightedness often causes us to run after other solutions - taking matters into our own hands and seeking help from other 'gods'. Even if the 'gods' we seek are not made of wood or stone, yet we trust in them.

- 30:21 There is guidance that is available to all who will be in communion with the Holy Spirit – *"this is the way, walk in it."* Praise God! (What decisions do you need to make right now?) Listen for the voice of the Lord in your spirit – He has promised to lead and to guide, if we will quiet our hearts, wait, and listen.

- 31:3 Egypt was a continuous temptation for these people. Egypt represents earthly help, the strong help of an ungodly ally. But with the help comes compromise, other gods, bondage, as well as a fickle commitment (based only upon the money provided for the help).

- God is committed to your good because of Who He is, and

because of His everlasting love for you.

- **Daniel 5** Belshazzar's Feast, "the handwriting on the wall".
- Belshazzar had no respect or reverence for the holy things of God. He worshipped gods made with hands, gods of "gold and silver, bronze and iron, wood and stone".
- And, he was filled with pride just as his father Nebuchadnezzar had been, even though he knew first-hand the story of his father's humbling.
- The issue for both of these kings was their heart. Both knew who the true God was, both understood His greatness – both chose to lift themselves above the Lord God, and allow themselves to be revered as gods.
- The Spirit of God searches the heart of every person. These kings are perfect illustrations of people with knowledge but no surrender, information but no application, respect but not reverence.
- Dan. 5:23b *"…and the God who holds your breath in His hand and owns all your ways, you have not glorified."*
- Darius is the third king that Daniel serves under.

QUOTE OF THE DAY

"I saw that the kingdom must be interior before it can be exterior, that it is a kingdom of ideas, and not one of brute force; that His rule is over hearts, not over places; that His victories must be inward before they can be outward; that He seeks to control spirits rather than bodies; that no triumph could satisfy Him but a triumph that gains the heart; that in short, where God really reigns, the surrender must be the interior surrender of the convicted free men, and not merely the outward surrender of the conquered slave."

Hannah Whitall Smith

DAY 314

⊙ K E Y   T H O U G H T S

- **Isaiah 32:8** (Look into your heart, is it the heart of a generous person? Make it a goal of your life to be a "generous man/woman" – devising generous things. Think for a moment, what would that look like?) Devise something generous today!

- Contrasting pictures of God's judgment and God's blessing.

- The prophet's ability in the Holy Spirit to describe the desolations of ungodliness and rebellion is ample proof of the inspiration of this passage.

- 35:3, 4 Someone reading this today is feeling weak in the knees, in other words, your resolve and hope has faded – you feel as though you cannot take another disappointment… hear the word of the Lord.

- *"Be strong and do not fear! Behold your God will come with vengeance…. He will come and save you."*

- **Daniel 6:3** Daniel is distinguished above all the other leaders in the land for one reason – *"because an excellent spirit was in him."* I would capitalize "Spirit" - Daniel had an anointing from God upon his life that he guarded by prayer and righteous living.

- Vs. 7 There are often times in our lives when those who are haters of God, or who are jealous of the blessing of God on our lives, will stir up trouble with lies.

- These people presented their petition to Darius saying that "all" the governors of the kingdom had signed it… obviously one governor, Daniel, had not signed it!

- Vs. 22 This magnificent account of God's favor and deliverance is truly a help to our faith. Daniel's understated response is so matter of fact in the face of a supernatural intervention. Daniel was not surprised or astonished by God's protection.

- Vs. 23 *"No injury whatever was found on him, because he believed in his God."*

"My life is a mystery which I do not attempt to really understand, as though I were led by the hand in a night where I see nothing, but can fully depend on the love and protection of Him who guides me."

Thomas Merton

DAY 315

📖 ISAIAH 40
📖 DANIEL 9

⊙ K E Y   T H O U G H T S

- **Isaiah 40:3-5** These verses are used by Jesus to describe John the Baptist.

- Vss. 13, 14 The Lord's wisdom is beyond the wisdom of any man, His ways are higher, wiser and stronger than any thought or plan of man.

- Vs. 28 Our God is everlasting, the Creator of all the earth, and He never faints or gets weary!

- Vss. 29-31 This passage is such a comfort and strength to us. The key is to wait upon the Lord. Renewal of strength, running without weariness, walking without fainting are all the result of "waiting" upon the Lord!

- The Lord is the One who gives power to the weak, and increased strength to those who have no might! Praise God.

- Daniel 9 Daniel's prayer for his nation is one that we ought to pray for our nation – vs. 15, *"we have sinned, we have done wickedly".*

- Vs. 17 *"Now therefore, our God, hear the prayer of Your servant."*

- Vs. 18 *"O my God, incline Your ear and hear; open Your eyes and see our desolations."*

- Vs. 18b *"For we do not present our supplications before You because of our righteous deeds, but because of Your great mercies."*

- Vs. 19 *"Oh Lord, hear! O Lord, forgive! O Lord, listen and act!"*
- Vss. 20-27 Daniel's vision of the seventy weeks, commentary from the Spirit Filled Life Bible:
- "The time frame of the seventy weeks or "Seventy Sevens of Years" is associated with Daniel's people, the Jews, and the holy city, Jerusalem. The fact that the weeks of years (490 years) are 360-day years is established by a comparison of 7:25 with Rev. 11:2, 3; 12:6,14; and 13:5. The weeks of years began with the commandment by Artaxerxes in 445 B.C. to restore Jerusalem. Chronologically, they are divided as:
- Seven sevens - 49 years – 445 – 396 B.C. (from Artaxerxes decree to the arrival of Nehemiah and the covenant renewal celebration at Jerusalem)
- Sixty-two sevens – 434 years – 396 B.C. to A.D. 32 (from the dedication of the second temple to the crucifixion of the Lord Jesus Christ)
- One seven – 7 years – unfulfilled."

QUOTE OF THE DAY

"God's greatest agency; man's greatest agency, for defeating the enemy and winning men back is intercession."

S.D. Gordon

DAY 316

📖 ISAIAH 41
📖 DANIEL 10

✱ K E Y   T H O U G H T S

- **Isaiah 41:10** This strong promise gives us the reasons to not fear or be dismayed:
  - He is our God.
  - He will strengthen us.

- He will uphold us!
- Vss. 11-13 During a time of trouble or a time when you are aware that you do have enemies, this promise will seem so very unlikely.
- And yet, this is the sort of deliverance that the Lord works on our behalf. He is the God who repeatedly through history has delivered, suddenly, improbably and completely.
- Do not fear. He says it this way, *"Fear not, I will help you!"* Awesome.
- **Daniel 10:12** This angelic response to Daniel's prayer gives wonderful insight into the spiritual workings of God.
- *"From the first day that you set your heart to understand... your words were heard."* So often we gauge the success of our prayers by what we see in the way of answers.
- How our faith would be increased if we remember that as we speak, our words are heard. Knowing the goodness of God, knowing His faithfulness – our motivation to pray and continue to pray will be greatly strengthened in the knowledge that we are heard.
- Vss. 17, 18 This angel has the role of bringing strength to Daniel. The spiritual weight of the revelation was too much for him, so he appeals to the angel for help and strength.
- Moses was ministered to by angels, Jesus was ministered to by angels and we too can be ministered to by angels, what a blessed thought!
- There are spiritual battles going on in the heavens over our communities. Bring this thought to the front of your mind and spirit today as you see people, businesses and neighborhoods – there is a battle raging for the souls of these people.
- Let us be the ones who partner with heaven's army for the good and the blessing of our community. Let us be the intercessors who lend our faith and strength to those at war in the heavens.

DAY 317

📖 ISAIAH 43
📖 DANIEL 12

⊛ K E Y   T H O U G H T S

- **Isaiah 43:1, 2** This is one of the classic promises of protection for the people of God. Again, as in previous chapters, there is the strong command to *"fear not"*.

- The One who protects us is the One who actually formed/created us. He has the authority and the power to protect us from the flood, from the fire and from every strategy of the enemy.

- We are able to live our lives confident that we are in the protective care of the Lord. No matter what the circumstances, we are assured that our lives are precious to Him. He knows all that is happening and we are safe in His hands.

- This doesn't mean that there will never be struggles. We still live in a fallen world of sickness and accident, but the Lord is with us. His purpose is being accomplished in our lives. Live life fully, be confident – He is watching and caring for you.

- Vss. 5-7 This is a call to the wandering and the backsliders. A wonderful position of faith in prayer is to actually call to those who are geographically positioned away from us to "come home", to return to the Lord, to His house and His ways.

- Vss. 18, 19 Powerful promise of "new things" in God. Our future is not simply made up of rehashing all that has happened before – there are new things in God. There are fresh breakthroughs, new revelations and new seasons of revival coming!

- Vs. 25 The merciful, grace-filled heart of God – only He can blot out sins. He does it for *"His own sake"*. He desires to do it, not out of pity, but out of love. Such love.

- **Daniel 12** A number of salvation-related prophecies concerning the end times. The book of life is mentioned, the resurrection is mentioned.
- Vs. 3 is a powerful call to evangelism – that those who bring others into relationship with Christ have the promise of shining *"forever and ever."* Eternal rewards, eternal blessings accompany those who labor at eternal work.

QUOTE OF THE DAY

"Cheap grace is the preaching of forgiveness without requiring repentance, baptism without church discipline, Communion without confession, absolution without personal confession. Cheap grace is grace without discipleship, grace without the cross, grace without Jesus Christ."

Dietrich Bonhoeffer

DAY 318

📖 ISAIAH 44
📖 HOSEA 1, 2

⊙ K E Y   T H O U G H T S

- **Isaiah 44:3** The Lord is the One who is able to quench the thirst of our soul - He satisfies, He renews.
- The Lord has been promising the out pouring of His Spirit for generations. We are blessed to be living in the time of His outpouring. (Have the results of the Spirit's deluge affected your life?)
- (Are you saying of yourself, as in vs. 5, I am "the Lord's"?)
- Vs. 6 We need to be constantly reminded that He is the first and the last, the only God, *"besides Me there is no other"*.
- There may be other gods, but no other living God! Vs. 8b there is *"no other Rock"*.
- Vss. 9-20 contains one of the most poignant descriptions of

the foolishness of worshipping any idol. The picture of using the tree partially for warmth and partially to shape an idol for worship is so revealing. It reminds us that man's desperation for God is constant.

- Man's determination for self-rule and rebellion against God is also constant – the shaping of any idol is an attempt to create a god that suits the person making it.

- This is backward worship, futile and frustrating. True worship must be for the maker. Our worship is shaped by His direction and authority - we surrender to Him. (vs. 12, 18)

- **Hosea** This beautiful, little book is the prophetic chronicle and love story of God and His people. It is also immediately applicable to individuals - illustrating the Lord's wooing, persistent love for us.

- The whole story is a prophetic illustration personified in Hosea and his wife, Gomer. (I'm hoping that there was some beauty in this name in the time of the writing, hard to imagine naming a pretty little girl Gomer!)

- The Lord is committed to the restoration of the backslider - His love is a faithful and redeeming love.

- The adultery and harlotry of Gomer (even after having come out of prostitution and having borne children to Hosea) must have caused immense sorrow and pain to Hosea and his family.

- Will you join with me today to pray for the backslider, the wanderer – how it breaks the heart of God, how it breaks our hearts.

- "Lord we ask, draw the backslider back to Yourself. Draw them with memories of better days in the house of God, draw them through the testimony of someone nearby, draw them through conviction of sin, and the realization that the taste of the world so quickly and consistently turns sour. Bring them home Lord, bring them home."

"Prayer is the way you defeat the devil, reach the lost, restore a backslider, strengthen the saints, send missionaries out, cure the sick, accomplish the impossible, and know the will of God."

David Jeremiah

DAY 319

📖 ISAIAH 45
📖 HOSEA 3, 4

⊛ K E Y   T H O U G H T S

- **Isaiah 45:8** A picture of the intention of the Lord in bringing blessing and revival to His people.

- The picture of the earth and heavens declaring and bringing forth righteousness and salvation is a wonderful expression of the original intentions of God for creation and for us.

- There is repeated reference to the Lord being the creator of the earth and heavens.

- Vs. 18b is a marvelously specific reference to the design of creation. The earth was intentionally created, by the design of the master creator *"to be inhabited"*.

- Thus far in science and astronomy no other planet even remotely close to being inhabitable has been discovered.

- The other major thrust of this chapter is to emphasize that the Lord is God, and that there is *"no other"*.

- There will be a time when every knee will bow in humility and every tongue will confess in surrender to the Lordship of Christ.

- **Hosea 3:3** When Hosea brings Gomer back into the life of the family, there is a season of discipline before all normal relations resume.

- When someone has stumbled or failed and is being restored, there is a necessary season of restorative discipline which is needed.

- 4:6 A lack of spiritual discernment and knowledge causes people to perish. Our assignment is to spread the good news of the gospel intentionally and persistently to all the world.

- *"How then shall they call on Him in whom they have not believed? And how shall they believe in Him of whom they have not heard? And how shall they hear without a preacher? And how shall they preach unless they are sent? As it is written: "How beautiful are the feet of those who preach the gospel of peace, Who bring glad tidings of good things!""*
Romans 10:14-15 (NKJV)

QUOTE OF THE DAY

"Universalism, fashionable as it is today, is incompatible with the teaching of Christ and His apostles, and is a deadly enemy of evangelism. The true universalism of the Bible is the call to universal evangelism in obedience to Christ's universal commission. It is the conviction that not all men will be saved in the end, but that all men must hear the gospel of salvation before the end."

John Stott

DAY 320

📖 ISAIAH 46; 48:12 – 22
📖 HOSEA 6; 10:12 – 15

✸ K E Y   T H O U G H T S

- **Isaiah 46:4** The Lord is contrasting how the carts used to carry the idols "totter" and are unstable, while He the Lord, will carry in strength into old age.

- The Lord is reliable, steady, trustworthy. He is able to carry. What a marvelous description of our God. *"Able to carry."*

- Vs. 8 *"Show yourselves men"*. Courage will be strengthened when we recall the faithfulness of God in the past and the judgment and trouble from times of rebellion and backsliding.

- 48:17 All knowledge comes from the Lord and specifically the knowledge of how to prosper! It is in the Lord's heart to prosper His people. He will teach you, He will show you, (from the scripture), how to advance financially.

- He gives us knowledge and teaches us how to prosper and then He also blesses our obedience to His commands. We are to return our tithes to the Lord (10% as a minimum guideline or starting point). Then we are to sow offerings of generosity over and above our tithes.

- Our God is extravagantly generous with us. We must reflect His character in every area of our lives. Generosity is one of the transformations of the heart that should be evident in every true follower of Christ.

- Vss. 18, 19 The blessings that follow heeding the commandments of the Lord are:

  - *"peace like a river"* – picture a large flowing river, deep, wide and powerful.

  - *"righteousness like the waves of the sea"* – constantly rolling, ever new, continuous, majestic and powerful.

  - *"offspring like the sands of the sea"* - multitudes, generations of blessing!

- Vs. 22 Peace is one of the greatest tangible blessings of God for those who enter into and walk in relationship with the Lord. The wicked do not have it.

- **Hosea 6:1-3** Pray in to this image of the blessing of God pouring down upon us like rain.

- The "latter rain" is a special blessing to bring the crops to bountiful harvest. It is a late rain that makes the different between a normal harvest and a bulging, supernatural harvest.

- Vs. 6 God is always more interested in the ways and intents of the heart rather than the outward appearances of religious practice.

- 10:12 This verse is one of the great calls for revival in all the scripture.

- Meditate upon this thought today in your own life. "Lord plow up the fallow ground of my life I pray."

- *"For it is time to seek the Lord."*

"Sow for yourselves righteousness; reap in mercy; break up your fallow (currently inactive, unseeded, land without crops, hardened), ground, for it is time to seek the LORD, till He comes and rains righteousness on you."

Hosea 10:12 (NKJV)

DAY 321

📖 ISAIAH 50, 52
📖 HOSEA 11:1 – 11; 14:1 – 4

⊙ K E Y   T H O U G H T S

- **Isaiah 50:4** *"a word in season."* The gift of prophecy and encouragement will often be this kind of word to another person - the right word at just the right time.

- Encouragement for the soul comes from the Bible - the Holy Spirit making something real to us, or a brother or sister speaking obediently in faith.

- This little phrase *"morning by morning",* gives us a picture of a devotional life that is not bound by obligation, but is characterized by a relationship and by open communication.

- Vs. 7 Although this passage is Messianic in its future fulfillment, there is comfort for each of us. There are times when we must set our faces like flint - because we know *"the Lord will help me".*

- So today, take courage, set your face like flint against the opposing headwinds and be assured that you will not be ashamed!

- 52:7 When news needed to be carried in ancient times the runner would have to travel over all types of terrain. Imagine the anticipation of the news as a runner is seen approaching across the hills.

- The gospel is the good news. When the Lord uses you to bring the good news to someone, it is one of life's greatest joys and privileges.

- Vs. 11 *"Be clean, you who bear the vessels of the Lord."* Serving the Lord in any type of ministry requires us to be in a continual process of cleansing and purifying. Do not allow the dust and stains of the world to linger on your soul. Come clean in repentance. Be cleansed so that as you serve, the blessing of God will flow through you.

- **Hosea 11: 7-11** Even though people are "bent" on backsliding, the Lord is the One whose *"heart churns within Me; My sympathy is stirred."* Pray today for the return of backsliders that you know. Why not make contact with them, invite them one more time!

- 14:2 Any repentance requires truthful and humble words, *"take words with you".*

- 14:4 This is the reception that every backslider can expect. If you have been drifting, here is how the Lord will treat you. He will:

  - Heal your backsliding (the backslidden bear many wounds from sin).

  - Love you freely.

  - Cease from anger against you.

QUOTE OF THE DAY

"Do not strive in your own strength; cast yourself at the feet of the Lord Jesus, and wait upon Him in the sure confidence that He is with you, and works in you. Strive in prayer; let faith fill your heart-so will you be strong in the Lord, and in the power of His might."

Andrew Murray

DAY 322

📖 ISAIAH 53, 54

◉ K E Y   T H O U G H T S

- **Isaiah 53, 54** These two chapters are filled with powerful and faith building prophecies and promises.

- Chapter 53 is one of the Old Testament's most specific

descriptive prophecies of the Messiah, Jesus.

- He provided the means by His death and resurrection for our healing. His wounds/stripes paid for our wholeness.

- Believe for healing, pray for healing, agree together for the Lord's working in our bodies and in the lives of those we know who are in need. This is one of the scriptural foundations that we base our practice upon.

- Vs. 6 This description so aptly describes our condition, *"all we, like sheep... have gone astray."* Our hearts are prone to wander, but, there is a means of restoration - because of Him!

- Vs. 12 What a marvelous Savior, what a friend and redeemer. Think of this hopeful concept – Jesus, our Savior is *"making intercession"* for transgressors - by His death, but also in prayer. *"It is Christ who died, and furthermore is also risen, who is even at the right hand of God, who also makes intercession for us."* (Romans 8:34b)

- 54:2-3 Vision, faith and promise. We are often beset by doubt and fear but this passage gives us the picture of the Lord's blessing and expansion. His desire for us is good. It is for the growth of succeeding generations and the refurbishing of things that become broken down by sin and wickedness.

- Affecting the actual "feel" or atmosphere of a community by our involvement and ministry, is the Lord's heart.

- Let's believe together for "expansion" for the glory of the Lord!

- Vs. 17 Make this verse one of your life verses! Get it into your spirit, speak it aloud in faith, "no weapon!"

- "Lord, today we stand in faith, believing for expansion, and protection from any weapon devised by the enemy. Be glorified through my life today Lord, increase my faith I pray, fill me with fresh vision for Your Kingdom's sake. Give me confidence in the face of enemies, that the battle is Yours and You will never fail!"

"Optimism is the faith that leads to achievement. Nothing can be done without hope and confidence."

Helen Keller

DAY 323

📖 ISAIAH 55, 56
📖 JOEL 1

⊛ K E Y   T H O U G H T S

- **Isaiah 55:1ff** The promises of God are guaranteed to satisfy the hungry and thirsty soul.

- (How often have we spent our wages for things that do not satisfy?)

- 55:6 A strong call to prayer and repentance – revival always has these two elements. There will be those who respond to the stirring of the Holy Spirit to begin increasing prayer and corporate repentance. Obey that prompting stirring in your heart.

- Vs.11 God's word is a fruitful and powerful force of heaven. When we spread the word of God, invest its wisdom and guidance in our lives, there will be an assured result.

- 56:7b This is to be the description/key characteristic of God's house – a house of prayer. For God's house to be a house of prayer there must be people who will pay the price of prayer. (Will you be that student in the school of prayer?)

- Vss. 9-12 A disturbing portrait of leaders who have lost their way, finally spiraling down to the place where they are strategizing on ways to get drunk. Whenever wine and intoxicating drink become a focus in any people or nation, there is trouble ahead.

- **Joel 1:14** (What is our response to the devastation of sin in our land, in our time?) The prophet calls the people to fasting and to prayer – *"call a fast, and cry out to the Lord"*.

- *"Cry out to the Lord."* (What does this look like in your life? When last did you cry out to the Lord?)

- When we are surrounded by wickedness and godless living, when our nation is characterized by indifference and rebellion to God, it is time to seek the Lord, to cry out to Him.

- Vss. 19, 20 describe the physical devastation of the land symptomatic of the spiritual aridness of the people.

- People of God, awaken from the slumber of prosperity and comfort, awaken from the anesthetizing influence of constant media bombardment and begin to seek the Lord.

- Do not be apathetic, do not be resigned to defeat – stand up, call upon the Lord – He is near to those who will call upon Him. He will hear and He will answer!

QUOTE OF THE DAY

"When may a revival be expected? When the wickedness of the wicked grieves and distresses the Christian."

Billy Sunday

DAY 324

ISAIAH 57:14 – 58
JOEL 2

⊜ K E Y   T H O U G H T S

- **Isaiah 57** Our Lord is deeply committed to the backslider. The key characteristics of those who would be restored from backsliding are contrition (repentance, shame over past sins), and humility.

- The result of these attitudes will be a revived spirit and a revived heart.

- Vs. 19 Healing for the broken is available in the Lord.

- Isaiah 58 The externals of religion are not what God is looking for. The people were practicing a "showy" religion – but their hearts and actions were evil.

- Benevolent treatment of the poor, righting injustice, sharing with the needy, clothing the destitute – these are all evidences of a heart right with God.

- The resulting influence – *"light will shine like the morning"*, is in keeping with the character of God.

- Vss. 8, 9 "Then" is a fabulous word. The results that follow right relationship with the Lord are stunning.

- 58:12b Contains two of the prophetic names for Jesus. Both are metaphors from a time of war - the walls had been breached by the enemy and wickedness, the streets were unsafe to dwell in.

- 12a *"many generations"* – God's intention for your family is many generations of godliness!

- Joel 2:12-14 A beautiful call to repentance and an encouragement to prayer and fasting. This image of a relenting God, allowing His mercy to respond to man's petition is such a motivation to pray.

- When He relents from judgment, He *"leaves behind a blessing!"*

- **Joel 2:28, 29** This is a very important prophetic link to the Day of Pentecost. Peter quotes Joel in Acts 2. He clearly connects this prophecy with the coming of the Holy Spirit on that Pentecost day that saw the birth of the Church.

- This is the only reference in the OT to a slave operating prophetically, (vs. 29) – all classes of people will enter in to this blessing, male and female will experience the fullness of the Spirit.

- The renewal of the 20th century characterized by the Holy Spirit has transformed the Christian world. This promise, this blessing, is for you!

- Invite the Holy Spirit to fill you right now. Simple invitations like, "come Holy Spirit" create an expectation and openness to receive all of the blessings that are available to you.

- These blessings are not for someone else, or for some other time or place – they are for you, for today, for here! Hallelujah!

"The promise is to you and to your children, and to all who are afar off, as many as the Lord our God will call."

Acts 2:39

DAY 325

📖 ISAIAH 59
📖 JOEL 3

☉ K E Y   T H O U G H T S

- **Isaiah 59:1** Living in the truth of this promise will give us increasing faith. Both His hands and His ears are active and for us!

- Vss. 2, 3 The real reason for a lack of response from God lies in the heart of the one asking. When hypocrisy and violence mark a life, the relationship with God becomes superficial and distant.

- Vs. 16 Think of our God looking for an intercessor! Oh the place of prayer in the workings of God! Oh for someone to stand in the gap and plead for the people as Moses did!

- Vs. 19 gives us a glorious picture of the restoration of the worship and spiritual vitality of the people.

- Vs. 19b When you are beset by the enemy's "flooding" waves of opposition, stand firm, the "Spirit of the Lord" is raising an irresistibly firm standard in your favor!

- Vs. 21 The Holy Spirit is active throughout the Scripture, but there is a forward looking prophetic longing for a day when the Spirit would be poured out on "all" flesh.

- This verse connects with Joel 2:28 and with Acts 2:17, 18.

- **Joel 3:14-16** This passage sounds like the foreshadowing of Jesus preaching in Luke 10.

- "Then He said to them, *"The harvest truly is great, but the laborers are few; therefore pray the Lord of the harvest to send out laborers into His harvest."* Luke 10:2 (NKJV)

- There is a continuous longing for the restoration of the glory of the Lord (vs. 16).
- Vss. 18-21 presents the scene of that restoration.
- As you pray today, allow yourself to dream of the restoration of the glory of the Lord upon our land. (What would it look like if there was a national return to Jesus?)
- (How would it affect government, education, entertainment, industry and business, family life?)
- "Oh God, restore, oh God we cry out to you, pour out Your Spirit upon us. We long to live to see an awakening in our city that could truly be called 'revival'."

QUOTE OF THE DAY

"Oh! men and brethren, what would this heart feel if I could but believe that there were some among you who would go home and pray for a revival men whose faith is large enough, and their love fiery enough to lead them from this moment to exercise unceasing intercessions that God would appear among us and do wondrous things here, as in the times of former generations."

Charles Spurgeon

DAY 326

📖 ISAIAH 60:1 – 5, 19 – 22; 61
📖 AMOS 7

✇ K E Y   T H O U G H T S

- **Isaiah 60:1** The rising of the Lord's glory upon a people or a person always results in people being drawn to the light.
- Jesus tells us that we are the light of the world, and that we are not to hide our light.
- Vs. 5 *"You shall become radiant."* This idea of those who are in the presence of the Lord actually having a radiance about them. Moses experienced this in the tent of meeting, as did the early disciples who experienced tongues of fire at Pentecost.
- Vss. 19-22 describe the blessings of a future time. This

description is similar to John's description in the Book of Revelation of the light of heaven being from God Himself.

- An *"everlasting light"*.

- Isaiah 61 This passage is made famous by Jesus' use of it when He read it in the synagogue (Luke 4:18ff). The key to the significance of Jesus' reading it is found in His own words after He finished the reading.

- *"Today this Scripture is fulfilled in your hearing."* Luke 4:21 (NKJV)

- It is Jesus who is the source of the good tidings. He heals the brokenhearted, brings liberty to the captives and opens the prison doors.

- It is Jesus who brings "jubilee" to the hearts of people, where spiritual debts are canceled and joy returns. Hallelujah!

- Vs. 3 Whenever someone is born again there is this fantastic exchange: beauty for ashes, the oil of joy for mourning, the garment of praise for the spirit of heaviness.

- (Is there someone reading today and the spirit of heaviness is troubling you?) Put on the Lord's garment of praise, sing to the Lord, put on some worship music and sing – let the Holy Spirit lift your spirit and replace heaviness with joy!

- Vs. 4 The people of God, filled with the Holy Spirit, ought to be the ones who are restoring the brokenness of sin and wickedness in our cities.

  - Rebuilding the old ruins.

  - Raising up the former desolations.

  - Repairing the cities.

- Long standing disrepair and desolations which has existed for generations will be rebuilt in the power of the Holy Spirit.

- Vs. 7 Claim this for you and your family today – *"double honor"*.

- Vs. 10 This is a lovely metaphor, *"the robe of righteousness"*. The parable of the prodigal son is Jesus' retelling of this scripture. Imagine the transformation when the Father places the robe of His righteousness upon the filthy, drooping shoulders of the wayward son? (Luke 15)

- **Amos 7:14** The Lord is able to gift and use people from all backgrounds. Amos was called as a prophet without the traditional priestly background - he was a sheep breeder.
- We must be willing for God to use us regardless of our lack of perceived qualifications. It is the Holy Spirit who qualifies us for ministry! Be open to all that God has for your life. Do not stand on the sidelines because you are intimidated by your background, let God do the deciding.

QUOTE OF THE DAY

"To be justified means more than to be declared "not guilty." It actually means to be declared righteous before God. It means God has imputed or charged the guilt of our sin to His Son, Jesus Christ, and has imputed or credited Christ's righteousness to us."

Jerry Bridges

DAY 327

📖 ISAIAH 62
📖 AMOS 8, 9

☾ K E Y   T H O U G H T S

- **Isaiah 62** This short chapter contains some motivating images on intercession and the powerful attraction of a city or church in a season of blessing.
- Vss. 4, 5 The immediate context of these prophecies applies to Israel and to Jerusalem. The broader context applies to the place of the kingdom of God and the people of God through Christ.
- Two unusual names, Hephzibah and Beulah. These names present an image of God in relationship to His children. They mean, "My delight is in her", and "married".
- The Lord is so committed to us, as a groom delights over his bride and is married to her. So deep and meaningful is the Lord's commitment and love for His bride, for you and for me.
- The Lord "delights" over us! How different from the view of the

ungodly, who see God as primarily angry and vengeful, just waiting for a chance to pounce in fury.

- Vss. 6, 7 One of the great calls for intercessors. I am motivated by the phrase, *"and give Him no rest till He establishes"*. This presents a picture of continuous, focused prayer.

- We are invited so very often, through the Scriptures, to call upon the Lord, to present our petitions, to intercede for the lost and broken, to believe for restoration from the destruction of wickedness.

- **Amos 8:6** God always forbids dishonesty and crooked business dealings. A true follower of Christ should be known by their integrity in business and financial dealings.

- Vs. 11 There is a spiritual famine in our land. There are so many people hungering and thirsting to hear the true word of the Lord. They are searching in endless directions that do not satisfy. They need to hear the word "of the Lord".

- 9:2-4 Once the Lord decides to bring judgment upon the wicked, there is no place where they can hide. The highest mountain and the deepest ocean will not provide shelter.

- Vs. 13- 15 These verses at the close of the book, bring hopeful prophecies of a coming day of blessing.

- Such great abundance and blessing that the cycles of planting and harvest will run into each other. "Oh Lord, bring your abundance to Your church, to Your people."

QUOTE OF THE DAY

"This blessed Book brings such life and health and peace, and such an abundance that we should never be poor anymore."

Smith Wigglesworth

DAY 328

📖 ISAIAH 64; 65:1 – 7, 17 – 25
📖 OBADIAH 1

☞ K E Y   T H O U G H T S

- **Isaiah 64:1** This prayer is one that should often be upon our lips. As when lightning divides the sky, our prayer and longing ought to be for the Lord to display His power and come among us in glory.

- Vs. 6 Here is the metaphor where sins are compared to filthy undergarments. There is nothing glamorous or attractive about the consequences of sin.

- Vs. 8 Allow the potter to shape you today, allow His strong and wise hands to mold you into the image that He has in His heart for you. It is futile to resist, or argue – He is the creator, He does know what is best.

- 65:1, 2 Thank God that He is open hearted to those of us who are not natural Israel, that His heart cries "here I am, here I am" to those of us who are Gentiles.

- Vss. 2-5 is a picture of His rebellious people. This is the context of the phrase "I am holier than you".

- This attitude is as pleasant to God, (claiming holy status without holy living) as smoke in your nose!

- 65:24 A powerful description of the attentive ear of God when His people pray.

- The last paragraphs of Isaiah 65 describe the conditions of the millennial reign of Christ on the earth. Compare this with Revelation 20:4-6.

- **Obadiah 1** The key to understanding this shortest book in the OT is this; Edom/Esau has mistreated Judah, beginning with the exodus when Edom would not allow Israel to pass through their land, and continuing through wars and harassment through the years.

- Pride is one of the main themes of this book. Edom is filled with pride.

- Vs. 3 This is a poignantly accurate description of the consequence of pride – deception and self-deception.
- A false confidence, an unhearing ear, a willful refusal to repent and make restitution.
- Vs. 15. Compare this with Galatians 6:7 (NKJV) *"Do not be deceived, God is not mocked; for whatever a man sows, that he will also reap."*
- Vs. 21 As with all the affairs of men and nations, in the end… *"the kingdom shall be the Lord's"*.

QUOTE OF THE DAY

"For since the beginning of the world men have not heard nor perceived by the ear, nor has the eye seen any God besides You, <u>who acts for the one who waits for Him</u>."

Isaiah 64:4

DAY 329

📖 ISAIAH 66
📖 JONAH 1, 2

◉ K E Y   T H O U G H T S

- **Isaiah 66** A primary theme in both Old and New Testaments is the contrast between true worship and false.
- False worship is made up of rituals, rites, traditions and exterior behavior - the heart remains unchanged.
- True worship is in the heart, as Jesus says; *"God is Spirit, and those who worship Him must worship in spirit and truth."* John 4:24 (NKJV)
- Isaiah 66:2 describes the condition of the one on whom the Lord looks: *"on him who is poor and of a contrite spirit, and who trembles at My word."*
- Vss. 22-24 The contrasting destiny of those who follow the Lord and those who go their own ways or choose idols.
- Both the blessings for the obedient, and the judgments for the

wicked are eternal, they have no end!

- **Jonah 1, 2** This book is far more than a Sunday School favorite. The big themes of this little book are fundamental to a heart aligned with Jesus, a heart passionate about all lost people, not just those we prefer.

- Vs. 1, 2 Jonah is prejudiced through and through toward the people of Nineveh. They were national enemies, a hated people and Jonah despises them thoroughly.

- He makes an intentional decision to go *"from the presence of the Lord"*. (Have you ever been this rebellious? Perhaps a different circumstance and maybe it sounds more like "I know this is wrong but....")

- Intentional rebellion will result in a hardening of the soul, a dulling of hearing, damage to your life.

- 2:7 Jonah's repentance is genuine. He had forgotten the Lord.

- Vs. 8 Regard for worthless idols moves a person out of the place of receiving the level of mercy that God desires to show.

- NKJV capitalizes "Mercy". It is an actual name for God - "forsake their own Mercy/God".

QUOTE OF THE DAY

"Let your tears fall because of sin; but, at the same time, let the eye of faith steadily behold the Son of man lifted up, as Moses lifted up the serpent in the wilderness, that those who are bitten by the old serpent may look unto Jesus and live. Our sinnership is that emptiness into which the Lord pours his mercy."

Charles Spurgeon

DAY 330

EZEKIEL 1
JONAH 3, 4

KEY THOUGHTS

- **Ezekiel 1** Although these highly symbolic visions are difficult to precisely interpret, there are some broad themes that can be picked up.

- Vs. 20ff The wheels with eyes. These could be a physical representation of the omnipresence of God. He is everywhere, at the same time, ever moving, ever seeing never surprised.

- Vs. 28 In a symbolic way Ezekiel is trying to create a picture of what God is like. *"This was the appearance of the likeness of the glory of the Lord."*

- *"I fell on my face."* (Do you long for the presence of the Lord. Have you ever experienced His presence in such intensity that you were unable to stand?)

- Ezekiel falls to his face numerous times in the book… oh that the Lord's glory was so real in our lives.

- **Jonah 3:5** This is an example of a "whitened harvest", a people ready to respond, willing to repent and change their ways, open to gospel.

- Up till now, no one had told them, they did not know how to get right with God, thus the need for the prophet/evangelist to come and tell them the way.

- What a beautiful scene, a city repenting and turning to God, (120,000 people!).

- Jonah 4 surely is one of the Bible's great teaching chapters on the heart of God for the lost.

- Jonah is self-absorbed, spiritually bigoted and full of self-justifying anger. Yet, he was the one used of God for Nineveh's salvation.

- Two major themes: Jonah is angry at God's mercy on his enemies – still; God's heart is for all people, everywhere!

- I hear God speaking the same thing over your city and mine.

Think of the millions who do not know their right hand from their left.

- In other words, they are in need of hearing the gospel, someone needs to show them the way of Christ!

- Your neighbors, your friends, your city – God's heart is to show them mercy. (Is your heart the same as His?)

QUOTE OF THE DAY

"During true revival, thousands of lost people are suddenly swept into the Kingdom of God. Scenes of the lost coming to the Savior in great, and unprecedented numbers, are common."

Henry Blackaby

DAY 331

📖 EZEKIEL 2, 3
📖 MICAH 3

KEY THOUGHTS

- **Ezekiel 2:2** There are many references to the "Spirit" in Ezekiel. Take note of his awareness of, and relationship with the Holy Spirit through this book.

- 2:6 When we are called upon to speak truth or a word that might be unpopular, we must take courage and fear God more than the disapproving looks of unbelieving people.

- Vs. 10 *"Receive into your heart all My words that I speak to you, and hear with your ears."* The combination of receiving along with hearing is what brings change to a life.

- Vss. 12, 14, 24 More activity of "the Spirit".

- Vss. 16-21 presents a powerful teaching on individual responsibility to get the message to those who have not heard. In this case the message is a prophetic warning.

- In our case, rather than a prophetic warning, we are tasked with the telling of the gospel, the good news. It is a grave error to assume that we have no responsibility to those with whom we could tell the message, false assumptions include:

- Someone else will tell them.
- If God wants them to hear He will tell them.
- I am afraid of rejection.
- I will tell them later.

- Ponder the phrase: *"you will have delivered your soul."*
- Ask the Holy Spirit to fill you again, right now, then with your soul full of love "deliver your soul" to those God has placed in your life.
- **Micah 3** The Lord is directing us today to focus upon the interactive relationship that we must have with the Holy Spirit.
- Both Ezekiel and Micah have strong emphasis upon the working and empowering of the Holy Spirit.
- 3:8 *"Truly I am full of power by the Spirit of the Lord."*
- Speak these words with me today: "come Holy Spirit". Make that your prayer, be open, be receiving, continue to receive.

QUOTE OF THE DAY

"Trying to do the Lord's work in your own strength is the most confusing, exhausting, and tedious of all work. But when you are filled with the Holy Spirit, then the ministry of Jesus just flows out of you."

Corrie Ten Boom

DAY 332

📖 EZEKIEL 11:14 – 20; 13
📖 MICAH 4:1 – 8; 5:2, 3

☺ K E Y   T H O U G H T S

- **Ezekiel 11:19, 20** This OT description of spiritual conversion is such a pristine picture of a life transformed by the power of Christ. (How many of us were that stony heart? How many of us would have been in the category of "the impossible to reach" group?)

- "Lord we present all the ones we know who are still living with a heart of stone. Put a new spirit within them Lord, give them a heart of flesh, a heart that feels, a heart that responds to your call."

- Ezekiel 13 These false prophets glossed over the impending judgment caused by Judah's sins.

- Untempered mortar would look good for a short while, but would not last the test of time. It would soon crack and chip away providing no safety or covering.

- There are many in our world who say what people want to hear. Some do it for profit or for popularity. Seek the truth of the whole of God's word, do not fall into the trap of majoring on single verses, or minor passages.

- Live in the balance of the whole tenor of scripture.

- **Micah 4** Although this picture has an immediate fulfillment for Israel, there is also a strong inference for a future revival of the Spirit.

- When God is moving by His Spirit there is a strong attraction to that place. Revival is like a magnet, people begin to "flow" to it.

- Saying: *"come let us go up to the mountain of the Lord, to the house of God... He will teach us His ways, and we shall walk in His paths."*

- 4:3 is a picture of a future time of peace, a time when wars will cease. Implements used for battle will be transformed into agricultural tools.

- 5:2 This most sublime and precise prophecy of Christ's birth in Bethlehem comes unexpectedly, in the midst of a prophetic word of judgment.

- Notice the names given to the Messiah, and also note His eternal existence

"His being does not consist of material substance, which is created. As uncreated, He is pure spirit. No human eye can hope to "see" Him except to the degree that He chooses to reveal Himself in some mediated form compatible with the finitude of man or in the incarnation of His Son. The glorious good news is that the invisible God became visible in the person of Jesus (John 1:18)."

Sam Storms

DAY 333

📖 EZEKIEL 14, 15
📖 MICAH 6:1 – 8; 7:1 – 7, 18 – 20

⊙ K E Y   T H O U G H T S

- **Ezekiel 14:5** Idolatry. Are there any idols set up in our hearts? It is God's desire to seize us by our hearts.
- The symptoms and consequences of idolatry are listed in Vss. 7-8.
  - Separate idols from God.
  - They are set up in the heart, (not just a physical idol).
  - They cause a person to stumble.
  - The Lord will set His face against that person.
- 14:12 and 15:8 use the phrase *"persistent unfaithfulness"*.
- (Examine your heart and your life. Is there any area of persistent unfaithfulness? If so bring it into light, and decide with God's help to walk in faithfulness instead of unfaithfulness.)
- **Micah 6:8** These things are good and are what the Lord desires from us:
  - To do justly.
  - To love mercy.
  - To walk humbly with your God.
- 7:7 When everything is at its worst, the best decision is to wait for the Lord.

- Our temptation will be to turn to other sources or gods, or to abandon the Lord altogether. Wait for the Lord, *"My God will hear me."*

- 7:19, 20 This is the reference that is so beloved, the image of God casting our sins into the depths of the sea, casting our sins and the remembrance of them so far from us that they are never dredged up again!

- Think of the power of this principle, those sins, those shameful things, once under the blood are gone forever from the record of heaven! Such marvelous grace, such glorious mercy.

- "It is not the greatness of God's power that these texts emphasize, but His immense compassion and His will to forgive and forget sin in covenant faithfulness to all generations." (SFLB)

QUOTE OF THE DAY

"Forgiveness is not that stripe which says, "I will forgive, but not forget." It is not to bury the hatchet with the handle sticking out of the ground, so you can grasp it the minute you want it."

D.L. Moody

DAY 334

📖 EZEKIEL 16:44 – 50; 18
📖 NAHUM 3

◉ K E Y   T H O U G H T S

- **Ezekiel 16:49** Further insight into the sinful behaviors of Sodom are given here:
  - pride
  - fullness of food
  - abundance of idleness
  - did not respond to the plight of the poor and needy
- Sodom represents the abandoned pursuit of hedonism and

fleshly self-indulgence.

- Vs. 50 also includes *"haughty and committed abominations"* as offenses.

- Ezekiel 18:4b *"the soul who sins shall die."* We will not be held accountable for other's sins, neither will another person's godliness count in the reckoning of our souls.

- Vs. 23 The Lord has no pleasure in the death of the wicked. His heart is always that the wicked should *"turn from his ways and live"*.

- Vss. 31, 32 are very important passages for understanding the ways of the Lord when it comes to repentance, spiritual transformation and God's true heart.

- We are to *"repent and turn"* so that iniquity will not *"be our ruin"*.

- We are to *"get ourselves a new heart and a new spirit"*.

- And then the great description of God's never failing heart of love for all people, *"Therefore turn and live!"* (vs. 32)

- **Nahum 3** This prophecy is focused in the time of its writing on the coming destruction of the Assyrian city of Nineveh.

- 3:5 This verse expresses one of the most fearful thoughts in scripture - that the wickedness of a person, or in this case a city, would be so complete that in righteous anger against sin and wickedness God says, *"Behold, I am against you."*

- Two great contrasting themes in our readings today. God's heart for the restoration of the lost to *"turn and live."* And God's ultimate determination to be against those who refuse and continue in rebellion and sin.

- Although difficult for us to balance in our limited understanding, these two concepts, mercy and justice are perfectly united in God. He knows every heart, knows every time and season – He only acts out of perfect goodness.

- Let us never be the ones as in Ezekiel 18 to say *"the ways of the Lord are not fair."* (18:25)

"In the deceitfulness of our hearts, we sometimes play with temptation by entertaining the thought that we can always confess and later ask forgiveness. Such thinking is exceedingly dangerous. God's judgement is without partiality. He never overlooks our sin. He never decides not to bother, since the sin is only a small one. No, God hates sin intensely whenever and wherever He finds it."

Jerry Bridges

DAY 335

📖 EZEKIEL 22:23 – 31; 33; 34

⊛ K E Y   T H O U G H T S

- **Ezekiel 22** A time of spiritual poverty is described, the spiritual leaders were in a place where they had *"not distinguished between the holy and unholy"*.
- Vs. 29 The people of the land:
  - act oppressively
  - commit robbery
  - mistreat the poor and needy
  - wrongfully oppress the stranger
- Vs. 30 Into the midst of this spiritual wasteland the Lord looks for someone to pray! An intercessor, someone who would stand in the gap, someone who would partner with God's heart for mercy instead of judgment.
- (Are you an intercessor? Is there anything that will move your heart to stand in the gap?) It cannot be, that among us, there are only one or two who hear this call. All of us have the call and the responsibility to carry the weight of the needs around us in prayer.
- Ezekiel 33 presents the job description of a *"watchman on the wall"*. There are people around us who are in the greatest spiritual danger. Someone must warn them.
- 33:11 The heart of God is presented so clearly, so openly.

God's great and loving heart for the wicked is that they would repent and turn, so that life instead of death becomes their destiny.

- Vss. 12-20 is an important passage in the whole counsel of scripture when it comes to the spiritual position of a person. Do not miss the underlying truth in this passage.
- Right living although not the means of salvation (which is only by grace, through faith in Christ), is an indication of a right heart.
- Vs. 18-19 God will not be mocked. People living as they choose, living in willful sin, defying His commands and yet expecting through some theological gymnastics that all is well, will find a different result than they thought "fair".
- 33:31 (Ask yourself these questions; "do I ever hear the word of the Lord and not do it?")
  - ("Do I ever speak words of commitment but my heart is after my own gain?")
- 34:1-10 Spiritual leaders are called to a higher standard. These "shepherds" were missing the mark completely.
- Combine vss. 11-16 with Psalm 23. The Lord truly is the good shepherd, He will;
  - feed his sheep in good pasture
  - make them lie down
  - seek those who were lost was lost
  - bring back those driven away
  - bind up the broken
  - strengthen the sick
- Vs. 31 *"You are men, and I am your God."* This will help us in times of confusion. He is God, we are flesh, He is good. That does not change.

"The Lord is my shepherd," is on Sunday, is on Monday, and is through every day of the week; is in January, is in December, and every month of the year; is at home, and is in China; is in peace, and, is in war; in abundance, and in poverty."

Hudson Taylor

DAY 336

📖 HABAKKUK 1 – 3

⊚ K E Y   T H O U G H T S

- **Habakkuk 1-3** We will take this brief book in one sitting. This is a good practice as you grow in your love of the Bible. Many of the smaller books (OT and NT), are good to read at once. You get a different feel for the flow of thought and the overall point of the writing this way.

- The scene in the first chapter is described by these words:

  - *"iniquity... trouble... plundering... violence... strife... contention... law is powerless... justice never goes forth....wicked surround the righteous... perverse judgment proceeds."*

- The end of the book is very different. Notice the contrasting words: *"rejoice in the Lord... joy in the God of my salvation... God is my strength... feet like deer's feet... walk on my high hills."* (3:18, 19) Praise God!

- 2:4 Although most of us are familiar with the phrase; *"the just shall live by his faith"*, just as many will be unfamiliar with the first phrase of this hugely significant verse.

- *"Behold the proud, His soul is not upright in him."*

- Pride is the antithesis of faith! Faith and pride do not mix, they are not compatible.

- This verse is the theological anchor that the NT message of salvation leans on.

- *"For by grace you have been saved through faith, and that not of yourselves; it is the gift of God, 9 not of works, lest anyone should boast."* (Eph. 2:8)

- Make note of the five "woes" of chapter 2.

- 3:2 Let us be people who make this our prayer, "Oh Lord, revive Your work in the midst of the years."

- 3:17-19 Read these verses out loud today, meditate upon the depth and meaning of this practical example of the faith spoken of in 2:4. Thank you Lord, we will trust in you, we will rejoice in You!

QUOTE OF THE DAY

"Lord, I have heard of your fame; I stand in awe of your deeds, (NIV). O Lord, revive Your work in the midst of the years! In the midst of the years make it known; In wrath remember mercy." (NKJV).

Habakkuk 3:2

DAY 337

📖 EZEKIEL 36:22 – 38; 37:1 – 14; 47:1 – 12

◉ K E Y   T H O U G H T S

- **Ezekiel 36** These passages emphasize the role of the Holy Spirit in the believer's life.

- 36:25, 26 The Lord's work in cleansing and purifying is such a refreshing for our souls.

- A powerful metaphor for the spiritual life of a believer - exchanging a heart of stone for a heart of flesh. Someone dead, someone unresponsive, for someone very much alive and vital.

- Vs. 27 Ezekiel has a keen sense of the work of the Holy Spirit. It is the promise of the Lord to put His Spirit within us!

- The result of the Spirit's dwelling within is the blessing of God! Seek the fullness of the Spirit. Invite the Holy Spirit to fill you.

- Ezekiel 37 The dry bones live! This prophecy is loved by many because of the encouragement in the application to our lives.

- (What are the dry bones in your life? What is it that would prompt you to say *"Our bones are dry, our hope is lost, and we ourselves are cut off!"*) (37:11)
- 37:14 It is by the Holy Spirit, His Spirit, that life and blessing flow.
- Pray prophetically to the dry bones of your life situation today! With the Holy Spirit's anointing speak saying: "O dry bones, hear the word of the Lord!"
- 47:1 Add this image of the river of God to the prophetic confidence of the dry bones passage.
- This wonderful picture of the ever increasing depth of the waters of the Holy Spirit is so helpful for us when venturing into the fullness of the Spirit.
- There is always more in God. Take some time to meditate on the picture of yourself swimming in the river of God that is flowing from the throne of heaven.
- There is healing in this river. Blessing and restoration comes in the river… hallelujah.
- John 7:38, 39 refers to the river of living water flowing from within, the Holy Spirit, who is available to all believers in abundance.
- This prophecy has a now and not yet character. The things of the Spirit are for now, and there will be a day in the future when in heaven, we will experience the full completion of the highest intention of God for our blessing.

QUOTE OF THE DAY

"Revivals begin with God's own people; the Holy Spirit touches their heart anew, and gives them new fervor and compassion, and zeal, new light and life, and when He has thus come to you, He next goes forth to the valley of dry bones… Oh, what responsibility this lays on the Church of God! If you grieve Him away from yourselves, or hinder His visit, then the poor perishing world suffers sorely!"

Andrew Bonar

DAY 338

📖 ZEPHANIAH 1:1 – 3; 3

◉ K E Y   T H O U G H T S

- **Zephaniah 1** One indicator of spiritual decline in a people is complacency.

- The description of complacency when people say, *"the Lord will not do good, nor will He do evil."*

- In other words, "God has removed Himself, He is not acting, therefore we will act as we please. We also don't care if we fall into spiritual apathy. It is His fault!"

- We live in a time where there is widespread complacency among "spiritual" people.

- God is always at work. There will be seasons when we do not see what He is doing, but He is always performing His will, always moving to see people return to faith.

- 3:12 The characteristics of a godly people are meekness, (submission), and humility. Rebellion and pride are the opposite behaviors of the ungodly or the backslider.

- 3:13 When a person or a people return to the Lord they will be known for their integrity. Lies, deceit and manipulation will not be part of their identities.

- We are to be known for honesty, straightforwardness and choosing the good for others. (Is this true of you, of me?)

- 3:17 This is a rare reference to the Lord's joy over His people rising to such a level that He actually begins to sing over them, rejoicing over them with gladness.

- Picture a parent overflowing with joy and thankfulness over their child, looking at them while they sleep and singing a song of blessing over their life.

- Most Christians do not see themselves in this type of relationship with the Father. We are prone to performance to gain God's approval. God's love for you is so deep and not at all dependent on how you perform.

- Zephaniah reminds us that the heart of God is to draw us close to Himself in relationship. That is why we were made.

- Try to uncomplicate your view of the Father today. See Him rejoicing over you, singing over you. Find your safety and trust fully in Him. Thank you Lord.

QUOTE OF THE DAY

"So for us, the condition and preparation on and by which we are sheltered by that great hand, is the faith that asks, and the asking of faith. We must forsake the earthly props, but we must also believingly desire to be upheld by the heavenly arms. We make God responsible for our safety when we abandon other defense, and commit ourselves to Him."

Alexander MacLaren

DAY 339

📖 HAGGAI 1, 2

✒ K E Y   T H O U G H T S

- **Haggai 1, 2** The Spirit Filled Life Bible provides a great outline of the content of Haggai. The book was written during the time when the returned exiles were rebuilding the temple (520 B.C.):
  - "The first problem is *disinterest,"* opposition had arisen to the rebuilding of the temple and the work had stopped.
  - "The second problem (they faced), was *discouragement"* – the present building was nowhere near as glorious as Solomon's temple, so some of the older people were weeping as they worked.
  - The third problem they faced was *"dissatisfaction",* the people were expecting immediate results, immediate gratification, not months of hard labor.
  - The essence of Haggai's response is "Do not expect the work of three months to undo the neglect of sixteen years." (SFLB)
- 1:6 describes the fruitless life of those who do not walk in the

ways of the Lord. (How many times, when we don't honor the Lord, does it seem like our money is being put into bags with holes?)

- The people had chosen to beautify their own lives and prioritize their own possessions instead of focusing on the work of the Lord.

- 1:14 The Lord is able to stir up the hearts of those who are consecrated to Him. He stirs up leaders' hearts.

- There are divinely appointed times and places where God's choice of leader mobilizes the church to action.

- 2:4 contains a great instruction for all of God's people to *"be strong… and work!"*

- 2:9 speaks to all the people who think that the best days in God are in the past. Regardless of the measure of blessing or revival you may have seen, God always has more glory for the "latter" move of God.

- Believe God today, intercede today that the Lord will pour out His glory in new and greater measure. "Oh Lord let Your glory be great in our generation!"

- 2:19 Even though the seed is still in the barn, (the evidence of multiplication is not tangible yet), the Lord promises:

- *"From this day I will bless you."* Receive it today, from this day!

QUOTE OF THE DAY

"Is the seed still in the barn? As yet the vine, the fig tree, the pomegranate and the olive tree have not yielded fruit. But from this day I will bless you."

Haggai 2:19

DAY 340

📖 ZECHARIAH 1:1 – 6; 4:1 – 10; 7 & 8

☉ K E Y T H O U G H T S

- **Zechariah 1:3** The Lord is always willing to restore His presence and anointing. We have a part to play in returning to Him. Take the initiative, return to the Lord.

- 4:6 Nothing is accomplished in the kingdom of God apart from the flow of the oil of the Holy Spirit.

- Everything in God is accomplished by the Spirit. It is not our own strength, might or wisdom, but the power and the anointing of God's mighty Spirit.

- 7:5-7 The practice of religious rituals without a heart surrendered to the authority of the Lord is pointless. It ends up being for ourselves and not for the Lord.

- 7:11, 12 This is a description of the spiritually bored, the disengaged, the hard soil of years of spiritual dryness.

- (Have you "shrugged your shoulders" to the word of the Lord? Have you "stopped your ears" to a word of correction or rebuke?)

- (Have you refused to consider that your ways, may be in need of change?)

- 8:16 When God is in charge of a nation/people these characteristics will be present.

- 8:21, 23 How we long for the days of restoration when the people of the world will "grasp the sleeve" of a man or woman of God, asking to go with them because "we have heard that God is with you."

QUOTE OF THE DAY

"God's mighty power comes when God's people learn to walk with God."

Jack Hyles

DAY 341

ZECHARIAH 9; 12; 13

KEY THOUGHTS

- **Zechariah 9:9** This picture of the Messiah is uttered 400 years prior to its fulfillment in Christ's triumphal entry (Matt.

21:5). Bible prophecy is one of the strongest evidences of the inspiration of the Scriptures. Hundreds of prophecies are fulfilled in Jesus. No director, producer or public relations person could ever have choreographed such accuracy.

- The scripture is a supernatural revelation of God, by God, for the strengthening of our faith.

- 9:10 For Canadians, this verse has national significance. We have been known as the Dominion of Canada for many years, because our founding fathers chose this verse as a basis for our identity.

- "Lord our prayer today: have Your dominion over our land, make Your glory known from sea (East), to sea (West), and the from the river (St. Lawrence), to the ends of the earth, (Arctic)."

- 12:10 A powerful prophecy looking toward the crucifixion. Remember that at the time of the writing there was no Roman empire, no such thing as a crucifixion.

- 13:7b Whenever the enemy is able to take out the shepherd, or spiritual leader, the ripple effect on the people of God is devastating.

- Pray for your pastors and leaders. Find ways to encourage and strengthen their hands. They are the prime target of the enemy for this reason.

- 13:9 The Lord is always searching for a remnant of people who are willing to serve Him with everything.

- There must be a refining, purifying process in every life. It is accomplished by different means - sometimes by fire, sometimes by difficulty - but the Lord is able to use the refining process to bring out the value in each life.

- The indicator of a person's heart for God is when they say, "The Lord is my God."

"God is more concerned with conforming me to the likeness of His Son than leaving me in my comfort zones. God is more interested in inward qualities than outward circumstances - things like refining my faith, humbling my heart, cleaning up my thought life and strengthening my character."

Joni Eareckson Tada

DAY 342

📖 ZECHARIAH 14:1 – 12
📖 MALACHI 1, 2

⊚ K E Y   T H O U G H T S

- **Zechariah 14:1** This reference prophesies the literal return of the Lord Jesus Christ to the Mount of Olives. This is called the second coming of Christ, different from the rapture of the church.

- A new order of things will be established from that point on in time.

- Vs. 12 Consider the horrors of atomic warfare, unheard of in Zechariah's time and yet so graphically described here.

- Church, we are living in those last days, we are living so very near to the day of the Lord! We must live right, be ready, be bold in proclaiming the gospel.

- Allow the urgency of the message and the finality of the time table of the Lord to grip your heart and motivate you to action today!

- **Malachi 1, 2** The last of the OT prophets.

- Mal. 1:8 is a powerful description of the heart attitude of the people. They have abandoned the principle of bringing the first fruits to the Lord.

- The first and the best of the crops and livestock were to be the offering to the Lord, acknowledging that everything we have is a gift from Him.

- The question posed is so insightful, *"would you give such a gift to your governor?"* Yet it is brought before the Lord.

- The second major issue examined by Malachi, in the people's backsliding, was widespread divorce among the people.

- Described in this way; you have *"dealt treacherously with the wife of your youth."* The men were abandoning their covenant with their wives and divorcing them for replacement wives from other nations.

- These new wives brought idolatrous practices with them.

- Vs. 16 The reason God hates divorce is that it *"covers one's garments with violence."* God does not hate divorcees, He hates the terrible violence that divorce always does to His covenant design for the family.

- Two things, people; if you and your spouse are in conflict and you are considering divorce, take this warning to heart today, *"take heed to your spirit, that you do not deal treacherously."*

  - Consider again, on your knees, before the Lord who knows all things, the covenant that you made before Him when you made your vows. God will help you. He will strengthen you and give you wisdom.

  - Secondly: if you know someone going through or who has gone through a divorce, be a faithful friend, be an encourager. Do not abandon those who are experiencing the violence of divorce. The Lord is the only One who can truly help them.

- Especially for the single parents, going from a two person job to a one person job is incredibly difficult. Help them, be there for them, without taking sides!

- Be a support without fueling the fires of bitterness and hurt, offer to pray when you don't know what else to do or say.

QUOTE OF THE DAY

"Many conflicts in a marriage result from living to please self instead of living to please the Lord. These conflicts can be resolved and are actually opportunities for spiritual growth when dealt with in a biblical manner."

John C. Broger

DAY 343

📖 MALACHI 3, 4

- **Malachi 3:1** John the Baptist is identified as *"My messenger"* that Malachi prophesies (4:5, 6) will come before the Messiah.

- Vss. 4-5 These verses contain a list of sins that indicate a lack of reverence for the Lord. To live in this condition shows that there is no concern for either obedience to the Lord's commands, or His judgment against those who live that way.

- Vs. 6 The Lord does not change! Hebrews 13:8 *"Jesus Christ is the same yesterday and today and forever."*

- Vss. 7-12 are the most concise, precise passages in the Bible on tithing. Allow the Bible to speak for itself. Let your spirit respond to the spirit of the Scripture.

- When it comes to our stewardship of the tithe, the primary question is, *"in what way shall we return?"*

- A person's dealing with God's portion is often a first indication of deeper issues of the heart. To withhold the tithe is usually a sign of deeper rebellious conditions.

- When taken in the context of the whole of the scriptural teaching on money, stewardship, first fruits, generosity, abundance – it is not possible for a person, who calls themselves by the Name of this mighty extravagant God to justify a miserly, closed handed refusal to give!

- Giving is one of the most practical proofs of faith!

- Take the tithe challenge – vs. 10. No other principle in scripture is open to "try" the Lord. This promise is sure.

- *"Bring all the tithe into the storehouse, that there may be food in My house, and try Me now in this, says the Lord of hosts, If I will not open for you the windows of heaven and pour out for you such blessing that there will not be room enough to receive it."*

- Vs. 11 Also consider the promise connected to the faithful tithe.

The devourer is rebuked – not only is blessing promised but protection from the enemy's devouring ways is promised.

- There will be abundance, plus that which you have will be sustained, unlike a previous reference to putting your money into a *"bag with holes"*. Haggai 1:6 *"You have sown much, and bring in little; you eat, but do not have enough; you drink, but you are not filled with drink; you clothe yourselves, but no one is warm; and he who earns wages, earns wages to put into a bag with holes."*

- 4:2 There is great promise granted to those who *"fear My Name"*.

- Jesus, the *"Sun of Righteousness will arise with healing in His wings"*. Wherever He is, there is a covering of healing.

- Look to the Lord for your healing, look to the Lord for your provision and promise - the day of the Lord is at hand.

QUOTE OF THE DAY

Luke 6:38 "Give, and it will be given to you: good measure, pressed down, shaken together, and running over will be put into your bosom. For with the same measure that you use, it will be measured back to you."

Jesus

DAY 344

📖 MATTHEW 1, 2
📖 PSALM 1

⊙ K E Y   T H O U G H T S

- **Matthew 1** presents the genealogy of Joseph, even though he was not Jesus' biological father, yet he still was from the line of David.

- 1:20 We do not have much in the scripture about Joseph, but notice that he is a spiritual man. Twice in our reading today Joseph is led by the Lord through dreams.

- He would have had to be a spiritual and godly man to have

husbanded the situation of Mary's pregnancy and Christ's unique identity.

- Matthew is also very diligent in presenting the many OT prophecies fulfilled in Christ.
- 2:6 Bethlehem is identified as the birth place of Jesus. So specific, so accurate.
- Fulfilled prophecy is one of the many proofs of the supernatural character of the Bible.
- 2:11 The wise men have travelled far and at great cost to come to see the Christ child. Notice their response when they arrive? They *"fell down and worshipped Him"*.
- "Lord we worship you today, we fall before You and worship You."
- **Psalm 1:3** The description of God's blessing is a picture of vitality and fruitfulness. *"Whatever he does shall prosper."*
- 1:4 The "ungodly" disappear like dust in the wind. There is nothing stable or lasting about their lives.
- 1:6 Contrast the ways of the righteous - they are "known" by the Lord.
- (Will the days and events of our lives be "known" by the Lord?) The wicked disappear forever, the righteous are "known" forever.
- Relationship and fellowship are in the heart of God.

QUOTE OF THE DAY

"...I don't have to worry about not meeting His expectations. God will ensure my success in accordance with His plan, not mine."

Francis Chan

DAY 345

📖 MATTHEW 3, 4
📖 PSALM 2

◉ K E Y   T H O U G H T S

- **Matthew 3:8** *"Fruits worthy of repentance";* true repentance means a turning away from the past behaviors and walking a new path.

- To "repent" without any change is not true repentance. Some people repent to receive the promised benefits, with no intention of changing. Without a change of heart the blessings do not follow.

- 3:11 Jesus is the One who baptizes in the Holy Spirit. We can ask Him to fill us. It is His blessed promise to submerge all who are willing in the person of the Holy Spirit.

- 4:1-11 Satan is the master of twisting the truth. There is nothing wrong with bread, God has promised to protect. Christ is the One who will have everything under His authority, and yet Satan distorts each of these true things into potential sin.

- There is nothing wrong with a relationship, and yet how many people choose a person over God?

- There is nothing wrong with money, and yet how many people succumb to the temptation to love money more than God?

- There is nothing wrong with children, and yet how many people place children upon such a pedestal that they become idols of the heart, displacing God's authority and priority?

- Jesus disposes of Satan's lying temptations with the truth of the Scripture. Darkness is banished by the power of the light of God's truth.

- 4:17 Jesus echoes John's message. Jesus says "repent". The preparation of the heart for the entrance of the Kingdom of God is repentance.

- 4:19 Fishers of men. (Is that what we are? If this is such a fundamental characteristic of the call of God, how fully are we responding to this call?)

- **Psalm 2:7, 8** It is God's purpose that all the nations would become the possession of Christ's authority and rule.

- This includes the "nations" of your neighborhood, school, and work place.

- As we seek the Lord for His Kingdom to come, His will to be done, let us return to a passionate commitment to present the nations to Christ. We must take the gospel everywhere to everyone!

QUOTE OF THE DAY

"What would we do about it if the 66,000 who die every day in unreached people groups were individuals trapped in a well?"

Phil Bogosian

DAY 346

📖 MATTHEW 5, 6
📖 PSALM 3

✏ K E Y   T H O U G H T S

- **Matthew 5, 6** These are some of the Bible's most famous chapters; Jesus' teaching called the Sermon on the Mount.

- Intensely practical, there are so many points of application, almost too many to mention. Make your own notations of what the Holy Spirit speaks to you today.

- Vss. 2-10 Presenting a kingdom perspective instead of an outward and ritual based righteousness. These markers of kingdom-hearted people are the opposite of what the 'world' would say should be done.

- Jesus is after your heart! If He has our hearts, He has us all.

- Vs.6 Hungering and thirsting for righteousness brings the promise of being filled. Filled with the goodness of God, filled with the abundance of His blessings – oh to be filled!

- Vs. 13 (What flavor do you bring to your world? If you weren't there, would your world taste different?)

- Anger in the heart, lust in the heart - a true relationship with the living God transforms the thoughts and intents of the heart. This is much deeper than just the appearance of holiness.

- 5:37 An elaborate system of vows had been developed with degrees of binding power. It would be a little like making a promise with your fingers crossed, a technicality releasing you from keeping your word.

- Jesus eliminates such pretense - honest, simple and true is His standard.

- 6:1-24 Giving, praying and fasting – all must be from the basis of the heart. To give alms for the approval of others negates the value of the gift for the giver. To pray so that people see rather than that God hears, is upside down. To fast for religious accolades misses the point completely.

- We are in a relationship. Jesus has come to establish a living kingdom, a kingdom of the heart, a kingdom without layers of hypocrisy and show. True followers of Jesus will walk with an authenticity and earnest desire for intimacy with God, not approval of men.

- 6:24 The god of Mammon, (money, material things) is as powerful and prevalent today as in any generation. You and I are not exceptions, we cannot serve two gods. Which will it be?

- 6:34 (Is worry a part of your daily routine? Would you be willing to obey Jesus on this one?) Give your worries to Him right now, release them, He will care for it in His time and His way!

- **Psalm 3:3** The Lord is your shield, protector, covering. He is the One who will lift up your head when you are bent over and weary.

QUOTE OF THE DAY

"God's commands are designed to guide you to life's very best. You will not obey Him, if you do not believe Him and trust Him. You cannot believe Him if you do not love Him. You cannot love Him unless you know Him."

Henry Blackaby

DAY 347

📖 MATTHEW 7, 8
📖 PSALM 4

◉ K E Y   T H O U G H T S

- **Matthew 7:7** Ask, seek and knock. All these requests are in the present continuous tense. They are intended to be a continued asking, continued seeking, continued knocking.

- The principle is from the earthly family - a good father will respond to the needs of his children, although not to every childish whim.

- 7:20 Do not be afraid to evaluate the fruit of a person's life, (especially a spiritual leader). If something doesn't make sense there is most likely a deeper reason for it.

- 7:24-27 Following Jesus is not complicated. This parable pictures the way of discipleship graphically. Obedience to His commands, or, disobedience to His commands...one life structure will stand during trial and adversity, the other will collapse with a "great" fall.

- 8:13 Faith, believing, so much of the activation of Kingdom power is based upon the willing response of faith. *"As you have believed"*, - how have you believed?

- 8:17 The basis of our faith for healing is rooted in the prophetic words the Messiah would bring, (Isa. 53:4), shown in the ministry of Jesus, and commissioned to the followers of Christ.

- When Jesus sent out the seventy to minister He said to them: *"And heal the sick there, and say to them, 'The kingdom of God has come near to you.'"* Luke 10:9

- 8:26 Again, faith is mentioned – *"Why are you fearful?"*

- **Psalm 4:7** This is the pathway that the Lord has prepared for you. (Is this promise true in your life? Are you living in the gladness of heart that the Lord has offered?)

- (How often do we miss the goodness of God by complaining and comparing?) Let your heart be full of gladness in the Lord.

- Peace is one of the most precious promises for those who are living in the fullness of the Lord's presence.
- 4:8 Only the Lord can make us dwell in safety!

DAY 348

📖 MATTHEW 13, 14

⊛ K E Y   T H O U G H T S

- **Matthew 13** highlights the emphasis of "the kingdom of Heaven", in recounting the parables of Jesus.
- 13:19 The gospel needs to be presented in understandable terms, and then followed up to be sure that there is a witness in the person's heart.
- Vs. 21 Always watch for a new believer who enters into a time of *"tribulation or persecution"*. They are vulnerable to discouragement and to giving up. Be an encourager in those times, make that call, include them in your fellowship.
- Vs. 22 – Luke reports this key verse this way: *"Now the ones that fell among thorns are those who, when they have heard, go out and are choked with cares, riches, and pleasure of life, and bring no fruit to maturity."*
- The result of these choking vines is that there is no fruit… immaturity is often the result of allowing distractions to have preeminence.
- Vs. 23 The goal of Christian living is fruitfulness. We should all take stock of the "fruitfulness" of our lives. (Is our testimony one of good behavior or good looks or is it the fruit of obedience to Christ's commands to love and to proclaim the gospel?)
- Vs. 30, 49 There are those present "in the kingdom" who are

false. It is Jesus' responsibility ultimately, to judge. Those who are hypocrites or pretenders will face a fiery and eternal consequence.

- Vs. 58 Think about the power of unbelief. We often speak of the power of believing, but unbelief has the power to limit the amount of miracles that Jesus could perform.

- Our calling as followers of Christ is to believe! To be like the man who cried out, *"I do believe, help my unbelief."*

- 14:23 The Son of God made time, valued the time, believed in the power of prayer enough to go, alone, to pray. Jesus needed and believed in prayer. (Do we? Enough to pray?)

- Vss. 27-31 We need not be afraid when facing any challenge to our faith. While walking in the power of God there will always be opposition or difficulty. The simple question of Jesus pierces so deeply, *"Oh you of little faith, why did you doubt?"*

- Put your own answer into that scenario. ("Why did you doubt?" Why do you doubt? How does the answer sound?)

QUOTE OF THE DAY

"It is just as important to trust God as it is to obey Him. When we disobey God we defy His authority and despise His holiness. But when we fail to trust God we **doubt** His sovereignty and question His goodness. In both cases we cast aspersions upon His majesty and His character. God views our distrust of Him as seriously as He views our disobedience."

Jerry Bridges

DAY 349

📖 MATTHEW 15 – 16:27
📖 PSALMS 5

⊛ K E Y   T H O U G H T S

- **Matthew 15:19** So much of Jesus' teaching is focusing upon the heart of a disciple. Jesus is interested in inner transformation, motivation that is genuine leaning toward God, not just an exterior "make-over".

- Vs. 19 Apart from a heart being transformed by Christ, and filled with the presence of the Holy Spirit, the natural heart brings out a lot of evil things.

- 15:33 and 16:11 (The question for each of us is this, "When will we become people who truly and finally will believe in the supernatural power of Jesus?")

- (How easily do we forget the previous miracle and assume it was the last; how often do we revert to the natural explanation instead of the supernatural?)

- 16:19 (SFLB) "The church will be empowered to continue in the privileged responsibility of leavening the earth with His kingdom power and provision. For example, if someone is bound by sin, the church can "loose" him by preaching the provision of freedom from sin in Jesus Christ (Rom.6:14). If someone is indwelt by a demon, the church can "bind" the demon by commanding its departure (Acts 16:18), realizing that Jesus alone made this provision possible (Matt. 12:29. How the church binds and looses is diverse and would most certainly extend far beyond the mere use of these terms in prayerful petitions."

- 16:23 (How often are we more mindful of the things of men than the things of God, and therefore in danger of offending Christ?)

- Vss. 24-27 One of the great passages in Scripture on the true life of the disciple, who must:
  - deny himself
  - lose his life for Jesus' sake
  - recognize nothing can purchase a soul, but Jesus blood
  - live knowing there will be rewards in heaven

QUOTE OF THE DAY

"Christianity without discipleship is always Christianity without Christ."

Dietrich Bonhoeffer

DAY 350

📖 MATTHEW 22:1 – 14; LUKE 14:7 – 24
📖 PSALM 6

◉ K E Y   T H O U G H T S

- **Matthew 22, Luke 14** Similar concepts in these two parables, yet a different primary thought.

- In Matthew Jesus is using the metaphor of a wedding feast to emphasize the Jews resistance to His kingdom, their unwillingness to "enter in".

- The eternal consequence of such rejection is very stark.

- Vs. 13 Weeping, gnashing of teeth and "outer darkness", are the destination and condition of those unwilling to accept the invitation of God.

- Luke 14:7ff One of the most moving of Jesus parables for the heart of evangelism.

- 14:18 Excuses do not stand up in the face of the invitation to eternal life – there will be no valid excuse on the day we are called to give an answer.

- Note the beautiful principle of bringing in those who are willing, finding good soil, finding those who acknowledge their need emphasizes the value of every soul.

- One person is not worth more than another in God's kingdom Their "never dying soul" is what matters to the "ever loving" heart of God.

- There is still room!

- Vs. 23 *"Compel them to come in, that My house may be filled."*

- Psalm 6:8-9 When we are going through deep trouble, we can be comforted with these wonderful promises:
    - *"The Lord has heard the voice of my weeping."*
    - *"The Lord has heard my supplications."*
    - *"The Lord will receive my prayer."*

"Evangelism is not a professional job for a few trained men, but is instead the unrelenting responsibility of every person who belongs to the company of Jesus."

Elton Trueblood

DAY 351

📖 MATTHEW 24 – 25:13
📖 PSALM 7

⊕ K E Y   T H O U G H T S

- **Matthew 24:6** When we are surrounded by troubling circumstances and events, we are to see that we are *"not troubled"*. The point of these passages is to emphasize that the Lord's timing is perfect and His ultimate plan of retribution to the wicked and reward to the righteous will come to pass.

- 24:13 Endurance to the end is required of the disciples of Christ. Many start well, but finishing well is the final evaluation.

- 24:14 Notice that the gospel is to be preached to "all the nations". While there are those who have never heard the good news, the work of God is incomplete.

- This responsibility is not just to the faraway places. In North America there are increasing multitudes who have not heard the gospel. This is a fundamental mission of the believer and of the church!

- The next passages to highlight all carry the same message in different ways. "Be ready."

- 24:36 The timing of the end time events are in the mind of the Father alone. Many have come and gone with predictions of Christ's return, bringing reproach on the Lord.

- When the time comes, all will know it! We are to be ready because: Vs. 44 *"The Son of Man is coming at an hour you do not expect."*

- Vs. 48 The temptation during a delay is to abandon the assignments and the trust that have been given. To expect the excuse of His delay to justify sinful and wicked behavior is folly.

- Vs. 51 That the hypocrites have a specific "portion" prepared by the Lord for their punishment is a sobering thought. So many complain about hypocrites - God is going to deal severely with them!

- 25:13 Summarizing the parable of the virgins, "watch therefore!" Be ready, prepare yourself, be current, fulfill your calling, do not delay.

- **Psalm 7** The psalmist struggles with the relevant issue of the apparent success and ease of the wicked. In our times there are so many wicked that seem to go free, suffer no consequence and mock the justice of God.

- Ps. 7:11 has the answer. The wicked will suffer the anger of God against their wickedness. There is a day of reckoning coming for all people.

- 7:17 Always end your prayer time and your day, focusing upon the faithfulness and the goodness of the Lord.

- In spite of every evil advancement and grievous perversion filling the land, put your heart in a posture of praise. God is God, He will triumph!

QUOTE OF THE DAY

"We talk about heaven being so far away. It is within speaking distance to those who belong there. Heaven is a prepared place for a prepared people."

Dwight L. Moody

DAY 352

📖 MATTHEW 25:14 – 46; 28
📖 PSALM 8

☉ K E Y T H O U G H T S

- **Matthew 25:15** The giftings or "talents" are distributed to each person *"according to his own ability".*

- It is the Lord who equips us for His service, He is the One who puts each piece together. There is no competition in Christ, only complimentary service.

- Ephesians 4:16 *"from who the whole body, joined and knit together by what every joint supplies, according the effective working by which every part does its share, causes growth of the body for the edifying of itself in love."*

- 25:15 Those who are trustworthy are honored with more opportunity and blessing. Those who squander their trust through neglect and self-pity will lose even the little that they had.

- So many dismiss the little that they could contribute by comparing it to the larger contribution of someone else. This misses the point completely. The body of Christ is only effective as *"every part does its share"*. Then synergy kicks in, then the multiplying starts.

- 25:40 The righteous acts of mercy that the King is looking for are to spring out of a genuinely transformed heart, a self-initiating heart of compassion, not a dispassionate rule, or quota (vss. 45, 46).

- 28:6 A powerful statement of foundational truth. He is no longer in the grave, because, "He is risen!" Fulfilling the prophecy that He himself made! Powerful.

- 18-20 This commission is the be the measurement of our lives. Are we living in obedience to this specific, universal task of the kingdom of God?

- **Psalm 8** The Lord's Name is above every other name, god or idea.

- 8:6 Jesus Christ has all power, all dominion (rule), and authority.

  - Ephesians 1:20-23 *"which He worked in Christ when He raised Him from the dead and seated Him at His right hand in the heavenly places, far above all principality and power and might and dominion, and every name that is named, not only in this age but also in that which is to come. And He put all things under His feet, and gave Him to be head over all things to the church, which is His body, the fullness of Him who fills all in all."*

DAY 353

📖 LUKE 1
📖 PSALM 10

⊚ K E Y   T H O U G H T S

- **Luke 1:4** Luke's purpose is clearly expressed. This book is written so that we can have certainty that what we have been taught is indeed true. Luke is a reliable witness.

- **1:20** There is always some consequence to unbelief. The offense of Zacharias does not seem that bad, and yet, the angel makes it clear that his refusal to believe in the face of a promise is a serious matter.

- We often think of what faith can accomplish, but unbelief also accomplishes something, although not a positive result.

- **Vs.37** The angel gives us a statement of fact that should be an anchor for all our lives.

- **Vs.38** Somehow Mary's question is not a symptom of unbelief, but rather a question of honor. Her response after the angel's explanation is one of the most beautiful childlike expressions of faith in all of scripture.

- **1:41** The Holy Spirit is very active in the lives of these godly people. *"Filled with the Spirit"* is one of Luke's favorite expressions.

- We can see that the infilling of the Holy Spirit is not a once for all experience. He is a person with whom we can have a daily relationship. Dependency upon the Spirit, and seeking of His working in our lives every day is one of the calls of the Spirit-filled believer.

- **Vs. 67** In contrast to his previous unbelief, Zacharias, in faith, is filled with the Holy Spirit. The result is that a prophetic mantle flows through him.

- Vs. 78 *"The Dayspring from on high."* The title given to Jesus refers to the morning sunrise. Jesus is the One who brings light upon a land filled with darkness. He is the One who brings peace to our hearts, in the same way that a morning sunrise brings the hope and promise of a new day.

- **Psalm 10:3** Frustration over the seemingly unchecked activity of the wicked (vs. 11). How current this description of the ungodly is.

- Vs. 12 The Lord will always arise against the wicked and against injustice.

- Vs. 14 As in Luke 1, the Lord has a special place in His heart for the barren and the fatherless. He hears their cry.

- If you are wanting children and are experiencing barrenness, the Lord sees you today. He will hear you.

- Join with me in faith right now that those who are barren will be healed and become fruitful. "We pray Lord, in faith, and ask for fruitfulness for our dear friends."

QUOTE OF THE DAY

"Persistent calling upon the name of the Lord breaks through every stronghold of the devil, for nothing is impossible with God. For Christians in these troubled times there is simply no other way."

Jim Cymbala

DAY 354

📖 LUKE 7
📖 PSALM 11 – 13

◉ K E Y   T H O U G H T S

- **Luke 7:9** Jesus commends this Gentile man's "great faith." (Would Jesus' observation of your faith and mine bring the same comment? Is my/your faith "great faith?")

- 7:22 Jesus' description of the coming of His kingdom presents a powerful point by point outline of the type of things that we should be devoting our lives to.

- Jesus' kingdom is a radical kingdom that reaches to all people. The concept of God's blessing at the time of Jesus was that only the prosperous and socially qualified were fit for the blessings of God's kingdom.

- Jesus brings a gospel that is to all people, everywhere!

- Vss. 44-48 Notice that there were three things this immoral woman did. The Pharisee neglects the same three things.

- It is as if this woman knows what is proper for someone like Jesus, and as the Pharisee does not provide, she steps in and brings what is fitting to Jesus, in her own broken way.

- (Do we have a relationship with Jesus that is one of curiosity, or a relationship that is genuine, fully committed and radically giving?) This woman is a powerful picture of what our worship should look like. She understood how much she was forgiven. There was no self-righteousness in her.

- **Psalms 11-13** The first verse of each of these psalms expresses the thought progression:
  - 11:1 *"In the Lord I put my trust."*
  - 12:1 *"Help, Lord, for the godly man ceases."*
  - 13:1 *"How long, O Lord? Will You forget me forever?"*

- But 13:5, 6 brings the whole matter to the proper conclusion.

QUOTE OF THE DAY

"But I have trusted in Your mercy; My heart shall rejoice in Your salvation. I will sing to the Lord, Because He has dealt bountifully with me."

Psalm 13:5, 6

DAY 355

📖 LUKE 12
📖 PSALMS 14, 15

◉ K E Y T H O U G H T S

- **Luke 12:2, 3** This is a very good test for the authenticity of our hearts. (Are the words we speak, in private or in secret, fit for all to hear?)

- This ultimate accountability for our words and attitudes when no one is watching brings strong instruction on the importance of the thoughts and intents of the heart.

- Vs. 8 We are instructed to be willing to confess Christ before men. Do not be ashamed of His Name.

- Vs. 15 A simple yet radical statement of truth - life does not consist in the abundance of the things we possess.

- Vs. 31 Seek first the kingdom of God...

- Vs. 37 (How can we become servants who are "blessed"?)

- **Psalm 14** God does not spare any feelings when He describes the one who says there is no God.

- Psalm 15 This question should be one that we ask ourselves often; *"who may abide in Your tabernacle? Who may dwell in Your holy hill?"*

- 15:2 This statement; *"who speaks the truth in his heart",* is such a powerful measurement of the kind of "truth" that we speak.

- Truth is much more than the words, integrity is much more than the appearance of honesty. All these characteristics must be borne out of the heart. There must be a transformation of the very core of our lives. Only the Holy Spirit is able to truly change us that much.

QUOTE OF THE DAY

"We must be the same person in private and in public. Only the Christian worldview gives us the basis for this kind of integrity."

Chuck Colson

DAY 356

📖 LUKE 18 – 19:27
📖 PSALM 16

☉ K E Y   T H O U G H T S

- **Luke 18** One of Jesus' favorite methods of teaching was to use a contrasting illustration. His point in this parable is to illustrate the "how much more" of our loving and good heavenly Father.

- If an unjust judge (being unjust) will eventually grant the petition of a needy person, how much more can we expect a just and speedy response from the Lord, who is good!

- 18:41 This question from Jesus to the blind man is one that we should always remember: *"what do you want Me to do for you?"*

- Jesus doesn't grow weary of our requests and needs. He does not grow frustrated by our weaknesses. His question is all about determining the level of faith in the heart. This man understood the power of Jesus and asked for a God-sized miracle. Do not miss a miracle because of small faith or artificial humility.

- 19:10 (If this is the mission of the 'Son of Man' should our mission be any different? If this is the most important task in Jesus' itinerary, is it right if this item has no place on our list of priorities?)

- **Psalm 16:11:**
  - the path of life
  - fullness of joy
  - pleasures forevermore

- Those people who decide to live in the presence of the Lord, and then follow through with purity and obedience will find these blessings flowing in their lives.

- A blessing is not luck. Blessing is not granted by personal merit. Blessing is found in "the presence of the Lord".

- Try to mark each day with an awareness of the presence of the Lord. Find a way to offer worship each day. Take the moments when the Holy Spirit speaks to your spirit to offer a prayer of thanksgiving, a word of praise.

- One brother coined the phrase – "practicing the Presence" of the Lord. You can purpose and practice being in His mighty presence.

QUOTE OF THE DAY

"The true, the genuine worship is when man, through his spirit, attains to friendship and intimacy with God. True and genuine worship is not to come to a certain place; it is not to go through a certain ritual or liturgy; it is not even to bring certain gifts. True worship is when the spirit, the immortal and invisible part of man, speaks to and meets with God, who is immortal and invisible."

William Barclay

DAY 357

📖 JOHN 1
📖 PSALM 19:7 – 14: 23

◉ K E Y   T H O U G H T S

- **John 1:1** John's immediate emphasis is upon the deity and eternity of Christ.
- The identity and character of Jesus are fundamental to our faith. Any lessening of Jesus' Godhood is an undermining of our standing in God.
- These first four verses form a grid for understanding who Jesus really is. Attacks against Christ's attributes and power have been the enemy's strategy from the time He walked the earth. Fully God and fully man, truly, *"this is the Son of God."*
- Notice the emphasis upon Jesus' creative power, *"the world was made through Him"* (vs. 10).
- Vs. 33 Jesus is the One who baptizes us with the Holy Spirit. Ask Jesus today, "Lord, baptize me with Your Holy Spirit".
- Vss. 39, 46 The phrase *"come and see"* is repeated here. What a beautiful invitation to offer to people that you know.

- Come and see what God is doing in people's lives, come and see what church is like today, come and see the good that your children can learn in Bible classes, come and see what God has done in people who have been in addictions – "come and see".

- Come and see who Jesus really is.

- **Psalm 19:12** Thank God that the psalmist expresses what we all feel, *"who can understand his errors?"*

- Vs. 14 This prayer should be a familiar one to us. Our words and our meditations are inseparably connected, one flows from another.

- Make it your aim to have both your words and the meditations of your heart acceptable to God.

- Psalm 23 Memorize these wonderful, strong six verses. One man of God made it his practice when beset by worry or stress to recite Ps. 23 as he was trying to fall asleep.

- Rather than counting sheep, look to the Good Shepherd and the shepherd's psalm.

QUOTE OF THE DAY

"Who can understand his errors? Cleanse me from secret faults. Keep back Your servant also from presumptuous sins; let them not have dominion over me."
Psalm 19:12,13a.

DAY 358

📖 EPHESIANS 1
📖 PSALM 27

⊛ K E Y   T H O U G H T S

- **Ephesians 1:3** Think about it. We are *"blessed with every spiritual blessing"* in Christ! There are no blessings missing when we fully embrace and enter into all that there is in Jesus!

- Vs. 6 The understanding of being accepted is a huge assurance for those who walk with Jesus. So many in this world are striving and wondering if they are accepted.

- In fact, in many man-made religions one of the key points of control is to make acceptance a mystery – so works and duty become a burden. In man's system you never know if you have crossed the line of acceptance.

- The gospel is good news because "in Christ" we are accepted. Because of Jesus and His grace, we are accepted by "the Beloved." Hallelujah!

- The supremacy and fullness of Christ is emphasized throughout this chapter:
  - Vs. 10 All things both in heaven and on earth are gathered together in Him.
  - Vss. 21, 22 He is far above all other powers and principalities.
  - He has all authority.
  - He is the head of the church – which is the fullness of Him in the world now.

- Vss. 17, 18, 19 Pray this prayer out loud over yourself and your family. Receive the prayer that the apostle prayed, for you today. Receive:
  - The hope of His calling.
  - The riches of His inheritance.
  - The exceeding greatness of His power.

- **Psalm 27:4** (Is it your desire to "dwell in the house of the Lord"? To be in His presence, to have daily fellowship with the Lord, to make His place your place, not just an occasional visit but an actual residence for your soul?)

- Vs. 13 The key to keeping your courage in the face of trial? Believe that you *"will see the goodness of the Lord in the land of the living"*.

- Vs. 14 (How do you do at 'waiting'? Do you allow the Lord to work His will in your life, in His time? He has promised to do it, He is faithful, His timing is perfect – will you wait for Him?)

"The Lord is my light and my salvation; whom shall I fear? The Lord is the strength of my life; of whom shall I be afraid?"

Psalm 27:1

DAY 359

📖 LUKE 2

◉ K E Y   T H O U G H T S

- **Luke 2:7** So simple, so sublime, the King of kings is born in the most humble circumstances.
- No room. Spoken so many times but still such a penetrating question - "is there room in my heart for You, Lord Jesus?" Or has all the space been taken up by other guests?
- Vss. 8-20 The attendants to His birth are both magnificent and obscure. The angels explode into the earth's atmosphere with praise and celebration.
- The shepherds - only God knows why they were chosen. Perhaps to indicate the wideness of the grace of God – *"to all peoples".*
- Vs. 25 Simeon represents all those who are longing for the coming of the Messiah. Looking, waiting, preparing for His arrival, by His Spirit into our lives, into our world.
- Vs. 49 Be about *"the Father's business".* (How would you describe "the Father's business" in your life? What has He called you to? What do you know in your heart that you are to be sowing into His Kingdom?)
  - serving
  - giving generously
  - witnessing to Christ's power
  - loving
  - showing mercy

"Thou didst leave Thy throne and Thy kingly crown, when Thou camest to earth for me; but in Bethlehem's home was there found no room for Thy holy nativity: Oh, come to my heart, Lord Jesus! There is room in my heart for Thee; oh, come to my heart, Lord Jesus, there is room in my heart for Thee."

E.S. Elliot

DAY 360

📖 MATTHEW 2:1, 2

◉ K E Y T H O U G H T S

- **Matthew 2: 1, 2** Find a few quiet moments today to "worship Him."
- Allow your heart to overflow with thanksgiving to God. Be thankful today, regardless of your circumstance. The King is born, we will worship Him.
- Enjoy family today. Set your mind to be a servant to the joy of others.

QUOTE OF THE DAY

"It is good to be children sometimes, and never better than at Christmas, when its mighty Founder was a child Himself."

Charles Dickens

DAY 361

📖 MATTHEW 28; MARK 16
📖 PSALM 28

◉ K E Y T H O U G H T S

- **Matthew 28, Mark 16** We must always connect the birth of Jesus with His death and resurrection.

- Jesus is the Son of God come in the flesh and He is the risen King triumphant over the Devil, hell and death.

- He has commissioned us to reach the whole world with the good news. Christ is risen from the dead, our sins and guilt can be forgiven, there is a way to be saved, a promise of assurance of salvation.

- Mark 16:11, 13 The immediate response of these 'disciples' is unbelief.

- Vs. 14 There are only a few references to Jesus rebuking His disciples. Unbelief is the cause of the rebuke on more than one occasion.

- *"Do be unbelieving, but believing."* (John 20:27)

- Mark 16:16-18"The signs accredit the gospel message, and cannot be limited to the apostolic age, any more than the Lord's commission to carry the gospel throughout the world. The signs, therefore, confirm the ministries of Christ's ambassadors in every generation. Casting out demons, speaking in tongues, and healing all appear in other passage in the NT, and there is no scriptural warrant for their cessation before the Lord returns....Many missionaries have testified to God's miraculous protection in heathen territories, where they experienced no ill effects from impure food and drink. All of the signs listed here have occurred repeatedly in Christian history." (SFLB)

- **Psalm 28:9** As we begin looking to a new year, orient your heart to the heart of God to "save His people".

- Begin today to have a new faith for the Lord to fulfill His promises of refreshing in our times.

- "Lord, save us, renew Your people, move in my heart in a fresh way."

"All other passions build upon or flow from your passion for Jesus. A passion for souls grows out of a passion for Christ. A passion for missions builds upon a passion for Christ. The most crucial danger to a Christian, whatever his role, is to lack a passion for Christ. The most direct route to personal renewal and new effectiveness is a new all-consuming passion for Jesus. Lord, give us this passion, whatever the cost!"

Wesley L. Duewet

DAY 362

📖 LUKE 24
📖 JOHN 21

◉ K E Y   T H O U G H T S

- **Luke 24:7** Jesus fulfilled His own prophetic words about His death and resurrection. The miraculous confirmations of Jesus' deity are important reference points of our faith.

- Vs. 47 The message of the gospel is to be preached, *"in His Name"*, to all nations!

- Vs. 49 is a key verse to understanding the importance and the place of the Holy Spirit in the life of the believer. Nothing else mattered after Christ's ascension, but to be filled with the Holy Spirit.

- No other pursuit is as vital, no other resource is as essential – do nothing else but be filled with the Holy Spirit!

- Jesus' final instructions were very general, but when it came to the Holy Spirit He was specific and firm.

- It is the Holy Spirit who will take the mission from Pentecost to the Rapture. We must be intimately in tune with the Holy Spirit!

- **John 21:6** (What is the right side of the boat for you when it comes to evangelism? Are there some people you have never invited, some that you may have overlooked or assumed they are not interested in the gospel?)

- There is no magic in the side of boat, the only difference is that one method does not have Jesus' blessing, the other yields a miraculous catch. Invite Jesus into your situation, ask Him for a miracle catch and then throw out the net again!

- Vs. 19 The simplest answer to all our questions is *"follow Me."*
- When we wonder what will happen, how things will turn out, etc… Jesus sums it all up … *"follow Me"*.
- It will work out the way it should, you will be on the right path, your life will be headed the right direction.
- Vs. 25 Always keep in mind that the writings of the apostles only capture bits and pieces of the life and ministry of Jesus and the early church.

QUOTE OF THE DAY

"Keep your eye simply on Him; let His death, His sufferings, His merits, His glories, His intercession, be fresh upon thy mind; when you wake in the morning look to Him; when thou lie down at night look to Him. Oh! let not your hopes or fears come between thee and Jesus; follow hard after Him, and He will never fail you."

Charles Spurgeon

DAY 363

📖 ACTS 1, 2

◉ K E Y   T H O U G H T S

- **Acts 1** As we are fast approaching a new year, set your heart and your focus upon pursuing a personal revival.
- 1:8 Power, witnesses - all through the "coming upon" of the Holy Spirit.
- The global mission of the church is only possible through the empowering of the Holy Spirit. Only He can keep us from declining into self-interest, and inactivity.
- Vs. 14 and 2:1 *"One accord"*. The Greek word *homothumadon*; unanimous, group unity, having one mind and purpose.

- In each of the occurrences of this word it shows a "harmony leading to action". (SFLB)
- Unity without action/purpose is not the unity of the Holy Spirit. True spiritual unity is designed to result in explosive action for God's glory.
- 2:16 Peter interprets Joel's prophecy as contemporary to their situation. He then casts the promise into the future, to our generation, our times.
- *"For the promise is to you and to your children, and to all who are afar off, as many as the Lord our God will call."* (2:39)
- Seek your personal baptism in the Holy Spirit. Expect to experience everything that they did in these magnificent chapters – it is all for today, it is all for you!
- Our commission is no less daunting today than it was for those 120 people that day. They were hopelessly outnumbered by religious people, pagans and the godless. Yet… by the power of the Holy Spirit the spiritual landscape as it was then, began to change radically.
- 2:42 Here is what they did.
- 2:47 Here is what happened. "Oh Lord Jesus, send the wind and the fire upon us again."

QUOTE OF THE DAY

"How we have prayed for a Revival - we did not care whether it was old-fashioned or not - what we asked for was that it should be such that would cleanse and revive His children and set them on fire to win others."

Mary Booth

DAY 364

📖 ACTS 3, 4

☉ K E Y   T H O U G H T S

- **Acts 3, 4** These chapters are so rich I am hesitant to comment at all. Allow yourself to be in the narrative, feel the spiritual intensity and vitality, measure your current condition against what was happening then.

- 3:16 The name of Jesus, *"through faith in His Name...Yes, the faith which comes through Him has given him this perfect soundness in the presence of you all."*

- 4:2 The resurrection is always the dividing line. It has greatly disturbed people since the time of the apostles, yet it marks Christianity apart from all other 'ways'.

- 4:10 By this point, within a couple of days of Pentecost, through the preaching and teaching of the apostles, the Resurrection was the focal point of their explanation for all that was happening.

- 4:13 *"they had been with Jesus"*. Ordinary people, like you and me, after having been with Jesus become those bold, miracle working radicals for Christ.

- 4:30 Make this your prayer today, "Heal Lord, perform signs and wonders, that Your Name, will be lifted up."

- 4:31 The result of their being shaken and filled with the Holy Spirit is <u>BOLDNESS</u>.

- This is not abnormal for the Spirit-filled believer and the Spirit-filled church. This dynamic power of the Holy Spirit is normal for those flowing in the fullness of the Spirit.

- Vss. 36, 37 The practice of the early church was to bring their tithes and offerings to the apostles. They were accustomed to bringing their "first fruits" to the temple. Now being led by the Spirit rather than the law, they began to expand the work of God through their giving.

- (Is it your practice to give? Are you consistent, generous, Spirit led in your giving? Do you pray about what to give, do you give your best, the first?)

- If you have not been honoring God with tithes and offerings, this is a fantastic time of the year to begin a new spiritual activity. The Bible is very, very clear about the calling and responsibility of the believer to honor God, from the heart, with our giving. Do not withhold what belongs to the Lord.

"It's increasingly common for Christians to ask one another the tough questions: How is your marriage? Have you been spending time in the Word? How are you doing in terms of sexual purity? Have you been sharing your faith? But how often do we ask, "How much are you giving to the Lord?" or "Have you been robbing God?" or "Are you winning the battle against materialism?"

Randy Alcom

DAY 365

📖 DEUTERONOMY 8, 28:1 – 14

◉ K E Y   T H O U G H T S

- **Deuteronomy 8** The Lord has promised blessings to those who will walk in His ways and obey His commandments,

- Jesus said: *"If you love Me, keep My commandments. And I will pray the Father, and will give you another Helper, that He may abide with you forever. The Spirit of truth, whom the world cannot receive, because it neither sees Him nor knows Him; but you know Him, for He dwells with you and will be in you."* John 14:15-17

- The desire to keep the commands of Jesus comes from a heart of love. As a result He promises to help us through the equipping power of the Holy Spirit.

- Jesus' command to obey is not unreasonable or unattainable. With the help of the Holy Spirit we can walk in the blessings of obedience.

- 8:11 *"Beware that you do not forget..."* This is a continuous theme throughout Moses' last words to Israel, *"do not forget"*.

- Our hearts are prone to wander, prone to pride, prone to taking the pathway of least resistance and ease.

- Do not forget the faithfulness of God, do not forget the mercy and goodness of God, do not forget !

- Vs. 17 The result of a forgetful heart is that we begin to take the credit ourselves for all that has happened.

- Vs. 18 Gives the straightforward explanation, *"it is He who gives you the power to get wealth".* He is the source of all blessing, He deserves all the glory, all the credit.

- He must be honored in our hearts lest we become prideful, forgetful and turn to other gods.

- The result of this rebellious and ungrateful behavior is disastrous for generations to come (vs. 19, 20).

- Deuteronomy 28 Know this dear brother, dear sister, it is the heart-felt and determined intention of God to bless you!

- He is able to bless in ways that you cannot even imagine. The blessing of God goes far beyond material blessings, it is a whole package of well-being.

- Physical health, mental and emotional health, relational health, purpose, provision, protection, intimacy with the Creator, empowering energy to serve in His kingdom, the joys of Christian fellowship globally, the hope of Heaven and reward, the promise of His soon return… you get the sense, right?

- 28:2 *"all these blessings shall come upon you and overtake you, BECAUSE you obey the voice of the Lord your God."*

QUOTE OF THE DAY

"And the Lord will make you the head and not the tail; you shall be above only, and not be beneath, if you heed the commandments of the Lord your God."

Deuteronomy 28:13.

DAY 366

📖 2 CHRONICLES 7:1 – 14
📖 JEREMIAH 29:11 – 14; 33:3
📖 HABAKKUK 3:2
📖 JAMES 5:13 – 20

KEY THOUGHTS

- As we arrive at the last day of this year, standing upon the threshold of a brand new year – turn your heart to the Lord.

Turn your heart to seek the Lord, to return to Him, to pursue Him. Four brief readings today, all to focus our hearts upon the call and power of prayer.

- Habakkuk 3:2 *"Lord, I have heard of your fame; I stand in awe of your deeds, O Lord. Renew them in our day, in our time make them known, in wrath remember mercy."* (NIV)

QUOTES OF THE DAY

"We must continue in prayer if we are to get an outpouring of the Spirit. Christ says there are some things we shall not get, unless we pray and fast, yes, "prayer and fasting." We must control the flesh and abstain from whatever hinders direct fellowship with God."

Andrew Bonar

"The coming revival must begin with a great revival of prayer. It is in the closet, with the door shut, that the sound of abundance of rain will first be heard. An increase of secret prayer with ministers will be the sure harbinger of blessing."

Andrew Murray

"I know of no better thermometer to your spiritual temperature than this, the measure of the intensity of your prayer."

Charles Spurgeon

BiBLiOGRAPHY

The Complete Biblical Library
Copyright © 1994 by World Library Press Inc. Database ©
2010 WORDsearch Corp.

Expositions of Holy Scripture
By Alexander Maclaren, D. D., Litt. D.
Database © 2009 WORDsearch Corp.

Easton's Illustrated Bible Dictionary
By Matthew George Easton
Database © 2008 WORDsearch Corp.

Spirit Filled Life Bible (NKJV)
Copyright, November 1991.
By Thomas Nelson, Inc.